The Coronavirus Crisis and Its Teachings

Studies in Critical Social Sciences

Series Editor
David Fasenfest (*Wayne State University*)

Editorial Board
Eduardo Bonilla-Silva (*Duke University*)
Chris Chase-Dunn (*University of California-Riverside*)
William Carroll (*University of Victoria*)
Raewyn Connell (*University of Sydney*)
Kimberlé W. Crenshaw (*University of California, LA,* and
Columbia University)
Raju Das (*York University*)
Heidi Gottfried (*Wayne State University*)
Karin Gottschall (*University of Bremen*)
Alfredo Saad-Filho (*King's College London*)
Chizuko Ueno (*University of Tokyo*)
Sylvia Walby (*Lancaster University*)

VOLUME 204

The titles published in this series are listed at *brill.com/scss*

The Coronavirus Crisis and Its Teachings

Steps towards Multi-Resilience

By

Roland Benedikter and Karim Fathi

Foreword by

Jan Nederveen Pieterse

Afterword by

Manfred B. Steger

BRILL

LEIDEN | BOSTON

Cover illustration: *Do Nothing*. Land art installation referring to the lockdowns during the pandemic. The artist wishes to remain anonymous. Talfer river, Bozen-Bolzano, South Tyrol, Italy, European Union. Image taken on April 25, 2020. Photo by Roland Benedikter.

The Library of Congress Cataloging-in-Publication Data is available online at https://catalog.loc.gov
LC record available at https://lccn.loc.gov/2021049602

Typeface for the Latin, Greek, and Cyrillic scripts: "Brill". See and download: brill.com/brill-typeface.

ISSN 1573-4234
ISBN 978-90-04-46952-5 (hardback)
ISBN 978-90-04-46968-6 (e-book)

Copyright 2022 by Roland Benedikter and Karim Fathi. Published by Koninklijke Brill NV, Leiden, The Netherlands.
Koninklijke Brill NV incorporates the imprints Brill, Brill Nijhoff, Brill Hotei, Brill Schöningh, Brill Fink, Brill mentis, Vandenhoeck & Ruprecht, Böhlau Verlag and V&R Unipress.
Koninklijke Brill NV reserves the right to protect this publication against unauthorized use. Requests for re-use and/or translations must be addressed to Koninklijke Brill NV via brill.com or copyright.com.

This book is printed on acid-free paper and produced in a sustainable manner.

Days, when they seem to be slipping away from us,
they glide quietly into us,
but we transform all time;
for we long to be ...

RAINER MARIA RILKE, 1907

Contents

Foreword XIII
Preface XV
Acknowledgements XX
List of Figures XXI
Overview and Summary XXII

PART 1
The Coronavirus Crisis

1 Introduction
"Do Nothing" or, an Epochal Crisis 3

2 Systemic Unpreparedness Inducing a Variety of Psychological
Reactions 10

3 The Branches and Social Strata Hardest Hit
A List to Be Carefully Remembered for the Next Systemic Rupture 13

4 Were Nature and the Environment "Winners" of the Crisis? Disputed
"Improvements" and Their Flip Sides 24

5 Children and Relationships 31

6 Labour and the Economy
"Generation Corona" 34

7 Corona and Re-Globalisation 1
*Sharpening Awareness about the Differences between Political Systems
and Their Growing Asymmetries* 38

8 A Battle for Values and Transformation Not Confined to Bilateral
Competition, but Spanning the Globe 44

9 Unprecedented Penetrative Depth
Uplifting Technology, Changing Sexuality, Questioning Science? 53

VIII   CONTENTS

10 Corona and Re-Globalisation 2
    Creating Conscience for National and International Reforms   57

11 Intellectual Rhetoric between Cheap "Humanistic" Appeal and
    Kitsch   61

12 "Humanised" Technology Instead of a New Humanism?   63

13 A Boost to "Post-human Hybrid Intelligence" Such as Biological
    Espionage and Sentiment Analysis?   70

14 Striking a Balance
    *Was Corona a Watershed for Western Humanism and the Basic
    Rationality of the Enlightenment?*   74

15 The Vast Variety of Political Instrumentalisations   81

16 Three More Far-reaching Aspects within Global Democracies and
    Open Societies
    Confirmation Bias, "Republican" Turn *and* Re-Globalisation Drive   85

PART 2
The Simultaneousness of Local, National and Global Effects

17 An Unprecedented Crisis Accelerating the (Temporary?) Rupture
    of Advanced Life Patterns – Including Gender Role Models in
    Democracies   93

18 "Unsocial Sociability" and the Re-shaping of the Global Order
    Anthropology and Politics Intertwined   99

19 Medical Diplomacy, or: The Great Divide of Principles over and after
    Corona
    More "Do It Alone" – Or More Cooperation?   103

20 Don't Forget the Bizarre, the Surreal and the Perfidious
    From Mona Lisa to Sharon Stone and Global Terror   107

CONTENTS IX

21 Coronavirus Crisis Social Psychology
Between Disorientation, Infodemic *and the Need to Understand* 115

22 Conspiracy Theories
Misusing the Crisis for Legitimating the Absurd in Times of "Fake News" 119

23 The Perspective
The Real Question Is Not about COVID-19, but about "the World After" 123

PART 3
The Corona Challenge: Multi-Resilience for an Interconnected World Ridden by Crisis Bundles

24 In Search of Examples of Efficient Resilience
From the Evolutionary Teachings of Bats to Regional Self-administration within Political Autonomies to a "Flexible" Handling of Constitutions 129

25 Crisis Resistance in the Face of Corona and in Anticipation of Potential Future Pandemics
A Short Overview of Different Options of Socio-political Responses 134

26 The Primordial Path to Follow
Enhancing Resilience. Basic Philosophical Assumptions and Their Implications for Crisis-policy Design 142

27 Revisioning the Concept of Resilience
A Necessary Step (Not Only) after Corona 145

28 Progressing from Resilience to Multi-resilience
Two Basic Approaches 149

29 Five Principles of Multi-resilience 167

30 Summary. Multi-resilience
A Crucial Topic to Shape "Globalisation 2.0" 184

PART 4

Requirements for a Post-Corona World

31 The Corona Effect and "Diseasescape"
Towards Weaker, but More Realistic Globalisation and Transnationalisation? 189

32 The Uncertainty about the Future of COVID-19
Short-term Scenarios versus Big-picture Trends 196

33 Technological Requirements
Six Trends 200

34 Towards a Post-Corona World
Seven Upcoming Conflict Lines Open Societies Should Prepare For 205

35 The Post-Corona World
Potentials and Visions for a "Better Globalised" International System 213

PART 5

Post-Corona Policy Design

36 Chances and Limits of Resilience
The Development Paradox and the Increasing Danger of Man-made Disasters with Multi-sectoral Side Effects 227

37 Towards a Broader and More Integrated Policy of Future Preparedness
Contributions from Selected Guiding Concepts 232

38 Fostering Local, National and International Paths towards Multi-resilience
Leverage Points for Interrelated Social Change Bottom-up and Top-down 244

CONTENTS

PART 6
Recommendations for a Multi-Resilient Post-Corona World

39 "Health Terror"? Towards an Adequate Framework for a Post-Corona Socio-political Philosophy
"Resistance" and Power Critique Will Not Suffice 261

40 Seven Strategic Recommendations for Pro-positive Multi-resilient Policymaking in the Post-Corona World of Open Societies 267

41 Recommendations for Global Post-Corona Policymaking in an Increasingly Multipolar World 284

PART 7
Outlook. The Coronavirus Legacy: A "New World" Ahead – or Back to Business as Usual?

42 The (Productively) Ambiguous Post-Corona Vision
A "New World" Ahead? 293

43 "Corona Positivism"
The Global Pandemic as an Unprecedented "Chance" for Radical Transformation – Or Even as the Epochal Example for What (Social) Art Should Achieve? 302

44 Corona as a Driver of Re-globalisation towards Post-Corona Globalisation 308

45 A Post-Corona Core Task
Re-positioning the Open Systems of Europe and the West by the Means of Multi-resilience 316

46 An End to Geopolitical Rivalry? Not Likely – Despite Some Positive Signals 319

47 Back to Business as Usual – Systemic Improvements at the "Evo-devo" Interface? 325

48 Integrating the Obvious
Post-Corona, Multi-Resilience and "Futures Literacy": "Bring Together What Belongs Together" 335

49 Corona and Emerging New Responsibility Patterns 342

50 Outlook: A Post-Corona World in the Making
Towards Difficult, but Feasible Innovation – For the Sake of a More Pro-positive Re-globalisation 347

Afterword 355

Bibliographic References 359
Index 426

Foreword

The COVID-19 crisis of 2019–21 exposed many problematic corners and frailties of governance across the world. Government capabilities, state-society relations and leadership were on the line. The limitations of political opportunism became evident. Economic opportunism did not work, either. Just as there was war profiteering, there was COVID-19 profiteering. Selling faulty personal protective equipment gear, promoting phoney remedies, vaccine speculation. Entire economic sectors collapsed. Retail, travel, tourism, fashion. The damage is still being mapped and processed.

The international consequences, both economic and social, are predicted to last for years. In addition, there are political ramifications. The opinions on the perspectives are split. While some assert that the world will go back to normal, others assert that the globe, and globalisation in particular, will never be the same as before the crisis.

COVID-19 also showed social strengths and resources. Countries with first-hand experience of pandemics – Ebola, SARS, MERS – in Asia and Africa had learned to take this seriously, react fast and not let nonsense get in the way. Countries with 'masking culture', such as Japan, were also in a stronger position.

The COVID-19 crisis was not just a pandemic but also, as the WHO pointed out, an infodemic. The quality of information, media and communication channels was at stake. Quackery was rife. Bots on social media were reposting and retweeting false narratives and made up 40 to 60 percent of social media traffic.

This is why the probing multidimensional and forward-looking approach of this work is an important contribution. It breaks with media fragmentation of issues, with the political segmentation of concerns and with the corona positivism that simply relies on numbers and vaccines. It acknowledges the wide-ranging, sprawling character of the crisis and represents a wide call to action in the name of broad societal and international resilience.

This book provides a thorough and inspiring overview of the main aspects to consider with regard to what the crisis implies and what its perspectives may be. It focuses on its political, philosophical and conceptual dimensions and outlines the concept of "multi-resilience" for the years to come, which could turn out to be the positive effect of the crisis, since it could unleash a push towards a more sustainable post-Corona conception of globalisation and modern life. As the authors explain, the Coronavirus crisis could become an impulse for creating a more resilient and better world. Whether this will be the case or not, the coming years must show.

I warmly recommend this book to all interested in the future outlook based on a critical assessment of elements and factors in play. My recommendation includes in particular students, youth movements and civil-society members, as well as policy and opinion-makers.

Jan Nederveen Pieterse
Duncan and Suzanne Mellichamp Distinguished Professor of Global Studies and Sociology
University of California, Santa Barbara

Preface

The Coronavirus – or COVID-19, or Sars-Cov-2 – crisis of 2019–21 was an international systemic crisis unprecedented both in its *global outreach* and *cross-border effects*, as well as in its *trans-sectoral* and *trans-disciplinary* penetrative power *within* fundamentally different societies. This double character made it one of the most encompassing systemic crises of the early 21st century whose full results remain open. Certain is that its experience and heritage provide many potentially exemplary teachings. The Coronavirus crisis proved that 21st century crises do not consist of segmented emergencies or isolated crises, but are, by their very nature, interconnected complex systemic crises, i.e., *crisis bundles* or *bundle crises*. Therefore, any concept of coping with similar and upcoming crises in the present and future must evolve traditional specialised concepts of *resilience* towards the new overarching concept of *multi-resilience*.

To begin with, the Coronavirus crisis was an exemplary case of what happens when a profoundly "penetrative" crisis hits a "hyper-globalised" and thus "hyper-connected" world. In March 2020, German Chancellor Angela Merkel defined COVID-19 as "the biggest challenge since World War II" (Crowcroft, 2020; Huggler, 2020; Der Spiegel, 2020b). In July 2020, WHO Director-General Tedros Ghebreyesus called it "the most severe health emergency ever declared" (BBC News, 2020cc):

> The head of the World Health Organization (WHO) [founded in April 1948, note by the authors] has said COVID-19 is easily the most severe global health emergency it has ever declared ... 'When I declared a public health emergency of international concern on 30 January [2020] ... there were less than 100 cases outside of China, and no deaths,' Dr Tedros said. 'COVID-19 has changed our world. It has brought people, communities and nations together, and driven them apart.' This is the sixth time a global health emergency has been declared under the international health regulations, but it's easily the most severe ... Although the world had made a huge effort in fighting the virus, there remained 'a long hard road ahead of us', he added (Ibid.).

In August 2020, the WHO in its Geneva headquarters assessment of the pandemic, including the connected, wider ramified systemic crisis, asserted that:

> This pandemic will last very long. The committee for emergencies ... underscored that this would be a longer process, probably taking years,

and it would have to be sustained by ongoing and lasting efforts on the communitarian, national, regional and global levels.

RAI – NOTIZIE TELEVIDEO, 2020

Also in the same month, a member of the UK government's Scientific Advisory Group for Emergencies (SAGE), Mark Walport, said that "Coronavirus will be present 'forever in some form or another' ", and that "Coronavirus would not be a disease like smallpox 'which could be eradicated by vaccination' " (BBC News, 2020j).

There are myriad causes for the way the pandemic spread: a combination of political obstruction (US, UK, Brazil), institutional capacities (in countries with and without meaningful and effective public health systems), political will ("scientific" leadership versus populist reaction), and, more generally, differing policy decisions which resulted in better and worse outcomes, including the socio-political economy informing the responses.

We believe that the need for a multi-resilience response post-COVID-19 must outline a global strategy, inasmuch as it seems to be a prescription for a reaction to what we perceived as a major rupture of international systems that was already underway before the Coronavirus crisis. That, in some way, presupposes the possibility for global governance of the kind that might seem, on the face of it, somewhat utopian, given the failure of global programmes around human rights, etc. In the following, we address the challenges and requirements for enabling such a solution and discuss the types of changes to structural and systemic forces that would be required.

In short, we argue that the pandemic is tied to a failure of neoliberal (and we assume austerity) policies under globalisation, and that the post-pandemic world has to transform itself via a process that, together with other scholars, we call re-globalisation (Benedikter & Kofler, 2019b; Gills, 2018). We interpret the latest movement towards anti-internationalism and a rise in key areas of nationalisation of economic systems as an impediment to this re-globalisation. At the same time, one must consider the realignment of regional economies – for example, the ascendence of China, both globally and in the Asian context, as well as the viability of the EU after Brexit, etc.

The teachings of the Coronavirus crisis 2019–21 therefore encompass the future of the interdependence of domestic and international dimensions. Corona was a systemic global crisis that included a multiplicity of interconnected effects on international, national, regional and local levels where global fault lines came together to produce practical impact on citizens' everyday lives, independent of and throughout very different political systems, countries, cultures, languages, traditions, mindsets and civilisations. The resulting shockwaves were both equally universal and concrete. They were both trans-normal and trans-systemic, as immediate, direct and palpable. In short, Corona changed people's realities and spaces, for most of the globe's populations, for months and sometimes longer, in unprecedented ways. It turned out that most of the world was ill-prepared for such systemic rupture, although the potential for and possibility of such a crisis had sometimes been (at least partially) anticipated.

The so-called "Coronavirus" contagion's spread started in China, reached out to Europe and then affected the West and the whole globe. The accompanying systemic process of fundamental unpreparedness was rightly branded "a story of complacency, overconfidence and lack of preparation" (Herszenhorn & Wheaton, 2020). Besides its countless tragic human implications across nations, cultures and civilisations, COVID-19 from a foresight, anticipation and prevention standpoint was, in many ways, an unprecedented case study of what to expect and how to prepare with regard to upcoming global systemic crises specific to the 21st century and inter- and trans-disciplinary in nature.

In this regard, the Corona crisis teachings went beyond the existing and expected dangers of "hyper-globalisation", i.e., over-intense interconnections, over-complexity and far-reaching interdependencies within and across socio-political and economic systems. The Coronavirus crisis crossed the borders between democracies and autocracies, private and state capitalism, and cultural nationalist versus multicultural systems. In many cases, the Coronavirus took the lives of the bravest, i.e., of those fellow citizens who, prior to the crisis, were often regarded as the most underestimated or those working in professions "taken for granted". In order to honour those who fought in this crisis against an invisible and powerful adversary, the COVID-19 teachings must be carefully registered and integrated into the long-term overall future projection. This is necessary in order to allow the international community to build, first, a complexity-adequate mindset with regard to upcoming crises, which in times of "mature globalisation" are not the same as those prior to the 2000s, and second, to develop better inter- and multi-disciplinary policies for incoming multi-dimensionally effective events.

In order to make the most of the teachings of Corona, regional, national, international and global institutions must integrate multi-level governance efforts in meta-ideological ways. They must proceed from concepts of "crisis" (in the singular) to strategies of preparedness and management for "crisis bundles" and "bundle crises" (in the plural). This includes, first and foremost, the need to advance the respective concepts of "resilience" towards "multi-resilience", i.e., from mono- to polyvalent resilience policies. In addition, those who want to be prepared for the next foreseeable systemic crises must introduce innovative and concrete concepts of mental preparedness and maturity such as "Futures Literacy", "Participatory Solution-Building" and "Mobilisation of Collective Wisdom", involving much larger parts of the population than was the case before Corona. This includes substantially higher investments in adequate education on the basis of advanced theory.

The two central questions are:

1. How can societies prepare for unpredictable bundle crises and crisis bundles?
2. And what are the chances for progress in the aftermath of this crisis?

The Coronavirus tragedy in 2019–21 triggered more than five million deaths (Abraham and Kavya, 2021) and immense suffering, also by those who were not infected but isolated or "socially distanced" in an unprecedented transnational lockdown with more than half of the global population forced to stay at home for months. Yet, if its teachings are properly used, it will not only have produced new heroes, but also attracted increased attention to professions and services often underpaid but, as it turned out, more essential than others. If "multi-resilience" will be the outcome in mental and instrumental preparedness, the Corona crisis may not have occurred in vain, neither on the systemic nor on the national or regional levels. In retrospect, it could become a step towards a better-prepared and more multi-resilient global community more conscious of its commonalities than of its divisions and more prone to solidarity and cooperation than to mistrust and competition. What is needed for this step are not "visions" or just good intentions, but inclusive concepts that foster concrete progress towards more complexity-adequate modelling which must both integrate and transcend the approaches in place over the past decades in order to retain their best aspects and take them to a higher level.

A global re-orientation after the crisis was indeed demanded by many, not least by the Catholic Pope Francis who, in October 2020, published his third encyclica "Fratelli tutti" ("All brothers"), in which he evoked a more human economic, social and political form of international cooperation by using the Coronavirus crisis as an occasion for reform and renewal of critical sectors of societies (CNA Daily News, 2020).

This book contributes to this endeavour. The following chapters provide an overview of the main problems and effects of the Coronavirus crisis on the basis of a critical assessment of the most important aspects and phenomena in play. The book hereby concetrates on the peak of the crisis in the years 2019–2020, when vaccines were still in development and the effects of the pandemic were in full swing, providing the most useful teachings for future crises. As a consequence, we propose the concept of "multi-resilience" as the main methodological and strategic path to follow over the coming years. This proposal is not made with a normative, but a heuristic and descriptive intention. The concept of "multi-resilience" is nothing finished or simply a tool or instrument to take and implement. It can be neither elitist nor grassroots but must be an open and evolutionary concept meant as consciously intermediate and conciliatory between top-down and bottom-up approaches. It must be a strategic and practical concept with a strong policy impact to which not only experts, decision-makers and civil-society activists but also ordinary citizens are invited to contribute equally and on the grounds of an ethics of sharing and merit, if the best results are to be achieved.

Acknowledgements

The authors thank Roland Psenner, Head of the National Committee "Global Change" of the Austrian Academy of Sciences and Vice President of the University of Natural Resources and Life Sciences Vienna, for advice on this text.

Figures

1   Talfer River, Bozen-Bolzano, South Tyrol, Italy April 25, 2020   xxvi

2   Talfer River, Bozen-Bolzano, South Tyrol, Italy June 17, 2020   xxvii

3   The four phases of the model of adaptive cycles. Source: Grundig/Hollerson 2002   161

4   Adaptive cycles as nested systems. Source: Grundig/Hollerson 2002   163

5   The Viable Systems Model (vsm). Source: Jackson, 2003: 92   165

6   The four basic dimensions of the Cynefin Model. Source: Snowden & Boone, 2007, 73   175

7   "Doughnut economics" related to the Model of Postgrowth Economy. Source: Raworth, n.d.   220

8   Categorising different types of risks. Source: Bostrom, 2013, p. 17   230

9   The futures cone. Source: Voros, 2003   271

10   The futures diamond. Source: Popper n.d., 2008a   272

11   Futures literacy framework. Source: Miller 2018, p. 24   275

12   Mapping futures literacy labs within the futures literacy framework. Source: Miller 2018, p. 40   337

Overview and Summary

The Coronavirus crisis of 2019–21 was a multi-sectoral global crisis triggered by the – at that time – worst pandemic of the century. This crisis was of pluridimensional characteristics, and of inter- and trans-disciplinary features and effects. It was both unprecedented in its *international outreach* and *systemic cross-border effects*, as well as in its *trans-sectoral* penetrative power *within* societies. This double character made the global outfall of the Coronavirus disease, called "COVID-19", one of the most encompassing, and disciplinarily most ramified crises of the early 21st century. This is why some branded it the first fully "global" crisis in the strict sense. Its full impact and results remain open, as is with regard to a potential "post-Corona world". Sure is, though, that its experience and heritage provide many potentially exemplary teachings. The Coronavirus crisis proved that 21st century crises do not consist of segmented emergencies, i.e., isolated or isolatable crises, but tend, by their very nature, to be interconnected and complex systemic crises, i.e., *crisis bundles* or *bundle crises*. Therefore, any concept of coping with similar, connected or new crises in the present and future must evolve traditional specialised concepts of *resilience*, which remain partially valid, towards the new overarching concept of *multi-resilience*. Multi-resilience must be developed to a theoretic, educational, strategic and policy application capable of guiding practice. Multi-resilience is the core challenge of the years ahead, if the teachings of the Coronavirus crisis are to be taken seriously. This book *first* describes and assesses the peak of the global Coronavirus crisis in the years 2019–20. *Second*, it draws the pillars for a more "multi-resilient" post-Corona world.

The global pandemic "Corona crisis" was a systemic crisis triggered by the virus SARS-Cov-2. It hit a widely unprepared world. Starting to become internationally noticed around January 2020, it most probably expanded already since the last quarter of 2019 from the Chinese city of Wuhan and the surrounding province of Hubei into the whole world, affecting millions of people and killing hundreds of thousands around the globe. It was the first pandemic of this size in the 21st century.

Equally catastrophic was the fact that it put half of the earth's population into an unparalleled forced lockdown for months. It thus interrupted both domestic communication and lifestyles, as liberty and individuality principles and value structures, and globalisation more generally like no event previous to it since the start of the new millennium. In terms of sheer numbers,

OVERVIEW AND SUMMARY

the Coronavirus crisis was the worst catastrophe in recent times, putting the global economy into recession and, perhaps more important in the long term, seriously harming the ideas of internationalism, globalism and cosmopolitanism, with global bodies such as the U.N. and the World Health Organization (WHO) manifesting a deepening crisis which had already started before the virus hit.

Overall, the global Coronavirus (or COVID-19) crisis of 2019–21 was a major rupture of the international system. It was caused by a virus infection that imposed its standstill for months, including aspects of international relations, and put elements of the global order in question, also for the years thereafter. For the first time in the history of the 21st century, large parts of the globe were simultaneously paralysed by one and the same crisis and forced under the motto: "Do nothing". The resulting questions for all sectors of society are manifold – as is the search for its main teachings.

In the view of this book, the main teaching of the Coronavirus crisis is the need for systemic "Multi-Resilience". To achieve it, resilience must be advanced from specialised and sectoral to systemic and trans-sectoral by applying an innovative inter-, trans- and pluri-disciplinary approach.

Originating in the rapid spread of a novel virus, the resulting international systemic crisis involved such a vast and multi-faceted bundle of trans-sectoral shock waves, societal ramifications and socio-economic side effects across the borders as well as of habits and cultures in different political systems all over the globe that it remains difficult to describe its complete scope and assess its full impact, let alone to anticipate a globalised system after its end in its full transformative consequences. Most of such analysis must be led to history, but the teachings for the future and for incoming new systemic crises must be learned now. What is probable is that in retrospect, this crisis will be less interpreted as a disruption of the neoliberal economic or financial global order that shaped globalisation as we knew it before COVID-19, but rather as an acceleration of a rupture and transformation of globalisation from a self-explaining process legitimated by the sheer functioning of its ever-expansionist machinery to "something else" – i.e., as a factor and driver of "Re-Globalisation". What exactly this consists of, this is what the international community will have to find out; single nations will have to choose their own ways towards a post-Corona (re-)order. It is highly plausible that multilevel governance will be affected by post-Corona re-globalisation, and it is probable that this will be the case not only in open but also in closed or authoritarian societal systems.

We first provide an overview of the main phenomena, aspects, implications and effects of the Coronavirus crisis (parts 1–2). Second, we ponder the options, potentials and probabilities regarding the coming-into-existence of a "post-Corona world". While evoked by many analysts, visionaries and (political and economic) prophets in often all too quick and exuberant ways, the concrete and practical outlines of such a world remain unclear in most prospects. We hereby try to combine the most important of the available drafts and concepts and integrate them into the overarching strategic policy concept of "Multi-Resilience". Our assumptions are that first, pragmatism and practice in building flexible and adaptive solution capacities of anticipation of and coping with the teachings of Corona are more important than ideology, rhetoric and political instrumentalisation; and second, that the Corona crisis has indicated – and to some extent proven – that the present and imminent future are and will not be shaped by single crises, but rather by "crisis bundles" (parts 3–5).

As a consequence, the core of the book's third part, its outlook argument, is dedicated to the need to develop an inter- and trans-disciplinary "post-Corona" approach embodied in an integrated strategy capable of guiding policy, including a multi-resilient mindset, and to elaborate a flexibly applicable concept of "multi-resilience" apt to master bundles of crises (crisis bundles), and multi-impact crises (so-called "bundle crises"), by integrating synchronic emergencies into viabilities while transcending the limits and borders of different socio-political systems towards cooperative patterns (parts 6–7).

Overall, the main teaching and perspective of the Coronavirus crisis is the need to develop Multi-Resilience as a practical tool that concretely helps by the means of concepts, strategies, instruments and applications, both at the regional, national and international levels and their respective intermediate settings. In essence, the Coronavirus crisis has shown that by transcending the limits of disciplinary and sectoral questions to interdisciplinary and trans-sectoral solutions, the goal of future preparedness and new crisis anticipation is not mainly about the universalisation of remedies but rather about their coordinated contextualisation, and not about developing all too precise "arrival scenarios" but creating scenarios of flexible and fluid process management in the first place. The task is to integrate the elements, features and characteristics of hyper-complex dynamics, not just of causalities, situations or single drivers, in systematic and planned ways that must combine top-down and bottom-up processes much better than in the past.

With all this, one thing is sure: Catastrophes tend to be quickly removed and forgotten by the broader public. They are in most cases left to historians as soon as possible – the more, the more profound and traumatic their

OVERVIEW AND SUMMARY

immediate impact was. The same might be the case with the Covid-19 crisis. The following two images depict an art installation made from natural materials such as roots, branches and twigs by an anonymous land artist in Bolzano, a small city in Northern Italy. The installation located on the banks of the Talfer river referred to the frequent lockdowns with their imposition to "do nothing" (a logical contradiction in itself, as some measures during the crisis appeared to be to the larger public). It played with the enforced "muse time" of "doing" nothing, which broke the hectic and busy everyday rat race and allowed greater self-awareness and concentration, and thus evoked the origin of creativity and art – something the crisis also provided to many rather unexpectedly. But it also showed how ephemerous crises are, and how in the end even the "do nothing" will vanish – and eventually might disappear as if nothing happened.

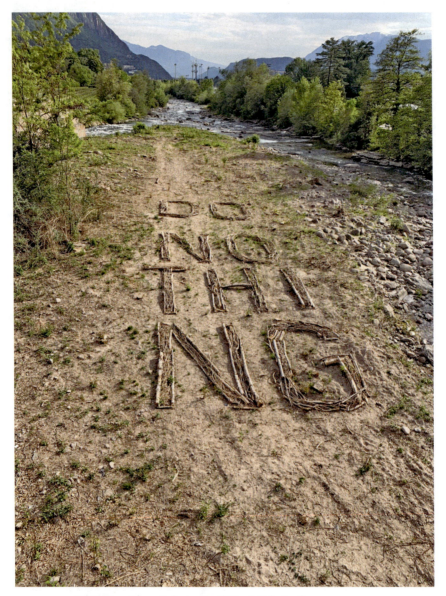

FIGURE 1   Talfer River, Bozen-Bolzano, South Tyrol, Italy April 25, 2020

OVERVIEW AND SUMMARY XXVII

FIGURE 2   Talfer River, Bozen-Bolzano, South Tyrol, Italy June 17, 2020

PART 1

The Coronavirus Crisis

∵

CHAPTER 1

Introduction

"Do Nothing" or, an Epochal Crisis

The global "Coronavirus" (or COVID-19) crisis started, at least for the world, in late 2019. In 2020, WHO Director-General Tedros Adhanom Ghebreyesus called the Coronavirus crisis "a once-in-a-century health crisis" (Aljazeera, 2020). The places where most people became infected were retirement homes, offices, and refugee and migrant shelters.

> "Corona" is the name of a family of highly contagious viruses; "SARS-CoV-2" the specific virus that caused the 2019–20 global pandemic; "COVID-19" the resulting, under given circumstances potentially deathly pneumonia-based disease which is, in many cases, interrelated with other complications.
> LAUREN & SAUER, 2020

Among the main identifiable symptoms are loss of smell and taste (Banner, 2020). The main medical conditions comprise severe difficulty in breathing, fever, headache, extremely sore throat and diarrhoea, all sometimes over weeks, with the last being an early warning sign. Many patients died of subsequent pneumonia or related inflammation. Among the lasting effects after recovery were, in many patients, a lack of concentration, fatigue and difficulty finding words. One result could also be a "decline in mental abilities" due to long-term COVID effects (NTV, 2020). The virus was believed to be particularly resistant on surfaces on which it could survive for up to four weeks (Bild Online, 2020e). As the three main infectious contexts, the magazine *Science* identified closed spaces, poor ventilation and domestic environments (Bild Online, 2020x).

"COVID-19" has been designated as exceptionally dangerous by institutions such as the World Health Organization (WHO) and Johns Hopkins Medicine because it combines a high infectiousness with a rather long incubation phase and a broad variety of different impacts on different people, reaching from no symptoms at all to weak flu symptoms to irreversible lung and other damage and death, which, particularly in the early stages of the pandemic, made it difficult to trace, identify, combat and prevent (Italian Ministry of Health, 2020; European Centre for Disease Prevention and Control, 2020). This variant of the Coronavirus presents a particularly wide spectrum of effects that make it

© ROLAND BENEDIKTER AND KARIM FATHI, 2022 | DOI:10.1163/9789004469686_002

apparently lethal to some and harmless to others, making predictions about disease progression difficult. Some experts explain the very different reactions to the virus with pre-existing immunity acquired by parts of the population before COVID-19 through contact with previous SARS viruses or herd immunity (Gupta & Kane, 2020). In addition, COVID-19 is said to produce side-effects which persist even after recovery, such as heart muscle inflammation, leaving up to 78 percent of the convalesced with long-term damage (Puntmann, et al., 2020; Bild Online, 2020f). The virus also seems to be particularly resistant, leading

> The World Health Organization's (WHO) Special Envoy David Nabarro [to state] ... that the virus is capable of 'surging back really quickly' and is 'returning all the time'.
>
> BBC NEWS, 2020nn

Studies suggest that a previous cold could provide some protection against the virus. Yet "mutated strings of the virus may jump back and forth" between humans and animals, prolonging the threat indefinitely for the years to come (Briggs, 2020b). According to (still non-conclusive) statistical studies, black people are twice as likely to catch Coronavirus than other ethnicities (Mundasad, 2020). This led to unproven speculations about the virus being a side product of potential weaponisation programmes, which could explain its selective dangerousness for different ethnic groups such as Caucasians, Africans, Afro-Americans or Asians, given that apparently according to some of these speculations, Sino-Chinese seem to be statistically less affected by death or severe, life-threatening course. There was also the question as to whether men die more often than women, as some observations suggest, and if so, why (Allotey, Schwalbe & Reidpath, 2020).

As a particular characteristic, the virus has presented extremely complex ramifications. Among them are fast and unpredictable mutations in animals which can be re-transmitted to humans, such as the so-called mink mutations detected in Denmark, and vice versa, which makes the development of vaccines more difficult (Bild Online, 2020y). A characteristic was that multiple infections seem to be possible in one and the same person, with the second course of disease usually worse than the first (Gallagher, 2020c). A partially resulting specific variant was "Long COVID", i.e., a comparatively very long course for a virus infection (Gallagher, 2020d). This could also be due to the fact that "anti-bodies fall rapidly after infection" (Gallagher, 2020b).

The *origin* of the Coronavirus was ascribed by both national and international experts and governments to the city of Wuhan, in Hubei province,

INTRODUCTION 5

China, probably as early as in autumn 2019. It remained not fully clarified as to whether the origin was a "wet market", most probably the Huanan Seafood Wholesale Market (Woodward, 2020), a live animal and seafood market in Wuhan's Jianghan district, or a laboratory, the P4 laboratory of the Wuhan Institute of Virology (The Japan Times, 2020) not far from it.

The first known European death was a man in France near Paris on 26 December 2019 (BBC News, 2020r). Yet it was only four days later that the Chinese authorities officially reported to the World Health Organization (WHO) that the virus had spread in the city of Wuhan and Hubei province (ibid.). A review report by the WHO of June 2020 nevertheless concluded that it was not Chinese information, but that on 31 December 2019,

> the WHO country office in the People's Republic of China picked up a media statement by the Wuhan Municipal Health Commission from their website on cases of 'viral pneumonia' in Wuhan. The Country Office notified the International Health Regulations (IHR) focal point in the WHO Western Pacific Regional Office about the Wuhan Municipal Health Commission media statement of the cases and provided a translation of it.
>
> WHO, 2020d

According to this report, the Chinese authorities officially informed the WHO only on 3 January 2020 (Ibid.). In reality, at that time the virus had long crossed the area's borders. It remains unclear whether the Chinese government officials purposely delayed information or not, and if yes, for what reasons exactly they would do so. There are scientific indications that the first Coronavirus cases occurred in December 2019 in other European countries, too, among them Italy (Südtirol News, 2020d). In Italy, the virus was, in retrospect, already traceable in the sewage water of two cities, Milan and Turin, as early as on 18 December 2019 (BBC News, 2020i).

The first U.S. deaths are thought to have occurred on 6 and 17 February 2020 in California's Santa Clara county, which comprises Silicon Valley south of San Francisco and features strong airway connections to China (BBC News, 2020p).

Some sources nevertheless declared a systemic multi-dimensional infection pattern, saying, for example, that "the virus came to the UK [i.e., one of the globally most affected countries and the most affected in Europe] on at least 1,300 separate occasions" (Gallagher, 2020) and not with just one "patient zero".

According to data based on official WHO information and on research of Johns Hopkins University Baltimore, the virus affected at least 216 countries (WHO, 2020b) and accounted for more than 23.6 million confirmed infection cases (as of August 2020, i.e., around 0.25 percent of the global population) (ibid.; Worldometer, 2020d). These numbers did not take into account a probably higher number of *de facto* infections due to a lack of testing, particularly in underdeveloped areas of the world. As of the first week of September 2020, only 10 countries worldwide remained Coronavirus free, all of them small islands in remote areas such as Palau, Micronesia and the Marshall Islands – but with insecure prospects (Globetrender, 2020; Amos, 2020).

In September 2020, the WHO asserted that two million direct virus deaths were "very likely", even with a vaccine at hand. Since the virus was thought to be selectively dangerous, i.e., of different levels of affectivity to different ethnicities and gene pools, it was particularly hard to calculate the exact impact on different regions in the world (BBC News, 2020kk). The COVID-19 disease caused at least 810,000 direct deaths within August 2020, while around 16 million people had recovered by then (Worldometer, 2020e; BBC News, 2020d). The country globally hardest hit was the U.S., with over 5 million cases and more than 162,000 deaths up to August 2020 (Worldometer, 2020f), making it also the advanced country worst affected. In the U.S., more than one million children had been diagnosed with COVID-19 in the first year of the pandemic (M. Fox, 2020). In Europe, more than 300,000 deaths were registered up to mid-November 2020, with 12.8 million cases (APA, 2020s). The hardest-hit nation was the UK with around 50,000 deaths, followed by Spain and Italy. Australia, South America and Africa were also particularly affected, but with the latter two having relatively lower registered infection numbers compared to the population due to a lack of testing, statistics, transparency and reporting (WHO, 2020b). According to experts, over the course of the pandemic, COVID-19 could cost humanity around 3.7 million human life years (Schäfer, 2020) and nearly 5 million human lives (as of December 2021).

Given that the crisis was systemic and caused a large number of side effects, the true harm and death toll of the pandemic remains disputed. What is certain is that many more "excess deaths" due to a variety of aspects and effects related to the crisis are assumed:

"At least another 130,000 people worldwide have died during the coronavirus pandemic on top of [the] officially recorded deaths from the virus, according to BBC research. A review of preliminary mortality data from 27 countries shows that in many places the number of overall deaths during the pandemic has been higher than normal, even when accounting for the virus. These so-called 'excess deaths', the number of deaths above the average, suggest the human impact of the pandemic far exceeds the official figures reported by governments around the world. Some will be unrecorded COVID-19 victims, but

INTRODUCTION

others may be the result of the strain on healthcare systems and a variety of other factors. Directly comparing the death toll between different countries is difficult. The accuracy of coronavirus data depends on how many people are tested for the virus and whether governments include deaths outside hospitals in their counts. As the virus has spread around the world, countries have reached different stages of their outbreaks at different times ... Analysing deaths from all causes during the outbreak and comparing them with deaths in the same period from previous years can begin to provide a more accurate, if still provisional, assessment of the coronavirus pandemic's true death toll" (Dale & Stylianou, 2020).

In response to the pandemic, most countries enforced harsh lockdown measures. The issue of borders, border closures and self-isolation became crucial in fighting the pandemic from early on. Many experts proposed a double strategy of "The Hammer and the Dance" (Pueyo, 2020a):

" 'The Hammer and the Dance' called for a 'hammer' (stringent measures to stop the virus) followed by a 'dance' (intelligent but less aggressive actions to prevent the pandemic from coming back) ... Many countries used a hammer: schools closed; businesses shuttered; public events were banned; masks were required; citizens were ordered to shelter at home. All those actions helped slow the spread of the virus. But as the world failed to dance the right way, it has been facing resurgences of the pandemic (Kingsley & Bautista, 2020; The New York Times, 2020) ... Measures like masks, testing, contact tracing, isolations, quarantines are still necessary, but one approach has not been emphasized enough: the fence. Countries that quickly closed their borders or carefully monitored anyone coming in have been most successful in slowing infections ... No country has been able to control the virus without a fence. Fences are not enough to stop the virus on their own, but they're a necessary part of the solution. European countries and U.S. states had hoped otherwise. They were deluded. They opened their arms to their neighbors too soon and got infected in the hug. They need to realize that not every country or state is effectively fighting the virus. Why should their citizens sacrifice so much for so long, with lockdowns and business closures, only to waste their efforts when their neighbors visit? And as long as states fail to control their borders, the coronavirus will come back" (Pueyo, 2020b).

The "Hammer and Dance" approach took on different forms in reality, and some "hammered and danced" better, while others did less well. Some countries had to impose second lockdowns, such as Israel (BBC News, 2020x), in a relatively early stage after a few months of relative calm, while others had a "dance" of their own, with rules repeatedly tightened and loosened without much of a system, such as the UK under Boris Johnson (BBC News, 2020pp).

According to a June 2020 study of Imperial College London published in *Nature*, the border closure and lockdown measures saved at least 3.1 million lives in Europe: "[Just] across ... six [European] countries, interventions prevented or delayed in the order of 62 million confirmed cases, corresponding to averting roughly 530 million total infections" (Hsiang et al., 2020; Bild Online, 2020u).

The lockdowns were imposed in local, regional, national, trans-national and multi-dimensional ways. Sometimes they were interconnected and planned accordingly, sometimes not. Most citizens could not leave their houses, their streets or their quarters and municipalities for months. Country borders were closed, flights cancelled, trains suspended and offices, universities, museums, bars, restaurants and all kinds of daily services such as hairdressers or vendors closed down. Police and voluntary units patrolled the streets, people mistrusted each other concerning possible infection, even within families, and suspended hugs and kisses. The path to the supermarket, with people standing metres away from each other, waiting immobile and anxious in the line at the entrance, felt like a Hollywood apocalyptic movie, and many described it like walking in a dream never experienced before. This, in the perception of the citizens, led to a "Do nothing" psychology that caused an unprecedented feeling of paralysis, rupture and change that was embodied and addressed, among others, by artists and psychologists. The "Do nothing" doctrine was even elevated to official national doctrine by Germany during the second lockdown in November 2020, hailing "couch potatoes" who declared to "do absolutely nothing in order to save lives" (BBC News, 2020s). Yet this did not lift up the spirits – on the contrary. Europe, for example, reported experiencing "pandemic fatigue", which became a buzzword of the times (M. Roberts, 2020). In Germany, every fifth citizen in autumn 2020 reported being more often in a depressive mood due to Corona (Bild Online, 2020l). The fact that over the duration of the pandemic, alert applications multiplied and became increasingly more sophisticated resulted in being not only an advantage but also problematic: more self-isolating alerts led to more concerns and psychological pressure, even in the absence of real threats (Kelion, 2020c).

According to the United Nations, the universality of the lockdown measures was one reason why, over the arch of 2021, there would be more than 31 billion US$ needed by the global community for the fight against the effects, remnants or recrudescence of the Coronavirus alone. This did not take into account probable subsequent fallout over the years to come, and it did not account for potential new viruses or other globally intertwined, i.e., systemic crises that, according to most specialising institutions of risk evaluation and anticipation, could spring up, adding further to the systemic long-term impact

INTRODUCTION

(UN News, 2020). Yet, according to estimates by the International Monetary Funds (IMF) of October 2020, in a more realistic scenario, Africa alone would need 1.2 trillion US$ over the years 2021–23 to recover from Coronavirus losses (BBC News, 2020a).

CHAPTER 2

Systemic Unpreparedness Inducing a Variety of Psychological Reactions

From relatively early on, there was a variety of statistical, academic and social science initiatives to help contain the virus and to make its eradication more probable by comparing best practices on a global scale and in real-time. Among them were, for example, the "COVID-19 Global Response Index" by the journal *Foreign Policy* (2020), and similar ones by other publishers. Others tried to develop popular narratives through simplified story-telling, such as the 30-year-old science journalist Mai Thi Nguyen-Kim who, in October 2020, received the German Federal Cross of Merit for explaining to the general public "how the virus would think if it could" (Bild Online, 2020q). Yet the beginnings of "serious" comparative analysis coincided with the paralysis of international law, and as one consequence, clearly comparable data referring to the same or similar background and reference frame were scarce (Connolly, 2020). Additionally, in the attempts towards an encompassing comparative analysis, realist versus idealist approaches in international relations often collided with each other (Basrur & Kliem, 2020).

This was one reason why, at the start of the pandemic, confusion was widespread among both virologists and politicians alike. Systemic unpreparedness became obvious to the general public. Some asserted for months that face masks were not necessary, others recommended them from early on. In many countries, behavioural rules changed so often and were sometimes regionally so diverse that, in retrospect, there were hundreds of thousands of cases where citizens fined for wrongdoing during the crisis started lawsuits against their governments and politicians to get their money back. This was the case, for example, in Austria where, when the worst of the crisis seemed over at the end of May 2020, the Socialist Party (SPÖ) demanded a "general amnesty" and the repayment of all fines inflicted in connection with infringement of Corona issues, including the lockdown regulations, due to unclear or fast-changing rules (Bischof, 2020). In the eyes of sometimes helpless, half-informed and confused citizens in open and closed societies alike, all too often the old saying seemed to be confirmed: "The people in front of the camera have nothing to say, so they say it".

The combination of shock, insecurity and uncertainty led to a wide spectrum of psychological reactions which were often diametrically opposed to

© ROLAND BENEDIKTER AND KARIM FATHI, 2022 | DOI:10.1163/9789004469686_003

each other. The desire of parts of the populations and opinion-makers to seize the shock for profound social, societal and systemic change for the better was polarised and disputed. Some, from early on, held that "our day-to-day" will hardly ever be the same again (Fogarty et al., 2020) – which others contested, as they thought the vast majority of people just wanted their normal lives back as soon as possible, and nothing more. Others in turn pointed out that the Coronavirus crisis helped to move back by one month the "Earth Overshoot Day" which, in 2020, was held on 22 August instead of 22 July, and thus that the virus had factually already helped to instil "deep" change towards a better world (APA, 2020f). Some prominent personalities welcomed the forced break in normal life of around three months (March to June 2020) caused by the pandemic lockdown:

"Nikolaus Bachler, an Austrian opera director from Munich, appreciates the corona-induced slowdown of everyday life. 'We have learned that you can experience the world more slowly because you were forced to get off this incredible hamster wheel,' the 69-year-old said. This also applies to the cultural sector. 'This international jet-set artist circus – must it go on like this, are there not perhaps other ways?', said Bachler, who believes that much has also changed as a result of the corona pandemic: 'Things will not be the same as they were. Something has happened to everyone during this time'" (Wiener Zeitung, 2020). Others, though, were not so sure that anything changed at all, and instead complained about the "countless errors in the system" (Von Westphalen, 2020).

Well-respected spiritual leaders, such as the Dalai Lama, also saw the crisis mainly as a chance – to transform one's emotions. In the Dalai Lama's view, emotional transformation is the most important psycho-social task humanity will be facing over the coming years and decades in order to master the main global problems, and crises such as the unprecedented Corona crisis of 2020 may help to fully understand this. According to the Dalai Lama, what the world now needs is "a sense of oneness of 7 billion people", which is the core spiritual challenge for humanity, and which could well become one heritage effect of the personal experience of the Corona crisis which has not only divided but also united the world – not only in sorrow, grief and anxiety but also in helpfulness and selflessness:

> The leader of Tibetan Buddhism sees reasons for optimism even in the midst of the coronavirus pandemic. People are helping one another ...,
> and if seven billion people on Earth develop 'a sense of oneness' they may yet unite to solve the problem of climate change. 'Many people don't care about their own safety but are helping, it is wonderful ... When we face

some tragic situation, it reveals the deeper human values of compassion. Usually, people don't think about these deeper human values, but when they see their human brothers and sisters suffering the response comes automatically.' The important thing is to try not to worry too much, he suggests. 'If there is a way to overcome your situation then make effort, no need to worry,' he explains. 'If truly there is no way to overcome then it is no use to worry, you can't do anything. You have to accept it ...' The important thing, he tells [us], is for us to recognise that we are not individuals alone, we depend on the community we are a part of ... 'In the past there was too much emphasis on my continent, my nation, my religion. Now that thinking is out of date. Now we really need a sense of oneness of seven billion human beings.' This, he says, could be one of the positive things to come out of the corona crisis ... The challenge ties into another of the Dalai Lama's great preoccupations: education. 'The whole world should pay more attention to how to transform our emotions ... It should be part of education not religion. Education about peace of mind and how to develop peace of mind. That is very important'.

BBC NEWS, 2020qq

CHAPTER 3

The Branches and Social Strata Hardest Hit

A List to Be Carefully Remembered for the Next Systemic Rupture

The psychology of anxiety and inquietude that took a grip on the whole spectrum of social strata and societal sectors in the global community was certainly not unfounded, though. Because of its particularly efficient infectiousness, the Coronavirus (COVID-19) put an unusual number of persons simultaneously in hospitals, unleashing a multi-dimensional health-care crisis which, according to experts, triggered many deaths due to side effects such as non-hospitalisation, lack of treatment and insufficient testing, but also because of impoverishment due to the closedown of stores and businesses.

Alongside overcrowded intensive care units, non-hospitalisation became a serious problem. In Germany, for example, more than 50,000 cancer surgeries were postponed due to Coronavirus concerns within seven months, inducing Gerd Nettekoven, Chairman of the Board of the German Cancer Aid organisation, to warn "of potentially fatal consequences. The great concern of the Cancer Aid organisation is that the postponements were not in all cases 'also medically justifiable'. This is a truly huge number of severely sick people not treated" (Der Spiegel, 2020c).

The assumed protracted consequences of the Coronavirus crisis as a whole – i.e., beyond its immediate effects as a disease such as fever, headache and life-threatening pneumonia – on single, particularly vulnerable segments of the population could, in retrospect, prove to have been even more tragical. Contrary to the assumption that "the virus does not distinguish between persons", it became indeed obvious that seriously sick and poor people – and poor nations – were hit much harder. In an indicative way for potentially upcoming global crises of the future, the effects of Corona pointed out which sectors and strata of society are particularly vulnerable to systemically interrelated "whole-complexity" crises. This list will be something to remember carefully for the years ahead.

First, as always, the poorest were the most immediate and hardest hit. This is why global NGOs called Corona "the hunger virus":

> COVID-19 is deepening the hunger crisis in the world's hunger hotspots and creating new epicentres of hunger across the globe. By the end of the year [2020] 12,000 people per day could die from hunger linked to

© ROLAND BENEDIKTER AND KARIM FATHI, 2022 | DOI:10.1163/9789004469686_004

COVID-19, potentially more than will die from the disease itself. The pandemic is the final straw for millions of people already struggling with the impacts of conflict, climate change, inequality and a broken food system that has impoverished millions of food producers and workers. Meanwhile, those at the top are continuing to make a profit: eight of the biggest food and drink companies paid out over $18 billion to shareholders since January [2020] even as the pandemic was spreading across the globe – ten times more than has been requested in the UN COVID-19 appeal to stop people going hungry. While governments must act to contain the spread of this deadly disease, [NGOs are] also calling for urgent action to end this hunger crisis and build fairer, more robust, and sustainable food systems.

OXFAM INTERNATIONAL, 2020

In July 2020, *Science* magazine warned of:

COVID-19 risks to global food security. Economic fallout and food supply chain disruptions require attention from policy-makers. As the COVID-19 pandemic progresses, trade-offs have emerged between the need to contain the virus and to avoid disastrous economic and food security crises that hurt the world's poor and hungry most. Although no major food shortages have emerged as yet, agricultural and food markets are facing disruptions because of labor shortages created by restrictions on movements of people and shifts in food demand resulting from closures of restaurants and schools as well as from income losses. Export restrictions imposed by some countries have disrupted trade flows for staple foods such as wheat and rice. The pandemic is affecting all four pillars of food security: availability (is the supply of food adequate?), access (can people obtain the food they need?), utilization (do people have enough intake of nutrients?), and stability (can people access food at all times?). COVID-19 is most directly and severely impacting access to food, even though impacts are also felt through disruptions to availability; shifts in consumer demand toward cheaper, less nutritious foods; and food price instability ... [critical responses that] policy-makers should consider to prevent this global health crisis from becoming a global food crisis ... Last, but not least, COVID-19 has highlighted the importance of early detection of new infectious diseases, 70% of which have their source in animals. Improving surveillance systems for zoonotic diseases arising from animals used in the food chain is vitally important for avoiding future catastrophes.

LABORDE ET AL., 2020

THE BRANCHES AND SOCIAL STRATA HARDEST HIT   15

The pandemic's toll on the hungry was indeed terrifying:

> More people are going hungry, an annual study by the United Nations has found. Tens of millions have joined the ranks of the chronically undernourished over the past five years, and countries around the world continue to struggle with multiple forms of malnutrition. The latest edition of the [U.N.] State of Food Security ... in the World, published today, estimates that almost 690 million people went hungry in 2019 – up by 10 million from 2018, and by nearly 60 million in five years. High costs and low affordability also mean billions cannot eat healthily or nutritiously. The hungry are most numerous in Asia, but expanding fastest in Africa. Across the planet, the report forecasts, the COVID-19 pandemic could tip over 130 million more people into chronic hunger by the end of 2020. Flare-ups of acute hunger in the pandemic context may see this number escalate further at times. As progress in fighting hunger stalls, the COVID-19 pandemic is intensifying the vulnerabilities and inadequacies of global food systems – understood as all the activities and processes affecting the production, distribution and consumption of food. While it is too soon to assess the full impact of the lockdowns and other containment measures, the report estimates that at a minimum, another 83 million people, and possibly as many as 132 million, may go hungry in 2020 as a result of the economic recession triggered by COVID-19. The setback throws into further doubt the achievement of Sustainable Development Goal 2 (Zero Hunger).
>
> WHO, 2020a

Among the disadvantaged often impaired by personal shortages were also the underpaid "heroes" who carried on putting themselves in harm's way, such as nurses or supermarket employees, who, despite all the praise, remained underpaid. There remained also the risk of a worldwide vaccination chaos for years, particularly affecting poorer countries (Bild Online, 2020o).

Among the particularly vulnerable segments were children in poor countries:

> In contrast to the direct impact of COVID-19, the broader effects of the pandemic on child health are significant. [...] Hundreds of thousands of additional child deaths could occur in 2020 compared to a pre-pandemic counterfactual scenario. This would effectively reverse the last 2 to 3 years of progress in reducing infant mortality within a single year.
>
> UN SECRETARY-GENERAL & UN SUSTAINABLE DEVELOPMENT GROUP, 2020

In addition, the Corona crisis represented an unprecedented challenge for social justice in the youth and educational sectors with harsh medium- and long-term consequences:

> Falling into poverty: An estimated 42–66 million children could fall into extreme poverty as a result of the crisis ..., adding to the estimated 386 million children already in extreme poverty in 2019. Exacerbating the learning crisis: 188 countries have imposed countrywide school closures, affecting more than 1.5 billion children and youths. The potential losses that may accrue in learning for today's young generation, and for the development of their human capital, are hard to fathom. More than two-thirds of countries have introduced a national distancelearning platform, but among low-income countries the share is only 30 percent. Before this crisis, almost one third of the world's young people were already digitally excluded (Ibid.).

On a side note and as a backdrop to school closures due to lockdown measures, the child infection and mortality rates were disputed throughout the whole pandemic process and led to partly fierce divisions about whether and under which precise conditions pre-schools and schools should be closed. This was one aspect that partly undermined the legitimacy of the "political rule of virologists", since these experts were divided on the issue as well and, as for example in Germany, acted ruthlessly against each other in a fight for recognition, influence and power (Hildebrandt, 2020; Rinke, 2020). While the Coronavirus crisis initially made the virologists "pop stars" (Welt, 2020), in many cases their reputation subsequently faded away due to too many opposed views and contradictions, not least whether it made sense to wear masks or not, and whether children had to be better or less protected than the elderly.

The resulting picture was mixed. On the one hand, cases became known where the Coronavirus was transmitted from a mother to her unborn child during the last weeks before birth, thus proving that children from infected mothers were at increased risk (Bild Online, 2020t). On the other hand, after months of empirical research, most experts asserted that compared to other age groups, the danger of child mortality was relatively low. According to a Europe-wide study, for children, the Coronavirus mortality rate was:

> Very low. Less than one percent of infected children and adolescents die as a result of the infection, according to a study published by the journal 'The Lancet Child & Adolescent Health'. In the vast majority of children

and adolescents infected with the coronavirus, the course of the disease was 'mild', explained Marc Tebruegge of University College London, who headed the study. For the study, the European research team evaluated the course of the disease in 582 minors aged between three and 18 years, who had been cared for in 82 healthcare facilities. All these children and adolescents tested positive for Coronavirus. Only four of them died. Two of the deceased had previous illnesses. In eight percent of the cases, the respiratory disease COVID-19 triggered by the virus took a more severe course, requiring intensive treatment. This is a small but 'remarkable' proportion, Tebruegge explained. In contrast, 16 percent of the minors had no symptoms at all. The low mortality rate is apparently due, among other things, to the fact that pre-existing conditions among minors are significantly less frequent than among adults. Only a quarter of the children and adolescents in the study had pre-existing conditions. The researchers also assumed that the probability of children and young people dying from coronavirus infection is even lower than in their study. It can be assumed that children infected with the virus with only a mild course of disease were often not taken to hospitals or other healthcare facilities. This proportion of infected children was not included in the study.

EURACTIV & AFP, 2020

Despite such – in principle – good news, this became publicly known only after months of school closures which inflicted both educational and psychological damage on children and teenagers. The side effects and indirect consequences were drastic, since the lockdown situation kept millions of children behind closed doors and within four walls, allowing only low exercise and poor motion and thus increasing de-socialisation and depression rates (C. Miller, 2020). In August 2020, the UN warned of a "catastrophe" because of world-wide school closures:

> The UN has warned that the world faces a 'general catastrophe' due to school closures caused by the pandemic. It warned that getting students back to schools should be a 'top priority' once the pandemic is under control.
>
> COLLERTON, 2020

In fact, missing school was worse for children than the virus itself, said Chris Whitty, the UK's Chief Medical Officer, in August 2020:

> Children are more likely to be harmed by not returning to school ... than if they catch coronavirus. Prof Chris Whitty said 'the chances of children dying from COVID-19 are incredibly small' – but missing lessons 'damages children in the long run ... Many more [children] were likely to be harmed by not going than harmed by going to school. There's also very clear evidence from the UK and around the world that children much less commonly get a severe illness and end up having to be hospitalised if they get symptomatic COVID ... There is much less transmission from children to adults than adults to adults'. He said reopening schools would connect households in other ways – for example by parents meeting at school gates, or mixing with others as a result of being able to return to work. 'The fact of schools being open will probably lead to some increase in transmission but much of that is indirect,' he said.
>
> BBC NEWS, 2020aa

The schooling situation contributed to a widespread psychological emergency, particularly among the global youth until then completely unfamiliar with such "universal" closure. As former OECD director for PISA research and Humboldt University Berlin representative Barbara Ischinger put it in a nutshell at the end of May 2020, Corona was a fundamental international educational challenge:

> The education sector was little prepared for such a crisis. From one day to the next, several countries closed all institutions of education, which caused a systemic shock: In early April, in approximately 150 countries nursery schools, primary and secondary schools, and institutions of higher education were forced to shut down. Politicians challenged parents and teachers and asked for home schooling and online teaching. Parents heard confusing messages regarding the timing of the closures. The weakness of national governance structures in education became apparent: Who makes the decision for closure and for re-opening of the institutions of education? In the future do we need a protocol for the education sector which recommends the necessary actions in a crisis, and could such protocol be drafted with international partners, for instance under the auspices of UNESCO or OECD?.
>
> ISCHINGER, 2020

Indeed, in the educational sector paradoxical developments were observed, as the UNESCO Chairs on Heritage Futures Cornelius Holtorf and Annalisa Brolin (2020) reported more in detail, touching upon the self-conception of education and thus upon the future of millions of young people around the globe:

> The use of distance methods and digital communication – whether in teaching, collaborating, or researching – has grown exponentially. In the immediate wake of the corona crisis, educators are engaged less in true distance education than in something more akin to emergency remote teaching: a patchwork of methods implemented without the preparation and experience that facilitate truly successful online education. But, especially depending on the duration of the pandemic, we are ... likely to see a shift toward a greater role for such methods, with a longer lead time enabling more adequate preparation for educators. The crisis has impacted the decisions of students as well. Sweden, for example, has seen a substantial increase in the overall number of applications to universities as a direct result of the crisis and a consequence of the loss of readily available employment for young people as they leave secondary school. Among those younger than 20, there has been a nationwide rise of more than 30 percent in applications to higher education compared with the figures from 2019, and there is a general increase in applications to nursing and medical programs (Ibid.).

Added to the complexities of the transfer to online teaching, such short-term rush put additional pressure upon many educational systems, particularly in developed countries.

Minorities worldwide were also facing challenges as a result of the COVID-19 pandemic. As the OSCE High Commissioner on National Minorities, Lamberto Zannier, and representatives of the United Nations reported in May and June 2020 at one of the model hotspots of European minority protection, i.e., in the trilingual city of Bozen-Bulsan-Bolzano in the Autonomous Province of South Tyrol at the border between Austria and Italy at the heart of the European continent (Eurac Research, 2020a), the implications and effects of Corona on all kinds of minorities were massive. They spanned from the reduction of positive discrimination and mechanisms of equality to new forms of discrimination, not least due to a revival of nationalism (Carlà, 2020). They included the partial *de facto* suspension of territorial self-governance and aspects of autonomy rights due to the closure of borders and changed inter-state relations regarding trans-national minority areas. There was also a grave situation of foreign workers in dormitories in Singapore and the Arab Emirates, but also in Germany and elsewhere, who were often forced to live and work under unhygienic, thus unsafe conditions. For example, among the hardest hit were the foreign workers in Singapore, where COVID-19 became a "pandemic of inequality" (Tan, 2020):

> Singapore is home to more than 300,000 low-wage foreign workers from countries like India and Bangladesh, who mainly work in industries like construction and manufacturing. Their right to live in Singapore is tied to their job and their employer must provide accommodation, at a cost. They commute from their dorms in packed vans to building sites where they work and take breaks alongside men from other crowded dorms – perfect conditions for the virus to spread. With no legal maximum occupancy rules, in pre-COVID times it was normal for up to 20 men to share a room in a dorm ... The authorities decided that the dormitories would have to be sealed off. Around 10,000 healthy migrant workers in essential services were taken out to other accommodation – a skeleton staff to keep the country running. But the majority were trapped in the dorms – some not even allowed to leave their rooms – while mass testing was carried out. Infected workers were gradually removed, isolated and treated. It was a remarkably different experience to the lockdown the rest of the country was going through, with shopping allowed, daily exercise encouraged and every type of outlet offering delivery. These people were well and truly locked down, with only basic meals delivered to them. 'Once the lockdown was in place, we were not allowed to come out of the room. We were not allowed to go next door too,' Vaithyanathan Raja, from southern India, told ... The turn of events forced many in Singapore to confront the living conditions of many of these migrant workers – the sudden attention, coupled with new hygiene measures, saw a surge of charitable collections, and many dorm operators working to improve conditions (Ibid.).

Furthermore, Corona led to particular problems for isolated indigenous people who, in times of the pandemic, were among the hardest hit since they were usually more prone to diseases which they historically did not develop or know. Also, the risk of death for ethnic minorities within advanced societies was significantly higher than for others:

> People from ethnic minorities are at a higher risk of dying from coronavirus, a report by *Public Health England* says. It shows age remains the biggest risk factor, while being male is another. The impact of COVID-19 is also 'disproportionate' for ... Asian, Caribbean and black ethnicities. But it remains unclear why. A trade union for doctors said the report was

a 'missed opportunity' for 'action' to be taken to protect health workers who are from ethnic minorities ... [UK] Health Secretary Matt Hancock told the House of Commons the public was 'understandably angry about injustices' and that he felt a 'deep responsibility because this pandemic has exposed huge disparities in the health of our nation'. 'Black lives matter, as do those of the poorest areas of our country which have worse health outcomes and we need to make sure all of these considerations are taken into account, and action is taken to level-up the health outcomes of people across this country,' he said

BBC NEWS, 2020ee

On the other hand, the "Corona summer" of 2020 also hurt migrants even in ultra-liberal Germany which, since the migration crisis of 2015, had been branded the most migrant- and refugee-welcoming nation on earth (Dallison, 2016) – yet they did so mainly by their own hand, as migration researcher Stefan Luft (2020) pointed out on the occurrence of repeated severe migrant riots in major cities, among them Stuttgart and Frankfurt in July 2020:

The corona summer has acted as a catalyst. According to conflict researcher Stefan Luft, the riots were caused by immigrants who had been unable to gain a foothold in Germany and were 'torn out of all structures' as a result of the corona crisis. The violent people were mostly migrants who immigrated to Germany in recent years but who, contrary to their original expectations, did not make it onto the labour market for skilled workers. Due to cramped accommodation conditions, they remained dependent on meeting places in public space. The Corona summer with its restrictions on residence in public space then acted as a catalyst. Basically, however, accumulations in public space – for example in Stuttgart – have been known for several years ... Luft recommended energetic regulatory intervention: In the power struggle for the public space, the conflict researcher believes that the authorities must react with local security concepts and penalties that quickly follow the crime (Ibid.).

The Chairman of the police union of the city of Frankfurt explained the riots: "These are young migrant men who do not want to integrate" (Bild Online, 2020n). According to him, these young men used the preceding Coronavirus lockdown and the respective tensions simply as a pretext to riot against all authorities, the rule of law and the public order of their host.

In Italy, irregular migrants from Northern Africa carried across the Mediterranean by private sea rescuers, mostly NGOS, continued to arrive in their thousands despite the pandemic measures, causing citizen protest. Irregular migrants repeatedly ignored the quarantine measures of the government and fled their compounds, stirring up further emotions against illegal mass immigration due to Corona anxieties:

> The corona pandemic made the refugee situation even more difficult. Citizens protest against migrants' arrivals on Lampedusa island: citizens of Lampedusa took part in a sit-in at the port to protest against the continuing arrival of migrants. The demonstrators demanded an immediate stop to immigration, Italian media reported. Earlier, 180 migrants who were in quarantine in the city of Caltanissetta in Sicily fled. In the night, 114 migrants arrived in Lampedusa on board two boats. The migrants were taken to a refugee camp, which already contained 650 people. The hotspot has only 95 places. On the evening, 520 migrants had been taken to other facilities in Sicily. 180 migrants, who had been placed in a two-week quarantine in a refugee camp in the Sicilian town of Caltanissetta, fled the hotspot. None of the fled migrants tested positive for the coronavirus, the authorities said. Dozens of police officers went in search of the asylum seekers, 120 of whom were subsequently located. They had to return to quarantine. The Mayor of Caltanissetta, Roberto Gambino, called on the Italian government to stop sending migrants to the city. 'It can't go on like this. The security conditions in the refugee centres are inadequate,' warned the Mayor.
>
> SÜDTIROL NEWS, 2020a

In many cases, stigmatisation made the infected themselves a minority, often independent of migration, ethnicity, age, race or gender. Some charismatic figures opposed these mechanisms even by or after dying, such as the daughter of Nelson Mandela, Zindzi, did with the help of her family in South Africa:

> Zindzi Mandela's family praised for revealing she had COVID-19. South Africa's President Cyril Ramaphosa has praised the family of the country's first black President Nelson Mandela for revealing that his daughter, Zindzi, who died on Monday, had COVID-19. The gesture will 'encourage acceptance' of those infected, Mr Ramaphosa said ... Zindzi was buried alongside her mother, anti-apartheid activist Winnie Madikizela-Mandela. Despite public awareness of how the virus is spread, its symptoms and effects, there have been some reported cases of stigmatisation of those infected. 'I would like to thank the Mandela family for the very important gesture of sharing this information with the nation. This is a

virus that affects us all, and there should never be any stigma around people who become infected,' he tweeted ahead of Zindzi Mandela's funeral. He added that revealing the cause of her death, was 'a final act of solidarity in the life of a woman who devoted her life to the cause of her fellow South Africans.' Zindzi Mandela, 59, was Nelson Mandela's sixth child and his second with Winnie Madikizela-Mandela, his second wife

BBC NEWS, 2020eee

CHAPTER 4

Were Nature and the Environment "Winners" of the Crisis? Disputed "Improvements" and Their Flip Sides

Was the pandemic with its strict lockdown and mobility and travel restrictions for more than half of the global population beneficial for the global environment, as some asserted? Was it even an artificial "rest period" for nature and the global climate context?

Scientific research proved: Yes and no. There were some good indications for "improvement", for example of water quality in otherwise polluted areas such as the city of Venice. But many doubted the effects were good enough in the medium and long term to speak of a real turnaround. Rather, Corona provided just a temporary break. As the national and international media reported:

> Because of the Corona crisis, CO_2 emissions have fallen sharply worldwide – at times by 17 percent. The CO_2 content of the atmosphere is nevertheless rising to record levels. One reason: the high stability of the gas. Because many countries have reacted to the pandemic, emissions have temporarily fallen significantly. At the peak of the strict Corona measures, daily global CO_2 emissions were temporarily reduced by about one sixth. Global daily values at the beginning of April 2020 were estimated to be up to 17 percent lower than the 2019 average. According to climate scientists at the University of East Anglia, an estimated 83 million tons of CO_2 were emitted worldwide on 7 April 2020 as a result of the burning of fossil fuels and cement production. In 2019 the daily average was 100 megatons. In some countries, emissions had even dropped by up to 26 percent on average at the height of the Corona restrictions. ... The measures taken against the spread of the Coronavirus have had a major impact on energy requirements worldwide. The fact that large parts of the world's population had to stay at home and borders had been closed has reduced traffic and changed consumer habits. These sharp declines are probably only temporary, as they do not imply structural changes in the economy, transport or the energy sectors.
>
> ZDF HEUTE, 2020

Some reports even suggested that Corona led to fewer deaths and to an overall improvement of health, at least in industrialised countries, as a result of cleaner air, less noise, less stress and less traffic due to the lockdown (Broom, 2020a; Watts, 2020a). Most of these assumptions were disputed, though, and dismissed by parts of the scientific community, while others confirmed some partial results. Harvard University analysed that air pollution made a Corona infection worse:

> 'If you're getting COVID, and you have been breathing polluted air, it's really putting gasoline on a fire,' said Francesca Dominici, a Harvard biostatistics professor. That's because the fine particles penetrate deep into the body, promoting hypertension, heart disease, breathing trouble, and diabetes, all of which increase complications in coronavirus patients. The particles also weaken the immune system and fuel inflammation in the lungs and respiratory tract, adding to the risk both of getting COVID-19 and of having severe symptoms.
> GARDINER, 2020

Instead of seeing progress, some environmental activists, on the contrary, feared that the climate change question could at least temporarily sink into oblivion due to what some called the "Coronavirus hysteria", and that interest-driven protagonists could exploit the crisis for their own plans. This fear was not completely unfounded. In May 2020, related to Corona "scientists said more than 50 billion years of cumulative evolutionary history could be lost as humans push wildlife to the brink" (Briggs, 2020a):

"A top Canadian official said this [was] a 'great time' to build a pipeline because Coronavirus-related restrictions ban large public protests. Alberta's Energy Minister Sonya Savage said people needed jobs and 'ideological protests' would not be 'tolerated' by ordinary Canadians. She was referring to the Trans Mountain oil pipeline, opposed by indigenous groups and environmentalists. It runs from Edmonton in Alberta to Burnaby, British Columbia" (BBC News, 2020ddd).

The good news was that Corona might have increased environmental consciousness, at least among Europeans – as, for example, found in August 2020 for the Central European nation of Austria:

> Study: Austrians attribute more importance to environmental protection since Corona: 30 percent find environmental protection 'more important' than before the Corona crisis.
> – Younger people in particular are more likely to separate their waste;

- more than 60 percent wish for more environmentally friendly policies;
- the initiative 'Every can counts' demands a #ReSTART for a better climate.

A world upside down, but nature is recovering! Worldwide, the Corona crisis has forced societies to suddenly stop. The question is: How has the crisis changed people and will we do things differently in the future? While the long-term effects on the labour market and the economy are still unclear, a positive development can be seen with regard to environmental matters: According to a recent survey by the recycling initiative 'Every can counts', 30 percent of Austrians attach more importance to environmental protection than before Corona. Concrete changes in behaviour are already becoming apparent: young people in particular are separating their waste more frequently, thus ensuring that valuable secondary raw materials such as aluminium are returned to the recycling cycle. In June [2020] around 500 people aged between 14 and 75 years were questioned throughout Austria ... and it appears that the virus could have a positive effect on environmental protection: 64 percent of all questioned would like to see more environmentally friendly policies, and among 14 to 29 year olds the figure is 71 percent. 'Because nature was visibly recovering in some areas within just a few weeks, there seems to have been a change of attitude among the population', reports Claudia Bierth from the 'Every Can Counts' initiative and Sustainability Manager at Ball Beverage Packaging Europe. For 30 percent of those surveyed, environmental protection has become 'much more important' or 'more important'; and for those under 30 it is more than 38 percent. In order to make their own contribution, they pay particular attention to waste separation and recycling (82.8%), avoid food waste (76.6%) and buy regional or seasonal foods (65.3%). Over 60 percent take care to avoid plastic as far as possible. In a comparative study from February 2019, the figure was at 48.3 percent. There has also been a significant increase in the avoidance of packaging waste: in 2019, 50 percent said they would contribute to environmental protection; in the [August 2020] survey, the figure was 60 percent. The Every Can Counts initiative founded in the UK in 2009 is one of the leading recycling programs for beverage cans in Europe. The initiative with 19 local country programs aims at motivating young people to dispose of empty beverage cans correctly and thus return them to the recycling cycle. The goal of Every Can Counts is to achieve 100 percent can recycling in Europe

APA, 2020p

Another issue was the reported reduction of the criminality rate due to the Corona-imposed lockdown which apparently hindered thieves, aggressors and murderers in the execution of their "business" – i.e., another crucial "improvement" of things in open societies. In reality, there were sharp differences, since some sectors of crime went down, such as physical crime, and others up, such as Internet-based crime and domestic violence. In Germany:

> The lockdown had something good: there was less crime. Many areas of life became safer. Corona reduced the crime rate. There were fewer burglaries, thefts or violent crimes. Even though these figures are provisional ..., they show a clear trend. Up to 90 percent less pickpocketing in Lower Saxony, only half the number of bicycle thefts in Berlin. When life in public places was as restricted as [in the Corona crisis], the opportunities for theft were lacking. In order to control curfews, there was also a lot of police on the road. According to the [German] police ..., this also applied ... to the registered thefts from offices, manufacturing, workshop and storage premises. Which means: During Corona there were fewer thefts in companies by their own employees. [There was] a decline in home burglaries of 25 to 30 percent (Hamburg), 35 percent (German federal state of North Rhein-Westphalia) to 50 percent (Lower Saxony). [Nevertheless], a strong increase in cybercrime was registered. The [German] Federal Criminal Police saw a massive increase in potential targets on the Internet. The Central German Crime Authority (BKA) assumed that criminals were increasingly exploiting the concerns of the population. Fake shops, false appeals for donations and more phishing mails could therefore be in circulation. In addition, the BKA also expects more cyberattacks on the health system: Crime remains very creative even in times of Corona.
>
> ZDF HEUTE, 2020

In neighbouring Austria, a similar phenomenology was registered:

– "The crime rate in Austria has almost halved [during the crisis], said Interior Minister Karl Nehammer. During the lockdown, he said, classic crime such as street robbery and burglary had shifted towards cybercrime. It was already clear that 'crime statistics will certainly not be comparable with normal years before or after ... Significantly fewer burglaries and body injuries were reported. In 2019, 52,618 criminal offences were reported, in 2020 28,208 offences were reported in the same period. In the sector of criminal offences against life and limb, there was a decrease of 37.3 percent to a total of 2,838 offences ..." (nachrichten.at & APA, 2020).

- Nevertheless, so-called home crimes, often among family members, went up due to the Coronavirus lockdown that forced people to stay together in smaller spaces over longer time periods than usual:
- "At the beginning of April 2020, the [Austrian] government had launched a campaign to offer women assistance with violent partners. 4,410 home entry and personal approach bans were imposed between the start of 2020 and 17 May. The average in Austria was 30 per day, in April and May 2020 it was 35 per day. The Federal Criminal Police Office subsumes under violence in the private sphere offences such as dangerous threats, (serious) bodily harm and (serious) coercion. From 16 March to the beginning of May [2020] there was an increase of nine percent compared to the previous year. The highest number of charges was 1,031 for bodily harm, 487 for dangerous threats, and 89 for aggravated bodily harm, according to figures from the [Austrian] Federal Criminal Police Office" (Ibid.).
- In the same period, as in other countries, Internet crime also strongly increased in Austria:
- "In some cases there were enormous increases in the area of Internet crime. Fake shops selling face masks and [anti-Corona] drugs shot up during the Coronavirus pandemic. In total, fraud on the Internet increased by 27.4 percent. 1,110 such reports were made between mid-March and the beginning of May 2020 [in Austria]. The trade of addictive substances also shifted increasingly away from the street to the online sector. The increase was even more pronounced in cyber-crime offences such as illegal access to computer systems with a plus of 72 percent, misuse of computer programs or access data with an increase of 207 percent to a total of 43 reports, and for fraudulent data processing abuse, where the number of offences rose to 560, an increase of 97 percent" (Ibid.).

Simultaneously, as Felia Allum and Diego Bolchini (2020) reported, while occasional and individual crime may have temporarily decreased due to Coronavirus, organised and collective crime was decisively strengthened – as happens during and after most other crises and catastrophes. In Europe, this was the case particularly in southern continental countries such as Italy where, to take just one example, the Mafia organised itself as usual on a large scale in order to make use of its social networks and to obtain a systematic grip "big style" on the financial post-Corona help provided by the European Union and single European governments, acting similarly to its previous systematic undertakings regarding the help after earthquakes or with social security payments to the poor, including migrants and refugees:

> Criminal organisations have always sought to benefit from new opportunities, even those arising from catastrophe ... The *Guardian* reported (Tondo, 2020) that criminal organisations were possibly gaining local influence and social consensus in some areas of Southern Italy by distributing free food to low-income families, providing needed services, and helping other market participants who have run out of cash because of the [Coronavirus] lockdown. Over the long term, the potential risk is that if criminal organisations are able to provide their services within a fragile human and economic terrain, they could gain a new degree of control and informal power over existing and new territories and local economies (Ibid.).

As Allum and Bolchini underscored, this is not a new phenomenon, but the Coronavirus crisis and its aftermath could have contributed towards taking it to a new systemic level:

> The power of clan prestige and local patronage is not a new phenomenon. Many clans made their fortunes in the aftermath of the 1980 earthquake in Campania, Italy. Although the earthquake was 'an act of God,' it proved to be an ideal money-making opportunity for companies close to Camorra clans. They were able to divert state reconstruct funds that poured into the region for public construction projects straight into their pockets, leaving many roads and houses unbuilt. As the world faced a pandemic, will the same thing happen in the post-COVID-19 context? A new global econometric outlook should especially focus on non-traditional territories and the new models of interactions ... that criminal organisations could exploit in the pandemic ... This diverse group includes Russian and Balkan mafia clans, French-Corsican cartels, Chinese Triads, Turkish or Nigerian groups, and more. Economist Milton Friedman would have probably invented a 'Mafia Helicopter Money' metaphor to describe the new risks of this possible alternative cash flow at a micro- and even meso-foundational level. We are perhaps entering an era of new dark profit-making activities and entrepreneurial strategies. Well beyond the symbols and rituals depicted in Mario Puzo's novel, *The Godfather*, states and liberal economies must win this battle through a persistent engagement strategy at all levels including with civil society (ibid.).

But not all criminals benefitted from Corona. In the United States, where prison conditions can be harsh, inmates at a California correctional facility tried to infect themselves with COVID-19 in the hope of being released or transferred to hospitals, a sheriff said on the basis of surveillance video material backing his claims (CNN, 2020b). In other countries, such as Italy, multiple prison uprisings occurred against the spread of the virus within restricted and overcrowded spaces. At the height of the crisis, Italy even released some of the most feared Mafia bosses because of the alleged life-threatening virus in the country's prisons, thus reacting to an exceptional situation for which the correctional system was completely unprepared (Borghese & Iddios, 2020).

The crisis even had some "positive" religious implications, welcomed by its representatives and the spiritual and religious in general. As Alison K. Ralph (2020) noted, as a consequence of the global Corona crisis, religion came back to some extent from the private sector to be noted as a "public" manner and benefit again:

> Americans used to consider religion a 'private' matter: Too emotional, too controversial, too studded by the minefields of culture wars and personal and collective hurts to discuss openly ... But something about this pandemic has made us think more about what communities of faith offer to their own congregants, but also to their neighbors. It's a turn toward thinking about religion as a 'public' matter. I heard a story ... on Mormons, who often have significant stockpiles of food and supplies as part of their ethos of self-reliance, sharing those stockpiles with neighbors down the street who [due to Corona] can't get to the store for fear of the virus. [There] was a story about cooking for Passover when you can't even get chicken for matzo ball soup at the store. Religious communities support not just their own well-being ... This action of sharing with neighbors is not limited to people of faith, but it is impossible to deny that religious traditions bring strong scriptural and cultural lessons to do just that ... In the words of Robert Putnam ..., faith communities are the largest store of social capital ... It is goodwill in action and it is definitely 'public' (Ibid.).

CHAPTER 5

Children and Relationships

There were, however, also more secular developments of civil courage and engagement, such as "the strangers reaching out to Kyrgyzstan's lonely teenagers" (Abdurasulov, 2020):

> The scheme – called You Are Not Alone – was launched after seven teenagers took their own lives in the first two weeks after Kyrgyzstan started the Coronavirus lockdown in March. At the time, the nation's attention was on the poor medical facilities, lack of protective equipment and impact of Coronavirus on the economy. But as news of the teenagers' deaths spread, a group of activists decided there was also a need to focus on the country's children and their mental health. 'I was dismayed. We had had one Coronavirus death and during the same period [so many] children committed suicide,' said Banur Abdieva, one of the project's founders. There is nothing to say the seven deaths were directly related to the lockdown, but people like Kurmanjan Kurmanbekova, a psychologist from a refugee centre in Tubingen, Germany, feared the strain it was putting on children's mental health. 'And as a symptom of depressive conditions, we get a suicide mood,' she explained (ibid.).

In Kyrgyzstan, as in other countries:

> Schools closing meant many children have limited options for interaction, especially in rural areas where education offers a respite from the relentless drudge of housework and a rare opportunity to communicate with other children. Added to this were concerns from experts over any potential increases in domestic violence, which could possibly be exacerbated by isolation and parents' loss of income ... Volunteers approached local schools and state education agencies which sent them a list of students in a 'group of risk' – mostly children without parents or who live with relatives and may lack attention and care. There [were] more than 100 volunteers and nearly 400 children aged 12 and older in their database ... Crucially, volunteers are not just on the end of the phone to talk about the problems their new friend is facing – unless the teenager brings it up themselves. Instead, they focus on their new friend's future goals and potential (ibid.).

© ROLAND BENEDIKTER AND KARIM FATHI, 2022 | DOI:10.1163/9789004469686_006

While such positive examples of enhanced care were also observed in other developing countries, it was worrying that according to the "Kids Rights Index":

> the Corona crisis affected children's rights. The measures taken to combat the Coronavirus have a catastrophic effect on many children. This is the conclusion of a report of the children rights organization 'KidsRights'. The worldwide school closures due to Corona alone affect 1.5 billion children and young people, according to the 'KidsRights Index 2020', which is based on UN data. This makes them vulnerable to child labor, child marriages and teenage pregnancies. The increase in domestic violence during the lockdown measures was particularly devastating for girls. The unprecedented pressure on the health system led to the suspension of vaccination programs against diseases such as polio and measles and could lead to an increase in additional child mortality by hundreds of thousands. In addition, the United Nations estimates that another 42 to 66 million children could fall into extreme poverty in 2020 as a result of the corona crisis. 'This crisis is undoing years of progress in the welfare of children,' said Marc Dullaert, founding chairman of 'KidsRights'. 'Showing children the cold shoulder can be disastrous in the short and long term, both for the present and future generations,' warned Dullaert
>
> VOLKSGRUPPEN.ORF.AT, 2020

Yet not only kids were affected; an unusually high number of partnerships also failed. As an effect of increased family conflicts due to restricted living spaces and forced togetherness, the divorce rate increased noticeably in many countries due to Corona, particularly in open societies, for example in Germany:

> Is Corona to blame for marriages ending, too? According to a survey, the divorce rate in Germany could probably increase significantly as a result of the Corona pandemic – by a factor of five! Lawyer Alicia von Rosenberg, on whose behalf the survey published by the opinion research institute *Civey* was conducted, said: 'Those who have been wishing to divorce since the so-called shutdown are divided into two case groups:
>
> 1. couples in whom spatial confinement was the straw that broke the camel's back;

2. couples who have been separated for a longer period of time and who, through the forced shutdown, now want to put their circumstances in order and definitely conclude with the chapter of marriage.

BILD ONLINE, 2020V; BRAUER, 2020

In response, the city state of Singapore offered a "pandemic baby bonus" to boost births and further family cohesion (BBC News, 2020yy).

CHAPTER 6

Labour and the Economy
"Generation Corona"

In the labour and employment sector, the Coronavirus effects were contradictory or even opposed in comparison between different nations. In Austria, for example, the number of days of sick leave decreased dramatically – by two thirds – due to the crisis in April 2020, from 436,619 in 2019 to 148,999 in 2020 (Austrian Press Agency (APA), 2020t). This was due to the large number of people working from home or temporarily unemployed. In neighbouring Germany, in contrast, during exactly the same timeframe, the number of sick leave days increased to record highs due to preventive unemployment registration (ibid.).

In Europe, there was the fear of a veritable "Generation Corona" due to the Corona-driven massive increase of youth unemployment in particular:

> There are large increases in unemployment among young people in Austria compared to the previous year – the increase in the Central European nation is 52 percent. What can be done to prevent a 'Corona generation' from growing up, who will continue to feel the consequences of the Corona crisis for a long time to come? When people enter the labour market, they have more and more problems finding a job. But unemployment makes young people sick. Further education, training and qualifications will be particularly important.
>
> APA, 2020m

Ironically, in such a dire situation, the Corona crisis did not only lead to an increased trust in remote-interconnecting technology such as videoconferencing or lecturing via "intelligent" video live-stream, but also accelerated the takeover of human jobs by Artificial Intelligence – in many cases precisely those jobs where humans are needed most, e.g. in journalism:

> The outbreak of COVID-19 has made jobless a lot of workers. And now Artificial Intelligence is starting to take over people's jobs. Several industries have already been affected in various sectors by the intrusion of Artificial Intelligence, and journalism turns out to not be an exception. Microsoft has recently fired dozens of journalists, who were responsible for arranging and editing news stories; they will be replaced by

© ROLAND BENEDIKTER AND KARIM FATHI, 2022 | DOI:10.1163/9789004469686_007

automatized systems. And at a time when Indian news media companies are sacking employees due to COVID related economic downfall, the possibility of intelligent robots is now becoming a major threat to ... job security. Artificial Intelligence is still in its early stages, but it will be interesting to see how it will change the fourth pillar of democracy, in the era of web journalism and shouting debates on prime time tv news. Will hysterical anchors in newsrooms be replaced by robots who'll talk with some sanity? [...] Yet can a robot bring the same feeling, the same compassion and humanity ..., which is an essential part of being a reporter? This is the reason why journalism needs to be human-centric always ... AI can help in gathering news ... but can never take over journalism as a whole.

TPT BUREAU AGENCIES, 2020

Perhaps most encompassing, the virus lockdown and related closure and protection measures by nations and states caused a deep global economic recession. It was estimated at around

-2% (Fitch Ratings, 2020) to -3% in 2020 alone (Gopinath, 2020), with developed countries projected to shrink more significantly at over -5% (Chan, 2020), and continued effects afterwards, most pronounced in 2021 and 2022. Corona thus caused what observers called "the worst economic downturn since the Great Depression" (Gopinath, 2020), worse than the 2008–09 "Great Recession" (The Economic Times, 2020; Boone, 2020), with repercussions over the years to come. As Gita Gopinath, the International Monetary Fund's (IMF) Economic Counsellor, declared: "... the crisis could knock $9 trillion off global GDP over the next two years" (Chan, 2020). In addition, potential persisting perceived psychological insecurity could make the economic downturn "especially deep and lengthy, with recovery limited by continued anxiety" (Goodman, 2020).

As a result, the Department of Economic and Social Affairs (DESA) of the United Nations (UN) estimates that the virus crisis will contribute to the rise of the most abject poverty in the world. About 34.3 million people are likely to fall below the threshold for 'extreme poverty' in 2020 due to the consequences of the virus. People in Africa (UN/DESA 2020), but also children worldwide will be particularly hard hit. According to UNICEF and Save the Children, child poverty worldwide has risen by 15 per cent to around 1.2 billion children (Bild Online, 2020i). According to the UN definition, 'poverty' is not only linked to income, but also to access to food, clean drinking water, sanitation, a roof over one's head and services for health and education" (UN/DESA 2020).

While recessions may per se not necessarily be a bad thing, since they can also have a cleaning effect which may, under given circumstances, increase the health and rationality of the economic system, it is a fundamental sense of uncertainty and insecurity that has been infused by the Corona crisis into the globalised economic, financial and, ultimately, also political systems which could turn out to be its lasting heritage. Corona has influenced the consecration of the term "uncertainty" to new lead term of international political economy and economic analysis for describing the state of the global economic system.

This effect was further intensified by the fact that while large parts of the middle and lower classes feared for their existence, the super-rich, as an effect of the Coronavirus lockdown, became massively richer:

> Despite the economic effects of the Corona crisis, the super-rich in the USA became even richer. The wealth of the 600 richest US-Americans grew between February and April 2020 by 434 billion US$. This is an increase of almost 15 percent. The fortune of Amazon founder Jeff Bezos increased by more than 30 percent, that of Facebook founder Mark Zuckerberg by more than 46 percent. Millions of people in the USA have lost their jobs in the Corona crisis, but online enterprises took strong profit from it
>
> APA, 2020q

Corona confirmed the economic law that crises and catastrophes always benefit the wealthy and top owners and earners. Paradoxically, even more profit than that of U.S. billionaires was gained by China's super-rich from the China-originating global crisis. According to specialised sources:

> The crisis produced not only losers but also winners: Billionaires from China in particular were able to increase their wealth during the lockdown thanks to a 0.2 percent increase in the Chinese stock market. First and foremost: Eric Yuan Zheng, inventor of the Zoom video platform, which is very popular with countless companies in the age of home office. Zheng was able to increase his assets by 77 percent to eight billion US dollars (7.27 billion euros). In addition to Zheng, eight other Chinese billionaires became richer despite the Corona crisis. It should be easy for these super-rich people to increase their enormous wealth even further. After all, the economic collapse caused by Corona is causing many companies to slide financially. The best starting conditions for an investment [of the super-rich]
>
> BILD ONLINE, 2020z

In this sense, the disputed – and to some extent misleading – term "social distancing", imposed by the global crisis management with the meaning of "keeping a physical distance of 1–2 m from each other in order to not get infected", acquired an additional meaning: "Social distancing" as widening the gap between the social strata, i.e., the "distance" between the rich and the poor.

CHAPTER 7

Corona and Re-Globalisation 1

Sharpening Awareness about the Differences between Political Systems and Their Growing Asymmetries

All in all, the Coronavirus crisis further increased both domestic and global inequality, confirming a general (typological) effect of multi-dimensional social crises. It thus contributed towards putting a question mark over the practices of neoliberal globalisation that dominated the past three decades (1990–2020). This included a new public awareness in Western liberal democracies for asymmetries within and between political systems (private versus state capitalism) as well as for the fundamental changes in the geopolitical relations between different systems that had occurred over the years which had immediately preceded Corona.

In fact, the Corona crisis *manifested*, *expressed* and *questioned* the new, increasingly volatile geopolitical power relations between the rising authoritarian superpower China (state capitalism), from which the virus originated, and the Western alliance of democracies (private capitalism). As observers analysed in mostly converging ways, COVID-19 in a relatively early phase not only became a "war" about defeating a virus, but also a competition between (at least) two different political systems and their underlying ideologies: mono-party dictatorship versus liberal democracy, (meta-)communism Chinese style versus open society as the European-Western model and as the basis of the international liberal order. As Bill Gelfeld (2020) put it:

> This pandemic has brought us to a critical inflection point in world history. Many scholars and pundits have observed that the world will likely be fundamentally different in its wake. The ascension of democracies since the end of World War II and particularly since the end of the Cold War is under threat. A new model of smart, technocratic authoritarianism, spear-headed by the Chinese government, has challenged its primacy. Tragically, the current American leadership … has bungled the response at every turn, failing to provide a coherent national strategy and shirking the international leadership that has been the hallmark of the U.S. in the post-Cold War world. And because of this vacuum, China has stepped into the void … to push its philosophy and pursue its hegemony. China now

© ROLAND BENEDIKTER AND KARIM FATHI, 2022 | DOI:10.1163/9789004469686_008

offers a competing vision of competence mixed with compliance. The Chinese Communist Party's propaganda machine (Wischer, 2020) is in full swing, arguing that their autocratic system ensured a more effective, efficient response to the pandemic. But the Chinese Communist Party's vision under Xi Jinping is an increasingly totalitarian one. Domestically, it is a vision of a surveillance state, controlled and manipulated by the government and reinforced through technology. Abroad, it is a surreptitious but expansionist power that extracts arm-and-a-leg concessions for aid and loans ...

According to Gelfeld (2020) from an early stage on, the Corona crisis was not only caused in China but also rather recklessly used by the Xi Jinping government to demonstrate the efficiency of a totalitarian system which finds no obstacles in closing down millions of people, in contrast to open societies. It can be added that most probably, the communist government will rewrite history in its realm of influence and point out that China was a benefactor and the best-organised and most effective fighter against Corona in the world, as always trying to turn a self-produced catastrophe into a historical highlight for the totalitarian regime and against the democratic world. In response, the West should weigh its own Corona and post-Corona strategy of "talking by doing" in order to "let values speak for themselves":

[China's government's] is not a philosophy that we in the democratic world should allow to go unchecked, but now [in the Coronavirus crisis of 2020] is not the time for open conflict; now is the time for wary collaboration ... The U.S. should become the arsenal of recovery, in particular for developing countries that will be hardest hit by the pandemic. We should mass-produce first the necessary supplies and later, once we have hopefully found it, the vaccine for the millions in the Global South who will invariably need our help. We should do this because it is the right and humane thing to do. Because democracies care about the well-being of people in other societies, be they under democratic or authoritarian rule. We should let our example do the talking [and] show that our philosophy is superior economically, politically, and morally (as we did in the Cold War) by producing the needed supplies, giving them without condition, and doing it not for political gain but humanitarian gain. Because if we do not do this, the Chinese government will step into the leadership void and push their more cynical, less representative, and less humane vision of governance and society ... (Ibid.).

Gelfeld goes even further and suggests that the post-Corona world is an unprecedented historical opportunity for the global alliance of democracies to show their real superiority by producing a humanistic supremacy and thus producing a new global democratisation push. In order to achieve this, an economic offensive is needed:

> The U.S. [and the West] may well want to consider a joint Marshall Plan for healthcare in the developing world, along with its OECD allies. These are extraordinary times that demand an extraordinary response. Because mass infection in developing countries like India, Nigeria, and Brazil, in a hyper-connected world, begets reinfection in the developed world ... This is how we win the battle against the pandemic and the war for democracy and liberal values (Ibid.).

Interpreting the global fight against Corona as a "war for democracy and liberal values" and as an opportunity against the rise of authoritarian and totalitarian regimes within a more multipolar international order was a take shared by many pro-democracy theorists and activists. Nation states and their governments were less inclined to such proto-ideological politicisation. Nevertheless, this (probably unnecessary) restraint created a situation where the West failed to re-ignite democratisation or to sustain it by deeds abroad, for example in Hong Kong or Africa. On the contrary, China could make propaganda through international Corona aid widely undisputed by Europe and the Western media. In this sense, Corona was a missed opportunity owed to the lack of a multi-dimensional, complexity-adequate long-term coordinated resilience and democratisation strategy of a West already in a crisis of self-confidence before the virus broke out.

This elapsed chance to turn a global strategic situation of democracies against autocracies from passive to active, and from defensive to offensive again could backfire in the post-Corona world and produce bitter fruits. It could allow a further expansion of non-democracies shaping re-globalisation even more strongly, i.e., the renewal of the global system, by dominating interpretation patterns by the means of putting the Corona *process* over the Corona *origins*. And this comes although China first tried to hide the dimension of the endemic and then used its "normal" strategy to stop it – i.e., suppression and surveillance. Italy, France, and Spain subsequently closed down millions of people, but without the surveillance system established in China, South Korea or Taiwan – but nobody in the West, with a few exceptions, has pointed this out as a decisive difference. Therefore, some observers saw China's behaviour not as "reckless", but rather as "normal", when contextualised to its own socio-political system and its authoritarian top-down order.

While the whole issue was never about the return to an old Cold War ideology, the failure to compare the systems and to confront the used procedures led, rather than to a critique of China's suppression, to the critical assessment that "the Coronavirus crisis proved the weakness of U.S. federal government" (Pearce, 2020), as, for example, Lawrence O. Gostin of Georgetown University pointed out. Although there may be some progressive potential of self-improvement here, in essence once again open societies tended to criticise (and de-legitimate) themselves in front of their citizens rather than unveiling the inhuman nature of authoritarian systems, thus uncovering their increasingly worrying lack of global consciousness in times of populism, polarisation and crisis of democracy which keeps open societies more engaged with themselves than with their global responsibilities to communicate and explain the advantages of their system.

This is all the more tragical given the fact that China, contrary to its helpful and modern attitude communicated by its government and state-controlled media, in reality – according to all estimates of international experts – partly hid and partly whitewashed its real Corona numbers, as it always does with state-controlled statistics, transforming the place of the outbreak, the city of Wuhan, "in a city of silence" (Sudworth, 2020). More importantly, it systematically used the Coronavirus crisis to further suppress its ethnic minorities and to demonstrate the absolute power of a violent regime against its population. For example, the Chinese regime in July 2020 declared an allegedly Corona-related "wartime state" over the capital of the Uighur province of Xinjiang, Urumqi, although there was no need to do so from an infection viewpoint:

'A wartime state' has been declared in Urumqi, the capital of China's western Xinjiang region, after a spike in cases of coronavirus. Officials on Saturday said 17 new cases had been recorded and strict measures on movement had been imposed. Although the figure appears low, China has [officially] recorded very few significant outbreaks since COVID-19 emerged in the city of Wuhan late last year. China is now not in the top 20 in terms of either infections or deaths. It has recorded just over 85,000 infections and 4,600 fatalities, according to Johns Hopkins University research. The capital of the Xinjiang Autonomous Region has a population of about 3.5 million ... The vast majority of coronavirus deaths and most of the infections in China occurred in Wuhan at the start of the year. Since then, the only large-scale cluster was reported in June in Beijing, where more than 330 people were infected before the outbreak was contained. However, some have questioned China's reporting of numbers on the outbreak ... Xinjiang is home to the mainly Muslim Uighur people and other Turkic minorities and is subject to intense state control ... There is the added sensitivity of controversial detention camps where hundreds of thousands of mostly ethnic Uighurs have been interned as part of a mass 'de-radicalisation' programme.

BBC NEWS, 2020f

Perhaps even more indicative for the turn against democracy, partly by the "use" of the pandemic for anti-democratic measures, the "meta"-communist government of China itself – where the virus originated – used the disaster to definitively put an end to Hong Kong democracy. In August 2020, the Hong Kong elections were "postponed" in an ultimate blow to the "one country, two systems" approach (Chinese: 一国两制), using the pretext of a third Coronavirus wave which had affected the city relatively early after initial success (Cheung, 2020):

The Hong Kong government has postponed September's [2020] parliamentary elections by a year, saying it is necessary amid a rise in coronavirus infections. However, the opposition has accused the government of using the pandemic as a pretext to stop people from voting. The government banned 12 pro-democracy candidates from running in the elections (BBC News, 2020ss). Opposition activists had hoped to obtain a majority in the Legislative Council (LegCo) in September's poll, capitalising on anger at Beijing's imposition of a controversial national security law in Hong Kong, and fears that the territory's freedoms are being eroded. Pro-democracy candidates had made unprecedented gains in [the 2019] district council elections, winning 17 out of 18 councils ... The overall numbers are still lower [in Kong Kong] than those of many other places – but the spike comes after Hong Kong appeared to have contained the outbreak, with weeks of few or no local infections ... The city has introduced tough new measures to combat the virus, banning gatherings of more than two people ... Opposition politicians say that, under local election laws, the polls can only be postponed by 14 days, and that a longer delay would 'trigger a constitutional crisis in the city'. Lawmaker Tanya Chan said she suspected pro-government politicians were more concerned about 'their own election prospects' rather than 'the severity of the pandemic'. Some experts have suggested that measures could be put into place to make elections safer, such as reducing waiting times at polling stations – and that a delay of a whole year is not necessary. Activist

> Joshua Wong, who was disqualified from running in the elections, wrote on Twitter that the pandemic was being used as 'as an excuse to postpone the election' and was 'the largest election fraud in #HK's history.' Hundreds of thousands of people took part in unofficial pro-democracy primaries earlier [in August 2020], in what was seen as a show of support for the pro-democracy movement.
>
> BBC NEWS, 2020tt

Independent of allegations and accusations about accurate or non-accurate reporting, cases like this make it clear that both the Coronavirus crisis and all future crises are and will always be related to questions of politics and, more importantly, to political systems and their use of the crisis for their purposes, including competition regarding efficiency, control, self-representation, and legitimacy. Anyone who wants to ignore this aspect for the sake of taking care of an emergency by designating it as "politically neutral", as mainly European democrats did during the Coronavirus crisis, wilfully blinds himself concerning a crucial dimension in play which is of similar or even bigger impact than the crisis itself.

CHAPTER 8

A Battle for Values and Transformation Not Confined to Bilateral Competition, but Spanning the Globe

Perhaps equally important for the future of re-globalisation, the "battle for democracy and liberal values" inherent in the Corona crisis was by no means confined to the competition between China and the West. In the biggest democracy of the world, India, it transformed into a fundamental fight for press freedom and the right to report unpleasant facts and publicly utter opinion:

> While the Coronavirus has focused much of the world on Europe and the United States, India promises to be the greatest victim of the disease. But other than a slick public relations campaign, the government of Prime Minister Narendra Modi has done little to confront the Coronavirus crisis ... Using a combination of financial pressure and outright censorship, Modi and his rightwing Bharatiya Janata Party (BJP) have silenced much of the media. Newspapers and broadcast outlets are finding that criticism of Modi or the BJP results in the loss of government advertising, a major source of revenue. Modi has also filed expensive and difficult to fight tax cases against opposition media outlets. In the case of the coronavirus, the government got the Supreme Court to order all media to 'publish the official version' of the health crisis, which, in practice, has [for an extended time period] meant feel-good stories. The success that the BJP has had in corralling India's 17,000 newspapers, 100,000 magazines, and 178 television news channels has been sharply condemned by media organizations. *Reporters Without Borders* rates India a lowly 140 out of 180 countries on its freedom index.
>
> HALINAN, 2020

In fact, according to Conn Halinan:

> One important independent outlet reporting on the COVID-19 crisis has been *Rural India Online*, part of the People's Archive of Rural India (PARI), a network of reporters and photojournalists who report on India's rural dwellers who make up 70 percent of the population. P. Sainath, PARI's founder and editor ... is sharply critical of the Modi government's actions,

and PARI's reporters have covered what the mainstream media has been intimidated from reporting: the massive number of poor who have taken to the roads to return home [because of the crisis], cancer patients sleeping outside of hospitals in the hope of getting treatment, and day laborers who cannot afford to miss any work [despite the dangers of the pandemic]. One told PARI reporter Shraddha Agarwal, 'Soap won't save us if we die of hunger first' ... The next pandemic is just around the corner, and unless there is a concentrated effort to make healthcare a human right, it is only a matter to time before the next mega-killer strikes (Ibid.).

India's problems with gender equality as a basic unsolved political problem of its democracy were also brought to the fore by Corona: Many Indian women who were abused previously lived in constant fear during the lockdown of suffering from even more domestic abuse and violence than before (BBC News, 2020aaa). There were even reports of a 14-year-old being sexually attacked in one of India's Coronavirus cure centres, while an accomplice of the attacker filmed the act (BBC News, 2020vv), demonstrating that India's public spaces are also often stages of abuse, even under the most precarious conditions. This is another notorious problem unworthy of a modern democracy, yet constantly ignored by Indian governments, thus undermining democracy's reputation among women. India, one of the countries with the world's highest infection rates over one of the longest periods of time, also saw a spike in other regressive social fallout, such as an increase in child marriages due to fears about the future of poor children in the pandemic (BBC News, 2020ww).

Not to speak of Brazil, one of the countries hardest hit by the virus, where populist, nationalist and anti-globalisation President Jair Bolsonaro acted openly against his own government's anti-emergency actions. In doing so, he tried to transform Corona into a political issue in order to demonstrate and legitimise his political stance of alleged "rightist liberalism", accusing officials that the Corona measures were "dictatorial" and, by so doing, indirectly suggesting that he himself was not – until he himself caught the virus:

> Stay-at-home orders and other restrictions were criticised by far-right President Jair Bolsonaro, who denounced them as 'dictatorial'. He even joined anti-lockdown protests in the capital, Brasilia ... Mr Bolsonaro has repeatedly played down the risks of what he calls 'little flu'... He has argued that regional lockdowns are having a more damaging effect than the virus itself, and accused the media of spreading panic and paranoia. The president has also been spotted meeting supporters while not wearing a mask, such as ... in Brasilia. And while many people share his concerns about

46   CHAPTER 8

the economic impact of lockdowns, health officials have disagreed with
his approach. In fact, two doctors have left their posts as health minister
since the pandemic began, one was sacked, one resigned. Mr Bolsonaro
also said he would not be seriously affected by the virus. 'I'm not going to
be brought down by a little flu,' he said in March. That's been put to the
test, as [in early July 2020] he tested positive for COVID-19.

BBC NEWS, 2020uu

As a consequence, the Brazil infection rate quickly became the second-worst in
the world after the U.S., with more than 3 million cases and more than 100,000
deaths up until August 2020. Observers described the situation in the nation as
"like a war" (BBC News, 2020k).

And what about Latin America as a whole, which, in the past, was most
often treated as the "forgotten continent" in global power plays, political relations, social innovation and international emergency measures in cases of
catastrophe and global change (perhaps with the sole exception of the BRICS
debate (Guriev, 2015; Bond, 2018), which concentrated widely on the continent's biggest country, Brazil, while Chile was more involved in the Transpacific
Partnership agreement process, or TPP)?

The former Chief of Strategic Content of the General Secretariat of the
Chilean Government, Carlos Cruz Infante (2020b), explained the particular
problems Latin America had to contain the disease with three factors that
favoured the spread of the virus: Firstly, high unemployment rates in most
Latin American countries, which forced people to go out to search for income
instead of obeying to the lockdown; secondly, the high urbanisation rate in
Latin America, which sees high numbers of people living together in restricted
spaces, which in turn favours the spread of infections; and thirdly, social
upheaval connected with a fundamental mistrust of those in power and civil
disobedience, which is common in these societies, as seen from the historical
experience with rulers:

"The coronavirus contagion has increased dramatically in Latin America.
Among the lamentable 'top ten' countries most affected by COVID-19, four are
in Latin America: Brazil, Peru, Chile and Mexico (Center for Systems Science
and Engineering (CSSE, 2020), in that order. Despite some claims that this
might have led to herd immunity in the region – hitherto, not the safest strategy, – the reality is that Latin America's public health infrastructure [was]
undeniable unprepared in the face of the pandemic (Infante, 2020b). If the
path continues to be followed, the plight will turn into a complete disaster. We
might have expected it for Mexico and Brazil, not for Peru and Chile".

Why? According to Cruz,

Considering Mexico's and Brazil's political situation, the massive and rapid spread of the disease was only a matter of time. Their populist leaders, Andrés Manuel López Obrador, and Jair Bolsonaro have bungled crisis management and scorned the pandemic's gravity. Moreover, governance in both countries is ineffective from a policy point of view. Both have extraordinarily complex and malfunctioning federal systems. Central administrations often struggle with state and local authorities, making it challenging to implement effective and quick responses to fight COVID-19 or any other national problem. In the cases of Peru and Chile, however, expectations were to contain the pandemic earlier. Why? Because both presidents, the Peruvian Martín Vizcarra, and the Chilean Sebastián Piñera, have used the lockdown as the primary tool to combat the virus. Nevertheless, neither could stop the virus' spread, and the contagion rate [went] out of control. Why, then, has the spreading accelerated so much? As we have seen throughout history, there is just one bullet-proof measure to prevent contagion: social distancing. Apparently, people in Latin America – at least in the four countries mentioned above – have not stopped going out (Ibid.).

Yet the most threatening part elucidated politically by the pandemic is, according to Cruz, a parallel "pandemic" that is chronic in Latin America, had existed long before Corona and had now been brought back prominently to the fore by it – the fundamental political pandemic of mistrust and lack of confidence in the system of democracy as such. This is one of the historical legacies of Latin America. As confirmed by most reports on the acceptance of democracy in public opinion polls and in the general mood of society, democracy on the continent is in retreat (Arana, 2019; Goenaga, 2016). Cruz pointed out that the approval for the political system of participatory democracy during Corona was below half of the population(!), causing a constant "legitimacy crisis" of the existing democratic rules and laws, including the Coronavirus measures. Anti-governmental feelings also involved the anti-Corona lockdown and other emergency measures which were often simply actively ignored in protest against the system, including malfunctioning democratic decision processes, elitism, party rule, state-capturing by parties, enterprises and governments, and corruption. The dysfunctionality of Corona measures in essence was based on a "rapidly deteriorating quality of democracy in Latin America" (Morlino, 2016; Zovatto, 2020):

"Latin America's legitimacy crisis is crystal clear. Latinobarómetro indicates that less than half of its citizenry supports democracy (Corporación Latinobarómetro, 2018). According to Transparency International (Pring &

Vrushi, 2019), one person in every four has been offered bribes in exchange for votes. Finally, the OECD (2020) reveal[ed] that 54 percent of the region's inhabitants justified not having paid taxes in 2016 ... The most threatening pandemic in Latin America is public mistrust, not COVID-19. It's irrelevant how large monetary transfers for the poorest will be, or how often the authorities will tout the necessity of adhering to the lockdown and social distancing. For most of its citizens, those are empty words coming from the powerful, 'the usual suspects.' Now is time for prudence. Public squandering must be avoided. Populism must be chided. If these governments do not take urgent policies and send long-term reform messages to redistribute political and economic powers, the pandemic will not recede until it is too late" (Infante, 2020b).

As a consequence, the problems of Latin America in containing the virus had equally deeply political, i.e., democracy versus anti-democracy related roots as in India and elsewhere. Corona manifested the global crisis of democracy, and in many cases deepened and sharpened it further. As a consequence:

> Cruz was concerned about Latin America's future after COVID-19. However, he also saw an excellent opportunity [in the Coronavirus crisis] to make profound institutional reforms in the region and to set the foundations for its development (ibid.).

Interestingly, the continent which many thought would be hardest affected – Africa – was, according to *Science*, widely spared by COVID-19 – and scientists struggled to explain why. Besides a lack of testing, it is probable that the reasons lay in a combination of factors, among them heightened resistance due to previous greater exposure to diseases and the youthfulness of Africa's population:

> Although Africa reported its millionth official COVID-19 case [at the start of August 2020], it seems to have weathered the pandemic relatively well so far, with fewer than one confirmed case for every thousand people and just 23,000 deaths so far. Yet several antibody surveys suggest far more Africans have been infected with the coronavirus – a discrepancy that is puzzling scientists around the continent. 'We do not have an answer,' says immunologist Sophie Uyoga at the Kenya Medical Research Institute – Wellcome Trust Research Programme ... Marina Pollán of the Carlos III Health Institute in Madrid, who led Spain's antibody survey, says Africa's youthfulness may protect it. Spain's median age is 45; in Kenya

and Malawi, it's 20 and 18, respectively. Young people around the world are far less likely to get severely ill or die from the virus. And the population in Kenya's cities, where the pandemic first took hold, skews even younger than the country as a whole, says Thumbi Mwangi, an epidemiologist at the University of Nairobi. The number of severe and fatal cases 'may go higher when the disease has moved to the rural areas where we have populations with advanced age,' he says. Jambo is exploring the hypothesis that Africans have had more exposure to other coronaviruses that cause little more than colds in humans, which may provide some defense against COVID-19. Another possibility is that regular exposure to malaria or other infectious diseases could prime the immune system to fight new pathogens, including SARS-CoV-2, Boum adds. Barasa, on the other hand, suspects genetic factors protect the Kenyan population from severe disease.

NORDLING, 2020

It was surprising to many that it was precisely Africa, seen as a whole (which of course is problematic due to the high diversity of the continent), where the politicisation of the virus towards a democracy versus anti-democracy issue was less explicit – perhaps because democracy was not and is not the primary issue of social and political struggles in many African societies these days. On the other hand, African innovators were among the most inventive in tackling the virus, containing it and helping to live with it (BBC News, 2020jj). As the BBC reported:

innovators on the continent have responded to the challenges of the pandemic with a wide range of creative inventions (Ibid.).

As the 10 most stunning, the broadcaster chose the following:

1. *'Doctor Car' robot.* Students from the Dakar Polytechnic School in Senegal have built a multifunctional robot designed to lower the risk of COVID-19 contamination from patients to care-givers (BBC News, 2020g). The device is equipped with cameras and is remotely controlled via an app. The designers say it can move around the rooms of quarantined patients to take their temperatures and deliver drugs and food.

2. *Automatic hand-washing machine.* Nine-year-old Kenyan schoolboy Stephen Wamukota invented a wooden hand-washing machine to help curb the spread of coronavirus. The machine allows users to tip a bucket of water to wash their hands by using a foot pedal. This helps users avoid touching surfaces to reduce the risk of infection. Stephen was given a presidential award in June.

BBC NEWS, 2020y

3. *The Respire-19 portable ventilator.* Amid a shortage of ventilators on COVID-19 wards in Nigeria, 20-year-old engineering student Usman Dalhatu attempted to help meet the shortfall. Dalhatu built the portable automatic ventilator to help people with respiratory problems – often a symptom of a severe coronavirus infection. He now plans to build up to 20 ventilators.

BBC NEWS, 2020gg

4. *3D mask printing.* Natalie Raphil is the founder of Artificial Intelligence company Robots Can Think South Africa. She is using 3D printers to produce 100 masks a day for use in some of Johannesburg's major hospitals. South Africa accounts for around half of all reported coronavirus cases in Africa.

PAUL, 2020

5. *Solar-powered hand-washing sink.* Amid a lockdown in Ghana aimed at curbing the spread of COVID-19, shoemaker Richard Kwarteng and his brother Jude Osei decided to design a solar-powered hand-washing basin (A Plus, 2020). When hands activate a sensor on the device, soapy water is automatically released. An alarm goes off after 25 seconds of hand-washing – in compliance with this timescale recommended by the World Health Organization (ibid.).

Among the innovations were, however, even more sophisticated ideas which could serve as models and could be exported to other parts of the world:

VALUES & TRANSFORMATION NOT CONFINED BILATERAL COMPETITION

6. *Web-based X-ray lung scans.* Engineers in Tunisia have created an online platform that scans lung X-rays to try to determine if a person could be suffering from coronavirus. When an X-ray is uploaded onto the platform, it runs a test to detect signs of a possible coronavirus infection. Researchers at the National Institute of Applied Science and Technology in Tunis say the tool is 90% effective in indicating the probability of infection. The platform is still in development, but thousands of lung X-rays have been fed into the system to enable it to recognise the impact of COVID-19 on lungs

EURONEWS, 2020

∴

7. *Police robots on lockdown patrol.* Authorities in Tunisia deployed police robots on the streets of the capital Tunis in April to enforce lockdown measures. The surveillance robots, called PGuards, spied on people walking on the street and approached them to ask why they were out. Offenders then had to show their ID and other documents to the cameras attached to the robots. The four-wheeled devices are equipped with thermal-imaging cameras and light-detection and ranging technology

JAWAD, 2020

∴

8. *Wooden money sanitizer.* Kenyan mobile money agent Danson Wanjohi has built a wooden device that sanitises cash notes that are passed through a slot in the machine. Wanjohi constructed the mechanism using a motor, a rubber band and gears which enable notes to pass through the machine. As the notes pass through the device, they are cleaned with a sanitising solution

DAILY NATION, 2020

∴

9. *Rapid 65-minute COVID-19 testing kit.* South African tech entrepreneurs Daniel Ndima and Dineo Lioma have created a COVID-19 testing kit which provides results in just 65 minutes. Typically, it can take up to three days for COVID-19 tests to produce results. The testing kit is known

as qPCR, and features a technology used to measure DNA. The testing kit needs to undergo regulatory approval before it can be rolled out.

GOPHE, 2020

⋮

10. *Socially distanced haircuts.* In Ethiopia, barbers have come up with a way to continue cutting hair for clients while minimising the risk of COVID-19 transmission. The barbers stand in a specially constructed booth which acts as a partition separating them from clients, minimising person-to-person contact

BBC NEWS, 2020XX

CHAPTER 9

Unprecedented Penetrative Depth

Uplifting Technology, Changing Sexuality, Questioning Science?

Without doubt, the most characteristic aspect of Corona was its unprecedented inter- and trans-disciplinary penetrative depth, quality and level. As the third truly global crisis since the fall of the Berlin wall on 9 November 1989 and after a preceding crisis duality that shaped the early 21st century, i.e., since

- the Islamist terror attacks on New York's World Trade Center of 11 September 2001 and
- the global financial and economic crisis of 2007–08,

the Coronavirus crisis of 2019–20 indeed affected all sectors of societies on the whole globe without exception. Although predicted since the 2010s by various researchers as part of an incoming bundles of crises of new quality, size and outreach, Corona was considerably more encompassing than its preceding crises (Ministry of the Interior and Kingdom, 2009) – it was a typical "bundle crisis". This notion implies that the Corona pandemic impacted multiple dimensions – it lead to a financial crisis, lead to societal divides, going along with an infodemic and a spread of conspiration theories and affected the health and welfare systems of any country. It questioned basically *all* fundamentals of modern life throughout most nations around the world. It put a halt

- to "business as usual" in the economy and the financial system;
- to the daily administrative practices of nation states;
- to international cultural and educational exchange and cooperation;
- to religious rites and rituals throughout the most diverse confessions and beliefs;
- and to mobility and demographic movements, including migration.

"Corona" changed behaviour and imposed "social distancing" and a dramatic limitation of space and physical outreach to more than half of the globe's population.

In turn, "Corona" decisively uplifted technology, enabling it to become a substitute of "real life" like no other transformation phase in recent history. It consecrated technology to become the perfect tool of "human extension", both communication-wise and beyond (for example with regard to Corona detection, surveillance and treatment), thus perfecting its rise to fully fledged "human technology" by conferring it the status of "essential" to more or less the same extent as food and shelter.

© ROLAND BENEDIKTER AND KARIM FATHI, 2022 | DOI:10.1163/9789004469686_010

This emergency-related transformation happened at a point in time where technology was already in the process of fundamentally changing human life and labour. As Microsoft President Brad Smith analysed in July 2020:

> The world is facing a staggering jobs challenge with a quarter of a billion people set to lose their job in 2020. Millions will need to learn new skills to get jobs, or even to hang on to their old one, as the digitisation of economies races ahead.
>
> JACK, 2020

In this situation, the perhaps first truly global "hashtag" was "istayathome" – which acquired the double meaning of being quarantined and unemployed and is a historical irony inbuilt in a phase of "re-globalisation". The Coronavirus crisis gave an unprecedented boost both to the Internet and, in particular, to its most important industry, porn, with some porn sites even experiencing difficulties in keeping their websites functional due to too much traffic during the "youmuststayathome" lockdown. People felt it easier to break the barrier to consuming commodified sexuality, and to further connect and relate technology and sexuality to each other – a greater trend that Corona massively strengthened and expanded to the "new normal". This included the commodification of the female body, which, in Corona times with its constant death threat, was diminished as a problem to minor, as was the importance and impact of most emancipative movements which had struggled for decades for gender and equality progress, such as feminist and queer movements which had already been brought into a problematic situation prior to the virus outbreak due to the ambivalences of an increasing merger of technology with gender issues (Benedikter & Gruber, 2019).

Of equal importance was that the Corona crisis, while elevating technology to a new "religion", ironically at the same time questioned science, i.e., the origin of modern technology, and its global institutions, denouncing them as both the potential *origin* (Wuhan laboratory) and *cure* of the virus. Such as, for example, U.S. President Donald Trump, who entered a constant propagandistic struggle against his own virologists and experts, suggesting that he was defending "freedom" against the reign of non-politicians. Trump, in July 2020, when the U.S. under his leadership became the worst-case scenario in the world, registering ever new records of infections:

> vowed not to order Americans to wear masks to contain the spread of coronavirus. His comments came after the country's top infectious disease expert, Dr Anthony Fauci, urged state and local leaders to be 'as

forceful as possible' in getting people to wear masks. Wearing face coverings, Dr Fauci added, is 'really important' and 'we should be using them, everyone'.

BBC NEWS, 2020O

As with his overall media strategy and the constant accusations of "fake news" which tried to undermine the claim of objectivity, Trump's (and others') attempt in the Corona crisis was to undermine the "religion of science" by putting diverging opinions of apparently all "empirical" nature against each other. He transformed the "war of the virologists" (Brady, 2020) into a "war of virologists against politicians", thus trying to legitimise its political approach against the overwhelming majority of political and other scientists who had regularly criticised him for his policies on a scientific basis. Corona, in Trump's hands, provided a tool to de-legitimise science and at the same time self-legitimise the president's own stand. At the start of October 2020, Trump and his wife Melania announced they had contracted COVID-19, which made Corona the single most influential factor in the U.S. presidential elections of November 2020. They announced they would comply with the rules set by science (BBC News, 2020n).

Overall, it was less the virus-triggered crisis as such, with its lethal consequences for so many, or the attempts of its political manipulation for undermining the credibility of scientists, than rather its multiple and interrelated practical effects that opened up the public's mind for a (self-)critique of postmodern scientific routine as related to capitalist contexts (be it private capitalism in the West or state capitalism in the East). Many policy- and opinion-makers explicitly realised for the first time the profoundly complex and often contradictory nature of contemporary science when confronted with a crisis that cannot be limited to just one scientific sector.

Corona made clear:

– that science is always political, and never neutral, although it does not intend to be so;
– that science is no monolithic bloc but consists of competing strands which interpret reality differently and are in competition against each other;
– that this includes, in particular, open processes difficult to oversee and steer, where normative standards are (temporarily) invalidated or suspended due to over-complexity, and where a clear destination space is impossible to consensually identify;
– and finally, that in times of crises which are inter- and trans-sectoral by nature, science may have no other chance than to evolve towards serious and both encompassing and capillary inter-, trans- and pluri-disciplinarity

with much more solemnity than ever before. Corona has indicated that this is valid for crises specific to the 21st century, i.e., hyper-complex and interconnected crises which do not consist of *segmental emergencies*, but rather of *crisis bundles*. What is needed for any potential "post-Corona world" is the ability for flexible and "open" scientific hyper-complexity management rather than for "definitive" solution-finding in single sectors dominated by the expertise of prevailing "single" sciences.

CHAPTER 10

Corona and Re-Globalisation 2

Creating Conscience for National and International Reforms

Perhaps most impactful in the long term, Corona interrupted the usual neoliberal narrative of globalisation as a "natural process" which – allegedly – cannot be stopped by its very nature. As the narrative went for decades, neoliberal globalisation therefore must be endured despite its obvious increasingly negative effects such as rising inequality among and within nations, asymmetric social stratification and exploitation, including the lack of migration control to provide cheap a workforce to companies, the rise of illiberal and state-controlled authoritarian economies to direct competitors in open markets, and the destruction of the environment. In so doing, the Corona experience provided a potentially far-reaching boost to reform efforts towards "re-globalisation" (Benedikter & Kofler, 2019b) which were already underway *before* the virus hit but were significantly intensified with it. This boost towards reform was related to a change of self-perception both of the "Imaginal Politics" (Bottici, 2011) and the "Contextual Politics" (Goodin & Tilly, 2006) of Western liberal democracies and their liberal global order that dominated the decades between the start of the 1990s and the end of the 2010s, i.e., from the fall of the Berlin Wall to Corona.

Indeed significant in the overall perspective, during the Coronavirus crisis, broader awareness arose regarding the fact that the current interpretation and practice of globalisation presents serious faults, that some aspects of globalisation had been exaggerated, that Western open societies had become too open for the penetration by closed societies, and that democracies were too self-confident and therefore became dependent on authoritarian regimes in crucial sectors such as medical supply or emergency equipment. Years before Corona struck, in 2018, scholars had explicitly and in detail warned of Western dependency on Chinese medical production (Gibson & Singh, 2018).

Overall, awareness rose that a better globalisation is therefore needed for the post-Corona world. This does not mean "better" of the same, but rather concrete steps towards new ways of interconnectivity, including the differentiation between more effective cooperation on the one hand and more layers of protection for open societies against their opponents based on more multi-dimensional anticipation, strategic foresight and resulting "precision politics" on the other hand. This includes more "glocal" ways of production

© ROLAND BENEDIKTER AND KARIM FATHI, 2022 | DOI:10.1163/9789004469686_011

and consumption (Benedikter, 2020a) and – as a basis for this – the more accurate distinction between the needs of different societal and value systems such as democracy (Europe, the West, India, South Korea, Taiwan and others) and communism (China), which, under globalised conditions, are unavoidably interconnected but continue to follow different rules of information, communication or concepts of good life and liberty, and to the present day are not mutually penetrable to the same extent, lacking reciprocity and thus presenting increasing asymmetries which openly manifested in the Corona crisis. Corona created the awareness that these imbalances have to be urgently corrected.

As the co-founder and director of the European Council on Foreign Relations (ECFR, n.d.), Mark Leonard, put it:

> Like other recent systemic crises, the coronavirus pandemic has confronted us with an inconvenient truth: the risks associated with international openness might very well outweigh the gains ... In the case of COVID-19, the world has been confronted with uncomfortable facts that are impossible to ignore. Like the 2008 financial crash and the 2015 refugee crisis in Europe, the pandemic has fully exposed a deep vulnerability to systemic threats. The ultimate role of the state – the very meaning of sovereignty – is to provide its citizens with adequate protection from existential risk. Yet globalization appears to have undermined the modern state's ability to cope with low-probability, high-impact scenarios. Just as the 9/11 terrorist attacks in the United States forced people to rethink security, the COVID-19 crisis compels us to take a fresh look at how we manage interdependence. It is tempting to ask whether this crisis will be resolved more effectively by nationalism or through international coordination. But that is the wrong question. The real issue is whether interdependence can be compatible with and complement the continued existence of nation states.
>
> LEONARD, 2020C

In view of these aspects, the Corona crisis can be regarded as one of the most impactful crises ever on the concepts of both globalisation and globalism. According to Bulgarian political scientist Ivan Krastev, the Corona crisis invigorated and brought to a new level the corrections which were applied during the major previous crises the world underwent. Firstly, the restriction of civil freedoms was still highly controversial in the "fight against terrorism" after 9/11, but little resistance was shown to the much more extensive restrictions during Corona. Secondly, the virus lockdown closed more borders worldwide than the migration and refugee crisis, with Corona leading to "territorial nationalism" ("Stay at home"), which the other crisis did not. Thirdly, the economic consequences of Corona were much more drastic than after the financial crisis of 2007–08. At that time, the economically richer EU member states from the north strongly opposed communising debts in terms of a transfer union (Krupa & Lau, 2020). Yet after Corona, 750 trillion euros in joint debt, mostly guaranteed by Germany, were mobilised within the EU to support the indebted southern member states (Krupa, 2020).

In its September-October edition 2020, *Foreign Affairs* published a piece about the "pandemic depression" (C. Reinhart & V. Reinhart, 2020), asserting that "the global economy will never be the same" (ibid.):

> The COVID-19 pandemic pose[d] a once-in-a-generation threat to the world's population. Although this is not the first disease outbreak to spread around the globe, it is the first one that governments have so fiercely combated ... To fund these and other public health measures, governments around the world have deployed economic firepower on a scale rarely seen before ... The pandemic has created a massive economic contraction that will be followed by a financial crisis in many parts of the globe, as nonperforming corporate loans accumulate alongside bankruptcies. Sovereign defaults in the developing world are also poised to spike. This crisis will follow a path similar to the one the last crisis took, except worse, commensurate with the scale and scope of the collapse in global economic activity. And the crisis will hit lower-income households and countries harder than their wealthier counterparts (ibid.).

Perhaps most relevant of all, Corona manifested the urgent need for a new concept of "multi-resilience" for a "re-globalising" scenery. The Corona crisis provided the insight that a "re-globalised" world cannot rely upon the same resilience patterns as the neoliberal globalised world did. Corona did not only prove to be a "bundle crisis" by affecting multiple dimensions like the social, economic, political and technological one. It showed also that the interconnected, complex and interdependent world of the 21st century does not consist of single crises or parallel crises, but of interwoven *crisis bundles* with complex ramifications, shockwave extensions beyond sectors and long-term systemic consequences. Thus, societies are not only affected by single multidimensional challenges like the Corona pandemic, rather than also bundles of them, including Corona, climate change, cyber attacks etc. In an interconnected world, all of these challenges prove to be intertwined. In the wake of the corona pandemic and the shift of all workplaces to home offices, i.e., cyber attacks have significantly increased worldwide. According to a study by Trend Micro, a global leader in IT security, cyber attacks increased by 20 percent to over 62.6 billion in 2020. (Trend Micro, 2021). Therefore, a "bundle resilience" is needed for potentially upcoming new crises. This is what we call "multi-resilience", i.e., a new, more complexity-adequate resilience concept for the "re-globalised" world after Corona.

All in all, as an effect of Corona, globalisation as we knew it has come under more scrutiny than it had before. It showed that "multi-resilience" brought forward in cooperation between different global protagonists stemming from different socio-political systems can be a fundamental building stone towards a positive and progressive re-globalisation era. In this sense, the Corona crisis of 2020 was, at least for the open societies of Europe and the West, an unprecedented call for a new balance between idealism (i.e., openness of open societies, even towards those which are not open and which do not follow the same standards and practices) and realism (i.e., reasoned protection from global competitors and a higher degree of ethical autonomy) in conceiving the now needed new phase of globalisation.

CHAPTER 11

Intellectual Rhetoric between Cheap "Humanistic" Appeal and Kitsch

Nevertheless, besides profound (although forced) insights, the crisis also produced an immense, probably unprecedented amount of trash rhetoric. Its common characteristic was a cheap emotional appeal to "being human", an over-generalised elite concept of global cooperation so abstract that it became meaningless (and sometimes harmful for practical efforts in the real world), as well as the poorly hidden desire to dispose of all problems the fast way through a purely appeal rhetoric which "solves it all in just one go". Fake-humanistic kitsch rhetoric was so cheap that it made its carriers unattackable: they had to be always right on such level of abstraction, thus avoiding any confrontation with practice and any challenge to develop concrete new concepts (such as we are attempting with the concept of multi-resilience).

For example, there were these words:

> Humanity needs to make a choice. Will we travel down the route of disunity, or will we adopt the path of global solidarity? If we choose disunity, this will not only prolong the crisis, but will probably result in even worse catastrophes in the future. If we choose global solidarity, it will be a victory not only against the coronavirus, but against all future epidemics and crises that might assail humankind in the 21st century.

While these words of star author Yuval Noah Harari (2020) in the *Financial Times* of March 2020 appear to be deep and wise at first, they reveal themselves as superficial, cheap and naïve at a second glance. While an easy-going elite faction may see the Coronavirus crisis, apparently with Harari, as a decisive push, even ultimate proof of the need towards further "simply human" internationalisation and strengthening cooperative patterns among and beyond different systems such as democracies (Europe and the West) and authoritarian and totalitarian regimes (China), others see such rhetoric as the "death knell" of all this: as an expression of the bad, superficial side of globalisation where different ethical and informational standards coexisted basically undiscerned to an increasing disadvantage of democracies against autocracies, but were constantly legitimated and defended by allegedly "meta-political" kitsch "humanistic" rhetoric. And while one side – like Harari – wants to strengthen

© ROLAND BENEDIKTER AND KARIM FATHI, 2022 | DOI:10.1163/9789004469686_012

global institutions and ultimately "old" globalisation to deal with upcoming crises by extending an elitist dream of "humanistic" trans-nationality (in reality never accepted by powers such as China which do not cling to humanistic ideals), others perceived the Corona crisis as the end of globalisation as we had known, perceived and accepted it over the past three decades. Some perceived Harari's (and similar) rhetoric exactly as the expression of the old neoliberal system, which just wanted to restore itself in order to retain the globalisation we had by using – such as Harari – a cheap and interest-driven "humanistic" pathos, meant only as a means to reproduce the given system indefinitely and to go back to business as usual under the smokescreen of easy-to-sell benevolence. The fact that Harari himself is known as a "transhumanist" who wants to overcome the human condition by the fusion of the human body and mind with the help of avant-garde technology, which includes modifications through bio-technology towards a super-human being close to a cyborg (Benedikter & Siepmann, 2016), but is now publishing an emotional piece on a new "global humanism" in an outlet such as the *Financial Times* did not exactly make his argument more credible.

On the contrary, it rather raised critique and suspicion, as well as the question: Why was such rhetoric on the title pages and not the investigation into new concepts and strategies; into who did and did not do what at which time; who was responsible for the virus outbreak; and what has to change in the global system, including its ideologies, rules and habits, in order to avoid future similarly catastrophic events? Instead of melting the hearts of an uninformed public without sufficient reliable facts at hand through the clichéd invocation of an even more undifferentiated and superficial "cosmopolitanism" than we had over the past decades, which ultimately played into the hands of irresponsible regimes, we should ask why there were apparently such different ethical standards in place between the different systems of Western democracies and emerging authoritarian powers such as China in crisis management and science in general, and in dealing with high-risk biotechnology in particular. And why global organisations such as the World Health Organization (WHO) apparently failed to work towards a functioning overarching practice appropriate to de facto high-risk global interconnectivity.

CHAPTER 12

"Humanised" Technology Instead of a New Humanism?

If the question is asked as to what the consequences of the Coronavirus crisis should be – for the sake of a "better humanity" this time not through emotional evocations, but in concretely pragmatic ways (which then, in the ideal case, may trigger ideological effects) –, the view on "Corona and the future of humanity" shifts noticeably. In reality, contrary to Harari, most current "humanists" who deserve the name do not think the COVID-19 crisis will result in a basically immediate "new global humanism" but could rather lead to a push towards "transhumanism", which is a meta-civilisational technology-enthusiastic ideology (Benedikter & Siepmann, 2016). One thing is the fact that the post-Corona effects will provide a boom to further automatisation in everyday activities such as shopping in supermarkets. For example, the cashierless Amazon Go model (Statt, 2020) will be boosted for the simple fact that the cashier is the most dangerous place in the grocery store as regards becoming infected – lesson learned also for future virus outbreaks (Meyersohn, 2020). Besides that, the Corona crisis gave a push to advanced robotics (Jawad, 2020) which, for example, have been employed in Tunisia to ensure people were observing the virus lockdown, and in airports such as Pittsburgh in the U.S. in the form of advanced cleaning robots equipped with UV light to kill the virus (Bild Online, 2020k).

In another crucial branch of society – the educational sector –, the utility of robotics as an immediate anti-virus tool triumphed in other ways. Such as on the occasion of the certificate-award ceremony in high schools in the federal state of Steiermark in Austria:

> High-school diplomas from a robot. In times of the COVID-19 pandemic, it is necessary to keep a distance. For this reason, the high school HTL Kaindorf thought up something special for the presentation of matriculation and diploma certificates: A robot handed over the certificates. It was a bit different, says director Günter Schweiger: 'The robot is actually just a robot arm, but to make sure it doesn't just look like one in a factory, we made it look a bit festive. After all, it is not a humanoid robot. The head of the class pressed a button, then the robot handed over the

© ROLAND BENEDIKTER AND KARIM FATHI, 2022 | DOI:10.1163/9789004469686_013

high-school certificate, and then the photo was taken with the appropriate distance between the awardees'.

STEIERMARK.ORF.AT, 2020

The school's headmaster described how this idea came about:

In addition to containing the virus, we did not want to deprive the pupils of their emotional peak after hard work. Students and parents had been looking forward to the award ceremony for years, and in times when hand-to-hand transfer is too dangerous – and because we are also a computer school – it was obvious for us to use a robot.' The photo of the testimonial handover with the robot arm looked a bit like science fiction – but it is not, as Schweiger emphasises: 'In reality, we are moving towards science fiction. So many things are already happening in factories and in normal houses that many people do not even realise ... there will be more science fiction in the world in the next few years than we now assume (Ibid.).

Was this, then, contrary to pseudo-"humanistic" kitsch rhetoric, the "real humanism" to be expected for a post-Corona world consisting of upcoming more global systemic crises transcending all limits of culture-related ethics and concepts of "humanism"?

Be it as it may, technology showed quite different faces during the crisis, showcasing its full spectrum of use and misuse, with both options often connected within one and the same application in an intertwinement that went beyond the dualism of "good and evil". For example, drone technology for surveillance purposes was employed in Britain (Castle, 2020), Rwanda (Uwiringiyimana, 2020), Kazakhstan (Terra News, 2020) and elsewhere. Ironically, on many occasions the drones looked, in shape and form, like the Coronavirus. In the most affected areas of Northern Italy, remote-controlled drones equipped with body-heat scanners were deployed at altitudes of 20–30 m above the heads of citizens in order to measure the temperature of people in public spaces, and the police then told those who had too high a temperature to go home (Agence France-Presse, 2020). Were these the first steps towards a universal surveillance state for "common health purposes", now also in open societies?

This question was posited from the start of the lockdown, and even more so after it ended. At the end of May 2020, the first jointly Google/Apple-based contact-tracing app was launched:

Automated contact tracing involves using smartphones to detect when two people are close to each other for long enough that there is a significant risk of contagion, so that one can be warned if the other is later diagnosed with having the disease.

KELION, 2020a

The question as to whether such unexpected technological partnerships among giant tech-rivals closely related to the mindset of neoliberal globalisation may lead to new monopolies or were instead just a "humanistic" crossing of competition habits for the sake of humanity was highly disputed. This was more the case as debates began as to whether apps like these should stay in place beyond the end of Corona, i.e., as a safety and anticipation measure. In Italy, the surveillance measures remained in effect even after the end of the strict lockdown on 4 May 2020, which released the Italians into what the Italian media – not by chance – branded as "surveilled liberty" (*libertà vigilata*). In the UK, self-surveillance contact apps were employed to trace the contacts of a person to find all those with whom she or he had had an encounter after potential infection – with an increased risk of misuse and mechanical incrementation by exponential information gathering (Kelion, 2020b). This risk was the reason why:

> the [UK] House of Commons' Human Rights Select Committee discussed fears about plans to extend the app to record location data. 'There is an inherent risk that if you create a system that can be added to incrementally, you could do so in a way that is very privacy invasive,' cautioned law professor Orla Lynskey [of the Department of Law of the London School of Economics and Political Science] (ibid.).

Similarly, Byun Hyun-Gyoun, the inventor of the main Korean tracing system, admitted that it could be misused by a dictator. He therefore argued for the creation of a new and improved data-protection agency, stating that the app both violated the private sphere and, at the same time, rescued the common freedom (Bauer, 2020).

As Natasha Singer reported for the *New York Times*, the trend that employers in the U.S. rushed "to adopt virus screening" (Singer, 2020) for their employees, such as "symptom-checking apps and fever-screening cameras [which] promise to keep sick workers at home and hinder the virus" (ibid.), could also induce some of them to violate privacy in the long term beyond Corona:

> Civil liberties experts said it was important for any virus-tracking of employees to be voluntary. Otherwise, by linking identification technologies like facial recognition to employees' health status, employers could

usher in an authoritarian, China-like system of surveillance and social control at workplaces. 'We are accepting encroachments on privacy here that we would not normally accept,' said Jay Stanley, a senior policy analyst at the American Civil Liberties Union. 'We need to be vigilant to make sure that they don't outlast this crisis' (ibid.).

This ratio appeared not totally improper, given the proven efficiency of these tools and measures, which could imply that aspects of them could be kept "in reserve", thus shifting the mindset of both officials and the public on the issue of surveillance – now also in open societies – towards more technophile, "transhumanist" and control-friendly positions. In April 2020, Amnesty International warned that the Corona crisis could lead to comprehensive surveillance as a "threat to your rights" (Amnesty International, 2020). In the same month, 100 civil rights groups jointly warned that:

> the world risks permanent surveillance with coronavirus controls. Don't 'sleepwalk' into permanent surveillance in the coronavirus pandemic's aftermath, warned 100 civil-society groups. Digital surveillance rolled out to curb the virus should be limited in time and scope, they said.
>
> DEUTSCHE WELLE, 2020

Similarly, Stanford University at the centre of Silicon Valley, a globally leading digitalisation hub, pointed out that increased awareness and respect for privacy with regard to some of the new tracing applications implemented in the Corona crisis will be crucial for the years to come and especially with regard to measures employed during possible incoming new challenges (Gidari & Driscoll, 2020).

Overall, during Corona, drone and remote-controlled technology not only pushed the surveillance issue by governments and public bodies, thus ousting some of the civic rights in place in open societies: During the crisis they were also used for civil-society purposes, among them bringing flowers to parents via drones in lockdown times, to "giving virtual tours of quarantined cities, identifying the sick, and even to walk the dog without leaving the house" (Jaffe, 2020).

Artificial Intelligence (AI), as with most other temporally advanced technologies, presented its full Janus face in the Coronavirus crisis: It served not only for surveillance with all its inbuilt problematics, but also for finding the cure against the virus, for which AI was employed to noticeably shorten the research time:

AI steps up in battle against COVID-19. It feels as if a superhuman effort is needed to help ease the global pandemic killing so many. Artificial intelligence may have been hyped – but when it comes to medicine, it already has a proven track record. So can machine learning rise to this challenge of finding a cure for this terrible disease? There is no shortage of companies trying to solve the dilemma. Oxford-based *Exscientia*, the first to put an AI-discovered drug into human trial, is trawling through 15,000 drugs held by the Scripps research institute, in California. And *Healx*, a Cambridge company set up by Viagra co-inventor Dr David Brown, has repurposed its AI system developed to find drugs for rare diseases ... The system is divided into three parts that:
– trawl through all the current literature relating to the disease;
– study the DNA and structure of the virus; and
– consider the suitability of various drugs.
Drug discovery has traditionally been slow. 'I have been doing this for 45 years and I have got three drugs to the market', Dr Brown said. But AI is proving much faster. 'It has taken several weeks to gather all the data we need and ... we are now at a critical mass,' Dr Brown said ... 'We will have output for the three methods ...'

      WAKEFIELD, 2020

In Colombia, Artificial Intelligence was used in daily activities to combat COVID-19, once again revealing itself precisely as the double-edged sword it is:

When the coronavirus outbreak first hit the Plaza Minorista market [in the heart of the Colombian city of Medellín], Edison Palacio knew that it would take more than disinfectant and face masks to contain it. So he decided to use artificial intelligence. Mr Palacio is the director of the densely packed market. Every day, up to 15,000 people flood into the giant building where more than 3,300 vendors sell fruits, vegetables, meats, eggs, spices, grains and clothes ... But such crowded markets have become hotbeds for the coronavirus to flourish across the region ... Minorista teamed up with researchers at the University of Antioquia to install AI technology to control and track the virus at markets ... They use facial recognition software connected to cameras at the entrances and to security cameras around the building to collect data on the vendors and market-dwellers. Among the data they collect is their age range, gender, and if the person is wearing their mask correctly in order to assess risks and more vulnerable demographics. Thermal cameras can take the temperature of 200 people per minute ... If someone has a high temperature or wears their mask incorrectly, an alarm will go off and alert market security. 'We have to learn to coexist with the virus,' Mr Palacio says ... [He] wants local governments to further harness the AI technology to curb the spread of the virus and implement it in other crowded public spaces like the metro system and government buildings. ...

JANETSKY, 2020

Yet the inbuilt risks were not fewer in Latin America than elsewhere:

Privacy watchdogs have warned of the potential danger of AI being misused and some consider that risk to be greater in Colombia where the authorities have in the past been involved in illegal wiretapping scandals, spying on political opponents, journalists and human rights activists

BBC NEWS, 2020rr; JANETSKY, 2020

Beyond that, all this may – in the transnational "civilisational mood" of the times – not only accelerate the "post-pandemic" employment of "intelligent technology" on a broad front (Hershock, 2020), but also the development towards "human enhancement" (Savulescu & Bostrom, 2009) in the medium term and trigger a new debate about "human enhancement ethics" in general (ibid. pp. 1–22). This could include the digitisation of vaccination options by the advancement of what Bill Gates in March 2020 called "digital certificates". Gates had anticipated the crisis in 2015 in a speech where he "warned that the greatest risk to humanity was not nuclear war but an infectious virus that could threaten the lives of millions of people" (Wakabayashi, Alba & Tracy, 2020). But it could also consist in developing new ways of making the human body itself more "resilient" through technological modification, as, for example, already proposed by "transhumanist" thinkers (John Cabot University, 2018) such as Stefan Lorenz Sorgner (2018) of John Cabot University Rome long before the crisis (Widmann, 2019), among other procedures by fusing the human body with animal tissue to make it more resistant or by melting the human body with machines to make it more independent of biological vulnerabilities (Benedikter & Fathi, 2019).

So, will the Corona crisis have accelerated a global push for "transhumanism" in the medium and long term?

Currently, there are both pro and contra signs. There are many who think a push towards "enhancing humans" as, for example, the "Global Future Congress 2045" (GF2045) exemplarily called for as early as in an open letter to the then U.N. secretary general Ban Ki-moon in March 2013 (Itskov et al., 2013), should now be better supported for the sake of post-Corona times in order to make humanity more resistant against global infections and other catastrophes. At the same time, though, many experts and citizens seem to have temporarily had enough of the "transhumanist" debate, precisely because of the virus-related omnipresent debate. Without doubt, a potential blow to "transhumanism" due to debate oversaturation could become particularly harsh if it should turn out that the virus was made in a laboratory, as was debated in highly disputed ways among experts, politicians and global powers, and thus would turn out to be a (by-)product of human bio-engineering. This would probably not favour immediate more bio-technological experiments to "improve" the natural condition of humans in the direction into which "transhumanists" envision it.

CHAPTER 13

A Boost to "Post-human Hybrid Intelligence" Such as Biological Espionage and Sentiment Analysis?

Some instead hold that the most important effect of the Corona crisis will be on national security as related to systematic spying against citizens (Corera, 2020b). Some cities and municipalities used the Corona crisis to introduce surveillance methods of unusual proportions (and otherwise difficult to implement), such as the city of Baltimore, Maryland, which, in 2018, featured an over-proportional homicide rate of more than 300, the second highest per capita in the U.S. Starting from May 1, 2020, the city used surveillance drones to control its 600,000 residents from the air (BBC News, 2020e). According to a US court in Maryland, this did not violate "the Fourth Amendment against unwarranted search and seizure" (ibid). Analysts hold that the Corona crisis nevertheless may change both fundamentals and priorities of national security as related to spying, also abroad, including a general shift to biological information-gathering and "biological espionage". Corona, in its long-term effects, could have made "health security" – as related to spying of national powers against each other – the new spearhead of global intelligence:

> Since the 9/11 attacks nearly 20 years ago, national security has been dominated by terrorism. But there have been voices over the years who have argued the notion of 'security' should be broadened, and the corona crisis has raised a significant question about whether global health security should be a more central part of national security. Under the last review, an international pandemic was classed as a Tier 1 national security risk in the UK – meaning it was judged to be of the highest priority – but that has not been reflected in the resources or the way in which the issue has been tackled when compared with the other three threats at the same level – terrorism, war and cyber-attacks. But just as in the wake of 9/11, there are people who feel they were not listened to when they warned the lights were blinking red about our health security. For spy agencies, adapting may take a significant gear change. A priority for policy-makers will be knowing the ground-truth about the health situation in another country. For agencies like MI6 and the CIA that recruit human sources, it may mean ensuring you have agents in the right place who can report back on what is really happening. There may also be shifts in what

© ROLAND BENEDIKTER AND KARIM FATHI, 2022 | DOI:10.1163/9789004469686_014

agencies who intercept communications look for and in technical intelligence, satellites may be tasked to look at medical or even burial sites. Just as technology was developed to remotely 'sniff' for traces of nuclear material, new devices may be required to scan for health and bio-threats.

CORERA, 2020b

According to British analysts, however, the change in the intelligence and espionage sector triggered by Corona could go well beyond that (ibid.), mixing "biological espionage" with "transhumanist" elements such as "sentiment analysis" and with new mechanisms and methods of how to anticipate potential virus- or pandemic-related futures for the own national benefit and against power competitors:

> But that is still largely the traditional world of intelligence gathering. The real future may be in the use of more complex data sets and artificial intelligence to spot, understand and predict developments in a population. Analysing meta-data from phones, online searches or other forms of activity could be used. Years ago, the then-director of digital innovation for the CIA told me about work the agency was doing to study population-level data of a whole country using AI and techniques like 'sentiment analysis' (Corera, 2016). The idea was to be able to spot events – like an approaching breakdown in law and order and the potential for a revolution – before it was necessarily obvious. Here the US and China are already engaged in a race for superiority, which many in Washington fear they may be losing as China has invested hugely in building capabilities and acquiring data ... Or it could be that borders close and countries turn inwards – refocusing the need for intelligence gathering on what other countries might be doing and hiding or new breakthroughs they may have made. 'Biological espionage' has a long history.

And the author of the British report concludes,

> In the future, the emphasis may be less about weapons and more about vaccines. The long-held fears that terrorists or other groups could unleash bio-weapons will also be turbo-charged by recent events with already some signs that far-right groups have thought about deliberately trying to spread the virus. The US Department of Justice has said those intentionally doing so could be charged as terrorists. The shift in the last few years to understand and counter disinformation by hostile states already looks to have a continuing importance in this world, but there are also

challenges domestically. One of the questions that may emerge from the current crisis is how far countries with a greater domestic surveillance capacity use it to spot the spread of any virus and also understand and control the movement of people to prevent further spread.

CORERA, 2020b

This is probably why international *vaccine espionage* has risen to new levels during the Coronavirus crisis:

Coronavirus: spies target COVID-19 vaccine research. Russian spies are targeting organisations trying to develop a coronavirus vaccine in the UK, US and Canada, security services have warned. The UK's National Cyber Security Centre (NCSC) said the hackers 'almost certainly' operated as 'part of Russian intelligence services'. It did not specify which organisations had been targeted, or whether any information had been stolen. But it said vaccine research had not been hindered by the hackers. Russia has denied responsibility. The warning was published by an international group of security services:

- the UK's NCSC;
- the Canadian Communication Security Establishment (CSE);
- the United States Department for Homeland Security (DHS) Cyber-security Infrastructure Security Agency (CISA);
- the US National Security Agency (NSA).

Understanding vaccine research and other details about the pandemic has become a top target for intelligence agencies around the world and many others, including Western spies, are likely to be active in this space. [...] Earlier in 2020, John Demers, an assistant attorney general for US national security, warned that hackers working for foreign governments were trying to steal vaccine research. He said that the first nation to find a vaccine first will gain clout on the world stage with a 'significant geopolitical success story'. For that reason, hackers have been pursuing vaccine research in several countries

C. FOX & KELION, 2020

In July 2020, the U.S. Justice department "charged Chinese COVID-19 research 'cyber spies'" (BBC News, 2020bbb):

The US justice department has accused China of sponsoring hackers who are targeting labs developing COVID-19 vaccines. Officials have charged two Chinese men who allegedly spied on US companies doing coronavirus research and got help from state agents for other thefts. The indictment comes amid a US crackdown on Chinese cyber espionage ... The accusations against former electrical engineering students Li Xiaoyu and Dong Jiazhi include charges of trade secret theft and wire fraud conspiracy. Prosecutors said the two men spied on a Massachusetts biotech firm in January [2020] which was known to be researching possible cures for COVID-19. They also hacked a Maryland company less than a week after it said it was researching COVID-19. Officials called the men private hackers who occasionally received support from Chinese intelligence agents, including an officer from the Chinese Ministry of State Security (MSS). They previously stole 'hundreds of millions of dollars' worth of trade secrets, intellectual property, and other valuable business information' beginning in 2009, prosecutors alleged (Ibid.).

Taking note of such potentially crucial trajectories, two options appear to be highly likely:

First, that the competition for vaccines – and the associated business-related and scientific evolution drivers – will give shape to a new centre of gravity of international intelligence plays and espionage of world powers against each other for the years to come, and beyond the possible end of the Coronavirus crisis in specific terms.

Second, that if the Coronavirus itself was not conceived as a pre- or proto-weapon, it may become one soon. Independent of the WHO's respective firm denial in April 2020, i.e., already in a very early phase of investigation, the Coronavirus – willingly or by accident – presented the most-desired features of a pre-weaponised biological entity, such as a long asymptomatic incubation phase with very high infectiousness without the knowledge of the carrier; slowly increasing fever; (relatively) sudden death after outbreak; as well as alleged high re-infection of recovered patients. Although scientists ascribed some of these aspects mainly to mechanisms of mutation (Corum & Zimmer, 2020), most powers may want to use such a provenly efficient virus as a basis to work on regarding its even deadlier yet restricted use for their bio-weaponry arsenal. Not to speak of global terrorists. The positive side here (if there is one) is, though, that these circumstances have made the global public more aware of ongoing virus research for bio-technological use of a different kind that has long been routine with all international powers, and of the dangers inherent in such research per se, independent of the intentions and applications involved.

CHAPTER 14

Striking a Balance

Was Corona a Watershed for Western Humanism and the Basic Rationality of the Enlightenment?

In the context of the rising post-Western and post-human world that had already surfaced before Corona (Benedikter & Gruber, 2019; Benedikter, 2018), many discussed the humanistic implications of the crisis – which were related to humanitarian ones, but not simply identical with them. The non-identity between "humanitarian" and "humanistic" is not least due to the fact that nations such as China, where the virus originated, do not dispose of a respective history of ideas and thus have no "humanism" in the Western sense, neither historically nor socially (Confucianism, Taoism and Buddhism are not "humanistic" in the European-Western sense of secular modernity and the enlightenment) (Benedikter, 2012b). In Europe and the West, the Corona crisis triggered a fundamental debate as to whether such catastrophes would harm "humanism", or rather further and promote its resurrection within the neoliberal setting. Many even saw the crisis as a watershed for the future of humanism in a "post-human" world increasingly dominated by globalised performative, utilitarian and materialistic logics. Others saw the measures against COVID-19 as the end of the basic rationality of the enlightenment, i.e., as an over-idealistic stance propagated by all too "leftist" ideologies inclined to always share the burdens and ask little about the costs. This debate reached much deeper levels than the usual academic or media discussions among the globalisation elites (including their approaches to "elite globalisation" (Danaher, 2001)) widely ignored by the broader public. Given the immediateness and urgency of the crisis, within the framework of COVID-19, the debate about humanisation versus de-humanisation – caused as much by the virus as by the anti-virus measures – produced a vast variety of social and political disputes about fundamentals. It manifested how encompassing the topic of humanism is at the core of secular Western societies and their value structures – for example, in their public rationalities and cultures of resilience and intervention.

The examples abounded, and none of them left the public untouched by its deep ambiguity and emotion. Among them was the debate about age, and whether whole societies should be closed down to safeguard the elderly and those particularly at risk due to existing preconditions. In Germany, Boris Palmer, Mayor of the city of Tübingen, representative of the otherwise strongly

© ROLAND BENEDIKTER AND KARIM FATHI, 2022 | DOI:10.1163/9789004469686_015

STRIKING A BALANCE 75

leftist Green party, stated that "we perhaps in Germany save elderly people who would be dead anyway in half a year" (Bild Online, 2020m), legitimating himself with his apprehension for children in developing countries who would be threatened in their very existence by the economic consequences of the lockdown, so that the Corona restrictions should be rolled back as soon as possible, even at the price of risking the lives of the German elderly. Despite subsequent polemics, Palmer was not excluded from his Green party (ibid.). Rather conservative critics, such as philosopher and former state minister of culture and science of the Federal German government Julian Nida-Rümelin, author of the best-selling book "Digital Humanism" (Nida-Rümelin & Weidenfeld, 2018), asserted that the lockdown was the biggest error of public policy in recent history out of a wrongly understood humanism which had become a pseudo-humanistic hysteria. He and others warned that the lockdown would undermine a basic good of open societies, i.e., open critical debate in which the real humanistic *succus* of open societies lies:

"Nida-Rümelin sees a 'conspicuous defence against critical debates'. [He] says that democracy in times of crisis includes discussion and controversy. 'Certainly the Coronavirus is a serious danger. At the same time, the images from Bergamo and New York have led to more people being under pressure to be conformist, and all divergent and critical opinions are having a hard time,' he said. Nida-Rümelin [with regard to how to deal with Corona] ... calls for the voluntariness and personal responsibility of everyone" (Focus Online, 2020b).

Indeed, in global comparison,

- Sweden trusted in "voluntariness and personal responsibility" but attained partly high infection numbers;
- Germany and other countries temporarily abolished freedom (and killed the economy);
- South Korea and Taiwan temporarily suspended the private sphere but kept freedom (and the economy) alive.

All of these procedures had their pros and cons, yet only some of them were justified and legitimated by "humanism". Some observers attributed the "humanism hysteria" in Western democracies to the romanticism of the European and Western post-1968 left parties which, according to critics, had transformed into a narcissistic generation and identified their own elitist left-cosmopolitanism as the only "true humanism" while remaining anti-economic and anti-individualist in their substance. Others rejected this allegation, since leaders who, although hesitantly, adhered to the stricter emergency measures, such as Boris Johnson, were certainly not representatives of "the left".

Nevertheless, and beyond partisan lines, in Europe a variety of public debaters and decision-makers stemming from the whole political spectrum questioned whether "humanism" would consist in saving lives at any cost, ruining the social and economic life of entire societies or regressing them for years. In the U.S., the debate among conservative congress members even circled around the question as to whether the elderly citizens should be ready to die for the economy. The question among U.S. Republicans was whether to ease public COVID-19 restrictions in order to save the employment rate, the level of wealth and growth prospects for future generations at the price of sacrificing the generations at risk – something which was rejected with abhorrence by the U.S. Democrats, thus deepening the ideological and emotional split in American society (The Washington Post, 2020).

The whole debate was, exemplarily perhaps for upcoming systemic emergencies, riddled by paradoxes. Stating that, in principle, the most important thing elderly people could leave to their children was a "good economy" and that a "bad economy" could be worse than death, Republicans closely related "the economy" to a "true humanism" – and thus paradoxically interpreted the choice of death as "true humanism", although the Republican party usually defines itself as the "defender of life", for example with regard to abortion. Similarly contradictory, Democrats pledged, with lots of pathos that often went beyond the border to interest-guided kitsch, to save every life at any cost, even if it came at the cost of thousands of "side casualties" due to deep economic regression and impoverishment of larger strata of the population. In April 2020, Indiana congressman Republican Trey Hollingsworth stated that:

> letting more Americans die from coronavirus is the 'lesser of two evils' compared with the economy cratering due to social distancing measures ... Hollingsworth asserted that, while he appreciated the science behind the virus' spread, 'it is always the American government's position to say, in the choice between the loss of our way of life as Americans and the loss of life, of American lives, we have to always choose the latter.' 'The social scientists are telling us about the economic disaster that is going on. Our (Gross Domestic Product) is supposed to be down 20 percent alone this quarter,' Hollingsworth said. 'It is policymakers' decision to put on our big boy and big girl pants and say [opening up again at the risk of more infections] is the lesser of these two evils. It is not zero evil, but it is the lesser of these two evils and we intend to move forward that direction. That is our responsibility and to abdicate that is to insult the Americans that voted us into office'.
>
> LEBLANC, 2020

Similarly, Texas Lt. Gov. Dan Patrick stated that " 'lots of grandparents' were willing to die to save the economy for their grandchildren' " (Stieb, 2020). Literally, he asserted that:

> 'No one reached out to me and said, as a senior citizen, Are you willing to take a chance on your survival in exchange for keeping the America that all America loves for your children and grandchildren? And if that's the exchange, I'm all in ... I just think there's lots of grandparents out there in this country like me – I have six grandchildren – that what we all care about and what we love more than anything are those children. I want to live smart and see through this. But I don't want the whole country to be sacrificed and that's what I see (Ibid.).

A fundamental question which was brought to the surface jointly by most of these statements which, in the eyes of some, both strengthened and fundamentally questioned the neoliberal mindset was: What is worth more: the economy or the life of elderly and sick people, and those with pre-existing conditions?

This question led to lasting polemics and further division, not least regarding the enormous number of statistics and information provided in often contradictory or even opposed ways by different public sources. Thus, the one called it the most aggressive virus of all times, while others published statistics that basically said mainly those with previous diseases would die. Others stated that the mortality of the virus was overestimated, others again warned against such "trivialisation". The ideological battle, mostly in the open societies of Europe and the West, opened up to a new discussion about the place and value of "humanism" in Western societies, which soon led to the question about how humanism could be interpreted rightly at all for a more globalised scenery through which the virus was spread and according to which it functioned. Besides opening up "human" abysses such as the case of a Chinese woman sneaking around a condominium and licking door sills to infect her neighbours, or the "Corona challenge", which went "viral" on the Internet, for which participants had to purposely lick toilet seats or other highly infectious places in order to show the affiliation to an alleged position of "rebels against disease" (who, in some cases, subsequently died through contracting the virus), the cases of non-adherence to the rules were many – including rebellions against the "solidarity lockdown" in the name of humanism, humanity and freedom (SadAndUseless, 2020; The Times of India, 2020; Cutway, 2020).

In light of such psychological extremes, philosophers such as Valentin Widmann spoke of "Coronaphobia" in the public social psychology (Widmann,

2020a). They saw the main "humanistic" benefit of the crisis in "a new opportunity and even need to talk about death" (Widmann, 2020d), rather than in its temporary change of public behaviour and order in the name of an alleged collective "humanism" or "enlightenment". In doing so, scholars such as Widmann questioned the public interpretation of humanism in the European-Western open societies, particularly with regard to human dignity and human rights which, in their view, are neither congruent nor the same (Widmann, 2020b). As Widmann summarised, critics of the German Corona lockdown such as:

> the president of the German parliament Wolfgang Schäuble, the members of the German federal ethics commission, the philosopher Ottfried Höffe and others did not want to absolutize the value of life. Yet they lacked a humanistic justification for their statements such as 'the protection for life cannot be absolute'. One should try to give rational and humanistic reasons for such ethical statements, which in the end are metaphysical statements. The ethical debate in the Corona crisis revolved almost exclusively around the question of whether the degree of responsibility for risk minimization can apply absolutely, or whether a balancing calculation of different interests is morally inadmissible and can still be called 'humanistic'. In this respect, the ethical dimension of the crisis became a question of weighing up young life against old life. Some Kantian philosophers and Christian theology forbid such a practice of balancing pros and cons when it comes to human life and denounce it as inhuman. Yet balancing-practices have always been part of the pre-theoretical lifeworld-practice. Human dignity, too, draws its normative power from the lifeworld-network and thus is a regulative principle and not a metaphysically sanctified one. This can already be seen from the fact that we also occasionally suspend human rights to guarantee human dignity.
>
> WIDMANN, 2020C

Yet, in the end, according to Widmann:

> the whole debate is nothing more than a symptom of our 'postmodern' aversion to death. In the past, death was much less under our active control. We regarded it as part of a *fatum* out of our control. Today, due to unparalleled intensive care resources and technology, we have the possibility to postpone the time of our death. One could also speak of a 'hegemony of technological feasibility'. Saving lives has become an industry. This has little to do with the preservation of human dignity. Due to the

lockdown, many people die lonely in nursing homes or intensive care units without having looked their loved ones in the eye for a last time. Do we really want this? It is clearly the primacy of the quantitative that is at the forefront here. It is an ideology of purely *biological securitization*. In the end, this leads to *inhumanity*, because a policy of individual incapacitation and sheer biological security can never promote a functioning democracy that promotes civic autonomy and human dignity. It must be possible to ask questions of balance; and we should learn to talk about death. This is the true 'humanism' we may learn from the Corona crisis (ibid.).

Last, but not least, one of the remaining strongholds of a humanism in the European-Western hemisphere still widely untouched by political interpretation and appropriation over the past decades was the healthcare sector, and, more precisely, medicine and healing in their socio-philosophical foundations. To some extent, the Corona crisis transformed even this remaining sector into a functional building stone of a greater socio-political and societal transformation, questioning its real humanistic value. As medical expert Hartmut Schröder wrote in May 2020 for a publication of the Berlin Senate of the Economy:

Today, everything is connected with everything else as in a great community of destiny and can only be understood through a systemic view. Against this background [the Corona crisis] health has become an 'indivisible' good: it can no longer be achieved exclusively or at the expense of others or at the expense of climate and nature. This ... links health policy with all other areas of politics – especially with climate and environmental policy ... It is becoming clear that even the best medicine can only help sick people to a limited extent when 'mother earth', the economy, politics and society as well as technology and science are 'sick' – when everything revolves around acceleration, profit maximisation and optimisation. The Corona crisis can be seen as a warning sign: a warning against a wrong, inhuman way in politics, economy and society. A new, more holistic concept of healing will therefore go beyond the purely medical. It will aim to also cure the conditions that made this pandemic possible in the first place. We have to understand disease as an interrelated ecological problem and, last, but not least, as a plea for a reassessment of the place of human beings in nature.

SCHRÖDER, 2020a; 2020bf

Thus, the Coronavirus crisis led to a politicisation even of the last remaining sectors of traditional "humanism", in essence leaving nothing of contemporary humanistic debates untouched. While the debate was to some extent indeed "enlightening", the main alternatives proposed as a result of it were widely not: "Keep the economy running and the elderly dying, or curb the economy to keep old persons alive".

Again, what about the third and very pragmatic way the "non-humanistic" Koreans chose: sacrifice the private sphere early and temporarily for safety, in order to then return to it unaltered when the worst was over? This was hard to understand for "humanistic" Westerners, who often reacted only after having debated, perhaps for too long, about the principle questions involved without discerning them accurately. Some Westerners admired the "Korean way" to the point that they even declared South Korea as "the winner" of the Coronavirus crisis – such as the popular German *Bild Zeitung*, which stated: "No complete lockdown, few deaths, economy stable: that's why South Korea is the Corona champion" (Leitmeyer, 2020).

CHAPTER 15

The Vast Variety of Political Instrumentalisations

Politicisation, including, in many cases, open and aggressive political instrumentalisation, abounded during Corona beyond such in-depth questions. It occurred widely without ideological borders or reasoned rhetorical limits and, more importantly, beyond different political parties – making it a case of modern populism even among those who usually do not count themselves as populists, or those who did not even want to be populistic. Daily briefings with every day the same politician's face turned out to annoy people and rather take away appeal than add it, since their appearances were unconsciously connected to the catastrophe. Astute popular politicians such as Russia's Wladimir Putin or North Korea's Kim Yong-un therefore disappeared almost completely from TV screens during the crisis, and with good reason: they obviously knew better than many in the Western democracies that after a nightmare crisis of unprecedented size and depth such as Corona was over, people would, after a while, remember it just like a bad dream. Then, the question is whether your image as politician will be collocated within this dream or not, unconsciously identifying you with it. If yes, irrespective of all the good and perhaps essential things you did, you are going down. If no, maybe you will survive.

Second, what people usually remember are not actions, strategies or ratio, but emotions and the heart, i.e., how they felt seeing things during the crisis. This applies to politicians, too. People often do not remember whether you did a good job, but whether or not you were "compassionate" enough (in their perception). And this, as was revealed, can be something quite hard to control – as, for example, the cases of Italy's premier Antonio Conte or U.S. President Donald Trump showed, who were perceived rather as poorly performing on the "compassion front", while some of their aids, including U.S. pandemic experts such as the director of the National Institute for Allergy and Infectious Diseases (NIAID) and one of the lead members of the Trump Administration's White House Coronavirus Task Force, Anthony Fauci, gained noticeably in media-driven "humanistic" reputation.

Given the penetration depth of the crisis and the confused mindset created among the public, the emotional factor inherent in the Coronavirus episode could be easily explained in view of strategic individual political positioning for the post-Corona world, for example for upcoming elections. Most protagonists grasped this either instinctively or consciously. As a consequence, the

© ROLAND BENEDIKTER AND KARIM FATHI, 2022 | DOI:10.1163/9789004469686_016

Coronavirus crisis was used for many different political purposes – which, ironically, were often interpreted by their "users" in diametrically opposed ways.

For example, some at the European Council on Foreign Relations (ECFR), a passionate and uncompromising Trump-critical institution from the very start, speculated that the US president would actively use the crisis for his re-election (Shapiro, 2020). This assumption was not interest-free, since most members hoped for a more pro-European next president. Yet others, similarly speculative and anti-Trump, bet on the very contrary: that the crisis would be the eventual end of Trump's charges. Other researchers again instead asked if "Coronavirus is bad for populism?" (Bufacchi, 2020), seeing populists succumbing to the crisis due to their inability to manage "real" situations properly, given that not only popular rhetoric but also skills were required (Gruber, 2020b).

Not surprisingly, arguments could be found simultaneously for basically all these theories and claims within one and the same publicly visible rhetoric. Never before were political actions so disputed as during the emotional chaos created by the Corona-break, nor interpretations so strongly embossed with bias and prejudice during non-war times.

Some politicians even used the crisis reputation-wise for retrospective rehabilitation and self-enhancement. For example, former U.S. President George Bush's emotional (others said kitsch "humanistic") solidarity video message to the Americans of May 1, 2020, "A call to unite" (Bush, 2020), produced by the George W. Bush Presidential Center which is part of the Dallas-based private Southern Methodist University, was meant to show the former president's "big heart". It had thus to restore some of his reputation lost during his presidency. Ironically, the message was launched on May 1st, the international workers solidarity day of decisively leftist imprint. The message stated:

> Let us remember how small our differences are in the face of this shared threat. In the final analysis, we are not partisan combatants, we are human beings equally vulnerable and equally wonderful in the sight of God (ibid.).

Despite all metaphysical pathos and the deriving ideological incitement, the message, together with other "emotional" statements such as from former President Barack Obama, was immediately promoted against acting President Donald Trump's alleged "heartlessness" by his arch-enemy CNN according to the slogan: "The enemy of my enemy is my friend" (CNN, 2020a). No doubt that both the liberal and the conservative media were also using Corona for their own purposes in the war between belief systems in deeply polarised Western democracies.

No doubt also that there was even worse and more shameless use of the "Coronavirus moment" for more specific and short-term political goals. For example, Venezuela's President Nicolas Maduro used the chaos to stage an alleged invasion of his alleged long-term foes Colombia and USA, claiming that a dozen soldiers had tried to "invade" his country by using the Coronavirus confusion (Herrero & Faiola, 2020). A dozen for an "invasion" seems not to be that much, though. Others traced the factual spread paths of the Coronavirus to use it for propaganda against single countries, as in the case of Iran, whose airways were apparently instrumental in spreading the virus around the Middle East (BBC News, 2020h). Not to speak of Chinese state media which, in retaliation against the Western communities' suspicions that the virus had originated in a Chinese city or even laboratory, "took aim" at Western politicians and media (BBC News, 2020m). They denounced alleged "lies" by German and Western officials, writing indignant letters to free Western media, such as in the case of the German Axel Springer publishing house which, in mid-April 2020, received a long letter of complaint from the Chinese embassy on Potsdamer Platz, Berlin about the "Bild Zeitung", which had dared to question Chinese information policies and the underlying politics (Reichelt, 2020). The Chinese officials more or less openly asked for the silencing of critical voices in open societies, thus interfering openly with the Western order not only "from abroad" anymore, but – using the Coronavirus emergency – now also "from within" open societies. Others again, in a more domestic move, made single aspects of the measures and circumstances that accompanied Corona a demonstration of political hatred and exclusion. As CNN reported on the example of *face masks*, during the crisis these became "a new fault line in America" (Tensley, 2020):

> The decision to wear or avoid them in the middle of the coronavirus pandemic signals whether people have chosen to adhere to public-health guidelines – a stress that's playing out on personal and political levels ... Percolating beneath the more general pandemic stress is a political divide ... over the role of government, science and even truth. On April 30, some 400 to 700 protesters descended on the Michigan Capitol building to demonstrate against Democratic Gov. Gretchen Whitmer's stay-at-home order, which was issued in March [2020] following the declaration of a state of emergency that was set to expire at the end of the day. Conspicuously, most weren't wearing face masks ....
>
> WAGNER, HAMMOND & HAYES, 2020

This was a clear sign of political polarisation:

> Many of those with objections cite the mistaken belief the requirement is unconstitutional, and under their theory, one cannot be forced to wear a mask,' city manager Norman McNickle said in a statement (The City of Stillwater Oklahoma, 2020), referring to what tends to be a conservative talking point in arguments in favor of flouting certain public-health guidance (Berman, 2020). 'No law or court supports this view. ... It is further distressing that these people, while exercising their believed rights, put others at risk.' (Notably, masks without medical-grade respirators were less for the wearers than the people around them whom they could unknowingly transmit the virus to (Tufekci, Howard & Greenhalgh, 2020). This followed a similar U-turn elsewhere in the country. On April 28, Ohio's Republican Gov. Mike DeWine reversed an announcement he made the previous day requiring state residents to wear face masks in stores (Dugyala, 2020). 'It became clear to me that that was just a bridge too far, that people were not going to accept the government telling them what to do,' he told. 'Generally, Republicans are less inclined to have the government tell them what to do (ibid.).

In sum, it became clear that the Coronavirus catastrophe made political statements out of basically all Corona-related medical and daily questions: of wearing medical face masks or of going out, of joining other people or of taking precautionary measures. This was further complicated by various government's often contradictory indications. More relevant, the politicisation of Corona in general, and on a global level, furthered a more reckless political behaviour, and a rougher, more propagandistic and uncompromising tone in debates around the globe.

To which extent was such political "interpretation" of Corona for, in many cases, partisan use symptomatic for a potentially upcoming "post-Corona world"? Will such open instrumentalisation of catastrophic events by politics take hold – and become the new normality, among both authoritarians and populists and even among alleged "non-populists"? Or will it simply alter the concept of "populism" itself, broadening it even further to include virtually everybody, so that everybody who shows her or his face during similarly profound crises is a "populist" from now on?

CHAPTER 16

Three More Far-reaching Aspects within Global Democracies and Open Societies

Confirmation Bias, "Republican" Turn *and* Re-Globalisation Drive

More penetrative than these appropriations which relied, in many cases, rather on allegations than facts – yet were partly sustained by all too pragmatic strategic nationalist thinking – were *three* more encompassing and deeper-reaching debates of perhaps even longer outreach in open societies (not in dictatorships, authoritarian and illiberal systems).

The *first* one is about the so-called "confirmation bias", as the European Council on Foreign Relations (ECFR) branded it in April 2020 (ECFR, 2020). Bias has been massively strengthened by the Corona crisis and has thus acquired hardened perception fixations, also in open and democratic nations:

> We are all suffering from confirmation bias. Nationalists claim that the Coronavirus shows the superiority of the nation state; multilateralists claim the same for multilateralism; the end of globalization has also been proclaimed; for the left it is the end of capitalism; and for climate activists it confirms the need for more climate protections. [We should] think [instead] beyond the immediate response to the COVID-19 crisis and overcome our pre-existing biases and beliefs to shape ... future role[s] in the post-corona world.

A closely related *second* aspect that some observers have questioned in its long-term consequences upon European and Western democracies is a socio-psychological variant of the "Stockholm syndrome" (Von Schönburg, 2020). It is the fact that in a profound, all-penetrative and comprehensive, i.e., systemic crisis, populations even in democratic nations seemed to prefer a "strong man" who offers a "clear way" and imposes it uniform and uncompromisingly orders to everyone, if necessary by the mans of force. At the peak of the Coronavirus crisis, millions of citizens in open societies suffered from money worries and existential angst that furthered such desires for "clarification" and personalisation (BBC News, 2020bb). For example, in Britain:

> Nearly half of people experienced 'high anxiety' as the country's lockdown began, an *Office for National Statistics* (ONS) survey suggests.

© ROLAND BENEDIKTER AND KARIM FATHI, 2022 | DOI:10.1163/9789004469686_017

Anxiety levels were highest among an estimated 8.6 million people whose income fell, according to the … survey on the impact of coronavirus. Renters and the self-employed were also particularly affected. Measures of well-being were at their lowest levels since records began in 2011, the ONS said. The survey's finding suggested that more than 25 million people – i.e., 49.6 percent of over-16s in Britain – rated their anxiety as 'high', more than double the amount who did so at the end of 2019. Those suffering the greatest level of worry were an estimated 2.6 million people who said they were struggling to pay bills. The survey data suggested that 8.6 million people had seen their income fall, with this group also reporting anxiety levels 16 percent higher than average. Women reported anxiety levels 24 percent higher than men on average, with the ONS saying the difference might be because a larger proportion of women were either economically inactive, in lower paid jobs or working part time (ibid.).

In Austria, with its widely different and more de-centralised institutionalisation of a democracy-cantered economy:

the Coronavirus pandemic manifested apparently strong effects on the psychological health of the population: symptoms of depression have multiplied, including sleep disorders and symptoms of *angst*. This is the result of a poll by Danube University Krems encompassing 1,009 people [in May 2020]. Among other aspects, the depressive symptoms have increased from 4 percent to more than 20 percent, the angst syndrome from 5 percent to 19 percent. Particularly stressful is the Coronavirus situation for adults below 35 years, women, singles and unemployed, the study author Pieh says. In contrast, people over 65 seem to be less psychologically affected

APA, 2020n

This is paradoxical, as this age segment was the most threatened by the virus. Yet, as the country's media reported in June 2020:

the worries and fears of most citizens have increased during the Coronavirus crisis. The biggest concerns are about rising unemployment and the growing gap between rich and poor (both 76 percent). Immediately thereafter is the worry about an economic crisis (75 percent). The climate crisis, previously ranked in position 1, was deferred to place 4, but remains huge (72 percent)

APA, 2020d

In July 2020, just one month later, the Austrian health ministry reported that the "psychological consequences" had grown to dramatic levels, although the immediate impact of the crisis was diminishing. The number of people with depression in the Central European nation had quadrupled to 21 percent over the previous three months. In addition, every seventh Austrian now showed moderate psychological symptoms. Every eleventh was considered "heavily depressive". A similar increase was reported by the Austrian health ministry regarding anxiety: within three months it had tripled to 20 percent. "And 15 percent of the population now suffers from sleeplessness, a number that has been more than doubled by Corona" (APA, 2020c).

It can be assumed that similar numbers were the case in other Central European countries.

In such stressful situations of disorientation due to a simultaneous bundle of crises, or *simultaneity of highly complex multi-dimensional crises (bundle crises)*, impositions from above seem to take away fear by "clarity" and "rule and order" in the eyes of many. For example, this was visible in the relatively smooth acceptance of the harsh limitation of civil liberties imposed during the Corona crisis in European nations, although the reasons and causes were often poorly communicated, based on contradictory information or non-existent evidence. Such collective acceptance of an – at least temporary – complete reversal of basic rights in open societies under the auspices of "strong measures" has shown how fragile open-society systems in their core values and structures are.

They also infused the fear into democracy activists that the learnings of the Coronavirus crisis, be they conscious (by politicians or voters) or subconscious (by voters or politicians) could reach far beyond the sheer duration of this crisis. They could lead to a return towards more "republican" patterns, i.e., stronger representative mechanisms in open societies. They could lead to democratic systems more focused on single strong persons, be their position objectively "right" or "wrong", which turned out to be rather secondary in "deep" crises, at the expense of collective-participatory basic democratic features.

Overall, Corona could turn out to be in favour of a rather "conservative" turn in the conception of open political systems – as already predicted before the crisis by, amongst others, scholars such as Harvard's Yascha Mounk in the framework of his analysis of the crisis of Western liberal democracy and "Re-Globalization" (Mounk, 2018). Mounk's analysis started well before the Coronavirus crisis and evolved to an international and global phenomenon perhaps further strengthened by Corona, but not due to it. Be it as it may, the Coronavirus crisis has proven that if not the political system, so in any case the juridical systems of open societies were hit as equally unprepared as their health systems (Eurac Research, 2020b).

Third, as mentioned there is an ongoing, far-reaching debate about the effects of the Coronavirus systemic crisis (not of the virus as such!) on globalisation per se. From a retrospective future viewpoint and in an encompassing perspective, the corona crisis may be even less related to "disease" but more closely to "Re-Globalisation" (Benedikter & Kofler, 2019b). To what extent, and why?

"Re-Globalisation" is a buzzword that we have coined to describe the present historical phase in which globalisation is changing its face in many crucial sectors and areas simultaneously, with profound trans-disciplinary and trans-sectoral consequences on the global system as a whole, including a profound rupture in its neoliberal self-conception (ibid.). The trend towards reforming, renewing and reframing globalisation was already in place before the Corona crisis. It produced symptoms such as re-nationalisation, the breakup or suspension of international agreements, new bilateralisms, a resulting deep crisis of all international and global institutions such as the International Organization for Migration (IOM), the International Monetary Funds (IMF) or the World Trade Organization (WTO), the doubling of global institutions by China, which is erecting its own parallel global order, massive global youth movements against the worsening environmental crisis, such as Fridays-for-Future or Extinction Rebellion (XR) which, in essence, have also been against the existing practices of globalisation, a technology sector out of national and international bounds which forms its own global "governance" outside political and social elections and negotiations, including its own currencies, thus trying to erode diplomatically founded political economy, and the rise of a more multipolar order, with China and other non- and anti-democratic nations becoming stronger and global democracies trapped in internal polarisation triggered by the effects of globalisation, such as migration and fake news on local realities, which together put them in a far-reaching systemic crisis.

All this led to a situation of "competing modernities" ((Stuenkel, 2020)) where different projections of what a good life on the planet, as related to overarching cultural narratives, is, competed with each other in rather chaotic ways. In this sense, the Corona crisis is nothing new, but it accelerated the trend towards Re-Globalisation: to rethink, modify, refine and perhaps renew a global system and its mostly neoliberal mechanisms which have created rising inequality among and within nations as well as uncontrolled mass movement and thus have destabilised the global community, towards more adequate forms, procedures and habits. This includes the search for new ways of coexistence among profoundly different socio-political systems whose differences have been worked out more precisely by Corona as well.

For *BBC Futures*, Jonty Bloom summarised the origins of re-globalisation trends in these words:

> Globalisation has been one of the buzzwords of the past 25 years ... Easier travel, the world wide web, the end of the Cold War, trade deals, and new, rapidly developing economies, have all combined to create a system that is much more dependent now on what is happening on the other side of the world than it ever was. Which is why the spread of coronavirus, or COVID-19 to be specific, has had such an immediate economic effect. Professor Beata Javorcik, chief economist at the European Bank for Reconstruction and Development, says that the pace of change in the global economy over just the past 17 years has been profound. 'When we look back at 2003, at the Sars epidemic, China accounted for 4 percent of global output,' she says. 'Now China accounts for four times as much, 16 percent. So that means that whatever is happening in China affects the world to a much larger extent.' Globalisation helps to explain while nearly every major car plant in the UK has shut down [during the Corona crisis] – they are dependent on sales and components from around the world. When both collapsed, they just stopped making cars. China's wealth and health therefore matter to us all far more than they used to, but this is not just a matter of scale – there is also a deeper problem with globalisation. Ian Goldin, professor of globalisation and development at Oxford University, and author of the book 'The Butterfly Defect: How Globalization Creates Systemic Risks, And What To Do About It', says that 'risks have been allowed to fester, they are the underbelly of globalisation'. That, he says, can be seen not only in this [Coronavirus] crisis, but also in the credit crunch and banking crisis of 2008, and the vulnerability of the internet to cyber-attacks. The new global ... system brings huge benefits, but also huge risks.
>
> BLOOM, 2020

The Corona crisis made these risks inherent to globalisation fully clear even to the average public – probably for the first time in 20 or 25 years or so, and perhaps even for the first time ever. It did so exactly by breaking the process of "natural" neoliberal globalisation and uncompromisingly interrupting the existing global system as had never been the case since the start of the 21st century.

Such a deep rupture would probably not have been possible as a result of economic, financial or political emergencies *per se*. With Corona, a more extended number realised the magnitude of the break, and many had time to think about what they did not like in the neoliberal period. Overall, part of the pendulum started to swing against the interpretation and practice of the globalisation we had been used to over the past 30 years, i.e., the mainly expansive and ruthlessly growth-oriented self-understanding of a system that produced as much wealth and productive interrelation as social and cultural unrest and blind activity, as well as the exploitation of many strata of global populations.

Some even go beyond this and posit the question in the light of COVID-19: Are globalisation and its accompanying ideology, globalism, in their very essence the real "threats" to a good life, or simply not in tune with "mother earth"? Or, in the words of Oren Levin-Waldman (2020) issued shortly before the Coronavirus crisis, i.e., at the start of January 2020: Are "globalism and inequality combined the real threats to our democracy"? And did we just not take notice before Corona?

PART 2

The Simultaneousness of Local, National and Global Effects

∴

CHAPTER 17

An Unprecedented Crisis Accelerating the (Temporary?) Rupture of Advanced Life Patterns – Including Gender Role Models in Democracies

Once again, we must underscore the following in order to take a step forward:

The profound turn in the perception of globalisation and the rise of the desire for re-globalisation was already *en vogue before* the Corona crisis. However, Corona accelerated it further, perhaps decisively; this remains to be seen.

Be it as it may, the unprecedented Coronavirus crisis opened a gap between more immediate shift efforts and the related practical questions on the one hand, and their overarching and theoretical aspects in a broader and longer perspective on the other. The more detailed applied socio-economic questions included, among many other detail questions for the future: Will the Coronavirus crisis be the end for environmental-killer cruise ships? Will there be more separations or more marriages due to the lockdown? And will there be more or fewer children born because of "enforced intimacy" (Majella Horan)? Will Coronavirus make:

> some people rethink where they want to live ...? After the pandemic passes, will some people choose to leave big-city life behind? That trend was already starting to emerge in some parts of the country, even before coronavirus hit. Now the pandemic is changing the way we talk about life in big cities. And some experts say it could change who opts to live in them.
>
> SCHOICHET & JONES, 2020

Some held that the time of the office as a working place was over – and that after the crisis, most people would continue to be working from home, thus changing the private-public nexus of the labour sector in advanced societies towards the private (Gillett, 2020).

Yet in turn in Germany, Federal family minister Franziska Giffey feared for the practical achievements of gender equality. She saw the Corona crisis as a regressive force that forced women back into old role models, i.e., to "stay at home" – with a clear discrimination pattern during lockdown times. The question is whether this was the case only in this crisis, or whether it may be a phenomenon during every crisis that advanced role models recede. For example, as was handled with female leadership of big global companies:

> In the Corona crisis, [the international enterprise] SAP needed 'clear leadership' for 'fast, decisive action', the software group recently explained the departure of co-head Jennifer Morgan. This means that the first woman at the top of a Dax company is already history after only six months. With Christian Klein, business is now once again being conducted by a single male. Even if the departure of Morgan is not exclusively due to the corona crisis, difficult times once again show how women in management positions are treated: modestly. Simone Menne, once Chief Financial Officer of Lufthansa and of the pharmaceutical group Boehringer Ingelheim and now a member of numerous supervisory boards, called Morgan's departure 'a disaster'. There were still men who claimed that there were no women in the industry suitable for top management positions. Janina Kugel, until recently a manager at Siemens, complained that there was little willingness for diversity in the [German] economy anyway. Now she fears that the corona crisis could be used as an excuse for regression [of female emancipation role models]. In fact, after seven weeks of shutdown, there are more and more voices warning of the serious consequences of the corona crisis for women.
>
> ANGER, 2020

Indeed, different treatment of men and women became routine during the COVID-19 lockdown:

> Under the title 'Back in the Men's World', Gruner + Jahr boss Julia Jäkel criticised ... that for thousands of women home office means above all 'home' and little 'office'. She came to the conclusion: 'Women are much less advanced than we thought.' The Corona crisis makes it obvious who in Germany 'really, really' decides, what the real structures are like, and that the dictates of diversity apparently only count on quiet days. The pandemic is aggravating all the problems and imbalances in terms of gender equality and women's policy, complains the German Association of Women Lawyers. Federal Minister of Women's Affairs Franziska Giffey was alarmed. 'Despite all their talents, excellent education, and all their efforts, women still too seldom make it to the executive floors', Giffey said. 'Unfortunately, the Corona crisis has intensified this situation.'...

'The Corona crisis poses a particular challenge to female managers', Commerzbank Board Member for Human Resources Sabine Schmittroth said. 'Even today, they still bear additional responsibility for childcare much more frequently than their male colleagues'.

IBID.; DARÜBER SPRICHT BAYERN, 2020

Some others speculated about a fundamental rupture regarding the future of jobs in particularly affected branches, such as the airline industry:

The wave of job losses that has come crashing down has had one silver lining: Many economists and investors think that a good portion of the layoffs are temporary. ... That may be true in some sectors. But for the airline industry, which has been battered by plunging demand as people hunker down at home, changes to its workforce will be more permanent. General Electric said that it is cutting as many as 13,000 jobs in its jet engine business for good. The move is designed to cope with an 'unprecedented' and 'deep contraction' of commercial aviation ... GE said the job cuts will help the company save $1 billion. Orders for jet engines and parts have plunged as Boeing and Airbus have slashed production of new planes. Demand for servicing jets has also collapsed. Meanwhile, a top executive at United Airlines is urging employees to consider leaving the company voluntarily ... These announcements underscore the gravity of the crisis facing the aviation industry, which is expected to take years to recover from the coronavirus shock. Ryanair, Europe's top budget airline, said that traffic plunged 99.6 percent in April 2020. Just 40,000 passengers flew [in that] month compared to 13.5 million in 2019. Shares of airlines reflect this turmoil. Stock in United, Delta Air Lines, Southwest Airlines and American Airlines all fell at least 5 percent after legendary investor Warren Buffett said he'd dumped his holdings, calling it a mistake to invest in the [airline] industry.

HOROWITZ, 2020; TAPPE, 2020; EGAN, 2020; MUNTEAN, 2020

Others though held that "the COVID-19 crisis [could be] the catalyst for eventually greening the world's airlines" (Watts, 2020b):

'The political moment is now' to address the climate risks posed by the aviation industry, analysts, insiders and campaigners say, as governments across the world weigh up bailouts for airlines grounded by the coronavirus pandemic. Rescue packages need to come with green strings, such as reduced carbon footprints and frequent flyer levies, they warn, or the sector will return to the path that has made it the fastest rising source of climate-wrecking carbon emissions over the past decade. Old passenger jets also need to be rapidly retired or cheap oil prices will encourage budget airlines to run services almost empty, which could push up emissions even if passenger numbers stay low, they say (Ibid.).

Most experts expected flying to become more expensive in the long term: "To get the 16,000 airplanes grounded during the Corona crisis in the air again, prices may remain low initially. In the long term, due to the fact that 85 percent of all airlines need state support through public funds, prices for flying may go up significantly" (APA, 2020g). Others again, positively, expected a "revolution in world's travel" (Rowlatt, 2020), but also in urban mobility, with many new pedestrian and bicycle zones created during the crisis due to restrictions and in order to favour social distancing which could remain in place.

The BBC in July 2020 estimated that the Coronavirus pandemic cost the tourism industry at least 320 billion US\$ (M. Jackson, 2020). There were, however, also aspects of a transformative forward effect of the crisis in the tourism sector, apparently precisely because it was "hardest hit" by the crisis (Tidey, 2020). Among the businesses hit hardest by the crisis was undoubtedly the hotel sector – for example in one of the major tourist hotspots in Europe, Austria:

> As a result of the Corona crisis, every third hotel in Austria is experiencing major problems. Compared to 2019, the establishments are registering less than half the number of guests on average. The situation is most dramatic in city tourism: in Vienna, hotel occupancy rates [in 2020] were only 10 to 15 percent on average
>
> APA, 2020k

In such situations, the Corona crisis has been seen by many local administrators and regional politicians as a once-in-a-lifetime chance for definitively turning the tide from rude mass tourism and so-called "overtourism" to qualitative and ecological tourism (Pechlaner, Innerhofer & Erschbamer, 2019), and more in general, from quantity to quality, such as on the Spanish island of Mallorca. As the local administrators declared, "booze tourism" came to an end with Corona and should be over forever – which had been the desire of the locals for decades, but could not be realised before the unprecedented, sudden and "total" Corona break:

> The regional President [of the Balearic Islands] Francina Armengol ... expressed the expectation that the corona crisis will help to ensure that

there will be no more party excesses in the Balearic Islands in the long term. 'Bucket drinking is history,' she said. 'The Balearic Islands stand for quality and sustainable tourism, sport, culture and culinary experiences. As early as 2019, the regional government had already taken measures to curb drinking tourism in the places El Arenal and Magaluf, which are particularly popular with tourists. This program will continue', Armengol said

> SÜDTIROL NEWS, 2020e

Yet according to expert Harald Pechlaner of Eichstätt-Ingolstadt University in Bavaria, the "overtourism" polemics might not be over with Corona – rather the opposite (Dignös, 2020). The opposition of parts of the population against "the return of tourism" may be intensifying due to second and third waves and ongoing cases, and it may do so widely independent of other facts because the anti-tourism perceptions of parts of the population, particularly in hotspots due to remaining Corona fears, will be greater and more pronounced than ever.

Another worry was for the future of retailers, many of whom "were too broke to go bankrupt" (Isidore, 2020):

Some retailers can't afford to file until stores reopen because they need money from liquidation sales. The 'everything must go' blowouts help get products off shelves and fund operations through bankruptcy proceedings. 'We probably would have seen more file by now if stores were open,' Reshmi Basu, an expert in retail bankruptcies told. 'We're clearly seeing a lot of companies engage [bankruptcy] advisors. But it's not a great time.'... It's not clear shoppers will return, and conditions remain difficult ... Shares of ... rental car companies] [we]re [also] down 29 percent.

> CNN, 2020c

On the other hand, some speculated that "Corona could remove barriers for women in the car industry" because of better consideration of generational and equality issues as a consequence of mass dismissals of workers as a result of collective anti-virus measures (Leggett, 2020). Obviously, among the most affected was the hospitality industry, including hotels and restaurants, for which Corona was at least temporarily "the apocalypse" (Vendettuoli, 2020):

The hospitality industry faces thousands of closures ... Kate Nicholls, chief executive of trade association Hospitality UK, said it was 'catastrophic for businesses and jobs. This ... will lead to thousands of businesses closing their doors for good, and hundreds of thousands of job losses,' she said.

'Over the past few weeks the industry has suffered unprecedented drops in visits and many businesses are on their knees'.

BBC NEWS, 2020W

Economic strategists were concerned with the fate of another particularly strongly globalised industry, the sports industry, and with the future of commercialised European football (soccer) – the world's most popular sport – in particular. As the most-read newspaper of Italy, the (always pink-printed) *Gazzetta dello Sport* (2020) estimated at the start of May that in Italy, football accounted for 7 percent of the national GDP – and like other branches of the entertainment industry in-large was wiped out by Corona completely for an extended period of time. In August 2020, one of the financially strongest clubs in the world, the FC Barcelona in Catalonia, Spain, symptomatically declared that "Barca generated 200 million Euros less than expected between March and June [2020] because of the Coronavirus pandemic" (BBC sport, 2020). As the club's President Josep Maria Bartomeu analysed,

> All the big European clubs are affected ... This isn't going to last a year, but three or four. ... If the situation of the pandemic doesn't improve, there will be no spectators, no museum, no stores open, and money will continue to be lost (ibid.).

The question was whether the football industry, and more generally the commercialised and mediatised sports industry in toto, would ever again be able to attract the masses to the stadiums where the "real experience" of sport is, or transform into virtual leagues with so-called "ghost matches", i.e., televised or streamed competitions with no physical public present. And, of course, whether this would have the same economic turnaround. The commercial value of sport was also the reason why U.S. President Trump insisted in restarting the American football, baseball and basketball leagues as soon as possible, despite concerns about an increase in infections.

CHAPTER 18

"Unsocial Sociability" and the Re-shaping of the Global Order

Anthropology and Politics Intertwined

Taken together, most observers took fundamental change for granted. If "in 2002 the sociologist John Urry defined contemporary man as subject with two fundamental drives: the compulsion to mobility and the compulsion to proximity" (Membretti, 2020), these times seemed to be over, at least for the post-Corona years. Rather, German philosopher Immanuel Kant's classical "unsocial sociability" (*Gesellige Ungeselligkeit*, (Wood, 1991)) of the human being (as sketched in the Fourth Proposition of his "Idea for a Universal History", 1784)(Schneewind, 2020) came to the fore with full power during the crisis. Kant thought that the human being is in a constant inner conflict between an endless search, if not pulsating drive for sociability (*Geselligkeit*) without which he or she cannot find satisfaction, and competition with others for supremacy which is his and her inborn instinct. The latter ultimately prevails, although with a compromise, making the human being a fundamentally torn being between social and unsocial. In the Corona crisis, it was something like this that seemed to make people particularly nervous under restricted space conditions. According to Kant, humans "cannot like each other completely" but at the same time they "cannot leave [or live apart] from each other" (Belwe, 1999). If anything, the Corona crisis, with its social distancing and related forced individualisation, added to the deep ambiguity between being close and far from each other. It was a close reminder that Kant knew humans all too well and that his anthropology is not far from reality. It seems to be valid, perhaps even regarding those "post-modern" born long after him, and even the Britons and Americans.

Among the more down-to-earth anthropological aspects, the more practical consequences also included the fact that Corona, for example in Austria, due to the high number of emergency cases and deaths, contributed to a decrease in autopsies, leaving many murders undetected (Südtirol News, 2020c). The sarcastic therefore described the Coronavirus as an "aide for murderers", i.e., for those truly "unsocial".

Yet beyond these more immediate and practical shifts, the Coronavirus crisis as mentioned also co-triggered an – at least temporary – search for an overarching better answer to globalised needs in a broader and longer-lasting

© ROLAND BENEDIKTER AND KARIM FATHI, 2022 | DOI:10.1163/9789004469686_019

perspective. It pushed the request for systemic modification, including better protection of open societal systems, against the increasing risks of unconditional interconnection, and against "elite globalisation" by an educated few against the alleged will of the majority of their populations who, before Corona, had already become more cautious against over-openness electing populists for their protection.

Dubbed the globe's "greatest test since WWII" by U.N. secretary-general António Guterres (BBC News, 2020u) and as a "geopolitical earthquake" by the European Council on Foreign Relations (Lopez, 2020), many expected that the Corona crisis' outcome would contribute to seriously "reshape globalisation", or perhaps even "reshape the global order" – among other aspects, by putting China at the steering wheel due to a "faltering America" in the crisis (Campbell & Doshi, 2020). Others, as mentioned, thought Corona may be the "death knell" for globalisation as such:

> The Coronavirus is killing globalization as we know it. The outbreak has been a gift to nativist nationalists and protectionists, and it is likely to have a long-term impact on the free movement of people and goods.
> LEGRAIN, 2020

And while some departing from the "death knell" theory developed scenarios for a "post-Corona world" which, in many cases, sounded like the return of the pre-Corona world just with sometimes radically altered prefixes, others, as mentioned, more pragmatically noted that the Corona crisis led to a temporary stop of *exaggerated* globalisation (Van Til, 2020). For example in the realm of medical supply and production, which Europe and the West had, until 2020, outsourced to around 80 percent to Asia and to China in particular, making themselves widely dependent on an authoritarian nation which is partly a strategic competitor, as the European Union branded China in its latest "EU-China Strategy" of March 2019 (European Commission (EC), 2019). Such lack of foresight and anticipation awareness was due to an exaggerated exuberance of European Union expansion and general Western overconfidence and miscalculation of new global power relations which the Corona crisis helped to bring to awareness.

On the geopolitical front, many saw the European Union in particular as the potential main victim of the crisis (Leonard, 2020a). Together with the U.S., the EU was a main co-creator of the existing liberal system of global rules and orders. The Corona crisis created disunity among the single member states and fully unveiled the missing power of a European superstructure. Europeans, in retrospect, may at least say that one insight from the European example

(R. Herreros, 2020) of struggling with Corona was: The Corona crisis helped European citizens and politicians to curb their exuberant cosmopolitanism towards a "weak cosmopolitanism" (David Miller) by understanding that open systems are more vulnerable to catastrophes than closed ones. Thus open systems in a hyper-interconnected world must transit towards a new balance between openness, self-protection and self-conservation. The decisive question is how exactly, and, more specifically, how this can be achieved without falling for the cheap simplifications of populist messages which tend to make things worse instead of better.

While some intellectuals such as Ivan Krastev saw the nation state strengthened by such debates, others rejected such speculation and pointed towards the need for pragmatic survival of existing supranational units and international bodies precisely for being able to reform globalisation (Krastev, 2020b). Others took more cautious intermediate positions. As, for example, the High Representative of the European Union for Foreign Affairs and Security Policy and Vice-President of the European Commission for a Stronger Europe in the World, Josep Borrell, wrote:

> The pandemic will likely magnify existing geopolitical dynamics and test the strength of Europe's democratic systems. Europe needs a new kind of globalisation capable of striking a balance between the advantages of open markets and interdependence, and between the sovereignty and security of countries.
>
> BORRELL, 2020

Without doubt, there were simultaneously all too many speculations around single policy questions related to Corona in sometimes overrated, disproportionate or unrealistic ways. For example, that Germany's response to the virus outbreak may "strengthen Europe" (Puglierin, 2020) and ultimately the Western alliance of democracies, or that the new geopolitics after Corona (Leonard, 2020b) may be more sober, less ideological and generally more balanced than before it (a claim that has found much opposition). There were some approaches towards a practical rethinking of the given international order that appeared to be more concrete, legitimate and plausible. Among them was, for example, the condemnation of neoliberal "bullshit jobs" by a new generation of civil-society thinkers such as David Graeber of the London School of Economics, who tried to use the Coronavirus crisis to recalibrate the transnational pay structure of low-paid jobs, with the ultimate goal of reducing inequality by eventually increasing the salaries of nurses, supermarket employees or waste collectors (Weisbrod, 2020). These intellectuals thought the time was ripe with Corona, since in their view, the crisis made clear to everybody that there are essential jobs in society that are underpaid and treated unfairly, while others which, in times of crisis, were revealed to be not absolutely "necessary", were by far overpaid. To change such asymmetry may indeed be one of the most pressing tasks as one main learning policy effect from the Corona experience.

CHAPTER 19

Medical Diplomacy, or: The Great Divide
of Principles over and after Corona

More "Do It Alone" – Or More Cooperation?

In sum, those critical observers holding that the Coronavirus crisis promoted "de-globalisation" highlighted that most nation states initially reacted unilaterally to the crisis and were likely to continue to do so in future crises. Within the European Union (EU), the respective actions included unilateral border closures and initial reluctance to help stronger virus-affected member states such as Italy and Spain (Rettman, 2020; Herszenhorn, Paun & Deutsch, 2020). As mentioned, due to the initial scepticism, China was able to step in to supply Italy with medical equipment, accompanied by great media fanfare and propaganda, both domestic and abroad. Disputes about the joint trans-national economic response, in particular the pros and cons of joint European debt-making through so-called Eurobonds to support the hardest hit countries, threatened to reopen conflict lines between the northern and southern as well as western and eastern EU nations which had already manifested during the 2007–08 financial and economic crisis. Many of the Corona crisis actions de facto questioned EU cohesion, as well as the unity of single nations such as the U.S. Federal and state institutions often argued against each other, for example about the right moment to reopen after the lockdown, or Italy, where a heated north-south dispute started with southern regions unwilling to take in compatriots from the north during the crisis months. In sum, a lot of reactions to COVID-19, both within and across nations, seriously questioned both national solidarity and international cooperation.

Moreover, the pandemic did not lead to a mitigation of populist rhetoric – rather on the contrary. During the Coronavirus lockdown, public rhetoric was often of nationalist colour, sometimes denying the pandemic's global outreach and calling it an imported "foreign" threat. US President Donald Trump, for example, repeatedly called SARS-CoV-2 a "Chinese virus" or the "Chinese plague", which was probably factually exact, but was also meant to actively designate a culprit to shift responsibilities and failures. The Chinese government acted similarly and worse, even trying to disseminate rumours that the virus was imported to China from "foreigners" and allegedly from the West. This was no surprise, since the Xi Jinping government's double strategy is always to blame the victims of its policies as the perpetrators, and for the rest to designate

© ROLAND BENEDIKTER AND KARIM FATHI, 2022 | DOI:10.1163/9789004469686_020

"the West" as the culprit for everything. In the EU, populists demanded the use of virus-related border closures to implement long-term immigration stops (Paun, 2020). Overall, both populists' and authoritarian government's COVID-19 rhetoric reinforced the nation state as a central authority and questioned international cooperation. Improper interferences between nation states were also reported, such as the attempt of China to influence German government officials to deny any Chinese responsibility for Corona, as officially confirmed by the German government in April 2020 (Bild Online, 2020g).

As a consequence, observers rightly stressed that the Coronavirus crisis pushed counter trends towards global interconnectedness. Yet, at the same time on a worldwide level, authoritarian governments such as in China and Iran, illiberal ones such as in Russia, and populist-led administrations in democracies such as in the USA, the UK or Brazil were weakened due to poor crisis management and procrastination, resulting in prolonged insecurity and disorientation of broader parts of the population with respective negative repercussions on social psychology, due a relatively high amount of infections and deaths (Käppner, 2020). Populists in general did not do well as crisis managers, losing in voter confidence and trust (Gruber, 2020b).

On the other hand, examples of strengthened international solidarity could also be found, although we might assume that their motifs were not always purely altruistic but also driven by geostrategic calculations: South Korea, China and Taiwan also sent medical equipment and staff to other countries (Silva, 2020). Russia donated medical equipment to the USA and Italy (BBC News, 2020mm). After some hesitation, Germany flew out Coronavirus patients from Italy and France to medicate them in Germany, equally to compatriots because they were EU citizens, ultimately saving their lives (Bateman, 2020). Some private companies also donated medical equipment worldwide, and benefactors – mainly from Western democracies – did the same (Lakritz, 2020).

Yet even generous help was politically instrumentalised for propaganda. For example, Taiwan was accused by China of "using" the Coronavirus crisis "to seek independence" – a veritable crime in the eyes of the authoritarian, if not dictatorial (meta-)communist Chinese regime of Xi Jinping:

> Taiwan ... st[ood] out with its relatively few cases of infection in marked contrast to previous estimates by experts and despite its close connection and proximity to China. With masks on, most Taiwanese seemingly carr[ied] out their daily business as usual, increasingly enjoying a sense of pride for being meticulously taken care of by the state and seeing Taiwan praised in international media as a model for confronting COVID-19. Moreover, the #TaiwanCanHelp campaign, initiated by President Tsai

Ing-wen, has drawn worldwide praise for its contribution to global health, and is expected to help Taiwan reduce its isolation in international affairs. Yet, the campaign has attracted backlash as well as recognition. WHO Secretary Tedros's recent emotional complaints against 'Taiwan' for making defamatory racist comments about him is one extreme episode that exposes the geopolitical fault lines under the pandemic crisis. In another, China has accused Taiwan of using the COVID-19 crisis to seek independence. A full-page ad in the *New York Times* sponsored by a crowdfunding campaign by young Taiwanese Youtubers and designers responded to this accusation, exemplifying Taiwanese determination to raise its standing in the world. The complexity of desire and anxiety beneath the increased sense of complacency in Taiwan in the midst of coronavirus pandemic ... may bring more uncertainty to the island state's effort to promote medical diplomacy ... The pandemic has brought new rays of hope to Taiwan but, at the same time, drawn it into a whirlpool of diplomatic drama, especially as regards its newly strained relationship with China

> HUANG, 2020

Despite these brawls, in the end, the Coronavirus crisis highlighted not only the need for more effective global cooperation but also for the differentiation of judgements about the narratives of "help" and "solidarity", both within and among nation states. This was due not least to the profound paradoxes inbuilt in the case, among them China giving origin to the virus, probably delaying information as long as possible in an irresponsible manner, denying responsibility post factum and simultaneously "helping the world" to cope with the virus (Markson, 2020). At the same time, even nationalist leaders accepted the importance of cooperation, particularly on information exchange and vaccine research, and the relevant role of international organisations for that task (Perthers, 2020). In addition, the roles, mistakes and failures of potentially leading organisations such as the WHO were also exposed clearly to the broader global public, calling for a reform of global bodies as a decisive aspect of any post-Corona re-start towards re-globalisation (Sritzel,Piatov & Ropcke, 2020).

Overall, with regard to the impact of the Coronavirus crisis on international conflicts, observers confirmed ambivalent developments throughout the process, concluding that the paradoxical simultaneousness of cooperation *and* conflict – particularly between the USA and China, but also in many other cases – was likely to continue beyond the crisis. This has various reasons.

Firstly, as mentioned, many of the aforesaid bilateral aid deliveries had the effect of promoting cooperation, but many were also driven by geostrategic motivations promoting ongoing paradigmatic rivalries. China, for example, having been initially "criticised for concealing the epidemic, [...] is now presenting its authoritarian system as superior to democratic models in dealing with such a crisis" (Perthes, 2020).

Secondly, most of the armed conflicts worldwide were proceeding during the pandemic, e.g. in Libya, Yemen and Syria, or Nigeria, relatively unimpressed by the UN Secretary-General's appeal to "put armed conflict on lockdown, too" in order to focus on fighting COVID-19 (Guterres, 2020). In May 2020, leading officials of Iran's totalitarian mono-religious government compared the sheer existence of the nation of Israel to the Coronavirus in the framework of an ongoing war rhetoric, triggering strong critical responses by open societies (Reuters & Landau, 2020). Among others, the EU High Representative for Foreign Affairs and Security Policy, Josep Borrell Fontelles, saw this comparison as a "threat for international peace" (APA, 2020l). Previously, neither of the two governments of Iran and Israel had been ready to coordinate their, as both branded them simultaneously, "war efforts" against the virus (Frantzman, 2020).

However, on the other side, there were a few positive responses to this plea coming from the Philippines and Colombia as well as trends in other governments to actively use the situation for confidence-building measures (Pace News, 2020). For example, the UAE and Kuwait sent aid to Iran which was – according to Middle East-expert Volker Perthes – not just a one-off, since it was meant as medical diplomacy, too. Nevertheless, these actions were not translated into lasting political reconciliation (Perthes, 2020). Thus, with regard to ongoing international conflicts, the Coronavirus crisis did not – and will probably not – mitigate the deeper-lying origins of international mistrust and competition. However, fresh forms of cooperation can be observed, and some of them are likely to persist for practical and pragmatic reasons. In the end, the shape of the world after the pandemic remains strongly dependent on political will, leadership, and the ability of international protagonists to cooperate.

CHAPTER 20

Don't Forget the Bizarre, the Surreal and the Perfidious

From Mona Lisa to Sharon Stone and Global Terror

Last, but not least, at the crossroads between the local, the national and the global, and mixed into the previously listed dimensions, there were aspects of the crisis which filled countless newspaper and gossip pages and reached from the bizarre to the apocalyptic. We must mention this column here, eventually, to not omit the profoundly surreal experience of this crisis which was strongly felt among those who lived through it, i.e., by more than half of the global population. Without doubt, the old wisdom that wherever there is an all-encompassing crisis mode that changes collective and individual life substantially and lasts for more than a short time, the bizarre and surreal are always lurking around the corner. The Coronavirus crisis was indeed no exception here.

For example, some perceived it as surreal when French public opinion-makers proposed selling the most representative pieces of the nation's art museums to finance COVID-19's cultural recovery:

> To get a grip on Corona, Frenchman demands: sell the Mona Lisa. From empty concert halls to closed museums – the French cultural sector is suffering from the Coronavirus. How can it be rescued from the financial plight? The influential French digital entrepreneur Stéphane Distinguin has the solution: He suggests selling the most famous painting in the world, Leonardo's Mona Lisa!.
>
> BILD ONLINE, 2020j

Apparently, Distinguin had in mind making the price 50 billion euros and selling the painting to the richest person in the world, Amazon's Jeff Bezos. According to Distinguin, the alternative would be to offer it to "any Arabic prince" (Ibid.). The fact that there even was a public debate on selling the nation's most prestigious cultural goods in order to finance its post-Corona culture showed how deep the COVID-19 had hit the nerve of artists and intellectuals in the "Grand nation".

Among the rather bizarre effects of the Coronavirus lockdown was also a steep rise in aesthetic surgery. This was due to the fact that facial (and other)

© ROLAND BENEDIKTER AND KARIM FATHI, 2022 | DOI:10.1163/9789004469686_021

108   CHAPTER 20

scars could be covered by the obligatory mask, and furthermore "I can recover at home":

> A number of cosmetic surgery clinics around the world [we]re report-ing a rise in people getting treatment during the coronavirus outbreak as they can hide their treatment behind a mask or work from home. Despite the virus shutting businesses across the globe, a number of plastic surgery clinics have remained open, adopting stricter measures such as COVID-19 tests and more frequent cleaning. Clinics in the US, Japan, South Korea and Australia have all seen a rise in patients coming in for treatment including lip fillers, Botox, face lifts and nose jobs. 'I decided to get procedures done during quarantine because it allowed me to heal at my own pace,' said Aaron Hernandez, who had lip fillers and buccal (cheek) fat removal in Los Angeles. 'Getting my lips done is not something that all men tend to do, so some people might find it different. Therefore, I preferred to stay home and recover fully and people not know what work I had done once I'm out.'... Rod J Rohrich, a cosmetic surgeon based in Texas, said he was seeing a lot more patients. 'Even more than I would say is normal. We could probably operate six days a week if we wanted to. It's pretty amazing.' He said usually people would have to factor in recovery at home when considering surgery but now that many people are working from home, this doesn't need to be considered. 'They can actually recover at home and also they can have a mask that they wear when they go outside after a rhinoplasty or facelift. People want to resume their normal lives and part of that is looking as good as they feel.
>
> WILLIAMS, 2020

On the other hand, there were the celebrities. Opera singer Andrea Bocelli first endorsed the COVID-19 measures of the Italian government of Giuseppe Conte, including giving a solo concert in the empty cathedral of Milan which was live-streamed and called "Music for Hope" – just to declare in July 2020 that he felt "humiliated" by the lockdown measures which should be ignored since he needed "sun and vitamin D" (BBC News, 2020b):

> Italian opera singer Andrea Bocelli has said he felt 'humiliated and offended' by lockdown measures imposed in the country due to corona-virus. 'I could not leave the house even though I had committed no crime,' Bocelli said. He also admitted to disobeying lockdown rules and believing the severity of the pandemic had been overblown. His comments will

surprise many as he had become a symbol of national unity at the height of the lockdown ... A national lockdown began in Italy in early March and was eased in stages over the following months. During Bocelli's speech, which he delivered in Italian, the 61-year-old said he disobeyed lockdown rules 'because I did not think it was right or healthy to stay home at my age'. He added: 'I am a certain age and I need sun and vitamin D.' Bocelli also suggested other citizens should 'refuse to follow the rules'. He said he thought the outbreak had been overblown and he didn't know anyone in intensive care. 'So what was all this sense of gravity for?' he asked. 'Let's refuse to follow this rule. Let's read books, move around, get to know each other, talk, dialogue,' he said (Ibid.).

In the ideological footsteps of Bocelli, among the bizarre events were not least demonstrations against the Corona safety measures imposed by many governments around the world. One of the most bizarre took place in Berlin at the start of August 2020:

> 20,000 protest against Corona rules. Anti-vaccinationists, neo-Nazis, conspiracy theorists: all united on one of the most insane demos in German history. From rainbow flags to imperial flags, from 'Merkel must go' to 'There is no Corona' conspiracy theorists, from demo hippies to party ravers: all united under the banner: No more Corona rules. According to the police, 20,000 demonstrators came to Berlin on Saturday 17 June [2020] to protest against the [German] government's anti-Corona measures, delivering a bizarre collection of people and political currents that could not be more different. The giant demonstration was organised by the initiative '*Querdenken 711*' [Lateral thinking 711] from Stuttgart and the Berlin 'Kommunikationsstelle Demokratischer Widerstand' (KDW) [Communication Office Democratic Resistance]. The motto was: 'The end of the pandemic – Freedom Day'; whereby 'Freedom Day' was already the title of a propaganda film by Nazi icon Leni Riefenstahl about the 1935 NSDAP party conference – whether this title was deliberate provocation or coincidence is not clear.
>
> BIERMANN, HAENTJES & WILKE, 2020

In these demonstrations against the German government's anti-Corona measures, 45 police officers were hurt, with more than 1100 police deployed and the demonstration eventually being ended by force through public officers. Many protesters did not keep the safety distances, wore no masks and had to be carried away by police. Even German Federal President Frank-Walter Steinmeier

110 CHAPTER 20

felt urged to launch a video messages warning that "the irresponsibility of just a few is putting us all at risk". (Bild Zeitung, 2020).

Simultaneously, in South Korea which, as early as in July 2020 confirmed a second wave of the Coronavirus, sect leader Lee Man-hee, 88, head of the Shincheonji Church of Jesus, was arrested because of spreading the virus (BBC News, 2020hh):

> South Korea has arrested the leader of a religious sect linked to the country's largest coronavirus outbreak. More than 5,000 of its members became infected, making up 36 percent of all COVID-19 cases in the country. The authorities accuse him of hiding information about the group's members and gatherings from contact tracers. The church says Mr Lee was concerned for his members' privacy ... A judge said there were signs that evidence related to the case was being destroyed ... In Korean, Shincheonji means 'new heaven and earth'. The group, which has 230,000 members, is considered a cult by many. Mr Lee identifies as 'the promised pastor' mentioned in the Bible, and his followers believe he will take 144,000 people to heaven with him after Christ's Second Coming ... The group is known for packing its followers tightly together during services (Ibid.).

Meanwhile, U.S. movie star Sharon Stone "lauded male human beings" (APA, 2020o), saying that due to COVID-19, they "were undergoing a change" towards becoming a little bit "more like real humans" as a result of the Coronavirus lockdown, which gave them more time to think about certain things:

> Hollywood star and men's dream Sharon Stone sees the Corona crisis as an opportunity for the evolution of men. Since men in isolation have had to cook for themselves and look after themselves, they have been calmed, the 62-year-old told the German magazine 'Bunte'. 'Some are even beginning to speak like real people.' Stone said men were all like tigers in a cage. 'They want out, but at the same time they are forced to think about themselves and their values. Men are changing right now, they are not quite as crazy as they used to be.
>
> SÜDTIROL NEWS, 2020b

More publicly serious than such profound socio-psychological observations were the multiplication of "terrorist narratives" during and after the crisis. As Annelies Pauwels analysed in the *EUobserver*, the Coronavirus provided fresh air to a terrorist scenery that, before the crisis, was in the process of dwindling:

The COVID-19 pandemic leaves no one unaffected, including terrorists. European terrorist networks are torn between protecting their own members against the virus and using the pandemic to further their goals … Like many state and other non-state protagonists, terrorist groups manipulate the global pandemic in their radical narratives. They do so to unify their followers, attract new sympathisers, and further their objectives. ISIS (Daesh) sees in the coronavirus 'a torment sent by Allah to his enemies'. China would be particularly hard-hit as punishment for its treatment of Uighur Muslims, and [in this view] it is no coincidence that Iran's holy Shiite city Qom is one of the new epicentres of the outbreak … The coronavirus pandemic has caused high numbers of deaths, massive economic disruption, and had a huge impact on the daily lives of millions of people. In short, everything terrorists would want to achieve with their attacks. No surprise thus that the global pandemic serves as inspiration and influences the modus operandi of terrorists, both in terms of tactics and target selection.

PAUWELS, 2020

For example:

Terrorist networks have encouraged followers to weaponise their own illness by trying to infect others. The pandemic might also serve as inspiration for their long-term strategies, leading to a potential rise of attempts to commit biological attacks … Terrorists have also found inspiration in the global pandemic with regards to their target selection, in particular critical health infrastructures. Recently, the FBI killed a far-right terrorist, who had accelerated his attack plan and changed the target to a hospital treating COVID-19 patients. For terrorists, the current crisis also serves as an ideal case study to learn about the threats and effects of atypical warfare methods and could thus inspire them to adopt innovative attacks, such as disruptions in the food supply or medicine and other health supplies … Violent extremists thus will most likely play out the apocalyptic narrative of the pandemic to spur their supporters to action.

Ibid.; BENEDIKTER, 2019

As a consequence, in May 2020, EU experts warned against terrorist 'bio-attacks':

Terrorism experts warn of a growing danger of attacks with biological weapons after the Corona crisis. The pandemic has shown 'how vulnerable modern societies are to virus infections', reports a paper by the

Council of Europe's Counter-Terrorism Committee. Extremists would not forget this lesson from Corona. The use of a biological agent can 'prove to be extremely effective'. The experts call for a strengthened and coordinated response by European states to this threat

APA, 2020h

Similarly, UN secretary-general António Guterres in April 2020 warned that:

The COVID-19 pandemic has provided a 'window' into how a bio-terrorist attack might unfold across the world. Guterres issued a strong warning that non-state groups could gain access to 'virulent strains' that could pose similar devastation to societies around the globe

NDTV, 2020

Yet on a smaller level, "everyday terrorists" and psychopaths were also "inspired" by Corona to pass from thought to action:

Politics had badly managed the Corona crisis: A man from Limburg (36) attacked the Belgian parliament. A man threw a Molotov cocktail at the parliament in the Belgian capital Brussels. Fortunately, only parked cars were damaged. The man was arrested. According to the public prosecutor's office, the reason for his action, according to his own statement, was that politics had badly managed the Corona crisis. The crime could not yet be attributed to a political conviction. The man denies having acted ideologically.

BILD ONLINE, 2020p

At the brink of the bizarre was also the attempt of Germany to hold crowded "study concerts" to see how many infections would occur among people respecting the safety guidelines:

Coronavirus: Germany puts on 'study concerts' with Tim Bendzko. Three pop concerts are being staged on one day in Germany to enable scientists to investigate the risks of such mass indoor events during the pandemic. Some 4,000 healthy volunteers aged between 18 and 50 were urged to sign up for [the] study in Leipzig, carried out by Halle University. Singer-songwriter Tim Bendzko agreed to perform at all three successive gigs. The concert study, called Restart-19 (University Hospital Halle (Saale) & Medical Faculty of Martin Luther University Halle-Wittenberg, 2020), was created 'to investigate the conditions under which such events can be carried out despite the pandemic', researchers said. Scientists planned to run three different scenarios ... The first aims to simulate an event before the pandemic; the second with greater hygiene and some social distancing; and the third with half the numbers and with each person standing 1.5m apart. Each staged scenario involves arrivals and departures from the stadium and performances by Tim Bendzko 'in order to depict spectator behaviour as realistically as possible.' All participants are being tested for COVID-19 and given face masks and tracking devices to measure their distancing. Researchers are reportedly using fluorescent disinfectants to track what surfaces audience members touch the most ... 'The corona pandemic is paralyzing the event industry,' Saxony-Anhalt's Minister of Economics and Science, Prof Armin Willingmann, said before the event. 'As long as there is a risk of infection, major concerts, trade fairs and sporting events cannot take place. This is why it is so important to find out which technical and organisational conditions can effectively minimise the risks.

BBC NEWS, 2020t

The "live experiment" with the Tim Bendzko concert series produced an "encouraging" outcome according to those responsible for the study (Bild Live, 2020). Similarly, but much more radical, unorganised and disputed, a mass experiment was carried out in Saxonia: the "Dresden experiment", branded by many as an "unethical human trial". The organisers instead said that "culture is needed to strengthen the immune defence against the virus" (RÖPCKE, 2020a). This was clearly perceived as a negative example by a majority of the population of how not to carry out "live experiments" with a deadly virus since "voluntary infection groups" were regarded as not ethical (RÖPCKE, 2020b).

Last, but not least, a tranquillising research finding was published in August 2020: singing is not riskier than talking for virus spread, if it is only as loud as normal voice speech. As the University of Bristol reported:

Singing does not produce substantially more respiratory particles than speaking at a similar volume. But it all depends on how loud a person is, according to the initial findings which are yet to be peer reviewed. The project, called Perform, looked at the amount of aerosols and droplets generated by performers. The findings could have implications for live indoor performances ... Aerosols are tiny particles which are exhaled from the body and float in the air. There is emerging evidence that coronavirus can be spread through these particles, as well in droplets which fall onto surfaces and are then touched. Twenty-five professional performers of different genders, ethnicities, ages and backgrounds – musical theatre, opera, gospel, jazz and pop – took part in the study that was led by scientists at the University of Bristol. They individually completed a range of exercises, which included singing and speaking Happy Birthday at different pitches and volumes, in an operating theatre where there were no other aerosols present. This allowed researchers to analyse the aerosols produced by specific sounds. They found that the volume of the voice had the largest impact on the amount of aerosol produced. For example, there was some difference – albeit not very substantial – between speaking and singing at a similar level. Whereas singing or shouting at the loudest level could generate 30 times more aerosol. Ventilation could also have an effect on how aerosol builds up. The larger the venue and the more ventilation there is could affect how concentrated the volumes are. Jonathan Reid, professor of physical chemistry at the University of Bristol, is one of the authors of the paper, which was supported by Public Health England. He said: 'Our research has provided a rigorous scientific basis for COVID-19 recommendations for arts venues to operate safely, for both the performers and audience, by ensuring that spaces are appropriately ventilated to reduce the risk of airborne transmission.

Culture Secretary Oliver Dowden said: 'I know singing is an important passion and pastime for many people, who I'm sure will join me in welcoming the findings of this important study" (Moss, 2020).

So let us sing, then!

CHAPTER 21

Coronavirus Crisis Social Psychology

Between Disorientation, Infodemic and the Need to Understand

If anything, Corona has proven that one aspect is a seemingly "universal" prerequisite for mastering crises, perhaps more than ever before: in order to get a grip on chaos and disorientation and to master anxiety and despair, first and foremost *understanding* is needed. In a crisis such as the COVID-19 global emergency, people do not want to only know the facts, they also want to know how to interpret and understand them properly. Too much information can be hurtful if not properly integrated into given conditions of processing and contexts of understanding.

"Understanding" indeed denotes an increasingly important aspect at the intersection of contemporary hypercomplexity, philosophy, popular education and policy. It touches many, if not all people in a very concrete way. It is also massively populism-relevant, because "deep" crises are unavoidably associated with both individual and collective disorientation that can be taken advantage of by pied pipers. Understanding is about putting order into chaos, and learning the lessons – although they might be scattered among the unimportant and disinformation – about how management procedures can best work in future crises. Most importantly, understanding in the present means that complex crises such as the Corona crisis are not and will never again be monocrises. Instead, they are bundle crises and crisis bundles.

Yet, if "understanding" is crucial in complex crises, then what is *perceived* as understanding becomes crucial, too (Yong, 2020). And this brings us to social psychology and its relation to contemporary science and the news industry.

First, Corona has once again proven, perhaps more visibly than ever, that crisis psychology in knowledge societies is also science psychology. It is a psychology which tries to rely first and foremost upon science for orientation. In one way or another, a good part of it always arrives at the conviction that "we cannot afford to not invest [more] in basic science" (Stauder, 2020). As, for example, Julia Stauder wrote:

> In February 2020, the EU Commission made 100 million euros available for immediate research into the diagnosis, therapy and prevention of COVID-19. Individual countries [we]re launching calls for funding to understand the biology and transmission of the virus. This *crisis* – the

© ROLAND BENEDIKTER AND KARIM FATHI, 2022 | DOI:10.1163/9789004469686_022

word comes from the Greek, and originally means *decision* – has clearly shown politicians and the general public the importance of basic research. It should herald a change in the way research and development are funded: The funds now made available should be the starting point for long-term investment in science more in general, so that mistakes such as those made during the [first and second] SARS epidemics are not repeated (Ibid.).

So, as a first effect, Corona has strengthened the *belief* in science – a veritable "science belief" that took grip of the whole of knowledge societies, widely removing other leading discourses and rhetorics of trust.

On the other hand, the Corona crisis disclosed considerable weaknesses of today's science and information societies. The highly inter-connected digital infrastructure brought about unprecedented effective and fast information transfer in nearly real-time simultaneously from different perspectives and ideological paradigms. This enabled governments worldwide to react much more quickly and informedly compared to past pandemics, such as, for example, the Asian Flu (1957–58) or the Hong Kong Flu (1968–70). The Corona pandemic was the first crisis which more or less anybody worldwide with the most basic access could follow up via live ticker. Another manifested strength was the very close cooperation between the political class, virologists and social scientists of various scientific sectors. Both elements led to a significantly more effective political response to the pandemic than would have occurred at the beginning of the 20th century. In Germany alone, the Asian Flu caused 30,000 deaths and the Hong Kong Flu about nearly 70,000, while the – in principle – worse Coronavirus pandemic accounted for less than 9,200 up until July 2020 (Wiegrefe, 2020; Worldometer, 2020d).

At the same time, the corona crisis also unveiled weaknesses and new vulnerabilities of today's information societies, which were best illustrated by the term "infodemic". Sylvie Briand, Director of the Infectious Hazards Management Unit at the WHO's Health Emergencies Program and architect of the WHO's strategy to counter the *infodemic* risk, explained:

> We know that every outbreak will be accompanied by a kind of tsunami of information, and also within this information you always have misinformation, rumours, etc. We know that even in the Middle Ages there was this phenomenon. [...] But the difference now with social media is that this phenomenon is amplified. It goes faster and further, like the viruses that travel with people and go faster and further. So it is a new challenge, and the challenge is the [timing] because you need to be faster ... What is

at stake during an outbreak is making sure people will do the right thing to control the disease or to mitigate its impact. So it is not only information to make sure people are informed; it is also making sure people are informed to act appropriately.

ZAROCOSTAS, 2020

During Corona, digitally disseminated "fake news" with inaccurate medical advice was considered to be spreading globally almost as rapidly as the virus itself. Fake news ranged from unproven or provenly incorrect medical advice to conspiracy theories about COVID-19. In parts of West Africa, for example, medically unproven rumours circulated claiming that high African temperatures can protect residents from becoming infected or that citizens are advised to drink hot water and to stay away from cold food and drinks. Often, these messages are wrongly indicated as coming from UNICEF (Backhaus, 2020).

As a consequence, combatting the spread of fake news required enormous resources. UNICEF, for example, has produced "myth-buster videos" and established coronavirus information centres in West Africa promoting the sharing of credible information, also via text message where not otherwise possible. On a global level, the WHO has partnered with Twitter, Facebook, TikTok and Tencent in order to ensure content on these open platforms is accurate and helpful. In January 2020, the WHO and Google joined forces to launch an SOS Alert system on COVID-19. Accordingly, information from the WHO's SOS alert appeared at the top of the Google page when people searched for information on Coronavirus. On YouTube, videos purporting to be useful updates on Coronavirus were framed by a banner which redirected users to the WHO web portal (WHO, 2020c).

But these aspects were not all when it came to public and individual psychology. Given the wide absence of in-depth studies for closed and authoritarian societies, for the Western World, observers stated a two-fold psychological effect of the Corona crisis:

- First, a rise of psychological tensions among citizens, and
- Second, a rise in conspiracy beliefs.

We previously already mentioned aspects of the first trend. There was a significant rise of psychological roblems among European and Western populations due to the pluri-month-long lockdown and perceived uncertainty. For example, in Austria:

there [wa]s a strong request for more psychotherapy. The limitation of social contacts, job pressure and financial woes as well as tensions within families [due to] the Corona crisis has been unfolding effects also on psychological health, as a study of the Danube University Krems has shown. This means that the psychotherapy options have to be significantly expanded, say experts. As a fallout of the crisis, Austria alone is in need of 20,000 additional psychotherapy places, which must be paid for by public and private health insurance.

APA, 2020i

CHAPTER 22

Conspiracy Theories

Misusing the Crisis for Legitimating the Absurd in Times of "Fake News"

Regarding the second trend, observers noted a rise of "pandemic populism"(P-feifer, 2020) correlating with the fact that "conspiracy theories generally bloom in periods of uncertainty and threat, where more people than usual seek to make sense of a chaotic world" (Ibid.). Conspiracy theories are about offering a "fast-track" explanation platform to understand everything here and now, immediately and universally just from one standpoint. In so doing, they concentrate mostly on a central narrative which is always more or less radically self-referential, i.e., its truth lies in its own existence.

Without doubt, Corona triggered a new search for orientation, meaning and the "real" mechanisms behind known life which was suddenly gone. The Coronavirus crisis lockdown motto: "Do nothing" led to a variety of "Coronavirus philosophies", in most cases not limited to mythologies and narratives but trying to span the globe. They were based, at least temporarily, on a "Coronavirus narrative" that often bordered "Coronavirus mythology" or even Coronavirus conspiracy theories. According to a representative survey among U.S. adults conducted by the Harvard Kennedy School on March 17–19, 2020, at least two conspiracy theories about COVID-19 were relatively popular. Around 31 percent of the respondents claimed "that the virus was purposefully created and spread" and "29 percent [...] agreed that the threat of COVID-19 has been exaggerated to damage [U.S.-]President Trump" (Uscinski et al., 2020). Research also showed that beliefs in these two popular variants of COVID-19 conspiracy theory were the joint product of two psychological predispositions:

- Firstly, to reject expert information and accounts of major events (denialism), and
- Secondly, to view major events as the product of conspiracy theories (conspiracy thinking), including partisan and ideological motivations (Ibid.).

Conspiracy theorists usually do not believe in coincidences but in personal universal control mechanisms, claiming there is a small group of elites successfully pulling the strings of complex processes behind the scenes, and conspiring against everyday people. Typically, such narratives are published by "alternative media" outlets, i.e., left- or right-wing publications that want to deliberately dissociate themselves from the political elite and the established media. "Alternative

© ROLAND BENEDIKTER AND KARIM FATHI, 2022 | DOI:10.1163/9789004469686_023

media" are basically reporting on the same, verifiable facts, but they lace the reports with speculation and propaganda. Typical "alternative media platforms" are *Russia Today*, the Chinese-controlled CGTN (China Global Television Network) or explicitly left- or right-wing magazines in the West (Pfeifer, 2020).

One of the most dominant conspiracy theories of 2020 was "QAnon". It detailed a supposed secret plot by an alleged "deep state" against U.S. President Donald Trump and his supporters (Shallhorn, 2020). The theory began in October 2017 with a post on the anonymous platform *4chan* by an individual or group self-named "Q", who claimed to have access to classified information about the Trump administration and its opponents in the United States (Rozsa, 2019; Rotschild, 2020). Hereby, Q falsely accused Democratic politicians, high-ranking officials and other celebrities of running an international child sex-trafficking ring and claimed that Donald Trump feigned collusion with the Russians in order to prevent a coup d'état by Hillary Clinton, Barack Obama, and George Soros (Laviola, 2018; Roose, 2019). With regard to the Corona situation, a popular QAnon theory described that Donald Trump imposed Coronavirus curfews and sent a large naval hospital ship to New York in order to secretly free thousands of abducted children being held in an underground tunnel system (Huld, 2020; Pfeifer, 2020).This belief was spread among some celebrities, increasingly also in Europe, including e.g. in Germany the singer Xavier Naidoo or the vegan-cuisine author Attila Hildmann. In October 2020, a presumably QAnon-related attack took place on the famous Berlin museum island, damaging more than 70 art works (Bild Online, 2020d).

There might be different reasons behind the increasing spread of conspiracy beliefs. Firstly, one might assume that these beliefs, particularly in the case of QAnon, are a tool of "information warfare". Simone Rafael from the Amadeu Antonio Foundation Berlin (n.d.) (dedicated to "reinforcing a democratic civil society that promotes pluralism and human rights while opposing right-wing extremism, racism and anti-Semitism" (ibid.)) stated that the purpose of "alternative media" outlets is to carry out targeted propaganda. She said:

> According to their own statements, 'alternative media' believe they are in an 'info-war' against democratic political parties and against parliamentary democracy. They spread uncertainty in order to overthrow the system.
>
> PFEIFER, 2020

Her colleague, Miro Dittrich, explained:

> Conspiracy theories are usually told from the perspective of the loser, not the powerful. But this serves to justify everything that goes wrong with

the ruler – because forces would work against him, the so-called deep state, and everything is part of a larger, still secret plan.

HULD, 2020

Evidence indicates that conspiracy beliefs contribute to create fringes and violent behaviour of political engagement, as Roland Imhoff, a professor of social and legal psychology at the Johannes Gutenberg University in Mainz, states. "This finding, together with the observation that many radical and terrorist groups employ conspiracy rhetoric in their pamphlets, might suggest that seeing the world as governed by hidden and illegitimate forces is a driving force for radical violent action as it a) seems justified and b) non-violent means seem futile", said Imhoff (Drinkard, 2020). If this is true, conspiracy beliefs in the Coronavirus emergency served as strategic means of information warfare and to instrumentalise social conflict potential among the population against perceived political enemies.

Another reason behind the high demand for conspiracy beliefs can be explained through the overwhelming extent and unprecedented effect of the Corona crisis itself. Conspiracy beliefs help to dramatically reduce complexity. "They often provide a simple answer to a complex problem and blame a clearly identifiable group of conspirators for a problem in society, which can make them very appealing. The 'official' answers do not always meet this need, are usually more complex, and are often provided by the government, a group that some people do not find trustworthy. People would prefer to focus on explanations provided by the underdog", as Daniel Jolley, a psychologist and conspiracy theory researcher, discussed in *Psychology Today* with the Trauma and Mental Health Report (TMHR) (Muller, 2020).

Yet, as Zaria Gorvett put it more "positively", what can be learned from conspiracy theories is that:

> people have gradually lost trust in experts, governments and powerful institutions. To fix the system ..., we need to re-legitimise democracy – reform our governments and retrain our institutions. In the United States that was done in the early decades of the 20th Century. It rehabilitated the government for new generations, and led to all sorts of progressive reforms, culminating in female suffrage ... There have been very few studies into why some [conspiracy theories] have extraordinary longevity, while others die out relatively quickly ... In fact, despite decades of research and an endlessly captivated public audience, there are still many unanswered questions in the field.
>
> GORVETT, 2020

Coping with the inherent information chaos of the Corona situation goes beyond the discourse on intentional and unintentional misinformation. Philosophers such as Markus Gabriel stated that in times of Corona, the natural sciences, particularly the discipline of virology, had become a "new religion". He criticised the fact that people increasingly cultivated an almost religious belief in the objectivity of the natural sciences, although their models were and are often not based on facts, but only on assumptions (Gabriel, 2020). Moreover, considering the complexity of the Corona bundle crisis, the focus on a mono-discipline might prove to be limited.

Thus, political decision-makers managing the highly complex present and future situation might have an increased demand for integrated or systemic philosophy as the science of inter-, trans- and meta-disciplinary understanding according to the old saying: "Philosophy blossoms in crises" (Mäder, 2016). Yet in what way exactly, and who needs what? These would be clues for future philosophical-theoretical approaches for politicians and the general public in order to facilitate understanding and decision-making in hyper-complex crisis contexts.

CHAPTER 23

The Perspective

The Real Question Is Not about COVID-19, but about "the World After"

Overall, as unprecedented and apocalyptic the COVID-19 crisis may have been, as urgent a sound in-depth discovery of its origins and of the related responsibilities remains, the latter of which are assumingly not mono-lateral, but multiple and interconnected. As surreal some of the ingredients, experiences and protagonists were, and as ugly some of the debates about the respective implications, political and socio-psychological instrumentalisations and long-term perspectives may be remembered: the two real overarching questions to posit are: *What are the teachings of this crisis?* And: *What should be done after the Coronavirus crisis is over* – or at least when it will appear to be just the remembrance of a bad dream, without (as is probable) ever being *completely* over?

As Stephan Ortner, the Director of Eurac Research Bozen (Italy), representative for many European and Western social science institutions, put it in April 2020 at the height of the crisis in the then worst-hit European country, Italy: "It is now essential to formulate the right questions to ensure a more sustainable world after COVID-19".

Given the great variety of – partly contradictory – phenomena and effects in play, it appears to be essential to ask not only science but also public institutions and politics for a *joint concept of better resilience*, given that the so far used – in their majority rather monolithic concepts – have proven to be not sufficient. The request for resilience, and in particular for *better* resilience is the main insight of the Corona crisis. The respective need will not go away but is here to stay, since Corona has shown the full complexity of contemporary global crises which require multi-dimensional concepts of anticipation and preparedness in order to be handled appropriately.

Given the phenomenology of Corona which we have illustrated on the previous pages, it is right to assume that overcoming this type of crisis in the direction of long-term sustainability will not only involve combating future pandemics, but also dealing with the many directly or indirectly related types of crisis, be these related types real or perceived by the public. Physical or imagined crisis makes little difference, since both create practical realities with wide-spanning effects, ramifications and implications. Many observers consider the possibility of an upcoming, longer-lasting global crisis as a consequence of climate change which could shadow and outlast the end of the pandemic. In addition, there are more global challenges ahead which will not disappear with the end of Corona, e.g. interconnected ecological risks and fights between different economic and political systems whose interconnected effects may, if worsening, interfere with the recipes to cure the aftermaths of Corona. For example, the *Global Risk Reports* of 2019 and 2020 rank environmental instability among the "most likely" and, at the same time, among the "most dangerous" crises that we may expect over the coming years (World Economic Forum, 2020).

A closely related main teaching to take away from the Corona phenomenology of 2019–20 is that there was not *one* Corona crisis, but that "crisis" in our days consists of *crisis bundles* which can only be handled if seen in their interconnection, and both in the "big picture" and in detail. Most "crisis bundle" effects have been brought in more or less close relation to the virus pandemic, some of them in more obvious, other in less transparent ways. For example, an economic downturn of the global economy as a consequence of COVID-19 seems, at least in the short term, unavoidable; yet to which extent global institutions such as the World Health Organization (WHO) may pay a price in trust and financing, and what this may trigger as an effect on other global institutions and the very idea of a joint global order, is open. Certain is that international connectivity, globalisation as an expansive endeavour that poorly differentiated between open and closed societies and their respective practices, and the idea of ever-more open borders spanning different protagonists and political systems have suffered massive harm through the crisis. In the eyes of many, they have reached their limits.

Third, perhaps the most pronounced effect of COVID-19 in the open societies of Europe and the West was a loss of trust in politics and in democracy and democratic decision-making processes more generally. As, for example, Jan Spurk of Paris Descartes University quoted a poll of French newspaper *Le Monde* of April 2020:

> most of the French population feels mistrust, gloom, weariness and fear. The French do no longer trust politicians (65 percent), who are expected to wage 'the war against the virus' (French President Emanuel Macron) as representatives of the people ... Brice Teinturier, the director of a large French polling institute, says that the 'nothing more to screw up attitude ... carries deeper anger and suffering. It is no longer a slow and almost underground process of detachment but a disgust which generates a desire for rupture, which can materialize through revolt or multiple forms of withdrawal'... The potential for revolt is great but ambiguous: there is no massive break with the established order. A poll [in 2014] ...

clearly showed the attachment to social gains and, at the same time, the desire for profound change. 84 percent think that 'France must be radically transformed or reformed in depth'. Change (87 percent), reform (75 percent) and revolution (57 percent) are mostly positively associated words. Yet, a quarter (26 percent) would leave the country if they had a choice, but their attachment to 'the country as it is' seems to remain deep (particularly to the pension system, health insurance, taxation and the country's territorial structure).

SPURK, 2020

According to Spurk, even more "transformative" is the "verdict on globalization" as a sum of the Corona-mood:

The verdict on globalization is final: 65 percent think that France should protect itself more from the outside world in the future. A large majority (67 percent) thinks there are 'too many foreigners' in the country. Following the corona crisis, almost two-thirds of French people (like the Germans and the British) think that immigration and borders must be better controlled. Is the future of democracy its transformation into an authoritarian regime? The corona crisis reinforces this call for authority not only in France. 88 percent want 'a real boss'. 18 percent would prefer an authoritarian system with a leader who decides without being embarrassed by parliament, unions or other opponents. In the context of the corona crisis, the fragility of democracy has been clearly shown by the fact that 44 percent of French people prefer an 'effective' policy to democracy, which is considered as ineffective. (Ibid.)

In essence, even more multi-dimensional scenarios than the Corona crisis must be taken into consideration for the future if we follow the indications of leading risk foresight institutions such as, for example, the Future of Humanity Institute at Oxford University. Among them is not only the breakdown of confidence in democracy as a form of efficient social organisation and the desire for "system change" which remains somewhat vague and opaque; systemic future risk scenarios are not only about new viruses, either. They are also about a prolonged large-scale collapse of critical infrastructures (i.e., supply of water, electricity, food or internet). Furthermore, as climate change progresses, the spread of more infectious diseases is likely to occur, which could be even more dangerous than COVID-19. According to a 2018 prediction of Oxford global historian Peter Frankopan, a worldwide spread of tropical diseases – such as Malaria, Ebola or Zika – as a result of rising temperatures in the global hemisphere and the return of old diseases such as smallpox or the plague as the effect of thawing permafrost are conceivable in the not too distant future (Mitteldeutsche Zeitung, 2018).

Against this background, the Coronavirus crisis of 2019–20 must be seen as an opportunity to gather experience and foster knowledge about better, more "multiversal", flexible and interconnected concepts of resilience in order to prepare for future scenarios. In developing adequate preparedness, international forms of cooperation could be expanded; not kitsch-wise and once again over-idealistically on the part of open societies, but first of all pragmatically, and existing pandemic plans and crisis communication strategies should be systematically improved in line with the comparison of best practices. Yet, most important, the Coronavirus crisis can and should be used to also develop a *social* multi-resilience – in other words, the ability to personally and collectively deal with confidence with diverse "crises bundles" that may occur simultaneously, and to emerge from them stronger (yet not necessarily identical) after a structured moulding and development process (Fathi, 2019c). What exactly would a new multi-resilience for diverse societies imply?

PART 3

The Corona Challenge: Multi-Resilience for an Interconnected World Ridden by Crisis Bundles

∵

CHAPTER 24

In Search of Examples of Efficient Resilience

From the Evolutionary Teachings of Bats to Regional Self-administration within Political Autonomies to a "Flexible" Handling of Constitutions

The copying approaches and strategies in the crisis in search of efficient resistance and resilience were many. And as horrific the Coronavirus crisis was, there were indeed some positive examples and hopeful approaches and developments.

For example, on the strictly scientific front, given that the Coronavirus supposedly originated from bats or virus research on bats, researchers at Yale and other universities studied in-depth "how bats have outsmarted viruses – including coronaviruses – for 65 million years". As the journal *Science Magazine* reported:

"Although the SARS-CoV-2 virus has sickened more than 14 million people, bats contract similar viruses all the time without experiencing any known symptoms. Now, the newly sequenced genomes of six species spanning the bat family tree reveal how they've been outsmarting viruses for 65 million years. [...] With more than 1400 species, bats are the second most diverse group of mammals on Earth. They ... are also known to carry many different kinds of viruses, including coronaviruses, with no ill effects. To discover their secrets, an international consortium launched the Bat1k project, which stands for bat 1000, in 2017 to sequence the genomes of all bat species. Six of those genomes are now complete, the consortium reported (J. Cohen & Kupfershmidt, 2020) . The genomes are more thorough and more accurate than previously sequenced bat genomes, says Jon Epstein, a disease ecologist ... 'That allows [researchers] to make some strong comparisons with other animals, including humans.' The researchers in the consortium did just that, comparing the newly sequenced genomes with those of 42 other mammals, from manatees to people. They found that ... bats have disabled at least 10 genes that other mammals use to mount inflammatory responses against infection. But they also have extra copies and modifications of antiviral genes that may explain their high tolerance for disease. Finally, their genome is littered with DNA pieces derived from past viral infections that got incorporated when the viral genomes were replicated. 'These non-bat genes leave a kind of medical record ... a diary of previous infections,' Yohe says. That diary reveals that bats have probably had more viral infections than all other mammals over time and have even been infected by viruses thought only to attack birds, the team reports. 'The findings highlight bats' ability to tolerate and survive viral infections more efficiently than other mammals,' says Sharlene Santana, an evolutionary biologist at the University of Washington, Seattle" (Pennisi, 2020).

In short, if bats succeeded in evolving over time with the help of "inbuilding" viruses in their genome system, why should humans not learn from this experience – and try similar developments perhaps by different means? This could certainly lead both to a "transhumanist" and to a practical path of dealing better with infections by "enhancing" human body resistance.

On the socio-psychological front, as an exception compared to national psychologies, in the Autonomous Province of South Tyrol (n.d.) at the centre of the European Alps adjacent to Switzerland and at the border between Italy and Austria, the mood was calm and positive (South Tyrol, n.d.). This was the case despite the fact that initially, the province, located at the most important North-South connection route of Europe and thus of high interconnectivity, experienced more deaths than the neighbouring areas. In a poll of July 2020:

> 2,140 South Tyroleans, who were randomly drawn from the registration registers, took part in the survey on the changes in lifestyle due to the containment measures of the coronavirus pandemic. At home, the mood was predominantly cooperative and relaxed, but a general feeling of concern is at the top of the list of the most common moods. Trust in politics and the media has declined, while personal autonomy has gained in importance. The lockdown was also characterised by healthier eating, lower alcohol consumption, more leisure time and more online shopping than usual. Of the smart workers, who are the most numerous among those with a university degree, one in four had technical problems, and among high school and university students one in three. 93 percent of South Tyroleans aged 14–80 who do not live alone reported that people living together have supported each other sufficiently or very much during the curfew. For 86 percent, the mood in the house was relaxed and for the same number there was little or no conflict. 79 percent described the domestic mood as not stressful. The data indicate that the home atmosphere was perceived more positively by older people than by the younger ones. It was also more positively perceived by households without children living together than by households with children living together. Furthermore, it can be stated that the more space in the houses per capita was available, the higher the percentage of persons who perceived the domestic atmosphere during curfew as cooperative, pleasant, not conflict-prone and not stressful.
>
> ASTAT, 2020

IN SEARCH OF EXAMPLES OF EFFICIENT RESILIENCE

Experts saw the Autonomous Province over the arch of the Coronavirus crisis as a positive model of how to successfully cope with a "universal" emergency, both policy-wise and psychologically. Some ascribed this to its high-degree autonomy statute. South Tyrol was until 1918 a core part of the Austro-Hungarian empire and was annexed by Italy afterwards. This was against the will of the population and ultimately led, after civil-war-like upheaval, to a wide-reaching autonomy for the area. Since 1972, South Tyrol has been an autonomous province within the Italian national state, with a special status anchored in the Italian constitution. It is composed of three main ethnic groups: Austrian German speakers, Raetoromans also of Austrian descent, and Italians. Together, they dispose of wide-reaching self-administrative powers and primary and secondary legislative powers for the territory in a variety of fields, including civil protection and emergency interventions (Peterlini, (2009); Alber & Zwilling (2016)). Analysts asked if its good mastering of the Coronavirus crisis was:

- because "small is beautiful", i.e., because small administrative and self-governed units like South Tyrol with its just 550,000 people but far-reaching autonomous powers can simply cope better with emergencies, since they can react quicker and act in more capillary and situation-oriented ways in people-to-people relationships;
- because there is generally more trust and cooperation on smaller scales with a strong sense of community than on bigger and more anonymous ones;
- or if it was because the local government which, according to the autonomy statute, must be *per legem*, composed of the three major historical ethnic groups in accordance with their respective political representation, simply did a good job, independent of the institutional and juridical framework, because in South Tyrol inter-ethnic cooperation is institutionalised by the autonomy statute and guarantees a public political model of "tolerance established by law" (Pflöstl, 2010)?
- A fourth factor could be the relative wealth of the inhabitants of the area, also due to the autonomy from the national state (Italy). On average, South Tyroleans of all ethnic groups had enough resources and space to get along with each other and not argue.

Probably, such positive exception was a mixture of all four factors, to be achieved in specific areas with a high degree of experience in self-administration, social and ethnic coexistence and autonomy – something to be remembered for the next crisis. The factor to which extent the 100 years of experience of South Tyrol with the (since 1972) institutionalised coexistence of different ethnic groups and languages – German, Italian and Raetoroman, or Ladin – as well as the long history of political and social battles for self-assertion and identity of the territory and the subsequent institution of a model of institutionalised power-sharing among the ethnic groups played a role in the supposedly increased resilience of the area remains to be researched in detail. This similarly applies to the question as to to what extent the geography in the midst of the mountains and, at the same time, at an inner-European cultural and linguistic border area with a very high confidence in the European unification process and in a trans-national "Europe of regions" were positive factors that co-produced the comparatively good coping with the COVID-19 crisis.

Given that local and regional autonomy and self-administration are not practised as widely within many other geopolitical areas – such as within the single states in the U.S. – compared to those European national states that compose the EU, the question after the Corona experience is to which extent positive examples such as South Tyrol can be transferred to other specific socio-political situations, and to which extent they may be valid in particular in "normal" federal models such as the U.S. where, as the Coronavirus showed, federal states are, to a high degree, independent but usually do not cultivate additional autonomy micro-models of ethnic and other nature (native Americans reservations perhaps excepted).

Last, but not least, on the applied political front, there were constructive in-depth debates on how to flexibly handle basic rights, as provided and guaranteed by the constitutions of open societies, in multi-dimensionally impacting crises (bundle crises) such as Corona, and in following similar emergencies. This helped the debate about the future of democracy to move forward, reaching into still widely unchartered territory. It included the fundamental assertion that "even in a well-managed crisis, critique must be possible" (Rauscher, 2020). The Coronavirus crisis both triggered and contributed to a democracy in crisis – [and a] crisis in democracy. The last months [of the Coronavirus crisis] have demanded a great deal from our [open] society and our democratic constitutional state – quarantine, shutdown, border closures, curfew. And anyone who did not comply was reported to the authorities. Questions of constitutional conformity were degraded to 'legal quibbles' [Austria's chancellor Sebastian Kurz] for which during the crisis would not be the time. Imbalances within nations and European society en-large were becoming more apparent than ever before; borders were again being erected everywhere, not only slowing down the spread of infection, but also hindering urgently needed cooperation and solidarity. In retrospect, however, the fog has lifted and communication strategies that remained hidden during the 'hot period' are now more clearly visible. After this impressive demonstration of what can be politically and governmentally possible in a crisis situation, the population is left with ... the burning question of how crisis-proof our democracies really are" (Lichtenberger & Pelinka, 2020).

And this is, in the *ultima ratio*, the question of what *resilience* as a contemporary systemic quality is and can be in open societies, and what not.

CHAPTER 25

Crisis Resistance in the Face of Corona and in Anticipation of Potential Future Pandemics
A Short Overview of Different Options of Socio-political Responses

On the most basic level and according to the bulk of available scholarship, resilience means crisis resistance. Yet what does, and what can and should crisis resistance exactly mean in the face of COVID-19 and potential future pandemics?

Corona has shown that crisis resistance is less about the ability of a society to beat a specific virus and be it one of the most dangerous and harmful ever. It is rather its basic systemic ability to prevent further damage and to maintain (or improve) its functionality during a crisis. Most crises are a "stress test" for some sort of collective immunity, which is not necessarily a virus immunity (Metzl, 2020).

In this more encompassing sense, countries have politically and socially responded in very different ways to the Corona crisis (see Our World in Data).[1] Although it might be interesting to derive "Best of"-strategies in preparation for future pandemics, international observers remain sceptical about the final outcome of such hope, since many countries cannot be compared properly. This includes, for example, differences in population density and average age of the population (e.g. Africa has a relatively young population, whereas Japan has not), data collection (Britain counts only COVID-19 deaths in hospitals, France includes also deaths in care homes), etc. (Kretchmer, 2020; C. Morris & Reuben, 2020).

Apart from the many differences between societies, there is, however, a typical set of socio-political measures of crisis management which applies to different countries, including those infected by pandemics, and which can be categorised as follows:
1) containing,
2) averting and
3) slowing down.

---

1 For an overview of the strategies and successes of all 207 countries, see Roser et al., 2020.

© ROLAND BENEDIKTER AND KARIM FATHI, 2022 | DOI:10.1163/9789004469686_026

CRISIS RESISTANCE IN FACE OF CORONA IN ANTICIPATION 135

In the case of a viral infection, the first "natural" core objective of crisis resistance is not to overload the health system and thus keep the number of fatalities as low as possible. An international overview of the effectiveness of measures against Corona demonstrated that although China was its geographical starting point, the spread of the pandemic in rather collectivity-based East and Southeast Asia was relatively slower than in the open and individualistic societies of the West. A brief overview of the most important measures indicates:

- In the initial stages, *containment strategies* have proven to be the most effective. These include identifying and isolating infected persons; tracing of contact persons; monitoring of self-quarantine; as well as tracing of infection chains. Since the SARS-CoV-1 pandemic 17 years ago, the countries of East and Southeast Asia, especially Taiwan, Singapore, South Korea and Vietnam, have further developed their contact tracing management, while others in the West have not (Yang, 2020; Senzel, 2020; Peters, 2020). Apps in which cases of infection are geographically listed and in which citizens are called upon to report their state of health were being used successfully during Corona. Additionally, broad-based testing made a significant contribution to early identification. South Korea, for example, systematically expanded its testing capacities and had tested around 146,000 people already between January 20 and March 5 (Yonhap News, 2020). According to Germany's most frequently quoted virologist Christian Drosten of the Charité Berlin, this was also a major factor that contributed to why the pandemic spread relatively faster in Italy than in Germany: In Italy, mainly people were tested who were admitted to hospital and already had severe symptoms, while in Germany there was anticipative testing (Drosten, 2020). Other measures included as early as possible border closures to countries with high infection rates and screening of travellers at border controls, such as those in Singapore, Russia or Taiwan (Senzel, 2020; Blanke, 2020; W. Yang, 2020).
- In the phase of further spread, *defensive measures* are taken with the goal of *averting* the virus now present in the population, usually in terms of social distancing. This includes, among other things, appeals and recommendations to reduce contact with the population; closure of public institutions such as schools and kindergartens; cancellation of events; restrictions on trade, business, traffic, etc.; up to the quarantine of entire areas. Here too, according to WHO estimates, the governments of China and neighbouring countries (including Russia) acted relatively quickly and consistently (Reuters, 2020). Vietnam's

handling was particularly praised. In the course of these measures, the country was able to prevent further new infections for three weeks until the beginning of March (Blanke, 2020). According to official reports, China is also said to have drastically reduced the number of new infections, but at the cost of a nationwide quarantine imposed in authoritarian and suppressive manner (Durach et al., 2020).

– The next set of interventions is aimed at *slowing down the spread* of the disease. It will take effect when the pathogen becomes endemic, i.e., when it is no longer controllable and cannot be eradicated. Typical measures to delay the spread of the pathogen are large-scale contact or exit barriers, or general lockdowns and shutdowns of whole regions or countries. Another goal is to maintain essential public services by further expanding supply capacities through field hospitals with extra beds, emergency teams and hotlines. In this phase, the primary goal is to flatten the curve of those infected so that as many sick people as possible can be treated without overloading the health system (Fock et al., 2001). Additionally, the function of effective crisis communication should not be underestimated, in order to inform and reassure the population and enable joint action and learning beyond lockdown paralysis.

All these measures seem to have proved more or less successful in individual cases, especially if contextualised or combined, but have also been subject to criticism. In 2020, the debate focused mainly on the pros and cons of restrictive measures, especially the curfew. Prominent critics in Germany, such as the physician Wolfgang Wodarg, the President of the World Medical Association Frank Ulrich Montgomery (2020) or the microbiologist Sucharit Bhakdi (Reiss & Bhakdi, 2020), doubted the effectiveness and proportionality of these measures and pointed to the manifold social, psychological and economic costs for the population if lockdowns are implemented (Richter & Hoffmann, 2020; Rp Online, 2020; Bhakdi & Reiss, 2020). Other contributions pointed out that, due to a lack of studies, there is hardly any robust evidence for the success of social distancing (e.g. school closures) (Rashid et al., 2015; Jefferson et al., 2011).

While most of the European countries began to loosen the restrictions in May 2020, the debate about the pros and cons of a curfew, lockdown or shutdown became increasingly ideologically and emotionally loaded. Referring to the fact that in Germany a dramatic infection process like in Italy or Spain did not occur, both critics and supporters of radical lockdowns argued that their positions were confirmed. While critics argued that the German health system was never overloaded, they stressed that measures such as lockdowns restricting fundamental rights such as free movement were totally exaggerated. In this regard, the popular "Bild" newspaper warned: "If the infection process continues to be avoided and if there is no second wave, the federal [German] government will be in need of explanation. The clock is ticking" (Piatov, 2020c). And, more in detail, elucidating the fundamental paradox of lockdowns:

> There were two scenarios that had been a source of concern to politicians since the beginning of the Corona crisis. The first fear was to underestimate the virus and be responsible for the collapse of the German health system. And the second fear was that nothing bad would happen. Because in this second case, politicians would have to justify everything that their actions had led to: Tens of thousands of companies facing bankruptcy, masses on short-time labour, an unprecedented state of emergency for months. The livelihoods of millions of citizens would have been sacrificed in vain, their fundamental rights restricted disproportionally. A political super disaster ... (Ibid).

By contrast, supporters of the lockdown argued with the so-called prevention paradox: that damages which do not come into existence because of the lockdown are invisible and uncountable. In their view, a worse scenario did not happen precisely because the restrictions were successful, but what was avoided was difficult to quantify in detail exactly because it was avoided.

Perhaps one of the most interesting experiments in this regard was the Swedish response model. Unlike other European countries, Sweden decided to follow its own path, avoiding lockdown and curfew and pointing to increased self-awareness and collective responsibility and care of its citizens. Over months, this model seemed to satisfy both opponents of lockdowns and those in favour of national collective measures, and it seemed to keep the infection rate low while protecting the economy. Yet after evaluation in July 2020, the model lost most of its shine. The answer to the question: "Did Sweden's coronavirus strategy succeed or fail?" seemed to point in a clear direction (Savage, 2020):

"More than 5,500 people have died with COVID-19 in this country of just 10 million. It is one of the highest death rates relative to population size in Europe, and by far the worst among the Nordic nations. Unlike Sweden, the rest all chose to lock down early in the pandemic. 'Maybe we should have taken some more care of each other,' says Dan Eklund, 31 ... Latest figures suggest Sweden is getting better at containing the virus. The number of daily reported deaths has been in single digits for much of July, in contrast with the peak of the pandemic in April, when more than 100 fatalities were logged on several dates. There has also been a marked fall in serious cases, with new intensive care admissions dropping to fewer than a handful each day. Though still not as low as elsewhere in Scandinavia, it's a clear improvement. 'It feels good. I mean, finally, we are where we hoped we would be much earlier on,' says Anders Tegnell, the state epidemiologist leading the strategy. He's admitted too many have died, especially in Swedish care homes. But he believes there is still 'no strong evidence that a lockdown would have made that much of a difference'. Sweden has largely relied on voluntary social distancing guidelines since the start of the pandemic, including working from home where possible and avoiding public transport. There's also been a ban on gatherings of more than 50 people, restrictions on visiting care homes, and a shift to table-only service in bars and restaurants. The government has repeatedly described the pandemic as 'a marathon not a sprint', arguing that its measures are designed to last in the long term. The unusual strategy has attracted global criticism, with even some of Dr Tegnell's early supporters saying they now regret the approach. Annika Linde, who did his job between 2005 and 2013, recently told Sweden's biggest daily newspaper *Dagens Nyheter* she believed tougher restrictions at the start of the pandemic could have saved lives" (Ibid.)

Taking into account both pros and cons of lockdowns, the German Network of Evidence-Based Medicine came to the preliminary conclusion that in the end, any measure would be better than doing nothing at all (Sönnichsen, 2020).

Overall, there are still many unknown factors which need to be better explored for a resilient handling of virus outbreaks and of future pandemics. For example, due to the lack of recent experience with pandemics, it remains unclear how long and possibly at what intervals the restrictive measures must be maintained in order to delay the spread of a virus, and what effects they will have in the long term.

Overlooking the options of political action, in political practice and the associated debate, decisions during the Coronavirus crisis in 2019 and 2020 (i.e. before diverse vaccines were successfully developed and released in 2021) were often based on *two extreme* pandemic scenarios. The *first* scenario involved the abandonment of restrictive measures and accepted an uncontrolled spread of the virus. The advantage would be a relatively rapid infestation of society, so that most citizens would have survived the infection within a couple of months and would have formed corresponding antibodies. This would lead to so-called "herd immunity" in the shortest amount of time. The disadvantage would be a serious overload of the health system and the associated risk of an out-of-control number of fatalities. According to calculations by the University of Basel, such a scenario would result in the need for simultaneous intensive medical care for up to 500,000 people in Germany, with approximately 30,000 intensive care places. It was estimated that in Germany more than 700,000 people would have died within a few months (COVID-19 Scenario, 2020).

An example of an approach based (more or less) on this scenario is the UK's initial pandemic policy. The hope was explicitly to develop collective immunity. Yet after a relatively short time, this approach had to be discarded due to total overloading of the British health system. Restrictive measures, mostly in the form of a general contact prohibition or curfew, were adopted instead, but as they were implemented relatively late, the UK suffered from one of the highest death tolls in Europe and in the world (Shulz, 2020).

A *second*, to some extent equally extreme scenario was implemented by most countries worldwide. This strategy aimed at "flattening the curve" of the number of infected persons. The priority were restrictive protective measures which would be maintained as long as necessary in order to keep the number of seriously ill people smaller than the number of places in intensive care units. According to this model of calculation, the number of infected persons in Germany was estimated not to peak until January 2021, then at about 450,000, producing a number of fatalities which would remain close to 100,000 by March 2021. The serious disadvantage of this approach is that it would take a long timeframe to tame the virus, i.e., in the given calculations, it was estimated at least until the end of 2021. Throughout that time, protective measures such as wearing masks or avoiding public transportation would have to be maintained, and the undesirable social, psychological and economic side-effects would have to be accepted as a kind of (temporary) "new normal".

In the political practice of most countries outside Asia, a back-and-forth between these two pandemic models could be observed. Initial hesitation was followed in many European countries by political actionism and restrictive measures. According to observers, this tendency correlated less with the actual spread of the virus, but rather reflected the political reactions to the decisions of neighbouring states in response to the virus (Maissen, 2020).

In our view and as a matter of fact in the very basics of any political approach, a resilient strategy in times of future pandemics does not necessarily have to weigh between these two extreme scenarios in the sense of "either/or". It must rather try to develop a situationally adequate strategy. An important strategy hereby would be to assess what concrete requirements and capacities exist nation- or region-wide, and to what extent the contributions for practical solutions made by individual measures can be integrated into an overall strategy without undesirable side effects. The extended discussions about an adequate "exit strategy" from lockdowns and curfews in several countries such as Italy, France or Germany illustrated that this is a process of trial and error that needs an overall perspective. An often-proposed "adaptation strategy" could imply relaxation of restrictive measures for non-risk groups while implementing targeted measures to protect risk groups. In the case of Corona, these were persons over 60 years of age or with pre-existing conditions such as cardiovascular disease. An "adaptation strategy" would make sense, since according to all gathered knowledge, about nine out of ten people infected with SARS-CoV-2 only develop symptoms of a mild or moderate cold. The number of fatalities to date has been almost exclusively among people in the risk groups (Worldometer, 2020a; 2021). As Christian Drosten, among others, suggested, further measures of "reasoned exit" would, in most cases, also include consistent early testing and anticipative admission to hospital as well as continuous working from home for risk-group members for an extended period. At the same time, solutions would have to be found to ensure that people belonging to risk groups could be isolated at home without being restricted to care homes or other "sickness facilities" and adequately cared for by the rest of society in all respects (Drosten, 2020; Zenker, 2020).

Since many countries outside East Asia still have little experience with pandemic management, developing the best contextualised crisis strategy for a given space is, above all, a trial-and-error process in differentiation and integration. Due to the many unknown variables, but also because of situation- and country-specific characteristics, it is not possible to derive a generalisable "one best pandemic strategy" that fits all – neither in the case of Corona, nor with regard to new similar crises.

It follows that the trial-and-error imperative also applies for the contested approach regarding "Infectious upper limits" (*Infektions-Obergrenzen*) as a measure to consider before any new imposition of lockdowns and curfews, as requested by the German chancellor Angela Merkel for Germany in May 2020 when the first wave of infections just dwindled away. To what extent could the introduction of general upper limits of infections per capita of regional and national populations be a useful constituent part of better preparedness for future crises? Do they have to be differentiated according to nations and regions, or should they be homogenised worldwide? On a binding or voluntary basis? Can there be sanctions, and who could be in charge of managing the interrelation between the "upper limits" of different countries and their often fundamentally different political and healthcare systems? Last, but not least: If "Obergrenzen" were to be introduced as a normality in the post-Corona world, making the implementation of political emergency measures such as lockdowns or restriction of civil liberties more objective, what, then, with the mutual assistance between countries and alliances of nations? Should there be common (although differentiated) standards, co-developed by science, or are they in reality an unnecessary reduction of democracies' constituent flexibility, potentially restricting day-to-day situation awareness and proper contextualisation? Would measures such as "upper limits", born out of the teachings of the Coronavirus crisis in expectation of new systemic crises, politically also lead to the introduction of "upper limits" in many other additional sectors of "over-penetrative" globalisation, such as for global migration? These and other questions remain open to the collective intelligence and smart decision-making of societies whose experiences differed during the crisis (Piatov, 2020a).

Due to the many unknown and context-specific variables, an approach towards better resilience will unavoidably be based on a more abstract, universally applicable systems level, including the ability of a society to systematically and swiftly use information, as well as to learn quickly from its own procedures and from others in the face of unexpected developments. Strengthening societies on this basic management level enables them to find situation-adequate answers on their own. The following guiding principles for better resilience should make a contribution to the development of effective strategies for dealing in integrative ways with systemic crises such as Corona and beyond, including future pandemics, but also other global challenges. We depart from the assumption that, as Corona has shown, any mono-resilience approach geared towards managing selected crisis elements will once again prove to be limited, if only because most contemporary and future crises are and will be "bundle" crises implying a variety of economic, social and psychological side-effects. Additionally, the future is not about addressing one global challenge after the other. Societies will have to learn to manage multiple systemic problems at the same time.

CHAPTER 26

The Primordial Path to Follow

Enhancing Resilience. Basic Philosophical Assumptions and Their Implications for Crisis-policy Design

The topic of resilience was already *en vogue* before Corona. Resilience is a timely concept that has steadily gained further importance throughout the global COVID-19 crisis. In the shadow of Corona, it is increasingly being addressed by governments and governmental agencies, with a particularly strong push by European initiatives – for example within the German government via the Federal Ministry of Education and Research (BMBF) by means of multiple projects and political medium- and long-term processes (BMBF, 2020; 2014). Resilience has become a guiding topic of the European Union (EU) Commission for the post-Corona re-building phase starting in mid-2020 (Martos, 2020; Buras 2020) and of the German EU Council presidency of 2020 under the motto 'Resilient Europe' (Goßner, Stam & Lawton, 2020). Resilience is destined to be the first overarching theme of the newly formed Franco-German Future Council (*Deutsch-Französisches Zukunftswerk*, whose one working motto is "Resilience in light of the COVID Crisis") (Bundesregierung, 2019; Jung, 2018). Within the German-European research program FONA (*Forschung für Nachhaltigkeit*, Research for Sustainable Development), resilience is also being taken up in multifold and interrelated ways (Fona, 2019). Last, but not least, resilience was the guiding idea behind the disputed vision of the Italian government to employ 60,000 voluntaries at village, town and municipal levels to enforce the post-Corona rules of continued social distancing as a kind of civic or civil force without sanctions at disposal. The idea was to mobilise and thus strengthen civil society through the "embedded resilience awareness" of average citizens helping other citizens to respect the post-Corona rules for their own and for common safety, to be achieved together, in a collective effort (Qui Finanza, 2020).

Overall, resilience is one of the great topics that emerged as mainstream from the Corona crisis, if not as its decisive cross-sectoral request – both as a foundation-laying answer to a "post-Corona world" and in anticipation of future crisis. While resilience is possibly too all-encompassing to be dealt with satisfactorily through single governmental initiatives, its very idea of strengthening networks and patterns instead of single strands of society points per se in a direction of structuring interconnectedness, interactivity

© ROLAND BENEDIKTER AND KARIM FATHI, 2022 | DOI:10.1163/9789004469686_027

THE PRIMORDIAL PATH TO FOLLOW   143

and interdependency. Yet although the concept of resilience is increasingly becoming part of the sustainability discourse and is sometimes being vaguely traded as the "new concept of sustainability", there is a more precise core idea behind it that is not simply identical with sustainability (Kramer, 2015; Zolli, 2012; HydroPoint, 2019).

Put simply, *sustainability* aims to prevent human-made global crises by guiding political and economic action in such a way that present generations meet their needs without restricting the needs of future generations. In this sense, sustainability includes the fundamental ethical principle of reversibility of actions and decisions that are made today by future generations.

By contrast, *resilience* assumes that (mostly human-made) unpredictable and multi-complex crises will happen anyway in always more complex forms, given that the world is becoming more complex by the means of modernisation and progress. Therefore, existing systems – be they individuals, organisations, cities, societies, ecosystems or the world community – should and must develop capacities to coexist with such crises, to survive and to adapt to them not once and for all, but continuously (Fathi, 2019c). That implies a continuous revision, adaptation, contextualisation and innovation of actions and decisions which are seen as ever-changing milestones in a process and not as "solutions" for specific problems in order to "switch them off" from the screen. From the view of resilience, instead of being implemented with heightened activity at certain crisis points, critical self-observation and self-revision must become a basic state of mind. In this sense, resilience can be understood as:

> ... the capacity of a system, enterprise, or a person to maintain its core purpose and integrity in the face of dramatically changed circumstances.
> ZOLLI & HEALY, 2013, p. 7

Taken together, the basic idea behind the concept of resilience is widely seen to be increasingly relevant in view of the insight that despite all traditional safety measures, the number of incidents in an increasingly connected world may rather increase than decrease, as the WHO and other scientific and science-based organisations such as, for example, the Future of Humanity Institute (FHI) at Oxford University, have been warning for years. The Corona crisis was certainly not the last encompassing, i.e., profoundly transformative, trans-disciplinary and trans-systemic global crisis. Thus, resilience becomes crucial for any world which wants to coexist with the inevitability of crises, i.e., a "post-Corona" world where crises become "viral" and "infectious" as one crucial effect of globalisation. Yet to mitigate the effects, and to transform the status quo towards a more sound "re-globalisation" pattern, the very concept and understanding of "resilience" itself has to be revised, adapted, advanced, modernised and contextualised, too: it has to proceed from "resilience" to "multi-resilience".

CHAPTER 27

Revisioning the Concept of Resilience

A Necessary Step (Not Only) after Corona

Originally, the term "resilience" comes from the Latin "resilire" and means, directly translated, "to bounce back". Since the 1940s, the concept has been adopted by various disciplines within the natural sciences, the social sciences and the humanities (Tusaie and Dyer, 2004). To date, the focus has been rather mono-disciplinary, analysing resilience as a response to more or less well-describable and, to some extent, confined crises, such as e.g. the austerity crisis, the migration crisis or the climate-change crisis. In contrast, we propose the advanced term "multi-resilience" to cope with pluri-dimensional and multi-disciplinary crises. Although this term may appear at first glance as a tautology, since resilience (similar to sustainability) is, in most cases, understood as either being encompassing or not being at all, the term "multi-resilience" as we propose it denotes a quite precise intention and practice.

Within the context of resilience, we assume that the increasingly interconnected world of the 21st century will be affected by crises that transcend national borders and in so doing are not sectoral crises, but complex "crisis bundles". Today's societies will increasingly have to develop "a general robustness" according to capacities, and to cope simultaneously with very different and, however, interconnected global challenges. Although many observers criticise the lack of in-depth theoretical and philosophical foundation of the resilience concept, some helpful contributions and models can be found, helping to derive the philosophical basics of critical importance to consider it for political practice.

From the perspective of resiliency, we can assume that problem-solving is a universal component of life, and thus one – if not the motor – of evolution. Referring to the popular work of science philosopher Karl Popper, we can assume that any decision in life implies a heuristic strategy that results from the perceptual framework of the world we create. Popper called these (un)conscious hypothetical presuppositions "expectations" (K. Popper, 2004). According to the most influential founder of the European social systems theory, Niklas Luhmann, an expectation is a "form of orientation" to deal with the inherent complexity and uncertainty of the perceiver's environment (Luhmann, 1993). This law can be found in any system, be it individual,

© ROLAND BENEDIKTER AND KARIM FATHI, 2022 | DOI:10.1163/9789004469686_028

communities-based, organisational or societal. They all deal with their environment and solve its arising problems. This also implies that – in the words of Popper – "a problem arises (...) when an expectation fails" and when its inherent hypotheses do not correspond with reality (K. Popper, 2004, p.16). During the millennia of cultural evolution, human communities have undergone many fundamental challenges such as famines, wars, pandemics, natural disasters, etc. In response to these, humankind has developed increasingly complex and detailed concepts about the world and respective technological and cultural tools. Building on this history of mastery, we can assume that resilience is essentially about constantly testing and re-defining our view on an evolving world and the related problem-solving strategies. The latter must be falsified, where needed, and improved where possible in order to generate more realistic problem-solving approaches.

Following the cybernetic core principle, i.e., *Ashby's Law*, we can assume that the capacity of a system to solve complex problems in its environment strongly corresponds to its own inner complexity.[1] In other words: The more inherent complexity there is in the system, the more effectively it can adopt and adequately react to the complexity of its environment. Ashby's Law is inherent to the *Viable Systems Model* (VSM), which describes the core principles of the viability, or put in a better term, resilience of a system within complex environments. Thus, every system can only cope with as much complexity as corresponds to its own inner complexity. The higher the intrinsic complexity of a system, the higher its ability to react flexibly to events and thus to control complexity (Beer, 1974; Ashby, 1956). Within the context of resilience, this means complex problem-solving requires managing and integrating different perspectives and already existing knowledge within the "wisdom" environment of a knowledge society, i.e., a complex body of knowledge which is continuously provided by mono-disciplines. It follows that perspective-integration does not only enable a more comprehensive understanding of overarching interrelationships of the phenomena but also developing innovative practices to master them in the first place.

---

1   If a system is to be stable, the number of states of its control mechanism [i.e., the variety and complexity of the system itself] must be greater than, or equal to, the number of states in the system which is being controlled [i.e., the variety and complexity of the system's inner environment]. William Ross Ashby summarised this law as "variety can destroy variety" (1956). This was reformulated by Stafford Beer for the management context as "variety absorbs variety" (1974). If we understand "variety" as "complexity", the systemic resilience of a given system (e.g. a society, a management strategy or a steering mechanism) is strongly dependent on its own inherent complexity and its ability to manage complexity in the first place.

Since according to its own inbuilt laws, available knowledge from multiple disciplines cannot be known and integrated sufficiently by a single person, complex problem-solving requires working in collectives; not always, but in principle. Due to their aggregated intelligence, collectives prove, in principle, to be more capable of solving complex problems (Surowiecki, 2004; Wooley et al, 2010). Thereby, we can assume that complexity management is a particular communicative challenge, and that successful communication is crucial to enable mutual understanding between different mono-disciplines. All forms of contemporary complexity management – whether in the organisational context (e.g. innovative product development) or in societies (e.g. geopolitical scenario-planning in political think tanks) – require successful communication between the participants assembled in agile teams.

This in turn means that optimising the communication processes among the members of action- and decision-preparing- and -making groups will improve the process of problem-solving and lead to more "complexity-adequate" results. Thus, improved transpersonal and transdisciplinary communication systems contextualised to a given society in space and time will increase its capacity to react, to forecast and to respond to different crises and to learn from the overall process.

Various measures can contribute towards optimising such communicative complexity management. *On the system level,* these include group-specific workshop methods to improve collective decision-making or problem-solving. On larger systemic levels, where direct, equal and simultaneous exchange between all participants of the system is no longer possible – i.e., on the organisational and social level –, other intervention factors are also relevant for consideration, e.g. digital infrastructures, communicative tools and styles, and institutions for cross-sectoral communication.

From a *methodological* perspective, this can most importantly imply improving transpersonal and transdisciplinary communication processes in groups of all those decision-related who can have influence upon larger system levels. Complexity-adequate workshop methods could, for example, enhance the capacity of committees of political think tanks to develop innovative practices in the face of unpredicted new crises, or they could enhance the capacity of effective and efficient decision-making by all concerned, including those who are participating passively (Fathi, 2019b).

From an *institutional* perspective, resilient societies tend more towards the philosophy of open societies than of autocratic systems. The underlying idea is less ethically justified in terms of individual human rights or the rule of law according to open society principles and ethics, but rather by pragmatic systemic functionality. It means that open systems prove to be more functional in generating creative collective intelligence, which has always been based on the creativity of individuals. This is, in turn, the core of any concept of advanced resilience, i.e., of any concept that could be called "multi-resilience".

Indeed, *multi-resilient process, action and institution design* features two basic strategic orientations:

- Firstly, to integrate as many perspectives and knowledge as possible from the members of any given social system; and
- secondly, to thereby maintain a subtle balance between centralised and decentralised decision-making.

This includes the philosophical assumption that at least those members who are directly affected by given problems might, in most cases and not under particular emotional, social or political pressure, know best as regards which decisions are the best ones to make for them. The "natural" institutional consequence for wealthy open-society policy-making (and perhaps initially limited to such societies) is multi-level-governance, incorporating decentralised decision-making by local entities (e.g. communities or cities) which is supported, audited and coordinated by a superordinate governance level (e.g. a federal or overarching government).

More detailed practical implications of how to coordinate communication and decision-making within a multi-resilient multi-governance system are outlined in the following pages by making use of transdisciplinary models. As of now, we can summarise at least four basic philosophical principles towards progressing from resilience to multi-resilience:

- Principle 1: Anything in life is problem-solving and constant, never-ending and not "once-and-for-all solvable" evolution.
- Principle 2: Enhancing resilient problem-solving corresponds with increasing inner complexity and perspective integration within information and decision-making systems.
- Principle 3: Optimising communication leads to better collective problem-solving and thus more complexity-adequate solutions.
- Principle 4: Better solutions require institutions of collective decision-making in a multi-level governance context under the conditions of freedom and open society standards such as rule of law and a strong interrelation based on equality between individuality and collective.

CHAPTER 28

Progressing from Resilience to Multi-resilience
Two Basic Approaches

Since its beginnings in the middle of the 20th century, the concept of resilience has been adopted step by step by various disciplines, spanning ecology, psychology, education, organisational sciences, urban planning, etc. What is less known is that resilience research has developed in *four* phases up to the present day:

- The *first two* phases, ranging from the 1950s to the 1990s, were dominated by psychological research observing people (particularly children) who lived under adverse conditions and, however, developed in a normal way or even became stronger. A famous study by Emmy Werner made a significant contribution to this, assuming that there are about seven universal resilience factors that characterise resilient persons (Cutuli et al, 2008). Later, in the 1980s, researchers noticed that it is difficult to assume generalisable resilience factors as fixed traits, since resilience takes different forms depending on context and time (O'Dougherty Wright, Masten and Narayan, 2013).
- The *third* phase of resilience research (for approximately a decade from the 1990s to the 2000s) was characterised by the development of resilience-promoting pragmatic sectoral interventions and their scientific evaluation, that wanted to be inter- and trans-disciplinary but did not always live up to this credo.
- The *fourth* phase (since approximately the 2000s) has been characterised by inter- and transdisciplinary research on several system levels, and by the attempt to integrate them. How do collective and individual resilience work together? This could open up further possibilities for research on resilience and, of equal importance, the practical policy implementation of resilience.

The most recent two phases (three and four) are, to date, still in their infancy and have not yet been fully developed (Ibid.). The following pages take up on the Corona crisis and its fallouts where the third and particularly fourth wave of resilience research stand. They examine current and future societal resilience against the background of an explicitly and consequentially inter- and transdisciplinary approach – which also is much rhetorically evoked, but still barely developed in reality.

© ROLAND BENEDIKTER AND KARIM FATHI, 2022 | DOI:10.1163/9789004469686_029

28.1 Prerequisites: Relevant Criteria

Although "resilience" has increasingly been adopted by different disciplines on the one hand and is frequently used as a "one-word answer" to different types of crises on the other hand, transdisciplinary concepts on resilient societies are still relatively scarce. The widespread mono-sectorality of resilience is the reason why Anna Scuttari and Philipp Corradini wrote in their critique and call for a trans-disciplinary evolution of the concept:

"We argue that evolutionary approaches to resilience might grasp complexity and long-term development, but they lack the capacity to understand limits of acceptable change ... and to assess the absorptive coping capacity of a system and its units to cope with disturbance. Therefore, we propose a broader interpretation of ... resilience, which acknowledges the presence of dynamic development and transformational capacities, but also assesses stability and flexibility of systems. According to this more comprehensive approach, the different disciplinary perspectives of resilience are not mutually exclusive, but rather complementary in ... resilience assessment. The more the system is complex, the more intense the disturbance, the higher the hierarchy level and the longer the time frame of resilience assessment, the more it is necessary to combine evolutionary approaches with engineering approaches to understand the resilience of the whole system" (Scuttari & Corradini, 2018).

So what could be the future relevant criteria of resilience?

In 2011, one of the first articles pioneered this issue, comparing the resilience of different cities – thus founding the prerequisites for multi-resilience. The article was written by Boyd Cohen from the *Triple Pundit* organisation. It ranked Copenhagen, Curitiba (Brazil) and Barcelona as the most resilient cities worldwide. In his article, Cohen defined resiliency from the relatively narrow, yet interdisciplinary focus of the climate issue, i.e., the adaptation to or management of systemic natural disasters in a future scenario of rising sea levels (B. Cohen, 2011; Center for Security Studies, 2009). A subsequent study from 2014, written by the *Grosvenor* organisation, ranked Toronto, Vancouver and Calgary as the three out of 50 most resilient cities in the world. It is noteworthy that this study referred to totally different criteria and a respective different concept of social resilience, namely the combination of the quality of:

1) Governance;
2) Institutions;
3) Technical and Learning Systems;
4) Planning;

5) Access to Funding
   BARKHAM ET AL., 2014

Taken as prerequisites for a contemporary, multi-complexity adequate concept of resilience, these criteria were starting points to enable a broader, cross-disciplinary application of the resilience concept towards more multi-dimensional and multi-lateral crisis contexts beyond natural hazards. However, both the 2011 and 2014 examples gave an impression of a resilience concept in transition. Despite its multi-contextual applicability, measuring the concrete resilience of complex social and societal systems like a city or even a whole society remains a huge challenge for further research. This is particularly the case with bundle crises and crisis bundles.

As typical bundle crisis, the Corona crisis contains various dimensions like medical and health policy risks, being expressed in infection rates, death figures and the risk of overburdening the health system, as well as impacts on other dimensions like the social, economic and psychological one. This does not make it easy to measure societal resilience which is shown in the discussion on the "Covid Resilience Ranking", i.e., suggested by the business news agency Bloomberg. This model measures "where the virus is being managed most effectively and with the least social and economic disruption" (t-online dpa, 2021), tanking into account not only infection and death rates, vaccination rates or quality of health care, but also how many people are going shopping or travelling to work, what restrictions there are on social and economic life and how many flights take off. According to the report, Switzerland and Austria rank 2nd and 6th respectively in July 2021, and Germany only 12th, out of a total of 53 countries covered. Norway is in first place, New Zealand, France and the USA in third, fourth and fifth place respectively (Bloomberg 2021). Hereby it is noteworthy, that Switzerland was considered a pioneer of easing measures in Europe, particularly in March and April 2021. Measures included a relatively short closure of schools (only in spring 2020), hotels could remain open, as could ski resorts. There was never a compulsory test for shopping or restaurant visits, nor was there a curfew. However, could be criticised that Switzerland has accepted higher infection rates, more corona patients in intensive care units and more deaths. The number of deaths in the first wave of coronas per million inhabitants was about 60 per cent higher than in Germany and the number of infected people was practically always higher than in Germany, in some cases up to three times as high in November 2020, so that in some cases it was necessary to decide which patient got an intensive care bed and who did not (t-online dpa, 2021). In Germany, on the other hand, which according to the

Covid Resilience Ranking is in a much worse position, the health system was never overloaded to the point that such triage had to occur.

This example illustrates two typical challenges that arise in the context of measuring resilient societies: Firstly, the measuring proves to be a difficult, even ambiguous undertaking, as the manifold crisis dimensions and associated objectives for resilience policy cannot be clearly weighted. In the context of corona crisis management, political decision-makers are usually confronted with a strategy dilemma which in the public debate is often reduced to an either-or confrontation: Should the crisis management strategy focus on keeping infection and death rates as low as possible through restrictive measures (including lockdowns)? Or should the focus rather be on not restricting the fundamental rights of the population and the economy as much as possible? Both strategy directions obviously emphasise different types of resilience. Secondly, and following on from these considerations, the example illustrates that resilience measures, especially if they have an overly limited focus on only one problem area, lead to undesirable societal side-effects. This can be seen in the resilience strategy of keeping the curve of infection case and death rates flat through lockdowns which has been and is often the subject of emotionally charged debate about implemented corona policies. The side effects for the population included economic problems and existential fears, increasing social isolation and loneliness as well as an increase in frustration, boredom, domestic violence and depressive disorders (Friebe et al. 2020). "Is the cure worse than the desease?" is a question that is indeed raised in many debates about the "right" or "resilient" corona policy (Dorling 2020).

Given the described multi-contextual challenges which are characteristic for the present and the imminent future of global crises, we assume that contemporary societies require a "broader" or "more general" concept of resilience which is trans-disciplinary and applicable to multiple contexts. We call it "multi-resilience", since we want to refer to a competency which is inherent to the resilience of a given societal system itself, as well as to its interconnections to other systems, and which can be applied to simultaneous crises contexts. The examples of Cohen's article and the Grosvenor report illustrated the difficulties in providing an integrative interpretation and implementation of the notion of resilience and the respective conceptual work. What does "transdisciplinarity" exactly mean in the resilience context? And what is the difference to the more popular concept of "interdisciplinarity"?

Julie Thompson Klein defines these notions as follows:

> Broadly speaking ... may interdisciplinary studies be defined as a process of answering a question, solving a problem, or addressing a topic that is

too broad or complex to be dealt with adequately by a single discipline or profession" (Klein & Newell, 1997). "Whereas 'interdisciplinarity' signifies the synthesis of two or more disciplines, establishing a new meta-level of discourse, 'transdisciplinarity' signifies the interconnectedness of all aspects of reality, transcending the dynamics of a dialectical synthesis to grasp the total dynamics of reality as a whole.

KLEIN, 1990, p. 66

As a consequence, at least two different approaches towards a transdisciplinary modelling of complex phenomena towards resilience can be found: the *"integral"* approach – we call it also "complexify" – and the *systemic* approach – we call it also "simplify". Both complement each other and significantly contribute to a meta-theoretical foundation directed towards multi-resilience.

28.2 *Complexify*: Multi-resilience in a Systemic Perspective

The *integral* or *complexify* approach tries to categorise reality in terms of non-reducible categories. Although this approach is relatively new, it has increasingly been referred to by different social sciences and by practitioners. Integral metatheories are the result of the contemporary challenge of dealing with increasing complexity of disciplines and methodologies reacting to more complex environments and aiming to complement rather than to contradict each other. In the meantime, a variety of models can be found, such as those of conflict worker John Paul Lederach (2003), the social scientists Roger Sibeon (2004) and Derek Layder (1997), or even renowned science philosopher Sir Karl Popper (2004). All of their approaches have one typical aspect in common: they use multi-dimensional schematics, assuming that social phenomena include correlating facets which cannot be analysed in a mutually exclusive manner. Usually, these schematics consider at least the variables "micro versus macro" and "subjective versus objective". The result is usually an integrative matrix of three or four social dimensions which cannot be reduced to their individual parts. Each of these dimensions brings a distinct methodological approach to the object of investigation. Therefore, they cannot be separated; they are part of a methodological pluralism and thus, in the ideal case, form a transdisciplinary map of the object of investigation.

In the following, we draft a brief, not exhaustive, outline of a typical "four quadrants" model which can be widely applied in transdisciplinary knowledge integration. For illustration, we categorise different indicators which directly or indirectly refer to pluri-dimensional social resilience versus vulnerability in a post-postmodern globalised society.[1]

The four typical "quadrants" are (see Table 1 below):

1) *Micro-subjective.* Characteristic for this dimension is an "I" perspective, referring to what internally motivates the individual conflict participant, including emotions, ideas, motivations (K. Popper, 2004), self-identity, individual perceptions (Sibeon, 2004; Layder, 1997) or simply "the personal dimension" (Lederach, 2003). In his tri-theoretical framework, Galtung (2008) referred to this social dimension indirectly as the "deeper" or inner aspect of behaviour. Accordingly, this dimension is accessed by qualitative investigation methods with a focus on "psycho-biography", individual phenomenology and introspection (Sibeon, 2004; Layder, 1997). With regard to resilience, this dimension asks: What motivates the individual from inside? Does she or he feel happy and satisfied with regard to the society in which she or he is living? Why? And how does this influence her or his resilience pattern in "deep" and complex crises such as the Coronavirus crisis?

   Various indices from happiness research might provide applicable answers. Among these, the "National Accounts of Well-being" by the New Economic Foundation (NEF) is of particular significance. Its well-being index implies relevant data on "emotional well-being", a "satisfying life" and "resilience and self-esteem" as well as on "social well-being" as the overall result (Michaelson et al., 2009). Also dealing with well-being are indices from the Gallup World Poll on positive and negative experiences (OECD, 2011). Another approach could be to determine the "average resilience quotient", which was developed by the founder of positive psychology and dominant-resiliency researcher Martin Seligman (Reivic & Shatté, 2003). These and other indicators try to elucidate the social-conflict potential of a society "from within" individuals (Fathi, 2019a), and how much it can be stirred up by external crises. However, if we take the typological dimension into account, they prove to be transferable to non-Western and non-open societies to only a very limited extent. They are also only to a limited extent applicable to differing, let alone to all types of crises.

---

1 For more detailed information about this approach of "meta-theory building" and the corresponding debate, see Fathi (2019a), or Fathi (2019b).

2) *Macro-subjective.* The macro-subjective dimension includes a "We"-perspective referring to the inter-subjectively communicated body of human experience and knowledge (K. Popper, 2004). This includes acquired norms, values, "symbolic interaction", "the cultural dimension" and Galtung's notion of "cultural violence",[2] including discriminatory and violence-legitimating myths, collective perceptions and metaphors (Sibeon, 2004; Layder, 1997; Lederach, 2003; Galtung, 2008). Access to this social dimension is provided by qualitative methodologies based on hermeneutics, including interpretative sociology, socio-psychology, and constructivism. With regard to the goal of multi-resilient societies, this dimension and its specific methodologies reflect on *interpersonal and cultural* risk and resilience factors. In this regard, country indicators such as interpersonal trust and tolerance may serve as indicators being provided, for example, by the Gallup World Poll and the World Values Survey (Medrano, 2012). Other insights are provided by the "social well-being index" of the various National Accounts of Well-being, measuring "trust and belonging" and "supportive relationships". A further indicator would be "trust and belonging" and "supportive relationships", surveyed by the New Economics Foundation (NEF) (Michaelson et al., 2009). In addition to these indicators, there are more recent studies, e.g. by the IRS Leibniz Institute for Research on Society and Space, which examine how societies as a collective perceive problems in general and how they communicate them through the media: Do they see them rather as a threat to be feared or as an opportunity (Christmann et. al, 2011)?

3) *Micro-objective.* This dimension is characterised by an "It"-perspective. It refers to all empirically observable or quantifiable factors being related to the sole conflict participant. This includes the behavioural dimension as highlighted by Galtung's notion of "direct violence", as well as by Lederach's "relational dimension" (Lederach, 2003). Indices on the physical living conditions driving the conflictual behaviour of the individual participant are important to complete the picture. This includes relevant economic data on factors such as income or employment. Accordingly, this dimension is best

---

2 The notion of cultural violence, introduced by Galtung in the 1990s, regards violence as embedded in culture, but not focused on a physical but rather on a legitimising function. Cultural violence is typically characterised by cognitive and emotional polarisation in terms of "We" or "I" versus "the other" (Galtung, 2008, p. 109).

approached through quantitative methods based on an empirical and positivist epistemology. With regard to social resilience, this dimension covers all empirical data available with regard to social cohesion, including pro- and anti-social behaviour as well as economic performance. As studies show, information regarding absolute and relative income, including poverty, as well as the unemployment rate and the de-commodification of labour are most strongly related to uncertainty leading to "unhappiness" (Fathi, 2013). For a more detailed analysis, one has to consider additional indicators. In particular, figures on economic performance, physical violence and criminal behaviour (which is already partly covered by the "anti-social behaviour" index) may strongly vary between postmodern societies. They can provide a hint regarding the conflict potentials of different welfare regimes (Fathi, 2013). Indices such as GDP, household income, or national budget deficit usually have less direct correlation with subjective conflict factors, such as "well-being", "trust", and "tolerance", but remain influential. Other important multi-resilience criteria would refer to self-sufficiency of the population (stockpiling), physical protection facilities (for example, available bunkers in the event of a nuclear catastrophe such as the one of 1986 in Chernobyl), economic resilience (e.g. productivity, diversity of sectors and low or high debt), and robustness of technical infrastructures. From a multi-resilience perspective, it is interesting to assess what practices a society and its subsystems use to implement its collective problem-solving capacity, especially in the face of unpredictable crises (Fathi, 2019c).

4) *Macro-subjective.* The inter-objective dimension, called "the structural dimension" by Lederach (2003), refers to an "Its" perspective, shedding light on systems and patterns behind single micro-objective aspects, including "patterns of power"(Sibeon, 2004; Layder, 1997) and Galtung's notion of "structural violence"[3] (Galtung, 2008). Specialised methodologies and theories such as systems thinking, or structuralism cover this dimension. From a structuralist perspective, social vulnerability and resilience can be traced back to major social fault lines which can result in social conflicts (Ibid.), such as, for example:

---

3 Galtung's notion of structural violence has been widely acknowledged since its introduction in the 1970s. The term implies impersonal mechanisms being exploitive or repressive in various contexts (such as social, economic, political, etc.) (Galtung, 2008).

- *Gender*: male versus female (sexism). This conflict line is a ubiquitous challenge to all societies through different manifestations, reaching from labour-market exclusion to domestic violence (Harrendorf et al., 2010).
- *Generation*: old versus "adult" versus young. This context is expected to become of increasing importance in the coming years, since the old-age support institutions are projected to decline in all OECD countries over the next 40 years, among them the welfare state as such (OECD, 2011).
- *Class*: economically powerful versus powerless. This fault line is also expected to increase in importance, since the overall trend towards inequality is rising within the OECD and worldwide (Ibid.).
- *Ethnicity:* racism. Together with the "class" fault line, this context may be considered as the most explosive one. Migrant integration has become a particularly important issue for European and Western countries, because a lack of integration combined with irregular mass migration, as in the framework of the European refugee and migration crisis of 2015/16 and illegal immigration into the U.S. or Russia, creates increased risk of social tension (Ibid.).

Another perspective in the macro-subjective view on multi-resilience is contributed by system thinking. According to this tradition, the context-adequate "viability" of a social system is largely dependent on its communication structures (Luhmann, 1993). In this view, any problem-solving and decision-making ability of cities, communities and other social systems, and even of whole societies, depends on how communication and knowledge exchange between their subsystems are institutionalised (Malik, 1992).

What, now, is the practical contribution of such a four-dimensional approach to improving resilience in fundamental and encompassing "bundle crisis" situations such as the Coronavirus crisis with its multi-dimensional impacts, and those upcoming ones which may follow?

Applied to the question of the potential multi-resilience of a contemporary society, the four-quadrant model would stress that there are at least these four non-reducible dimensions of resilience which can be investigated and promoted by the means and instruments of different disciplines and their inherent methodologies. Accordingly, any society wanting to become more resilient would employ at least these four facets and integrate their respective paths of investigation.

TABLE 1 Systematic methodological pluralism for investigating the four systemic dimensions of societal resilience and conflict potentials

Subjective vs. Objective / Micro vs. Macro	Subjective	Objective
Micro	Perspective: "I", personal dimension, inner drivers of behaviour Methodology: Qualitative investigation of emotions, ideas, motivations, psycho-biography *Psychological conflict potential*: Degree of personal happiness / well-being and rates of positive and negative experiences as a result of basic needs satisfaction	Perspective: "It", relational dimension, behaviour Methodology: Quantitative methods, based on empiricism and positivism *Economic and political conflict potential:* Pro- and anti-social behaviour Hard facts: Absolute and relative income (e.g. Gini coefficient), unemployment rate, etc.
Macro	Perspective: "We", cultural dimension, norms, values, myths Methodology: hermeneutics, including qualitative sociology and (de-) constructivism *Cultural conflict potential* Cultural violence versus "trust and belonging" and "supportive relationships" Resilience Culture	Perspective: "Its", structural dimension, systems, order patterns Methodology: systems thinking, structuralism *Structural conflict potential* Structural violence: social fault lines Social structure Communication systems

SOURCE: ADOPTED FROM FATHI, 2013, PP. 41–74; BASED ON GALTUNG, 2008; LEDERACH, 2003; SIBEON, 2004, PP. 108–110; LAYDER, 1997, PP. 2–4

Apart from that, the integrative or "complexify" approach lacks a more concrete practical perspective, leaving open in what respect there may be other "universal" orienting principles to strengthen the multi-resilience of societies. This could be the contribution of the second transdisciplinary thinking tradition on resilience: Simplify.

28.3 *Simplify*: Multi-resilience in an Action-oriented Perspective

While the complexify approach of multi-dimensional categorisation tries to trans-disciplinarily integrate the contributions of different perspectives, the simplify tradition, notably its most representative approach *systems thinking*, understands itself as a "trans-discipline" per se. It focuses not on mapping complex phenomena in their "whole complexity", but rather on identifying their inherent systemic *mechanisms* and *structures*. Today, modern systems theory is considered to be an approach in which fundamental aspects and principles of systems are used to describe and explain complex phenomena. Systems cope with complexity by grouping them into "wholes", i.e., "simple" mechanisms and rules.[4] Systemic Thinking and its various sub-disciplines, such as Cybernetics (Beer, 1974; Ashby, 1956), Systems Dynamics (Senge, 1990), Soft Systems Methodology (Checkland, 1981), and Chaos Theory (P. Smith, 1994) can be regarded as some of the most well-known and most comprehensive approaches in the tradition of simplifying complex phenomena.

With regard to a deeper understanding of a potential multi-resilience of societies, at least *two* standard-setting models of "simplifying" can be identified: The *Panarchy Model of Adaptive Cycles* and the *Viable Systems Model* (VSM).

The *Panarchy Model of Adaptive Cycles* describes the process of "evolutionary" or "transformative resilience" (Hodgson, 2009) which a system undergoes in the face of "serious" crises. It was developed in the mid-1980s by Buzz Holling through his observation of the adaptive cycle of forests (Holling & Gunderson, 2002). While most resilience researchers traditionally understand resilience as the ability of systems to bounce back to an invariable, original balanced state when being exposed to adversities, the Panarchy Model points out that balanced states can dynamically change over time. The model details how systems and their inherent subsystems (i.e., a society and its sectors) evolutionarily develop through perpetual cycles in the face of crises and thereby also change

---

4 For a more detailed definition of and introduction to systems thinking, see Strachan, G. (2009).

processes (Resalliance, n.d.a, b; Pendall, Foster & Cowell, 2010). Hereby, adaptation and resilience depend on a variety of circumstances. The Panarchy Model is based on the assumption of systemic adaptation cycles which, in essence, include four phases (Figure 3). These phases are dynamically interwoven:

- *r-phase (growth)*: The evolution of a system, e.g. a forest, starts with a phase of exploration and growth (Holling & Grunderson, 2002). In terms of resilient districts or cities, this could imply populational or constructional expansion. According to Schnur, this phase usually progresses with relatively high resilience, since the system's structures are under construction, enabling a flexible integration of external influences (Schnur, 2013).
- *K-phase (conservation)*: The initial growth eventually reaches a fairly stable state, where the levels of the constituent parts (e.g. the flora and fauna of a forest) reach a sustainable point (Holling & Gunderson, 2002). In the context of resilient districts or cities, this phase could imply social and constructional consolidation. In this phase, system errors (for example constructional decay, financial bubbles) and thus social vulnerability may start to show (Schnur, 2013).
- *Ω-phase (release)*: Put under great stress (for example a fire), the system becomes brittle and falls into a release of all accumulated potentials. In the context of forests, a fire would clear dead flora and fauna, release nutrients back into the soil, and help to disperse seeds quickly (Holling & Gunderson, 2002). In the context of resilient districts, this phase would correlate with a decrease and release of district potentials and/or social capital in terms of population and space. By contrast, there would be new potentials for "space pioneers" finding new and creative ways to put the released potentials to use (Schnur, 2013).
- *α-phase (reorganisation)*: Finally, the system enters into the reorganisation phase. The system's components as well as the system itself are adapting to the new environment and provide the basis for new growth. In the context of forests, this could mean new plants spring up which are particularly suited to surviving the fire conditions (Holling & Gunderson, 2002). This means not only renewal, but an evolution from the previous condition that reacts to the environmental threat. In terms of resilient districts in cities, this phase implies increasing change potential. The initiatives of the "space pioneers" and of solidarity networks of crisis-affected people have an impact towards better life conditions. As the dynamic reorganisation process occurs, these networks become less important, and overall resilience increases (Schnur, 2013).

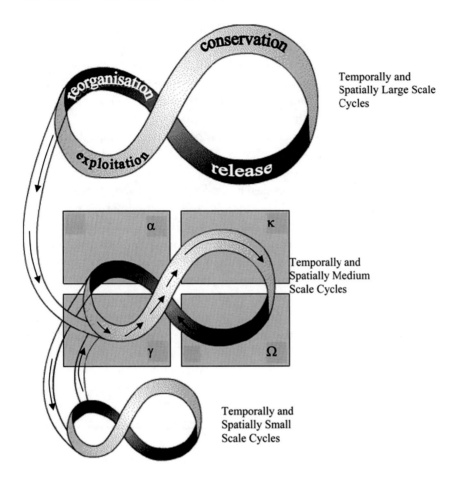

a System Cycles.

FIGURE 3 The four phases of the model of adaptive cycles
SOURCE: GRUNDIG/HOLLERSON 2002.

With new growth, the same building-up process starts again from the beginning, yet on a different level. New conditions (for example the fire) caused a change in the type of the system's components (i.e., new plants). The system (i.e., the forest) may still reach a stable state, but it is not exactly the same as the one before (Holling & Gunderson, 2002). However, the transition into a new r-phase can be triggered or even stopped by unexpected events. With regard to resilient districts or cities, these events could positively imply gentrification or innovations of well-priced house building (Schnur, 2013).

Thus, the four phases of the Panarchy Model can dynamically cross-influence each other. The shift from the growth phase (r) to the conservation phase (K) is called "forward loop", being characterised by incremental change – a process which is slow, but also large. The shift from release (Ω) to reorganisation (α) is a "backward loop", being characterised by disruptive changes and systemic transformation (Holling & Gunderson, 2002).

Given the fact that systemic changes can occur due to abrupt shocks (for example, political upheaval, Coronavirus) or through gradual changes (for example, climate change), Holling/Grunderson assume that adaptive cycles are nested in other adaptive cycles. For example, an economic region is at once "a subsystem within a global economic system and a super-system within which individuals, households, firms, local governments, and organizations act and interact" (Pendall, Foster & Cowell, 2010, p.78). Subsystems and overall systems are interconnected through two different functions being called by Holling et al. "revolt" and "remember" (Holling, Gunderson & Peterson, 2002). Subsystems can pressurise or change overall systems via innovations. This would be a "revolution"-function from stage Ω (reorganisation) to stage K (conservation). In terms of multi-resilient societies, this aspect could illustrate spillover effects from the local level to the overall societal level, for example in the context of social innovations or protest actions by civil-society participants, or disruptive technological innovations by organisations from the private sector.

By contrast, overall stable systems can govern subsystems. This function is called "memorising" or "remembering". It happens from stage K (conservation) to stage α (growth). In terms of multi-resilience, the revitalisation of banks by the superordinate system "government" during the subprime crisis (2007–2009) would be a typical example.

In this regard, the term "panarchy" mirrors the ambivalent relation between superordinate systems and subordinate subsystems leading into positive and negative cascades of change (Holling & Gunderson, 2002). Not by chance, "Panarchy" refers to "Pan", the Greek god of nature who can cause both well-being and its opposition, "panic", to the same extent, depending on circumstances, time and context (Holling, Gunderson & Peterson, 2002). The ambivalent dynamics between the nested adaptive cycles (Figure 4) can be drafted as follows:

The Panarchy Model makes it clear that there is not only *one* "normal" state of "status quo" to which a system should bounce back in order to be resilient. Rather, there are multiple possible normal states that are located within an evolutionary (Hodgson, 2009). Given the irreversibility of some contemporary crises, such as natural catastrophes or a terrorist attack, the Panarchy Model

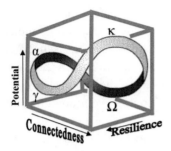

b The three characteristics

FIGURE 4 Adaptive cycles as nested systems
SOURCE: GRUNDIG/HOLLERSON 2002.

enables the drafting of strategic visions and respective innovative practices. This will be explained in greater depth in the following chapters with particular regard to the Coronavirus crisis.

Complementary to the Panarchy Model, the *Viable Systems Model* (VSM) does not describe the exterior evolutionary process of social systems in the face of crises but focuses on inner mechanisms and communication structures of these systems which could contribute to transformative resilience.

The Viable Systems Model stems from the *cybernetic* tradition, introduced by Norbert Wiener in the 1950s. Cybernetics can be briefly understood as the scientific study of how humans, animals and machines control and communicate with each other. Ashby's Law is inherent to the VSM, describing the core principles of the viability, which is, to some extent, used identically to resilience here, of a system in complex environments. Resilience here means that and how a system continues to function after an unexpected catastrophe hit, for example the Coronavirus. A major practical conclusion for implementation of multi-resilience is to find a balance between decentralised, autonomous decision-making by local units and effective, comprehensive (centralistically aligned, homogenised and combined) knowledge distribution and "bundling" between units (Malik, 1992). The contribution of the VSM for resilience research lies in its generality that can be applied to all types of systems and subsystems of organisations and societies to make them work better. In terms of multi-resilience, it provides us with information on those aspects of a system which are essential to viability (M.C. Jackson, 2003). According to the VSM, a viable system is composed of five interacting subsystems, pictured in the following Figure 5 as 1–5:

– *System 1* includes the primary activities being conducted by the local management of a given system (for example communities). Each

System 1 itself must be a viable system. In systems thinking this is called "recursive", which means that each System 1 is an autonomous sub-system and includes a VSM with all five systems in itself. Each System 1 needs to be as autonomous as possible to deal in the most efficient ways with its environment. Thus, they should develop their own policy, development, operational control, coordination and implementation functions.

– *System 2* represents the information channels and bodies that allow the primary activities in System 1 to communicate between each other. It thus fulfils a co-ordination function and ensures harmony between the parts of System 1. This allows System 3 to monitor the activities within System 1.

– *System 3* checks on their performance, quality, conformance to regulations, and maintenance of System 1. Its key role is the operational control of System 1 and services management. In organisational systems, this role is typically conducted by the human resources management. Systems 1, 2 and 3 make up what Beer calls the 'autonomic management' of an organisation (Beer, 1974).

– *System 4* is responsible for integrating internal information provided by System 3 and external information of the system's total environment. If the organisation is to match the complexity of the environment it is dealing with, it needs a model of that environment which enables predictions about its likely future state. System 4 must provide this model and communicate the information to System 3 if quick action is required, or to System 5 if it has longer-term implications (M.C. Jackson, 2003). This is a key activity for the resilience of a given system operating in complex environments – be it an organisation dealing with a highly competitive environment and disruptive innovations, or a state dealing with geostrategic or world economic developments. In general, System 4 is home to activities such as strategy, planning, research and development, marketing, and public relations.

– *System 5* is responsible for policy decisions within an organisation or a state as a whole. It formulates policy based on the information received from System 4 and communicates this to System 3 for implementation by the divisions. An essential task is balancing the often conflicting internal (System 3) and external demands (System 4) placed on the overall system (Beer, 1974; M.C. Jackson, 2003).

Overall, the System 1 parts receive confirmation of their goals and objectives from System 5 being refined into targets by System 3 and are (at the same time or in cycles) subject to co-ordination by System 2 and audit by System 3. They

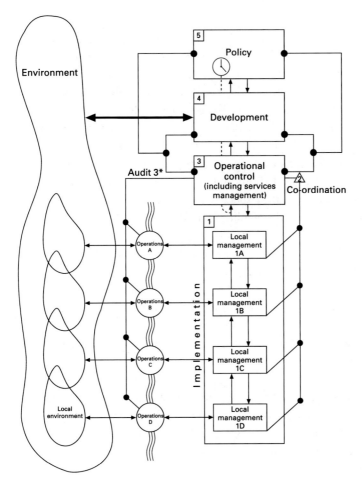

FIGURE 5   The Viable Systems Model (VSM)
SOURCE: JACKSON, 2003: 92

report back on performance to System 3. It is noteworthy that System 1 is the most important and that Systems 2–5 merely facilitate the proper operation of System 1 (Ibid.).

The contribution of the VSM for (multi-)resilience research lies in its generality that can be applied to all types of systems and subsystems of organisations and societies to make them persist and work more effectively in crisis situations.

Summing up, what is the teaching of these two "simplifying" models, the Panarchy of Adaptive Cycles Model and the Viable Systems Model, with regard to a more multi-resilient answer to major systemic ruptures such as the Coronavirus crisis and its aftermath?

Referring to both models, we can derive one major practical implication towards more multi-resilient societies: Societal subsystems should be granted autonomy so that they can absorb some of the environmental variety that could otherwise overwhelm reasoned management on governance levels. In turn, this implies a governance approach based on co-ordination and audit instead of exclusive hierarchical control. In other words: multi-resilience implies multi-level governance. Multi-level governance in this perspective wants to serve as empowerment of a multi-polarity of forces to become (diverse and pluralistic) agents of a more resilient social structure in continuous development. The superordinate governance level should be open enough for spill-over-effects from the bottom (e.g. technical or social innovations generated on the local and regional levels), allowing for evolutionary development "from below" in crisis situations. On the other hand, it should also have the capacity to support and maybe also regulate top-down, if crisis situations require it.

In the case of the Coronavirus crisis of 2019–20, this implies that a model of autonomy of multi-level governance subsystems like the one briefly sketched above – the South Tyrol model of self-administered and self-governed autonomy from the nation state of Italy – is positive and should be able to transfer its specific teachings to the "whole", i.e., to the national government; and vice versa, in this cooperation the nation state as the overarching system should be able to integrate and align these teachings in the greater picture of its systemic needs of functioning and stability. Something similar applies, in the case of Western and European democracies, to the relation between the U.S. and the EU as superstructures and the single states and nation states as their (relative) substructures, which are then internally structured in further subsystems. The goal of stability in crises and of learning from crises must always be a balance between a system and its subsystems, on any given level.

CHAPTER 29

Five Principles of Multi-resilience

Overall, the idea of multi-resilience is meant as a tool for improving the efficiency of "bundle crises" management. It is about integrating a multi-disciplinary approach with pluri-valent policy solutions. Multi-resilience aims at developing the "systemic robustness" of societies, including enhancing stability, functionality and systemic learning during and from crises and fostering an enhanced innovation and problem-solving capacity on the basis of an applied inter- and trans-disciplinary mindset. It is about an increased ability to respond to widely different or even "incommensurable" (Lyotard, 1988) crisis contexts, including crises in different political systems and socio-economic context suddenly interdependent on each other, as in the Coronavirus crisis. The Corona crisis of 2020 was perhaps *the* most pronounced global example of such a "multi-complex" crisis in the 21st century. In this regard, multi-resilience is about both *enlarging* and *engaging* "normal" mono-systemic resilience (Benedikter & Fathi, 2017) beyond typical contexts, including usually poorly or non-compatible societal eco- and subsystems.

In so doing, multi-resilience necessarily creates cross-links between different problems (e.g. economic downturns, cyber-vulnerability, social conflicts, pandemic management) and the corresponding mono-systemic crisis-management approaches. These links are insofar necessary as any mono-systemic measurement often leads to man-made new vulnerabilities, or even unprecedented rebound effects. Often, however, these vulnerabilities are not noticed within the respective narrowly defined mono-systemic context where they have been (unwillingly) developed but can manifest in a different context. Typical examples in this regard are unprecedented economic impacts and vulnerabilities for medium and small businesses (SMEs) as a result of crisis-management strategies, for example in the Coronavirus crisis to mitigate the pandemic. For example, positive economic stimulus measures such as the German government's VAT reduction from July to December 2020 to mitigate the Corona lockdown effects and to increase private consumption and spending were effective in the first instance, but produced new vulnerabilities in the medium-term perspective:

> The effect of the value-added tax reduction after the Corona crisis: a consumption boom. But experts warn of a bubble. Germany is booming again: consumption is picking up! This is reported by market researchers and

experts, who attribute this to a large extent to the reduction of the VAT. 'The propensity to buy has risen very sharply', says consumer researcher Rolf Bürkl. 'Consumers apparently intend to bring forward planned major purchases, which will help consumption this year', Bürkl continues. Since July 1, in Germany the normal value-added tax has been reduced from 19 to 16 per cent and the VAT reduced tax from 7 to 5 per cent. The reduction was part of the billion-euro economic stimulus package of the federal German government for its post-Corona economy. In addition, parents received a bonus of 300 euros for each child. The researchers continued: 'Even independent of tax effects, the consumer climate is again clearly and surprisingly steeply on the rise – which indicates a recovery in consumption! Aid from the federal government and the EU is cushioning the effects. According to research, [in Germany] the consumer climate has risen by 23 points since the low point [at the peak of the European Coronavirus crisis] in spring. The calculated forecast was slightly negative in July at minus 0.3 after minus 9.4 in July. The longer-term average value is around plus 10, and the income expectations of Germans also seem to be improving again – even though expectations are still significantly lower than in the previous year. According to experts, this also has to do with the expected payment of a child bonus. Overall, the government aid had an enormous cushioning effect ....

BILD ONLINE, 2020aa

Yet there was a flip side:

But: Are we in a VAT bubble? Consumer researcher Bürkl warned of a VAT bubble. Even in the run-up to past [German] tax increases, for example from 2006 to 2007, there have been anticipatory effects: 'Retailers and manufacturers must prepare themselves for the fact that the propensity to consume could decline again when the original VAT rate re-applies again starting from January 2021. Meaning: From January onwards, it is to be feared that people in Germany will buy significantly fewer things. But even if the effects are not sustainable – the tax cut is an important support for domestic demand in the current year [2020]. Yet despite the recovery, which in some cases has been significant, there are still major concerns about the potential for the most severe recession in post-war German history. The questions of whether a second wave of infection is imminent, whether there will be an increased number of insolvencies and how the situation on the labour market will develop have not been conclusively answered. Methodology: The findings are taken from the 'GfK Consumer

Climate MAXX' survey and are based on around 2,000 consumer interviews conducted each month on behalf of the EU Commission. The consumer climate relates to total private consumption expenditure (Ibid.).

Thus, any mono-resiliency (for example, successful pandemic mitigation by lockdown measures and subsequent economic stimulus programs) can be accompanied by new vulnerabilities in other system contexts (e.g. social and economic stress or cycle breaks). As a consequence, multi-resilience must take interlinkages of problems and unprecedented side-effects into account.

In this regard, we distinguish between *five orientation principles* of multi-resilience, as actively challenged by the Coronavirus crisis. They are directly derived from both transdisciplinary traditions, "complexify" (integrative thinking) and "simplify" (systems thinking). Each of these five principles refers to a dimension of the four-quadrants model of the integrative tradition, and each considers practical implications of systems research on viabilities and enhanced functionality in the direction of multi-resilience.

29.1   Principle 1: Fostering Individual Resilience

A fundamental systemic component of multi-resilient societies must be the psychological resilience of the affected citizens. This includes, above all, the ability to deal with one's own stress and to act calmly, helping to prevent solo political actionism and panicky herd behaviour more effectively. A core competence required for this is "keep calm and carry on", i.e., the ability to (self-) regulate stressful thoughts, perceptions and feelings.

Psychological resilience can be learned and should be integrated more systematically into educational and healthcare policies in anticipation of future crises, including new pandemics. It correlates with Peter Senge's discipline of "personal mastery" in his often-cited book "The Fifth Discipline", which drafts the principles of learning organisations (Senge, 1990). Correspondingly, this principle of individual resilience contributes to a "learning society" and incorporates the concept of life-long learning. Life-long learning should incorporate competency development on the professional, personal and social level, and also best practices towards psychological threats. For instance, a country which is often exposed to earthquakes might place emphasis on other aspects than a country which is exposed to financial crises, but both will have to take care of psychology, i.e., of individual resilience capacities.

The case of the so-called "Cuban Way", for instance, illustrates the importance of education and competency development in promoting a resilient population despite the otherwise many faults of the system. Cuba is not only a communist country but also regularly exposed to natural disasters. Between 1996 and 2002, six major hurricanes hit Cuba, killing 16 people, which is a minimum of the total 665 deaths in the affected countries. In some cases, for instance Hurricane Charlie, fewer people died in Cuba (4 people) than in Florida (30 people), although both countries were affected in a similar way and despite the relatively high poverty in Cuba and its lack of technical resources compared to Florida. The International Secretariat for Disaster Reduction (ISDR), the UN body that focuses on disaster reduction, points to "glocally" contextualised and anticipation-related education as one of the main reasons for the low level of hurricane mortality rate in Cuba compared to its neighbours. Disaster preparedness, prevention and response methods are part of the general education curriculum in Cuban schools, universities and at workplaces. People are continuously informed and trained to cope with natural hazards from an early age onwards (Mohideen, 2010). In the Coronavirus crisis, Cuba did well for a population of 11.5 million, with officially 2,478 cases and 87 deaths, and with 2,345 recovered up until the end of July 2020 (Worldometer, 2020b).

Overall, during Corona, the question of individual resilience arose through at least three respects:

- Firstly, the Corona crisis raised questions about strengthening one's own immune system and organising personal hygienic protective measures (protective mask, disinfectant, etc.).
- Secondly, this context also touched on economic issues of personal protection and stockpiling.
- Thirdly, the Corona crisis was also accompanied by psychological stress, not only in the course of isolation due to the curfew, but also in the fundamental handling of one's own fear and uncertainty about the future. The latter, i.e., the ability to deal with one's own stress and act calmly, has, as mentioned, proven to be probably the most important component of individual resilience and is also important beyond the Corona crisis for all other future crisis scenarios, as it helps to prevent political actionism, self-justice, domestic violence, looting or other deeds performed out of despair, and, more generally, panic herd behaviour. People who master themselves directly and indirectly help others to master themselves, too.

This is why, besides individual crisis management, individual resilience competency contributes to collective resilience. This includes, as to be outlined in more detail later, social competencies and tools of effective collective decision-making by the means of individual determination. It also comprises "Futures Literacy" (R. Miller, 2018; 2019, 2017), the ability to anticipate and co-create desired futures. "Futures literacy"(R. Miller, 2017; R. Miller, 2019) is about the ability to individually and collectively anticipate and imagine futures, and to design effective collaborative processes of action-learning under conditions of uncertainty (Ibid.). Consequently, this approach includes life-long development of basic personal and social competencies, but also concrete methodological competencies to develop best practices through the use of emerging and innovative tools that have to be constantly updated. The promotion of individual resiliency has to be based on best coping practices derived from the lessons learned from past crises. Individual competency development provides the basis for the realisation of the principles that follow.

29.2 Principle 2: Integrating Centralised and Decentralised Decision-making and Implementation

In hyper-connected and thus hyper-complex contexts such as the Coronavirus crisis one, almost every successful form of interdependent and collective crisis management – as particularly requested to solve a pandemic among people living closely together – is accompanied by fast and effective decision-making.

This is also the case with regard to what we saw in the Corona crisis. While authoritarian and dictatorial governance such as in China and centralistic governance such as in Italy or France allowed for relatively fast und uniform implementation of measures, democratic nations with decentralised decision-making structures in semi-autonomous sub-entities with strong delegation and subsidiary powers, such as the Federal Republic of Germany, Switzerland or Austria, i.e., the German-speaking countries, enabled more locally flexible, differentiated and contextualised responses. Contrary to these, the rather centralised federalist system of healthcare and emergency response in the U.S. came under scrutiny – which had to do with poor performance of the federal authorities which could not always differentiate between the national and specific local and regional needs, and, as a reaction, de facto allowed the single U.S. states to basically do what they wanted, triggering chaos and non-alignment that led to record infection rates (Duff-Brown, 2020).

On the other hand, the handling of a pluri-complex emergency such as the Corona crisis has to do with the size of the territory. Perhaps the U.S. as a nation state is simply too big, as China and Russia may be, too, to properly handle a profoundly penetrative and territory-wise asymmetric crisis and to be able to properly differentiate *and* integrate measures according to differing realities on the ground.

Considerations of differentiating the international, national, regional and local levels due to differing but interdependent requirements also arose in the context of international cooperation, i.e., on the UN, transatlantic and EU levels. As mentioned, the teachings of the many failures of the international system in coping with the crisis are clear: Multi-resilient international structures which aim at integrating the best aspects of centralist and decentralised decision-making should be oriented on the subsidiary principle of multi-level governance (Fathi, 2020).

Effective global crisis management in joint emergency cases requires trans-systemic political integration, which, however, must not dissolve nation-state sovereignty or transfer it to a centralised supranational structure, as, for example, in the case of the EU, since this would weaken contextualisation on the ground. An adequate response must rather preserve nation-state sovereignty and integrate it into an internally and externally differentiated multi-level system. This means:

- Firstly, that some sort of policy integration on a meta-level will be required, with international institutions in charge to not only provide recommendations to the national level but to also have the ability to sanction single participating nation states, if they fail to comply with jointly established rules. This was not the case in the Coronavirus crisis of 2019–20, but the international community should prepare such a mechanism in anticipation of future crises.
- Secondly, at the same time, multi-resilience also implies the highest level of local and national independence possible, particularly in terms of (temporary) self-sufficiency and self-responsibility. Self-sufficiency and self-responsibility cannot be delegated. One main challenge of (multi-)systemic interrelated action is to trust the other to solve the problem. Yet, on the other hand, if everybody behaves *only* like this, i.e., if everybody just places trust in the action of the other, the problem will not be solved despite all attempts towards multi-resilience and trust, since everybody will wait for the other to act.

Both aspects must be carefully pondered and balanced.

29.3   Principle 3: Problem-solving Practices with Knowns and Unknowns

In 2002, former U.S. Secretary of Defense Donald Rumsfeld (1975–1977 and 2001–2006) issued his own version of "quadripolar" resilience. His pointed words can serve as a good summary of what we may expect to be addressed by integrated resilience strategies in the coming years. As Rumsfeld put it, there are four categories of problems to be addressed by policy-making based on an encompassing radar of awareness:

> [T]here are *known knowns*; there are things we know we know. We also know there are *known unknowns*; that is to say we know there are some things we do not know. But there are also *unknown unknowns* – the ones we don't know we don't know. And if one looks throughout the history of our country and other free countries, it is the latter category that tend to be the difficult ones.
>
> U.S. DEPARTMENT OF DEFENSE, 2002

What Rumsfeld omitted was the logical fourth quadrant which must read:

> There are *unknown knowns*, i.e., things we don't know that we know (Ibid.).

Although he used this primordial conceptual differentiation as a rhetoric tool to justify the US intervention in Iraq in 2003, his statement clarified very precisely the contemporary challenge for societies and states in managing the unexpected. Rumsfeld's statement was inspired by Nassim Talebs notion of "Black Swans", describing unpredictable events combined with potential major impact (Taleb, 2008). The two resulting challenges are: *First*, unexpected events cannot be exactly predicted. *Second*, they are very different in their specific contexts and often require widely different measures and reactions which can hardly be repeated in new contexts and can therefore usually not be transformed in a simple "recipe".

In the face of events that cannot be predicted or even known, and which are therefore hardly categorisable, multi-resilience implies an enhanced learning aptitude in order to become able to adapt and to react more quickly and adequately to structurally and characteristically very different and evolving challenges. This indeed implies a differentiation between various types of "knowns" and "unknowns" and the development of more accurate management strategies.

One example of such strategies is the so-called *Cynefin Model* by Dave Snowden (see Figure 6 below). He developed it in the late 1990s, trying to extract "quintessences" of various systemic disciplines, such as integrating chaos theory and complexity theory, into one and the same framework. A brief overview of the four dimensions of *Cynefin* reveals the following basic pillars (Snowden, 2000; Snowden & Boone, 2007):

- *Simple phenomena* can be termed as "known knowns". Here, the relationship between cause and effect is obvious, and the resulting approach is *Sense-Categorise-Respond*. Since the affected decision-maker has access to the information necessary for dealing with this situation, a command-and-control style for setting parameters works best. Functions are automated and adhering to best practices or the *one best practice* is useful.
- *Complicated phenomena* are "known unknowns", since there is a clear relationship between cause and effect, but not everyone can see their interrelation and, particularly, the cause. Thus, complicated phenomena require the induction of expert knowledge in order to be understood. A typical example of complicated phenomena are most issues regarding advanced technology such as, for example, reparations of industrial plants. The typical approach here is to *Sense-Analyse-Respond*. This means that there are multiple right answers, for example in the search for oil or mineral deposits: The effort would usually require a team of experts, involving complicated analysis of origins, causes and consequences at multiple levels before responding by the means of an adequate strategy. Since responding to complicated problems contains multiple right answers, Snowden/Boone recommend creative applications generating multiple options. This may include simulations of working in unfamiliar environments, for example by putting marketing professionals in military research environments or by letting executives work on a simulated "alien planet". "The goal of such games is to get as many perspectives as possible to promote unfettered analysis" (Ibid., p.74). Thus, the main responses to complicated problems are good practices.
- *Complex phenomena* are "unknown unknowns". Other than complicated systems (i.e., an industrial plant), complex systems (i.e., a South American rain forest) are not the sum of their parts. Thus, the behaviour of complex phenomena cannot be predicted, and the relationship between cause and effect can only be perceived in retrospect. Typical for such phenomena are the effects of inter-group conflicts or of acquisition mergers. The approach for dealing with complex phenomena includes the steps *Probe-Sense-Respond*. Practices emerge during the problem-solving process through experimentation. An essential aspect of *experimental understanding* is an enhanced tolerance towards failures, which is not common for those decision-makers who assume that a situation requires a traditional command-and-control response. Decision-makers who "try to impose order in

a complex context will fail, but those who set the stage, step back a bit, allow patterns to emerge, and determine which ones are desirable will succeed" (Ibid.). The key approach to solving complex problems is to generate *emergent* practices.

– *Chaotic phenomena* are "unknowables". They correspond to Nassim Taleb's "Black Swans", such as the 9/11 terrorist attacks, natural disasters or disruptive innovations, and, to a large extent, the many ramifications of the Coronavirus crisis itself. At this level, there is no obvious relation between cause and effect. The approach is to *Act-Sense-Respond*, which is typical for "real-world labs" (Schäpke et al. 2015; Schneidewind, 2014), sometimes also specialised towards "urban living labs" (ULL) (Wolfram, Ravetz & Scholl, 2020). The goal is to manage the immediate crisis and to discover *novel* practices *at the same time*. In the face of a crisis, this could imply appointing a reliable crisis-management team to resolve the issue and, at the same time, picking out a separate team focussing on the opportunities of such a process for doing things differently. Typically, this domain is useful for highly advanced resilience research and practice based on sound preparedness.

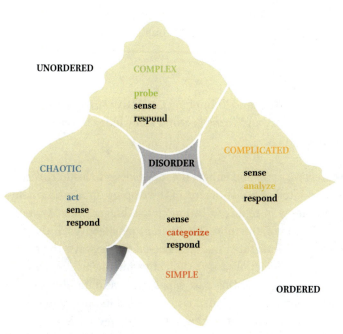

FIGURE 6   The four basic dimensions of the Cynefin Model
SOURCE: SNOWDEN & BOONE, 2007, 73

Snowden asserts that political and organisational leaders often tend to respond to crisis phenomena with an inadequate approach. For example, they focus on a "best practice" approach (known knowns) in the face of a chaotic problem (unknowables). Good and best practices are mostly related to *risk management* which, in essence, tends to assume predictable and calculable risk factors. Integrated *resilience policy*, on the contrary, manages the highly complex and unexpected. Thus, *risk management* and *resilience management* resulting from resilience policy are not the same.

Resilience management has mostly been explored in the context of organisational resilience (Weick & Sutcliffe, 2001; Müller-Seitz, 2014), while the much wider context of resilient societies remains mostly under-considered. However, the recent contributions on organisational learning may provide at least some guidelines which could be transferred to societal systems.

Overall, the main challenge today is to create systemic environments which foster "automatic" resilience learning through a network of mutually enhancing mechanisms. "Automatic" here does not necessarily mean "self-referential" or "self-sufficient"; and it is in any case not limited to such categories. Rather, "autonomy" may be a more apt translation of what "automatic" may and should be under conditions of enhanced contemporary resilience. The first (and most important) goal for reaching such an elevated level of resilience must be to instil an enhanced learning aptitude into a given system: to create a "learning culture" as the indispensable prerequisite of timely resilience. What would this imply?

29.4 Principle 4: Supporting and Enhancing Collective Intelligence through Participatory and Cross-sectoral Knowledge Management and Integration

First and foremost: relying upon and enhancing the abilities to foster *collective intelligence*. Collective intelligence is the art of developing appropriate solutions to complex problems in teams or in interactive bigger social systems. From a systemic point of view, the more the different perspectives of the participants are different and integrated in difference-adequate ways, the better the solutions will be (Woolley et al., 2010). Collective intelligence is not only necessary for systematically evaluating past experiences and developing collectively proven best practices. Above all, it is also needed in order to develop, test and modify innovative solutions in new, unprecedented crisis situations such as Corona.

FIVE PRINCIPLES OF MULTI-RESILIENCE

Examples of systematically generating collective-intelligent problem-solving practices in the Corona crisis were *hackathons* in Germany (Bundesregierung, 2020) or in Estonia (Broom, 2020b). A hackathon is a design competition in which participants try to solve tasks in interactive groups, mostly via Internet, within a few days. It is a typical measure to systematically mobilise and use collective intelligence for innovative responses to a complex crisis. In Germany, 42,000 participants took part in the #WirvsVirus hackathon which took place on three days in March 2020, submitting problems arising from the Coronavirus crisis for which solutions were then to be developed. The organisers identified the most promising proposals and sorted them into categories, e.g., effective testing of new cases of infection, distribution of aid, neighbourhood support, etc. (Bundesregierung 2020). Estonia's initiative, also launched in March, sponsored five ideas with 5,000 euros for practical implementation, under the condition that the ideas could be prototyped within 48 hours. The initiative was organised in a matter of hours and went global, attracting participants from 20 nations, across 14 time zones (Broom, 2020b). Knowledge-exchange measures which are, at the same time, integration measures – like these hackathons – should and could also be implemented systematically in transnational constellations.

The teachings can be extended to upcoming crises. In the context of advanced societies, enhancing collective problem-solving intelligence through mobilisation by adequate tools and mechanisms is largely operated through cross-sectoral knowledge management. As transdisciplinary studies assert and as we have repeatedly underscored, contemporary challenges cannot be sufficiently covered by the specialist knowledge of a single societal sector anymore. As a result, multi-sectoral knowledge integration and multi-sectoral cooperative learning are increasingly the subject of efforts towards more resilient societies (as discussed e.g., by Scharmer, (1995) and Schneidewind & Singer-Brodowski (2013)). As social differentiation and multi-sectorality at the same time mirror key vulnerabilities of today's societies, multi-sectoral dialogue and knowledge integration are increasingly needed as appropriate answers to these challenges. How such a dialogue, combined with integration, could be institutionalised in the long term and on a meta-systemic level is still widely unexplored, but is the subject of active debate, particularly in the German-speaking European countries and in Scandinavia. Such debate, if properly continued, can provide certain bases for an approach of *multi-resilient governance* being applicable to different crises.

Multi-resilient governance is about coping with complexity by differentiating tasks but keeping the main functions of government integrated and stable despite multiple threats. Following the principles of management cybernetics, particularly the aforementioned Ashby's Law, the ability to manage the complexity of a given environment mainly draws upon the inner complexity processing ability of a given system. This also applies to governance. Modern societies are systems composed of different societal sectors whose activities are intertwined and lead into incidental side-effects – the more, the more they are complex. Since none of these sectors could sufficiently cope with today's challenges, resilience management should be based on cross-sectoral knowledge management. This would not only result in a holistic view of the problem – a principle which also correlates with "discipline five" of Senge's approach of organisational learning (Senge, 1990). It also contributes to conflict prevention within a society, fosters social solidarity and promotes a more effective and efficient resource allocation within its participants. A variety of tools could significantly promote it, such as transdisciplinary think tanks and regular formats of cross-societal dialogue which may also include societal mediation and meditation.

The latter is particularly relevant for social crises like, before Corona, the U.S. and European migration crises starting in 2015, which were regarded among the most relevant crises worldwide (World Economic Forum, 2020). In Europe, this crisis did not only challenge most societies' integration policies and their welfare systems; it also led to deep social divides, political polarisation and multiple meso- and micro-conflicts.

A concrete case example: Being engaged with the consultation and training of personnel in refugee and migrant camps in Germany, we had a direct impression of "rhizomatic" (Deleuze & Guattari, 1980; B. Olivier, 2015; Clinton, 2003; Benedikter, 1999) conflicts across societal segments. We observed major fault lines between the personnel (particularly the security personnel) of refugee camps, the refugees' and migrants' NGO initiatives, the media, politicians from different parties, the population and, of course, the refugees themselves. One widely underestimated conflict fault line was between the personnel of the refugee camps and the refugee NGO initiatives. During our conversations, it was striking that both parties had strongly polarised views on the other while both were perceiving themselves as being on the side of the refugees. The NGOs perceived the personnel as racist and incompetent, willingly doing harm to the refugees. The personnel, by contrast, felt highly overburdened with their situation, acting as a buffer between the politicians, the refugees, the media and the NGOs. They accused the NGOs and the politicians of exploiting the refugees and self-staging in the media. Yet both, the NGOs and the personnel, perceived themselves as acting in the interests of the refugees. A mediation process which could be conducted as a "shuttle process", back and forth, with one-on-one dialogues, could contribute towards deconstructing the polarised views of the parties and help in allocating necessary resources for the good of all involved and of social peace (which is in the "natural" interest of most of the involved parties (Fathi, 2019a)).

In contrast, during the Coronavirus crisis, in most European countries we could observe a rather close cooperation between representatives from politics and science, especially from virology. From the perspective of transdisciplinary informed multi-resilience, it could be criticised, though, that the crisis management was one-sidedly focused on measures to reduce the epidemiology in the strict sense (Hergersberg, Hoffrogge & Beck, 2020). Contributions from experts of other sciences such as economy, finance, the humanities, sociology, political science, psychology or futurology, but also from sectors such as private businesses or civil society were, for a considerable amount of time, widely neglected. Yet, as we have seen in the "mature" phases of Corona, taking them into account is and will be necessary to anticipate undesirable complex rebound effects of counter-pandemic plans and to develop holistic and lasting preparedness. In Europe, during Corona, scientifically informed politics was not systematically organised in a transdisciplinary fashion; this would, however, be an essential prerequisite for multi-resilient problem anticipation and solving.

Additionally, the Coronavirus crisis in countries such as Germany illustrated a typical conflict line between the science and the media sectors. The conflict escalated in May 2020, when the popular German newspaper "Bild" claimed under the headline "Drosten study on infectious children grossly mistaken" ("Drosten-Studie über ansteckende Kinder grob falsch" (Piatov, 2020b)) that virologist Christian Drosten had used "questionable methods" to suggest that kindergartens and schools be closed down (Ibid.). Hereby, "Bild" quoted four scientists who commented on different aspects, such as the small sample size among children and adolescents (only 49 samples in the Drosten study came from children under ten years of age) or the conclusions that the virologist drew from the statistical analyses, i.e., to leave schools and kindergartens closed. The "Bild" author interpreted Drosten's study as "increasingly coming under criticism" by "scientists from several countries" accusing Drosten of having "worked uncleanly" with "disastrous consequences". Additionally, "Bild" headlined "How long has the star virologist known about this?", suggesting that Drosten even withheld information about the real danger of infection of children. As a source for the "explosive" – so the wording – insinuation, the newspaper quoted its own research, which it did not further elaborate upon (Ibid.). In reaction, several scientists quoted in the article demented the comments, emphasising that they had been wrongly cited and without having given permission. Furthermore, some clarified that the study would not be "grossly wrong", but "not very accurate", and that their criticism against the study would be a normal part of scientific dispute culture (Mast, Schumann & Simmank, 2020).

The case elucidated the difficulties of creating and cultivating collective intelligence in profound crisis situations such as Corona in the midst of a torn socio-political climate ridden by emotional polarisation, as is the case in most European and Western democracies, contributing to the "global crisis of democracy" (Diamond, 2019; Wike & Fetterolf, 2018; Edel, 2019) or "democratic decline" (Journal of Democracy, n.d.). According to media scientist Johanna Haberer, Vice-President of the University Nürnberg-Erlangen, this conflict is a symptom of a deeper misunderstanding rooted in profoundly different communication rites and processes of the political sector, the media sector, and the science sector. While the scientific debate works by the principle "I have a thesis that might be disproved, but afterwards I'm smarter than before", parts of the press would interpret this as a weakness. Furthermore, the boulevard lives from fear and insecurity, driven by the motivation of presenting an "interesting story" (Grimm, 2020).

In the end, the scientific sector and the journalistic sector will have to learn to adapt to each other in a better way if collective intelligence is to be fostered. To better master systemic crises, profoundly different systemic logics expressed – as natural in differentiated societies – by strongly different and mutually independent branches and sectors will have to manifest their active will to cooperate instead of trying to harness short-term gains on each other. This does not take away from the natural critical function of the media in open societies which remains indispensable. Journalists should cite scientists correctly and publish articles under consideration of ethical standards. This would also include avoiding personal attacks, i.e., going "ad personam". By contrast, scientists will have to learn to become much better at explaining what they are doing and to accept critique, not only by peers but also from citizens and the broader public, since they are part of a democratic discourse in which they have to explain themselves (Ibid.).

29.5 Principle 5: Fostering "Resilience Culture" by Stimulating and Facilitating Collective Reasoning and Cohesion

A component that is often not sufficiently taken into account and, at the same time, proved to be highly relevant during the Coronavirus crisis is the "resilience culture" of a group, a community, a county or a country, or of any other practical collective. The term "resilience culture" is still not very widespread

FIVE PRINCIPLES OF MULTI-RESILIENCE

and is scientifically poorly developed. Among the most recent scientific contributions are studies by the IRS Leibniz Institute for Regional Development and Structural Planning. In a two-year study published in 2012, they revealed that the resilience of a society with regard to a profound and complex threat depends primarily on its perception of that threat. Such perception is almost always simplifying.

This can be illustrated by using the "resilience culture" example of the Netherlands. Throughout its history, the country has always been plagued by flood disasters. Until the 1990s, the resilience strategy was aimed at dyke construction, reflecting the perception of "keeping the water away". The new resilience strategy "Leven met water" (2020) since the 1990s provides a classic example of a crisis transformational approach – in other words, the use of new opportunities arising from a crisis. Since then, floating architecture has dominated the cityscape of the Netherlands (Christmann et al., 2011).

With regard to the Coronavirus crisis and future challenges, at least three questions can be deduced: What exactly is collectively perceived as threatening? How do societies co-create the threat in the sense of both a mental construct and a practical reality? What is the "resilience-promoting" or "resilience-unpromoting" role of gossip, informal communication and the media?

A limited but, however, still insightful approach to quantify it is a 10-point scale of *Politico* developed during the Coronavirus crisis assessing the panic level of societies in Europe in mid-March 2020 considering items such as, for example, panic buying. According to this study, the panic level in Sweden (3), Estonia (3), Croatia (3), Finland (4), Luxemburg (2), and Latvia (1 point) were comparably low. By contrast, the Netherlands (6) and Denmark (5) were at the medium level and the other countries in continental Europe (including Germany, France, Belgium, Austria, all at 7), South Europe (including Italy and Spain at 8) and East Europe (including Slovenia, Czech Republic and Hungary at 8 points) were at a high level (Politico, 2020). Respective media activity can be related to these results but is still under scrutiny. In many cases, the media play the role of an amplifier, creating a *circulus viciousus*, whilst in others they serve as tranquillisers or tools for removal.

A last but not less important aspect of "resilience culture" crucial to any efficient collective crisis management consists in a shared awareness of "pulling together". "Pulling together" is a soft, contextual and sometimes temporary form of (secular) civil religion (Benedikter, & Göschl, 2014; Benedikter, 2014a; Helfer, 2014). The resulting collective cohesion or feeling of "deep togetherness" and solidarity is not only fundamental for directly supporting each other in the face of upcoming challenges, thus creating "citizen consciousness", i.e., better perception and awareness of the co-creation of living spaces, including habits and unwritten rules that often touch upon joint values. Collective cohesion also helps to implement bottom-up approaches (by citizens) which, as mentioned, in complex crisis constellations are necessary completions to top-down regulations (by governments).

In Vietnam, for example, this was evident with the function of the so-called "neighbourhood committees" (Fathi, 2020). In addition to supporting people in need of help, they voluntarily exercised shared social control, especially in the initial phase of the pandemic, to detect infected persons and ensure compliance with contact and hygiene regulations. According to Harvard University, there were also impressive "collective mindfulness" teachings in Thailand (Limphaibool, 2020). The principle of solidarity can manifest in culturally different and civilisation-specific ways. An example is the term "Whanaungatanga", which comes from the Maori culture, meaning "to care for others because their fate is inseparable from one's own". As a collective resilience practice, Whanaungatanga was explicitly demonstrated in New Zealand after the terrorist attack on a mosque in Christchurch via active and expressed empathic reactions of the vast majority of New Zealanders (C. Olivier, 2019). The fact that New Zealand, as one of the first countries worldwide, reported having "factually eliminated" the Coronavirus as early as in April 2020 (BBC News, 2020dd; News Wires, 2020) means that this may not be just an accident. Something similar is true for the concept of "Teraanga" in Senegal, although its specific effects on the Coronavirus crisis in the country are still unclear (Coleman, 2020).

Yet on the level of international relations, too, the principle of collective cohesion is essential in dealing with present and probable future global challenges. As mentioned above, some striking examples of international solidarity could be found during the Corona crisis. Solidarity initiatives between nations during profound and lasting crises such as the Corona crisis prove to be an effective approach for trust-building and to form strategic ad hoc alliances which can turn into more stable relations after the end of the crisis.

As we could observe in the context of the Coronavirus crisis, not only the media, but also political action can strongly influence collective crisis perception and resulting de-solidarisation or solidarisation processes. Recent examples can be found in Singapore: The head of state, all ministers and all members of parliament waived a monthly salary in favour of the so-called "heroes" of the Corona crisis who, despite all odds, continued to work in systemically important but notoriously underpaid professions, such as cashiers, nurses, cleaners or taxi drivers. Another example is the "We fight the Virus" song or "Corona Rap", which swore the people of Singapore to the common fight against the virus, referring to the fact that everyone can rely on each other (Senzel, 2020). These examples point to the importance of effective crisis communication for social cohesion, particularly in information societies. Today, in view of the high level of networking and the influence of the Internet, this applies more than ever on the broadest possible level and should be taken into account more systematically in the crisis-management concepts of governments.

CHAPTER 30

Summary. Multi-resilience
A Crucial Topic to Shape "Globalisation 2.0"

These five guiding principles of multi-resilience can be applied to any crisis. In the Coronavirus crisis, they demonstrated the necessity of effective communication not only within but also among nation states and non-governmental protagonists. If this prerequisite is met, multi-resilience, if properly implemented, can contribute both directly and indirectly to the paradigmatic discourse on Re-Globalisation, or "Globalisation 2.0". What exactly do we mean by this?

At all times in human history, nations have been developing more or less lasting forms of bilateral and multilateral cooperation, meant as some sort of systemic integration – mostly in the context of military security and economic prosperity. Recent global challenges and, particularly, the Coronavirus crisis could contribute to a new context for global cooperation of increasing importance for the 21st century: Multi-resilience of international relations and security patterns. Meaning: Alongside already existing economic and political global institutions, agreements and forms of multilateral cooperation, multi-resilience could provide an additional methodological, strategic and contextual incentive for re-globalisation – pushing farther both global political integration as local self-sufficiency towards "glocality" (Meyrowitz, 2005) and "glocalisation" (Blatter, 2013). To what extent?

To date, no fully developed formalisations of multi-level governance can be found in the sphere of *international relations*. Even the European Union, which features the highest degree of political nation-integration in the world, is still far from the evolutionary stage of a "United States of Europe", different from the United States of America in the sense of a "unity in diversity", i.e., a unity with a high degree of subsidiarity and sub-federal autonomisation. A first important starting point for promoting better global cooperation could be implemented through post-Corona solidarity initiatives among nation states – e.g. the formalisation of active bilateral offers of support after this and during upcoming crises, which ultimately means a new "crisis automatism" under the umbrella of international organisations. The Corona crisis could be the positive trigger for such effort.

Before and during the Coronavirus crisis, China had already suggested a similar approach to consolidate its "New Silk Road" from China to Europe or, as it is officially called, the Chinese "One Belt One Road" (OBOR) Initiative. OBOR can be regarded as one of the major strategies of the rising superpower China to shape and consolidate its own vision of "Globalisation 2.0". For a couple of years, China has increasingly been dominating the discourse on globalisation – and some expect that the Coronavirus crisis, originating in China's partly irresponsible handling of wildlife markets and, as the U.S. assumption goes, perhaps even high-risk laboratory research, may paradoxically strengthen China's position in global relations due to some symbolical solidarity actions (Cabestan, 2020) and increased "debt hold" on struggling nations (Davidson, 2020; Burgers & Romaniuk, 2020). Be it as it may, any "victory over coronavirus will be heralded as a boost for Xi Jinping's brand of Marxism" (Brown, 2020). The result is that while "China's model of control has been blamed for the Corona crisis, for some it's looking increasingly attractive" (Griffiths, 2020a). China's model – i.e., its systematically self-mystified "great leader" Xi Jinping's "Chinese dream" – foresees a new coexistence of authoritarian and non-democratic with democratic systems within a new multipolar order without any clear common value or rule of law. In Xi's view, it is an order led by China as the new superpower at the centre of the world. Western observers such as Ian Bremmer have branded this centerless vision as "G-0 world" (Bremmer & Roubini, 2011). The EU in particular and partly the USA have failed to define and communicate an appealing competing vision for re-globalisation yet (Godehardt & Kohlenberg, 2017).

In such situations, cooperation-based multi-resilience would be the chance for the democratic powers of the West to formulate such a "different" vision on the basis of Western values and for the sake of a new unity on the globe after the Corona crisis. Reformulating globalisation after Corona by providing the global community with a concept of participatory multi-resilience could provide a unique opportunity to frame a more unifying vision for the global future more apt for European-Western participation than the "multipolar world" vision of illiberal powers. The EU in particular could become an example for such a bridging approach on the basis of multi-resilience (Dennison, Dworkin & Shapiro, 2020). Branded "the de-globalisation virus" (Ortéga, 2020) by the European Council on Foreign Relations (ECFR), the Coronavirus could thus turn out to actually become the opposite: "the re-globalisation virus". This can happen if "multi-resilience" as a policy approach substitutes (at least partially) attempts of mutual appropriation in the sense of competition for avant-garde technology, such as seen in U.S. President Donald Trump's efforts in 2020 to acquire the German firm behind a potential cure for Corona, *CureVac*:

186   CHAPTER 30

> In 2020, as the Corona crisis took hold, the German government received a new fright in the form of *CureVac*: it appears that no less a figure than Donald Trump himself made a technology transfer attempt. The US president reportedly offered a great amount of money (The Guardian, 2020) to acquire *CureVac*, a globally important biotech company that may prove critical to finding a vaccine against the coronavirus. *CureVac* itself has stated that no formal purchase offer was made, although Germany's economy, interior, and finance ministers all confirmed the American interest in the business – and they all reacted accordingly too, making clear their anger at the move.
>
> HACKENBROICH, 2020

Instead of such irresponsible interior competition in front of a multipolar global order in the making at the disadvantage of democracies where European and Western open societies are threatened to become a minority, the Atlantic partner's efforts should be directed towards strengthening multi-resilience by, for example, investing jointly in future vaccine research and technology and institutionalising respective mechanisms, and by learning from those countries which fared best in the crisis, which, in many cases, were smaller countries with experience in subsidiary processes. Multi-resilience requires new Atlantic agreements, and thus the readiness to cooperate despite political differences instead of competing at any cost by unnecessarily politicising the crisis issue in partisan ways.

Apart from a stronger cooperation among global democracies on shared multi-resilience, further important steps for the 27 remaining post-Brexit EU nation states after Brexit could be to firstly reflect, design and communicate a vision of multi-resilience in the context of the Atlantic partnership and, more encompassing, to Western constructive thinking about re-globalisation. Secondly, the U.S. and Europe should actively initiate cross-national mechanisms of global crisis coordination at the formal level, including the existing alliance of democracies, and then of supranational institutions (e.g. at WTO and UN level). This could be thirdly backed by bilateral talks between nations and respective initiatives at the informal level, as already proved efficient during the first months of the Corona crisis.

PART 4

Requirements for a Post-Corona World

∵

CHAPTER 31

The Corona Effect and "Diseasescape"

Towards Weaker, but More Realistic Globalisation and Transnationalisation?

Taken together, the Coronavirus crisis of 2019–20 manifested a previously rather undervalued fact: that highly interconnected alliances (and assemblies) of countries are apparently faster, more easily – and more heavily – affected by global systemic crises than those which do not present these features. For example, in Europe the Eurozone countries seemed to have been harder hit than those countries which retained their national currencies (Anderson et al., 2020; Ewing, 2020). The EU as a whole is a good example of highly interconnected nation states which were particularly hard hit as an exact result of their mutually open borders. The United States is another example, albeit on a politically different level.

In response, countries that form trans-border alliances and take particular profit from them, as the European Union has done for decades, in the post-Corona scenario must learn that there is also a price for such profit. They must more fully integrate trans-border unification into their plans and programs – with all the consequences and effects. This price will consist, among other aspects such as lowering the standards of certain sectors, in higher and more appropriate joint preparedness measures which will have to include higher investments and shared financial support with regard to the crisis resilience of substantial sectors, including laws that prescribe such standards as an integral part of a *conditio qua non,* and with regard to coordinating these sectors towards multi-resilient patterns as described above.

Furthermore, Chan Yuk Wah of Hong Kong University and David Haines of George Mason University pointed out another important aspect at the interface between globalisation and the Coronavirus spread. It is the rise of an "intersectional flow" type of globalisation they branded "diseasescape":

> Originating in China ..., what does this pandemic teach us about [the] global governance of a health crisis? While the human world has championed globalization since the last century, are we now witnessing a more detrimental side of globalization? While the crisis is surely one of public health, it also alerts us to the different and intersecting areas of government, society, and culture. The *intersectionality* of coronavirus ... takes a toll not only on human life, but on cultural perceptions, medical

© ROLAND BENEDIKTER AND KARIM FATHI, 2022 | DOI:10.1163/9789004469686_032

discourses, racial relations, regional and international health governance, and global politics. Arjun Appadurai has assessed global cultural flows in terms of five scapes – ethnoscape, mediascape, financescape, ideoscape, and technoscape – and stresses that such scapes overlap and do not flow in a single direction. The coronavirus outbreak suggests we need to be heedful of one more scape, a *diseasescape* that intertwines with other scapes and likewise flows in multiple directions.

YUK WAH & HAINES, 2020

According to the authors, this means that:

In the age of hyper globalization, everything moves faster: people, ideas, money, media information, images, and diseases too. Viruses spread faster with faster human movements. Governments that used to welcome foreign tourists and businesspeople have been mostly unprepared when border-crossers bring inflows of disease. While most of the globalized scapes that Appadurai discusse[d] are largely welcome and likely to facilitate human progress in some ways, the diseasescape is detrimental and harmful. Today, the threats of disease have increased tremendously because of the great expansion of human mobility (Ibid.).

Indeed, according to Wah and Haines, it was the dramatic increase in mobility, particularly of Chinese citizens and diaspora in the first place and at the start of the Coronavirus spread. Tourism and travelling prepared the stages for the scale and magnitude of the Coronavirus distribution, both geographically and speed-wise:

Compared to the 2000s, national borders nowadays are much busier. In 2003, [also China-originating] SARS was a more deadly but less contagious virus. Another reason it could be contained within a single region (mainly in Asia) was the much smaller scale of human movement at the time. In the early 2000s, Chinese did not cross borders as frequently as today and most Chinese nationals did not even have a passport. The market for outbound Chinese tourism had barely begun to develop. Around 20 million outbound trips were taken by Chinese annually and over two-thirds were to Hong Kong, Macau, and Taiwan (Ibid.).

Yet according to the authors, things have changed towards the outside world:

Since that time, policies to ease cross-border travel boosted the flow of people from China to Hong Kong, exceeding 50 million visits per year. At the same time, Chinese outbound travel was extending to all corners of the world. By 2015, Chinese tourists had topped the international tourism market with over 100 million trips. Increased movements of people facilitate faster spread of diseases and viruses, imposing threats posed by human mobility and changing the implications of globalization. The coronavirus, a globally shared disease, has turned all borders into portals of danger and raised suspicions about mobility. China was the original source of transmission, but now the People's Republic of China (PRC) must guard itself from transmission into the country from outsiders and returning nationals. Conversely, the United States was originally in the position of guarding against this immigrating virus, but [became] the country with the highest infection numbers and death toll, and [wa]s viewed by many as a danger zone(Ibid.).

The teachings seem to be clear, at least in the first instance, according to Wah and Haines:

The complexities – and dangers – in this fully globalized system result not only from its scope but from the disjunctures between the flow of the disease itself and the flow of medical information, media discourses, medical practices, and even medical images. All these may enhance or slacken the containment of the virus. One result is a forced opportunity to rethink globalization and the synchronization of its many different forms and flows ... (Ibid.).

Which would be to *think re-globalisation* (Benedikter & Kofler, 2019a). A similar reasoning leads Wah and Haines to draw their conclusion: Coronavirus was, to some extent, the start of a new phase of globalisation – of a period of international development which may be destined to at least partially re-think globalisation:

Different systems, cultures, and politics created different national and regional responses to a shared global pandemic ... The diseasescape revealed by the pandemic illustrated some unfortunate disjunctions in globalization. It appears that disease is much more effective at crossing national and cultural borders than is information about disease and how to manage it. On top of cultural barriers, there are disturbing indications of how irrational the purportedly rational policy-making process can be, and how some countries trade off transparency in policy for control, either due to incompetence or governmental arrogance about not informing – or even misinforming – their people for their own good. The pandemic has been a teacher: about disease, mobility, people, and government. There have been jarring failures in politics as leaders pursue blame for gain. The failures in policy have rendered a disease – and diseasescape – more dangerous, have shaken global connections, and raise questions about whether there is either the human will or capacity to understand a pandemic pan-globally, much less to act on it effectively.

YUK WAH & HANIES, 2020

Overall, the Corona crisis seems to have strengthened re-globalisation awareness and efforts in general. And in so doing it may have given, maybe as a side effect, a push to concepts such as "weak cosmopolitanism" (D. Miller, 2018; Knight, 2011) and "compatriot partiality" (D. Miller, 2005; Riker, 2011) coined primarily by Oxford scholar David Miller. In essence, these two concepts describe a moderate conservative turn towards less idealistic and more realistic practices of globalism, sometimes branded as "prudent openness". The intent is to reduce the exaggerations of "total openness" which European and Western citizens, parallel to the growing direct negative effects of globalisation on their own lives, increasingly reject. In response, Miller and others want to introduce a more pondered and balanced cosmopolitanism for the years to come, which must also take note of the new power relations in a more multipolar world. As Miller himself summarises his approach, which some hold could become, in one way or another, one typical post-Corona approach:

> I argue that we should abandon the 'strong' version of cosmopolitanism in favour of a weaker one, which recognises that we have duties to human beings as such, in the sense that we must respect their human rights, wherever they may be; and that we must always consider the effects of our actions on those who will suffer the consequences, regardless of whether there are links between us. This concern, which is genuinely cosmopolitan, is not, however, incompatible with the expression of a greater degree of attention and commitment to our fellow citizens. That is, to admit the existence of a certain partiality towards our compatriots; hence the concept of 'compatriot partiality'. This is the general idea, I would say like a starting point, because we must then ask ourselves in depth what obligations we have towards people who are not our fellow citizens.
>
> D. MILLER, 2018

THE CORONA EFFECT AND "DISEASESCAPE"   193

Corona has certainly strengthened such basic ideas of "our own citizens come first" in quite "natural" ways. Self-isolation and lockdown have questioned cosmopolitanism like no other collective experience in the 21st century among most citizens throughout different political, economic and social systems. While these and similar ideas of reducing the radicality of globalisation by introducing layers of differentiation were debated rather critically by the European and Western mainstream prior to the Corona crisis (De Shutter & Tinnevelt, 2011), the crisis experiences and practices have given them a decisive new legitimation in the perception of many. Corona has triggered a search for a "better" globalisation by means of re-globalisation, also in the field of international relations – to the point that some forward-thinkers are weighing how the globalisation project can be "salvaged" at all in a post-Corona world. For the European Council on Foreign Relations (ECFR), co-founder and Director Mark Leonard put his doubts and search for an answer into these words:

> As soon as the coronavirus was recognised as a global threat, most national leaders' first instinct was to close their borders. Calls for international coordination through the G20 were an afterthought. And yet, while the initial spread of the virus owes much to interdependence, the health crisis it has created within individual countries will not admit of nationalist or autarkic solutions. Once COVID-19 is being transmitted within communities, closing borders will Do nothing ... The COVID-19 pandemic has struck an international order that was already in crisis. It has been obvious since at least 2008 that, contrary to what was long claimed, not everyone wins from globalization. A more open and interconnected world is conducive to strong economic growth and prosperity, but also to rising inequality and ecological destruction. The freer movement of people has provided new opportunities for millions, but it also has increased the upward pressure on public services and downward pressure on wages in host countries, while fueling a brain drain from the places left behind. Long before the pandemic, these trends had provoked a backlash, particularly in developed countries, where populist parties and leaders have seized the political agenda from the mainstream parties that defended the post-war liberal international order. ...
>
> LEONARD, 2020c

For the historically unique global experiment of trans-nationalisation between different cultures, languages and nations which is the European Union, in particular, according to Leonard the Corona crisis could mark a historical turn

194 CHAPTER 31

towards a new, "weaker" but perhaps more realistic conception of the relation between the union and its member states:

> Against this background, it is inevitable that the [Coronavirus] crisis will remake globalization one way or another. But how? The pandemic represents an opportunity for a number of different political movements, from environmentalists who have long demanded more sustainable development to those who are worried about inequality or the fragility of global supply chains. For their part, Europeans should use the occasion to rethink their notion of sovereignty. The challenge is to figure out how European integration itself could serve as a backstop for national sovereignty, rather than posing a threat to it. As this and recent previous crises have shown, European governments must be allowed to protect their citizens from the threats introduced by interdependence, be they environmental, cyber, contagious, migratory, or financial in nature. To that end, Europe's leaders need to develop a vision of 'European sovereignty' that mitigates the need for autarchy by creating channels for national governments to make certain fundamental decisions for themselves, and to bargain effectively within broader frameworks of interdependency ... (Ibid.).

From this, Leonard draws the conclusion that:

> Ultimately, the COVID-19 crisis could allow the European project to return to its roots: reconciling the prerogatives of the nation state with the realities of interdependence, rather than sacrificing national sovereignty on the altar of neoliberal dogma. Better yet, developing a coherent vision of European sovereignty would help to prepare for the next crisis of interdependence (Ibid.).

Confirming the core elements of such reasoning, Bulgarian political scientist Ivan Krastev and Dutch historian Luuk van Middelaar pondered a better federalisation of the EU as a direct result of the crisis (Krupa & Lau, 2020). Firstly, as Krastev stated, in a post-Corona world more than ever, every EU country has to answer the question of how it wants to survive in a much more hostile global environment dominated by Chinese aspirations to become the next superpower and Trump's "America First" policy. Until now, conflicts in the EU have often occurred between the nation states and Brussels. For Krastev, it is not a coincidence that France and Germany, not the European Commission – the EU's de facto government –, took the initiative to prepare joint mechanisms in post-Corona healthcare and preparedness, including a pan-European post-Corona economic reconstruction fonds (Blume, 2020).

Secondly, van Middelaar observes the emergence of a "European arena", characterised by the fact that during Corona, Europeans have learned to pay more attention to their neighbouring countries. This is illustrated by the fact that politicians are increasingly invited to other EU member countries to explain their positions.

This thirdly correlates with the positive trend of increasingly comparative politics within the EU. An example for this is, according to Krastev, that governments are increasingly controlled by their populations through comparisons with other governments. For instance, the Austrian decision to withdraw Corona public restrictions had much influence on the debate in Germany.

Fourthly, both Krastev and van Middelaar pointed out that many still underestimate how radically the EU is changing after Corona and becoming more internally flexible and consolidated. This would be illustrated by the fact that the EU has reduced its claim to want to change its member states. At the same time, external pressure has increased on national governments to work together despite their differences. As a result, external consolidation will lead to the EU becoming more flexible internally (Krupa & Lau, 2020).

This is fifthly supported by the attempt to introduce a system of at least partially shared expenditure and revenue within the EU which in extremis could, according to German Finance Minister Olaf Scholz, lead to something similar to a "Hamilton Moment". This refers to Alexander Hamilton (1755–1804), the first American Finance Minister, who, in 1790, implemented a joint debt system which lead to the factual emergence of a truly united "United States of America" (Koch, 2020). Although this might be still out of reach, as are the "United States of Europe" in the strict sense, according to Krastev, due to the post-Corona requirements the EU is experiencing an unprecedented moment of integration, although in most countries there is no strong public enthusiasm for the EU. However, the main driver is not some "new European dream", but rather the pragmatic motivation to jointly survive (Krupa & Lau, 2020).

CHAPTER 32

The Uncertainty about the Future of COVID-19
Short-term Scenarios versus Big-picture Trends

In the short- and medium-term perspective, many analysts in 2020 speculated on scenarios about the potential next (and perhaps in some way never-ending future) waves of the pandemic. Most of them refered to the example of a study of the Center for Infectious Disease Research and Policy (CIDRAP) of the University of Minnesota of April 2020 (Moore et al., 2020).

The CIDRAP Model considers historical experiences of and comparisons among pandemics and aims at further developing them through experiences drawn from the Corona pandemic. To date, it is likely that this model will be a reference point for scenario assessment regarding future pandemics. In 2020, before the successful development and distribution of any vaccines, the CIDRAP Model assumed three future scenarios:

1. "Peaks and valleys": The first wave of COVID-19 in spring 2020 would be followed by a series of repetitive smaller waves. These would occur through the summer of 2020 and then consistently and gradually diminish over a 1- to 2-year period. The occurrence of these waves may vary geographically and depend on the pandemic policies in place. Depending on the extent of the wave peaks, this scenario would require periodic change between reinstitution and subsequent relaxation of restrictive measures over the framework of 2021 and 2022, i.e., over 1 to 2 subsequent years (Ibid.).

2. "Peak in autumn": The first wave of COVID-19 in spring 2020 would be followed by a larger wave in the fall or winter of 2020–21 and one or more smaller subsequent waves in 2021. This pattern would require the reinstitution of restrictive measures in the fall, and to some extent afterwards, in an attempt to drive down the spread of infection and prevent healthcare systems from being overwhelmed (Ibid.). This pattern is similar to that of other pandemics, such as the Spanish flu pandemic of 1918–19 (CDC, 2018), the Asian flu of 1957–58 (Saunders-Hastings & Krewski, 2016); Miller et al., 2009), or the H1N1 pandemic of 2009/10 (Saunders-Hastings & Krewski, 2016).

3. "Slow burn": The first wave of COVID-19 in spring 2020 would be followed by a "slow burn" of ongoing transmission and case occurrence, but without a clear wave pattern. This pattern may vary geographically

© ROLAND BENEDIKTER AND KARIM FATHI, 2022 | DOI:10.1163/9789004469686_033

and be related to the degree of restrictive measures in place. Although this pattern was not observed in past influenza pandemics, it remains a possibility for COVID-19. This scenario would probably not require the reinstitution of restrictive lockdown or other measures, although cases and deaths would continue to occur (Ibid.).

Every single one of these three scenarios has different political implications. However, it remains a crucial part of the problem that there are several unknowns regarding the full extent of short- and long-term effects of the coronavirus and the COVID-19 disease. These include, for example, the question as to how long the immunity after recovering from the disease may last and whether it is possible to become reinfected (Cooley, 2020). Even in 2021, with several vaccines available, these questions remain relevant due to further mutations of the virus. All of these and other unknowns largely influence the choice between the two main resulting pandemic-management strategies, also for future pandemics:

- The "restrictions and vaccine" strategy implies slowing down the spread of the virus (Iati et al., 2020) by taking precautions such as social distancing, wearing face masks in public and washing hands correctly and frequently (D. Smith, 2020) until there is an effective vaccine. By the beginning of 2021 diverse vaccines have indeed been successfully developed and released, which to date (December 2021) nevertheless appears not yet to be conclusive since the virus still mutates.
- The "collective immunity" (or: "herd immunity") strategy assumes that there would be no significant reinfections and – since the virus is highly contagious, but most of the infection cases occur with low or even no symptoms – there would be a high number of unreported recovered and already immune people. Optimists like the Norwegian authorities estimated an unreported figure so high that only 3 in 1000 would die when infected (Nielsen, Eilersen & Sneppen, 2020). If collective immunity were possible, most experts in 2019 and 2020 estimated that at least 60 to 70 percent of the population should have been infected to achieve it (Fottrell, 2020). With the release and distribution of vaccines in 2021, political decision-makers and observers estimate likewise herd immunity to be achieved with an amount of at least 60 to 70 percent of full-vaccination in the population.

Both these basic pandemic-management strategies are prerequisites for a post-Corona world yet imply speculative, widely unknown variables. Since June 2020, most countries worldwide relaxed their lockdowns, but still kept the "restrictions and vaccine" strategy implemented. The uncertainty was exemplified by the fact that initially successful societies such as Hong Kong relatively early in the recovery phase, at the end of July 2020, faced a massive return of cases and were "on the verge of 'large-scale' community outbreak, risking collapse of the city's hospital system" (BBC News, 2020v) and "urging people to stay at home" (Ibid.). Vietnam, with 95 million inhabitants, had o deaths due to early state measures and was very proud of its system, which had even cured the Scottish pilot Stephen Cameron after months of treatment and ten weeks in a coma. According to his own words, Cameron would have died in any other system, since everybody else would have given up (Barnes & The, 2020; Barnes, 2020). Yet, at the end of July 2020, i.e., after half a year of Corona crisis and when everybody thought the worst was over, Vietnam suddenly registered the first death, "a devastating blow for a country proud of its zero deaths" (BBC News, 2020ccc).

On 31 July 2020, when many Asian and European countries thought the worst was over, according to the WHO, a new record of daily infections was registered, reaching 292,000 infections within 24 hours, most of them in the Americas with 172,000 new daily cases, among them the U.S. with 65,000 new cases in just one day and Brazil with 69,000, then India with 55,000 (RP, 2020, p. 120). In the whole of Europe, 25,000 new infections were counted on that single day (Ibid.).

And it was as late as nine months into the crisis, in August 2020, that the state of Victoria in Australia, after initial, much-applauded containment, declared a new state of emergency: the "state of disaster", and imposed a harsh lockdown, demonstrating to the world that early success does not immunise against a later return of a pandemic or any other similar emergency (BBC News, 2020ll). In detail:

> The Australian state of Victoria has declared a state of disaster and imposed new lockdown measures after a surge in coronavirus infections. Under the new rules, which came into effect at 18:00 (08:00 GMT), residents of the state capital Melbourne are subject to a night-time curfew. There will be further restrictions on residents' ability to leave home. Australia has been more successful than many other countries in tackling COVID-19, but cases are rising in Victoria ... Premier Daniel Andrews said the measures were working but too slowly. 'We must go harder. It's the only way we'll get to the other side of this,' he [said] ... Melbourne residents will only be allowed to shop and exercise within 5km (three miles) of their home. Exercise outside of the home will only be allowed

for one hour at a time. Only one person per household is allowed to shop for essentials at a time (Ibid.).

In August 2020, on the occasion of the new lockdown, some of the more than 1500 police officers employed to enforce the restrictions were attacked and "bitten" by angry parts of the population who opposed the measures (BBC News, 2020z).

As a result, perhaps more than ever in recent human history, societies are mutually observing one another regarding failures and successes in crisis management – and with regard to the emergence of best practices, not least in view of the return of the Coronavirus in specific contexts. Based on these experiences with the COVID-19 pandemic, we can assume that worldwide awareness and responsiveness towards future pandemics will be significantly enhanced for the coming years and perhaps even decades.

However, the two basic models and the unknown variables as outlined above will most probably remain similar or the same. Dealing with lasting uncertainty will require collective awareness and the ability of responsive learning processes, based on trial and error. Ongoing worldwide digital interconnection will be a major resource for this. Hereby, the Corona crisis itself can be regarded as a major driver for further digitalisation and related technological trends. Most publications about a potential post-Corona world refer to this.

CHAPTER 33

Technological Requirements

Six Trends

It can indeed be said that the Corona crisis brought about tremendous unprecedented and unpredicted changes in the everyday lives of people in most countries worldwide. Although it is early to speculate about the longer-lasting future impacts of COVID-19, some trends can already be observed. Most speculations about the long-term effects of the crisis concentrate on describing its influence on digital transformation and related cross-industry trends. The assumption hereby is that all areas of the digitalisation trend would receive a further "push" from the Corona situation and its aftermath. These areas include an increasing use of digital communication technologies, monitoring through IoT and Big Data Technology, increasing automatisation and respective reliance on robots. As a result, most observers point out at least these following *six* technological trends and related social impact patterns.

33.1 Remote Working

One of the probably most obvious structural changes triggered by the Corona crisis is that suddenly millions of people are working from home. In pre-Corona times, concerns about home workplaces might have had more to do with the employer's lack of control over his or her employees. During the Corona crisis, companies such as *Interguard, Activetrack, Vericlock* or *Time Doctor* tripled their sales within a few months, according to the German newspaper "Süddeutsche Zeitung". Among other things, their software allows employers to log the keystrokes of employees (Moorstedt, 2020). Additionally, many observers point out that working from home increases the employee's productivity and working motivation (Jacobs, 2020) and, in general, leads to cost and time savings. Thus, it is quite conceivable that working-time models and travel activities in professional life will change in the long term (Rohwer-Kahlmann, 2020).

Yet, remote work also imposes challenges on employers and employees. As Yan Xiao and Ziyang Fan from the World Economic Forum point out:

> Information security, privacy and timely tech support can be big issues, as revealed by recent class actions filed against *Zoom*. Remote work can also

© ROLAND BENEDIKTER AND KARIM FATHI, 2022 | DOI:10.1163/9789004469686_034

complicate labour law issues, such as those associated with providing a safe work environment and income tax issues. Employees may experience loneliness and lack of work-life balance. If remote work becomes more common after the COVID-19 pandemic, employers may decide to reduce lease costs and hire people from regions with cheaper labour costs. Laws and regulations must be updated to accommodate remote work – and further psychological studies need to be conducted to understand the effect of remote work on people.

XIAO & FAN, 2020

33.2 eLearning

Similarly, to home office, eLearning is expected to increase. However, it will not completely replace going to school. Instead, many observers talk about "an intelligent combination of classroom and distance learning" (Steinschaden, 2020). By 2024, the market for digital education is expected to more than double, from 23 billion dollars in 2019 to more than 56 billion dollars. The Corona situation is an important door-opener (Ibid.). Starting from March 2020, Harvard and other trend-setting universities transferred most teaching online, saying at least part of the arrangement would stay in place (Harvard University, 2020). However, while the working-from-home trend is accompanied by an increased use of "spying" and controlling software, the eLearning trend is expected to increase disadvantages for students who are less technically gifted or who cannot afford advanced computers or broadband connections. Thus, the technologies could create a wider divide in terms of income level and digital readiness. Furthermore, this trend can also create economic pressure on parents (in reality still mostly women) who need to stay home to support their children with eLearning and may themselves work less (Xiao & Fan, 2020). Last, but not least, it could put a question mark over tuition fees, since many parents are less or not at all willing to pay high fees for their children studying de facto at home in front of their computers (Farrington, 2020). This could put business as usual in the traditional education sector into jeopardy, particularly in the higher and university sectors, which are also among the most important business branches of advanced societies as regards income, such as, for example, of Australia and the U.S (Great Britain, Department for Business, Innovation and Skills, 2013; Roser & Ortiz-Ospina, 2016; Globalization 101, 2016; UNESCO, 2020). According to research, the global higher education market alone was worth 48 billion US$ in 2015 and expected to grow to around

71 billion US$ by 2020 (Market and Market, 2020), with the global online education market showing a trend towards strong increase (Research and Markets, 2020) and the U.S. holding the biggest share. Some see the total global education spending comprising all categories and training until 2030 expanding to up to 10 trillion US$ due to the expansion of developing countries (Holon IQ, 2018), i.e., around 10 percent of the global GDP, of which, after Corona, a good part could be located online. Independent of the exact numbers, this trend is likely to continue if the general direction towards knowledge societies persists or is even virtually strengthened by Corona. Knowledge increase is a major factor of multi-resilience, not least because it is a "naturally" interconnected process among social strata, governance levels, countries and civilisations.

33.3 Telehealth

Telehealth utilisation has increased during the COVID-19 pandemic as an effective way to contain the spread of the virus while still providing essential primary care. Telehealth implies personal IoT devices tracking vital signs and chatbots making initial diagnoses (Xiao & Fan, 2020; Steinschaden, 2020). Several questions remain open for a post-Corona world. Similar to eLearning, telehealth also requires a certain level of tech literacy, as well as a good internet connection (Xiao & Fan, 2020). Moreover, medical care can typically only be provided to patients living in the same jurisdiction. Can a European psychotherapist treat a patient in the US, where the psychotherapist is not licensed? Where does the psychotherapy take place: where the client is, where the therapist is, in both places, in cyberspace, or in all three places? (Zur, n.d.) With the expected increasing use of telehealth in a post-Corona world, definitions of the location of treatment will have to be adapted to modern digital environments.

33.4 E-commerce and On-demand Economy

The notion "on-demand economy" means that products and services are brought to the customer within a short time after tapping on a smartphone app (Schultz, 2016). In times of lockdowns, such push-button services are among the big winners – especially when they satisfy basic human needs. Food suppliers or online pharmacies are recording gigantic growth rates (Trend Watching, 2020; Marr, 2020). However, observers highlight unprecedented negative side-effects correlating with the trend towards e-commerce (Trend Watching, 2020). On-demand companies sometimes employ precarious solo self-employed

TECHNOLOGICAL REQUIREMENTS

persons – without standard wages, occupational health and safety insurance (Schultz, 2014). According to an analysis by the Cologne Institute for Retail Research, the dying of shops in the stationary retail sector is also likely to accelerate until 2030 due to the Corona crisis (Der Spiegel, 2020d).

33.5 Automatisation

The Corona situation significantly pushed most if not all technologies of the Fourth Industrial Revolution. These include the Internet of Things (IoT), Big Data Analytics, Cloud Computing, Robotics, Additive Manufacturing, Blockchain, Augmented Reality and Artificial Intelligence (Frederico, 2020). As mentioned, robots have been used to disinfect areas, to walk dogs (Eadicicco, 2020) and will increasingly be used – in line with increasing e-commerce – for delivery (Lewis, 2020). Labour-intensive jobs are expected to be more and more substituted by robots. According to a study from Oxford Economics, from June 2019, more than 20 million jobs worldwide will be affected by automatisation up until 2030. This will include more than 1.5 million jobs in the United States, 11 million in China, and almost 2 million employees across EU member states (Oxford Economics, 2019). Particularly poorer local economies relying on lower-skilled workers will be affected; societies will therefore have to prepare for increasing income inequality correlated with increasing robotisation. However, the researchers of this study also predicted that the rise of robots will bring about increased productivity and economic growth. "This equates to adding an extra $4.9 trillion per year to the global economy by 2030 (in today's prices) – equivalent to an economy greater than the projected size of Germany's", the report said (Ibid., p.6).

33.6 Increasing Use of Immersive Technologies

The Internet has always been able to do both: active and passive consumption. The latter includes e.g. passive scrolling through *Instagram* or *Facebook*, while active consumption implies active participation and connection, making use of *Skype*, *WhatsApp*, Internet house-party apps or similar applications. In times of lockdowns, the active-connecting side seems to flourish. Similar to eLearning, virtual activities are not (yet) an equivalent substitute for a physical meeting. But it is a gain, in principle, that dozens of new forms of pro-active social behaviour on the net are emerging (Shultz, 2020). Immersive new technologies are also expected to receive a boost in post-Corona times, enabling people to obtain their experience-based status fixes, satisfaction of needs for entertainment and communication from increasingly improving virtual experiences, too. Hereby, social media, virtual museum tours, interactive VR gaming and e-sports are already dominant manifestations (Trend Watching, 2020; Xiao & Fun, 2020).

As can be deduced from these trends, the Coronavirus crisis has demonstrated the importance of "digital readiness", allowing businesses and private life to continue as usual during the pandemic. In order to remain competitive, societies in the post-Corona world will have to further develop the necessary infrastructure to support a more digitised world (ibid.). In this regard, according to *The New Yorker*, Estonia may be the nation best prepared for the post-Corona world, since it has been treating technology as critical infrastructure for decades and could thus serve as an inspiration for other societies to follow in the sign of the Corona teachings (Gessen, 2020).

What is probable is that these trends combined will further decisively strengthen the role of the Internet and of ICT in general, thus giving a further push to globalised business and finance Internet giants, mainly of American and Chinese origin, perhaps also including a new chance for global Internet and crypto-currencies. They will probably also co-drive fast innovation towards 5G technology, although the latter is contested concerning its dubious health impact (Nature Research, n.d.; Eliassen & Pena, 2020). Of increased importance will be the scrutinisation of the growing global and international power of Internet tech giants, as is the case in the U.S. with the congress antitrust hearing "Online platforms and market power, part 6: Examining the Dominance of Amazon, Facebook, Google and Apple" of July 2020 (U.S. House Committee On The Judiciary, 2020), considered by many to be "historic" (Lyons, 2020; Clayton, 2020). Similar developments of increasing scepticism and scrutiny are underway in the EU. From a multi-resilience perspective, it will be important to consider promoting not only technological innovation, but also social innovations and to anticipate rebound effects and new vulnerabilities arising from such new techno-environments in the future.

CHAPTER 34

Towards a Post-Corona World

Seven Upcoming Conflict Lines Open Societies Should Prepare For

What polarisations and conflict lines can be expected to shape the main discussions in a post-Corona world?

The post-Corona debate is not only full of contributions about chances, potentials and visions, but also implies a variety of pessimistic estimations and critical questions open societies should prepare for. In the summarising words of Stephen Walt, professor for International Relations at Harvard University:

> In short, COVID-19 will create a world that is less open, less prosperous, and less free. It did not have to be this way, but the combination of a deadly virus, inadequate planning, and incompetent leadership has placed humanity on a new and worrisome path.
> ALLEN ET AL., 2020

Other contributors remain – as we will see in more detail later – far more optimistic and hopeful. Yet the main potential threats in a post-Corona world have to be taken into account and considered carefully. Based on our findings and reflections in the previous chapters, we can summarise at least *seven* polarisation patterns and social conflict lines which are likely to increase as an effect of and after Corona and for which societies should therefore prepare for. Among these are three main polarisations that dominated the emotionally loaded debates during the Corona crisis and which are expected to continue in the post-Corona world.

34.1 Nationalism versus Globalism

One of the most contested topics in the post-Corona debate is about the nationalism versus globalism polarisation. To survive, most governments unilaterally closed borders and implemented measures widely falling back into national patterns and beliefs. At the same time, in some countries increasing racism could also be observed, particularly between Asians and Westerners and Africans.

© ROLAND BENEDIKTER AND KARIM FATHI, 2022 | DOI:10.1163/9789004469686_035

From an economic perspective, observers such as Richard N. Haass, President of the U.S. Council on Foreign Relations, or Laurie Garrett, former senior fellow of global health at the Council on Foreign Relations, predicted more accentuated moves towards selective self-sufficiency and decoupling, given supply chain vulnerability during Corona; even greater opposition to large-scale immigration; and a reduced willingness or commitment to relate regional to global problems (including climate change) (Ibid.). Similarly, the Foreign Ministry of Israel expects:

> the combination of ... tension and international economic distress, as well as a grounded aviation industry, to create 'new rules' about international trade. (...) International trade will change [after Corona], with nations pulling up the drawbridge and re-creating their own manufacturing and supply chains, particularly in areas critical to national security, despite the costs it would entail.
>
> KAHANA, 2020

Laurie Garrett anticipated that companies would reverse the just-in-time model of globally dispersed production. As mentioned, the result could be a dramatic new stage in global capitalism, in which supply chains are brought closer to home and filled with redundancies to protect against future disruption. This may cut into companies' near-term profits but render the entire system more resilient. Confirming this, Shannon K. O'Neil, a senior fellow at the Council on Foreign Relations, concludes that profitability may fall, but supply stability should rise (Allen et al., 2020). Additionally, since not all states will have the resources to develop the according resilience and to recover from the crisis, Richard Haass expects state weakness and failed states to become an even more prevalent feature in the post-Corona world than before (Ibid.).

Correlated with the trend towards nationalism and decoupling, geostrategic observers expect further global destabilisation in the post-Corona world in terms of intensifying competition between countries (Ibid.; Kahana, 2020). For example, Robin Niblett, Director and Chief Executive of Chatham House, states that it seems "highly unlikely (...) that the world will return to the idea of mutually beneficial globalization that defined the early 21st century" (Ibid.). Niblett asserts that "it will take enormous self-discipline for political leaders to sustain international cooperation and not retreat into overt geopolitical competition (and) to blame others for their failure" (Ibid.).

John Allen, President of the Brookings Institution, predicts that the pandemic will continue to depress economic activity and increase tension between countries. Over the long term, the pandemic is likely to reduce the productive capacity of the global economy, especially if businesses close and individuals detach from the labour force. As a result, the international system may, in turn, come under growing pressure, resulting in instability and widespread conflict within and across countries (Ibid.). In addition, some geostrategists, as mentioned, expect that the pandemic will accelerate the already ongoing shift in power and influence from West to East, maybe towards a more "China-centric globalization" (Ibid.; Kahana, 2020; Khan, 2020).

From another perspective, an increase in international cooperation could also be possible, including forms of bilateral solidarity initiatives and multilateral crisis coordination, particularly in terms of a strengthening of joint global public-health governance. Shivshankar Menon, former national security advisor to Indian Prime Minister Manmohan Singh, and a visiting professor at Ashoka University, India, states that "this is not yet the end of an interconnected world. The pandemic itself is proof of our interdependence". Despite increasing nationalism, Singh sees also signs of hope and good sense for increasing international cooperation. As an example, he refers to a recent initiative of India to convene a video conference of all South Asian leaders in order to craft a common regional response to the threat. "If the pandemic shocks us into recognizing our real interest in cooperating multilaterally on the big global issues facing us, it will have served a useful purpose" (Stiglitz et al., 2020). Also, as mentioned above, between the EU member states, geostrategic observers such as Ivan Krastev and Luuk van Middelaar identify a trend towards increasing political integration, even supported by nationalist governments, which are simply driven by cooperation needs "in a hostile environment" (Krupa & Lau, 2020).

Both extremes of nationalism and decoupling versus a new drive to cooperative globalism show ambivalent sides. They are likely to coexist in a post-Corona world. According to G. John Ikenberry, professor of politics and international affairs at Princeton University, the polarisation Corona has further accentuated might dissolve over time. Nationalist responses (including nationalism, great-power rivalry, strategic decoupling) have, in most cases, been tendentially stronger in the short term. Referring to the recovery processes after the 1930s' collapse of the world economy and in the Post-WWII era, Ikenberry assumes that over the longer term, European and Western democracies "will come out of their shells to find a new type of pragmatic and protective internationalism" (Allen et al., 2020).

34.2 Freedom versus Safety

A rather undisputed observation is that the Coronavirus crisis will bring the government back in a bigger way than before. Assumingly, people will rely more upon the government to organise a collective defence against future pandemics and other emergencies, and the government also has to save a sinking economy. The reputation of the state is expected to rise through this influence. This trend could be also observed in past crises, not only pandemics, but also economic crises (Subran, 2020). However, the Corona crisis brought about measures such as lockdowns and tracing-systems, reducing data protection and personal rights. In this regard, as mentioned, some observers and human rights activists are worried that the Corona crisis will increase the appeal of big data authoritarianism which has already been employed in countries such as China (Krastev, 2020a). As a result, it is expected that the increasingly emotionally loaded "freedom versus safety" debate will further spread in post-Corona times.

34.3 Professionalism versus Populism

Thirdly, some observers expect that major successes of populist politicians in the past ten years will be reversed by the Coronavirus crisis. To most people, dealing with the crisis meant, in practice, also having to trust experts, resulting in a growing legitimacy of professionals having led the fight against the virus. Although some state that professionalism is back in fashion (Ibid.), as mentioned earlier, we could also observe a rise of alternative media and conspiration-belief populism precisely due to the "reign of virologists". It remains open whether this scepticism will significantly fade away in post-Corona times. A society's policies of education, information and communication will have to consider that.

Besides these three main dialectics, many societies, particularly in the Western world, are affected by at least four more post-Corona social-conflict lines. These conflict lines refer to typical structural vulnerabilities, as outlined in a previous chapter. Almost all of the following are expected to gain in impact after the Corona crisis. Future preparedness in a post-Corona world will have to take them into account.

34.4 Class: Rich versus Poor

Many critical observers point out that the Corona pandemic has widened social and economic divisions (Fisher & Bubola, 2020). Several studies conducted in different countries such as the USA (Wimer, Collyer & Jaravel, 2019), Singapore (Abeysinghe & Yao, 2014), or Iran (Gholipour, Nguyen & Farzanegan, 2016) pointed out that high inequality correlates with rising costs of living and housing for people at the bottom of the income-distribution chain. Emergencies which reduce income hit these people hardest. The Center on Poverty and Social Policy of Columbia University calls this phenomenon "inflation inequality" (Wimer, Collyer & Jaravel, 2019). In the Corona crisis, this forced more lower-income families to live paycheck to paycheck. At the same time, the rise of part-time work and precarious solo self-employment means that low-income workers have fewer protections such as paid sick days. Lack of these protections and large numbers of uninsured increase risks of spreading the Coronavirus and potential future pandemics, and make emergencies worse (Gould, 2020). Highly competitive societies like the USA, with a modest welfare regime structure being characterised by high individual freedom but, at the same time, by high social inequality and low social protection, risk falling into a "Pandemic-Inequality-Feedback-Loop" (Fisher & Bubola, 2020). "Declining economic status leads to rising rates of chronic illness. That, in turn, further depresses productivity and raises healthcare costs, leading to more poverty, which leads to more disease" (Ibid.), as Fisher/Bubola state. The Royal Society B (Biology) confirms this with its "poverty-trap theory" (Bonds, M.H. Keenan, D.C., Rohani, P. Sachs J.D., 2009).

Social and economic divisions could be also observed in the employment sector. As the BBC and the International Labour Organization (ILO) estimated, a total of 81 percent of the global workforce of 3.3 billion people have had their workplace fully or partly closed during Corona. For the post-Corona world, the crisis is expected to "wipe out 6.7 percent of working hours across the world ... that is the equivalent of 195 million full-time workers losing their jobs" (BBC News, 2020q). The Arab region is predicted to be the worst-hit, with an 8.1 percent decline in working hours, equalling five million full-time workers (Ibid.).

As outlined earlier, automatisation is expected to be a further driver behind profound changes in the employment market. Hereby, particularly manual professions and jobs which do not require high education are expected to be substituted. These and other aspects of social and economic inequality have been accentuated and accelerated by Corona. They imply high conflict potentials which societies in the post-Corona world will have to prepare for, including measures promoting quick economic recovery and new demand for labour, respective skills education as well as effective welfare policies.

34.5 Ethnicity (Racism)

As described in previous chapters, the Corona pandemic has led to a rise in (covered and open) racism, including anti-Asian discrimination because of the Chinese origin of the Coronavirus (Larsson, 2020), but in this lane also against non-Asians (Vanderklippe, 2020). Within most modern societies, the fault line of racism is strongly correlated with the fault line of social inequality. "African Americans and Latinos are less likely to be able to work from home and more likely to be forced to take public transportation, increasing their risk of exposure to Coronavirus. Minority and low-income communities are more likely to experience food insecurity, which is linked to higher rates of obesity and diabetes, and less able to stockpile supplies", as Laughland/Zanolli pointed out (Laughland & Zanolli, 2020). The social upheavals, particularly in the USA and France, triggered by the murder of Floyd George were strongly associated with social inequality and structural racism, which the strong impact of the Corona pandemic on disadvantaged communities may have further accentuated.

As a sort of *antidoton*, the world may copy a concept used in New Zealand: "Ethnic solidarity" (Liu & Ran, 2020). As Liangni Sally Liu and Guanyu Jason Ran of Massey University, New Zealand, reported:

> A … key reason for New Zealand's success in containing the pandemic [wa]s the country's recognition of the importance of ethnic and racial solidarity in their response to it. While the deep-rooted racial discrimination and stigmatization towards certain ethnic groups, especially the Chinese, were catalyzed in some countries by their governments' COVID-19 rhetoric and mainstream media's racist sentiment, New Zealand's handling of ethnic and racial relations during the pandemic was much better. Following the WHO's suggestion that the naming of a human infectious disease should not indicate disease-related geographic locations, people's names, or cultural, population, industry, or occupational references, the New Zealand mainstream media engaged in very little anti-Chinese stigmatization narratives in its reporting. The government's slogan 'Unite Against -19' underlined the importance of solidarity across races and ethnicities from the very beginning of its pandemic response. Also, anti-racist government leadership was advocated, and a joint force comprising several governmental and civil organizations (including New Zealand Police, Crime Stoppers, NZ Human Rights Commission, and Netsafe.org.nz) has been organized specifically to deal with reports of racial hostility and discrimination during the pandemic (Ibid.).

TOWARDS A POST-CORONA WORLD

This leads the authors to the conclusion that:

> New Zealand's successful campaign against the virus are related to the country's external geopolitical relations and internal rationalization of public health priorities and resources. In general, success in combatting the pandemic in the country largely comes from the government's apolitical response, transparency, and belief in science. The collective effort made by public health institutions, opposition politicians, and general public also contributed to the success. In many countries outside of New Zealand, however, this pandemic has fueled blaming and stigmatization of many Asian ethnic communities, especially the Chinese. Stigmatizing discourse capitalizes on blame as a strategy for political gain. New Zealand's success story demonstrates how important it is to deal with a pandemic with less political intervention, as well as strengthened cross-cultural understanding and racial coordination. In all, is shows how important social solidarity is during a public health crisis without judgement of race, ethnicity, and culture (Ibid.).

34.6 Gender

The Coronavirus conflict context was a ubiquitous gender challenge throughout all societies in different manifestations. It reached from labour market exclusion of women to more pronounced domestic violence against them. With regard to the post-Corona world, some observers assume an "upgrading" of systems-relevant professions, including non-paid care, which typically still tend to be carried out rather by women than by men (Frey, 2020). This could regress achievements of gender emancipation, as it coincides with new challenges to them by technological advances per se (Gruber, 2020a). Not only feminists criticise the increase in domestic violence during the lockdown which affected women significantly more than men and apparently lowered the general threshold (both emotional, moral and societal) for applying violence in general. This was denounced as a social, not only as a gender problem.

34.7 Generation: Young versus Old

In some Western societies, the Corona crisis sharpened already existing intergenerational dynamics. These were present in the context of debates about climate change and the risk it presents, whereby younger generations were increasingly critical of their elders for – in their view – not thinking properly about the environmental future as the surrounding whole of any possible future. Paradoxically, the Coronavirus to some extent reversed these dynamics: being the risk group of Corona, the older members of society were much more vulnerable and felt threatened by millennials who were unwilling to change their way of living and sometimes manifested undisciplined behaviour. This intergenerational conflict could intensify, if lockdowns or curfews have to be re-imposed over the coming years due to new outbreaks (Krastev, 2020a); and it is likely to continue in principle in post-Corona times when the debate on climate change will be resumed.

CHAPTER 35

The Post-Corona World

Potentials and Visions for a "Better Globalised" International System

Aside from sometimes apocalyptic and often mixed-feelings trend predictions, many publications about the post-Corona world concentrated on identifying opportunities and chances to shape future preparedness. Most of these visions responded to ecologic, social and economic challenges that already existed before Corona. Many of them hereby related to major advanced society concepts, namely "the developed society" and "the sustainable society". In some respects, these contributions were also responses to social-conflict lines and unprecedented side-effects of the Corona crisis. Two types of contributions with particular value for our concept of "multi-resilient society" referring specifically to the post-Corona world can be distinguished:

- *Firstly*, contributions focusing on just one or several change-potential patterns for a better globalised system.
- *Secondly*, visions based on explicitly trans-sectoral models which have formerly been regarded as "utopian" and now present concrete references to post-Corona, linking it with concepts of sustainability and resilience.

We have discussed some of the ideas relating to the first type previously, and there are some more. Among the second-type visions, the universal basic income model and the idea of post-growth economy are mostly dominant in the European and liberal post-Corona discourse.

35.1 Idea Potentials: Policy-relevant Contributions by Intellectuals, Ecologists and Futurists

There are a variety of contributions about a post-Corona world which do not imply elaborated trans-sectoral approaches. However, they deal with potentials which could also part of a bigger post-Corona vision.

This applies particularly to the topic of gender equality, which is regarded by some observers as having now been improved under the effect of the Corona crisis and its teachings (Christoph, 2020). For example, the authors of a study about "The Impact of COVID-19 on Gender Equality" (Alon et al, 2020), conducted by the University of Mannheim, concluded for the future:

© ROLAND BENEDIKTER AND KARIM FATHI, 2022 | DOI:10.1163/9789004469686_036

Beyond the immediate crisis, there are opposing forces which may ultimately promote gender equality in the labour market. First, businesses are rapidly adopting flexible work arrangements, which are likely to persist. Second, there are also many fathers who now have to take primary responsibility for child-care, which may erode social norms that currently lead to a lopsided distribution of the gender division of labour in house work and child care (Ibid.).

From an ecological perspective, contributors such as the European futurologist Matthias Horx point out that 2020 was the first year in which human CO_2 emissions dropped, indicating that satellite images showed the industrial areas of China and Italy widely free of smog. "That very fact will do something to us" (Horx, 2020). Accordingly, countries being particularly affected by climate change, such as Australia, whose fire risk has been boosted by 30 percent over the past years and whose fires have lately become worse than any prediction, are advised to take the Corona situation as a chance for a shift to more climate-friendly green energy. Further contributions emphasise that the necessary post-Corona transition to renewable energy would create an opportunity to design the next energy system "community-owned" (Angell, 2020). As an example, Alaska owns the state's most valuable oil fields and collects rent from companies which use them and returns the resulting dividends to the residents of Alaska by means of a paycheck every year. As community-owned renewable energy projects are growing, they could create a new similar income source for individuals in the future (Ibid.).

This participatory approach applies also – according to other contributions – to the discussion about the future of work in a post-Corona world which should have to become more inclusive of all workers. There is the hope that the pandemic may force people and the elites to become more solidary with workers across all sectors, particularly with unjustly treated sectors and industries (Leberecht, 2020a). Referring to this, contributors from the *Journal of Beautiful Business* saw the crisis as an opportunity to catalyse what they hoped would be "The Great Reset" (Jiang, 2020). This – at first glance – rather romantic approach would also imply, as business consultants such as Jessica Orkin, CEO of SYPartners, stated, that the teachings of the Corona crisis function as a "remover of illusions" and as a chance for companies to build better ways of working together. The hope is that the crisis ultimately helps leaders "design their organizations as organisms whose output is whole and healthy people, not just financial returns or consumer value" (Leberecht, 2020a).

THE POST-CORONA WORLD

Further contributions pointed out opportunities resulting from what they called "the art of stillness" (Leberecht, 2020b). This would gain more relevance taking on the experience of times of confinement where the world came to a halt. This experience may offer opportunities for a new interest in wisdom practices like meditation in order to avoid distractions from everyday life hectic. "Solitude is the loneliness in which you can hear something wiser than yourself" (Ibid.), as the meditation expert and author Siddharth Pico Raghavan Iyer stated (Iyer, 2009). Iyer viewed Corona as a chance for everyone to reassess one's priorities and see the world anew, beyond the many distractions of micro-interactions and -business on social media, etc. The hope is that the post-Corona "world, at the core, will remain calm and serene, as will our lives, empty of clutter and noise" (Leberecht, 2020b).

Muhammad Yunus, who was awarded both the Nobel Peace Prize and the Alternative Nobel Prize (The Right Livelihood Award) for founding the Grameen Bank and pioneering the concepts of microfinance and microcredits, sees the central role of a post-Corona world in a "New Recovery Program" (NRP) in the private sector. He suggests investing in social businesses, meaning "a business created solely for solving people's problems, without taking any personal profit by the investors except to recoup the original investment. After original investment comes back all subsequent profits are ploughed back into the business" (Yunus, 2020). According to Yunus, after Corona, governments could foster social businesses through "Social Business Venture Capital Funds" and even prioritise them and undertake additional measures, such as reviving and expanding healthcare and socio-economic essential services. Yunus stressed that "people are born as entrepreneurs, not as job-seekers" (Ibid.). NRP should:

> break a traditional division of work between citizens and the government. It is taken for granted that the citizens' role is to take care of their families and pay taxes; it is the responsibility of the government (and to a limited extent of the non-profit sector) to take care of all collective problems, like climate, jobs, healthcare, education, water, and so on. NRP should break this wall of separation and encourage all citizens to come forward and show their talent as problem-solvers by creating social businesses. Their strength is not in the size of their initiatives, but in their number. Each small initiative multiplied by a big number turns out to be a significant national action (Ibid.).

From a business perspective, journalist Frankie Wallace summarised for the post-Corona world:

There will be far more accountability and transparency in expense accounting, with automation playing an increasingly important role in this process. Demands for higher minimum wage rates will grow and will likely be more successful than they have been in the past due to greater recognition of the massive wage gap that currently exists. Finally, online banking systems will become more robust, secure, sophisticated, and ubiquitous in our changed, post-corona reality.

WALLACE, 2020

35.2 Universal Basic Income as a Driver towards Better Socio-economic Resilience?

As stressed earlier, the Corona crisis had severe socio-economic impacts on nearly all affected societies, putting their welfare systems under pressure. Many governments have decided to implement unconditional fiscal aid to support the population strata being mostly affected by the economic downturn. In most cases, these were short-term measures in terms of "helicopter money", i.e., money distributed unconditionally and without particular criteria or specific aim. However, the concept of universal basic income, which has been debated for decades, may be gaining more supporters after Corona. According to an opinion poll by Oxford University's professor of European Studies, Timothy Garton Ash, after Corona and its economic fallout on small and medium enterprises, almost 71 percent of Europeans were in favour of introducing a universal basic income (Garton Ash, 2020; Garton Ash & Zimmermann, 2020), and Spain was about to institutionalise it as a permanent system in its welfare policy (BBC News, 2020ii).

The concept, in principle, implies unconditional, periodic payment delivered to all people, i.e., without a specific prerequisite or work requirement. The amount of the payment varies from model to model, often between 500 and 1,500 dollars; however, the inherent common idea is that it should be sufficient to meet a person's basic needs, at or above the poverty line. Some approaches consider a combination of universal basic income with negative income tax in which the payment is gradually reduced with higher labour income in order to incentivise the people to work and not to "Do nothing". Since 2010, basic income has become an active topic in political debates in many countries. So far, no country has introduced an unconditional basic income by law (Sheahen, 2012).

For at least three reasons, the Coronavirus crisis favoured the development of the Western public debate towards universal basic income.

THE POST-CORONA WORLD   217

Reason 1: Overcoming the Pierson trilemma. Firstly, it is noteworthy from the resilience perspective that any existing welfare system features typical vulnerabilities and inherent conflict potentials. These are outlined in Paul Pierson's so-called "trilemma of the service economy" in which, in his view, "the goals of employment growth, wage equality and budgetary constraint come into increasing conflict" (Pierson, 2001). Accordingly, each of the existing typical three welfare regimes offer a different response to this trilemma (Ibid.):

- The liberal welfare regime is characterised by a high level of market dominance and private provision. Workers' protection and social security are relatively low; however, individual freedom and the possibility to find a job (at least low-paid) are relatively high. Representative countries are mostly Anglophone, including the USA, the UK, Australia and New Zealand (Esping-Andersen, 1990). A liberal welfare regime avoids the problems of budgetary constraints and unemployment through policies resulting in the expansion of low-wage private sector service employment. Thus, inequality is relatively high (Pierson, 2001).

- The *conservative welfare regime* offers a higher degree of social security, based on social insurance schemes. Based on statist, corporate and paternalistic structures, workers enjoy higher protection and social security but, at the same time, flexibility on the employment market and respective individual freedom are relatively lower. Representative countries are located in Continental Europe, such as Germany, Austria and France (Esping-Andersen, 1990). The conservative welfare regime has a medium budgetary constraint, resulting in relatively low income inequality. Due to limited public-service employment, labour-market regulations and high fixed costs, private-service-sector employment is, however, more difficult and less flexible (Pierson, 2001).

- The *social democratic welfare regime* provides universal access to social services based on citizenship. Accordingly, social equality is higher than in the other regimes. State regulation is relatively high, granting a high degree of social security and, at the same time, "steered" integration on the labour market. Representative countries can mostly be found in the Scandinavian region (Esping-Andersen, 1990) according to the "Nordic Model"(Toben et al., 2007; Hilson, 2011), sometimes also branded the "Northern Model" (Traegardh, 2007), which, to some extent, after WWII was based on teachings and elements of German Classical Idealist philosophy of the 18th and 19th centuries. By expanding the public-service sector, the social democratic welfare regime can maintain high employment without worsening income inequality. This leads, however, to high bureaucracy and high costs (Pierson, 2001).

Hence, all three typological welfare regimes have typical strengths and weaknesses. In non-crisis times, the social democratic welfare regime appears to have the lowest conflict potential; paradoxically, the liberal welfare regimes, which are characterised by high inequality and low social safety, appear correlated with higher degrees of psychological well-being and trust than the conservative types (Fathi, 2013). During the European (and partly American) migration crisis in 2015/2016, the relatively bureaucratic and highly regulated social democratic regimes proved to be relatively quickly overloaded and thus poorly able to copy with sudden crises but rather relying on stability and unchanging conditions (Djuve, 2016). In 2020, during the Coronavirus crisis, liberal welfare regimes, notably in the USA, characterised by low social support and high inequality, appeared to be particularly challenged when it comes to the aforementioned "Pandemic-Inequality-Feedback-Loop". Within the scope of socio-economic multi-resilience, a fundamental challenge in the post-Corona world will be to overcome the "Pierson trilemma".

Thus, it might be recommendable for policymakers to remain open to new solutions finding an intermediate solution in welfare policy design addressing relevant factors such as employment, equality, decommodification and low bureaucratic costs. A model inspired by a "universal basic income guarantee" could provide answers to some of these questions, although it would have to be, in any case, contextualised and adapted. It implies a relatively high universal social security guarantee with relatively low bureaucratic costs and social expenses (Bien, 2017). Further empirical studies should scrutinise the main counterarguments to that model, namely potential work disincentives and the rise in public expense. However, empirical evidence on the high correlation between social conflicts and unemployment suggests that unemployment or "Do nothing" is not a situation which most humans typically choose willingly, since humans on average like to be creative and active rather than non-achieving and passive (Fathi, 2013).

Moreover, as the Coronavirus crisis is expected to push the trend of digitalisation and automatisation further, information societies will, as mentioned, in any case have to find ways of dealing with increasing substitution of human workers by machines and resulting technological unemployment (Pouliakas, 2018). At the same time, increased automatisation is expected to bring about increased productivity and economic growth worldwide, which could be taxed. Thus, according to prominent supporters such as Andrew McAfee or Erik Brynjolfsson, universal basic income combined with a Negative Income

THE POST-CORONA WORLD   219

Tax (NIT) may be the answer to a post-Corona economy which will be "heavy on technology, but light on labour" (McAfee & Brynjolfsson, 2014). However, even among supporters, the concrete design, financing and implementation process of a universal basic-income concept which could be driven by the automatisation trend is highly contested. Zoltan Istvan, founder of the American Transhumanist Party, estimates a successful implementation would take at least two decades from 2020 on, "when driverless cars, robot food servers, and AI attorneys – just to name a few – do everything for us, leaving tens of millions unemployed forever" (Love, 2017).

What does all of this mean for post-Corona multi-resilience? It remains open to further exploration and testing, whether universal basic income really contributes to a more resilient welfare policy with potentially low, ignorable or non-existent side-effects. Multi-resilient policy design, which will be described in more detail in the following section, would require mechanisms to explore and develop these concepts, not least by including means of collective intelligence and wisdom.

35.3 Post-Growth and Degrowth as Responses to the Economic and Ecological Challenges in a Post-Corona World?

In addition to the universal basic income concept, the concept of post-growth and degrowth economy is gaining increasing attention in debates about the post-Corona world. These concepts refer to the limits-to-growth dilemma (Post Growth Institute, n.d.). They assume that, on a planet of finite resources, populations and economies cannot grow infinitely (Jackson, 2009). The concepts usually acknowledge that economic prosperity has beneficial effects up to a certain point,[1] but beyond that point, it would be necessary to look for other indicators and techniques to increase human wellbeing (Jackson, 2009). Typically, post-growth and degrowth do not specify the answer to the limits-to-growth challenge, but instead develop emerging solutions that are appropriate with regards to place, time, resource and cultural factors (Treehugger, n.d.). Although both post-growth and degrowth (or: "zero-growth") differ in the radicality of their demands, both terms are often used synonymously. Currently, Kate Raworth's model of a post-growth "Doughnut Economy" and Niko Paech's

---

1   According to estimations in the field of happiness research, that point might be at $25,000 GDP/capita. Beyond this amount, there is no significant increase in psychological well-being (Wilkinson & Pickett, 2009).

"zero-growth" approach (however, he often used to call it "post-growth") belong to the most popular ones shaping the discourse.

Based on the Oxford University economist Kate Raworth's 2017 bestselling book "Doughnut Economics: Seven Ways to Think Like a 21st-Century Economist" (Raworth, 2018), the city of Amsterdam has officially decided to adopt and to implement a variation of the post-growth concept as the first city worldwide (Purdy, 2020). Raworth's "Doughnut Model" attempts to balance the needs of people without harming the environment. Hereby, there are two "rings" to consider (Figure 7): the basic needs of the population (inner ring of needs) and the ecological needs of the planet (outer ring of needs).

The inner ring implies the minimum context for leading a good life, derived from the United Nations' Sustainable Development Goals (SDG's) long agreed

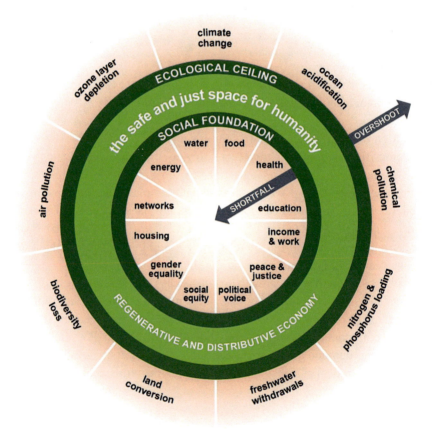

FIGURE 7   "Doughnut economics" related to the Model of Postgrowth Economy
SOURCE: RAWORTH, N.D,

THE POST-CORONA WORLD

by world leaders of every political stripe. These needs range from food and clean water to a certain level of housing, sanitation, energy, education, health-care, gender equality, income and political voice. Anyone who would not attain these minimum standards would live in the doughnut's hole. The outer ring represents the ecological limits being drawn up by earth-system scientists. It highlights the boundaries of the planet's resources beyond which humanity should not go. These limits are to avoid damaging the climate, soils, oceans, the ozone layer, freshwater and biodiversity. Between the two rings is the dough, where people's needs and that of the planet are being met (Raworth, 2018). Thus, the "Doughnut" is a model to consider "the core needs of all but within the means of the planet" (Boffey, 2018) in the economic activity of a society.

Similar to the Doughnut Model, Carys Roberts, Executive Director of the British Institute for Public Policy Research (IPPR), considered the recovery from the Corona crisis as an "opportunity to build a better kind of economy and society". This would imply the moment to think "beyond a blind pursuit of GDP" and to reconsider what is valuable in society (Roberts, 2020). According to her, this should be a "green recovery", including work and training programmes in low-carbon heating, water efficiency and flood-protection (Harvey, 2020) on the UK's path to net-zero carbon. The recovery should not just focus on boost-ing the GDP, but should target "well-paid, high-quality jobs" across the country, providing ordinary people with access to secure incomes and providing the state with a sustainable tax base (Roberts, 2020).

A more radical approach of post-growth, which could be also regarded as "zero-growth" or "degrowth", is stressed by Germany's most popular "plural-ist economy" representant, Niko Paech, Professor of Pluralist Economics at the University of Siegen. He questions economic growth in total, even green growth, and pledges for a rethinking of prosperity. Paech emphasises the need to reduce global consumption and production in order to achieve a socially, economically and ecologically sustainable society based on well-being as an indicator of prosperity instead of GDP. Paech advocates deglobalisation, con-sidering that it would reduce the cost advantages of unlimited division of labour and thus would lead to higher prices but, at the same time, would lead to more crisis stability and new jobs, albeit less in the academic than in the craft sector. According to Paech, living in a post-growth economy would con-tribute to a more stress-free and responsible life at the price of less consump-tion and travel opportunities, which might perhaps not be a bad deal at all (Paech, 2020).

In order to achieve re-globalisation in the sense of de-globalisation, Paech suggests that if products for which global supply chains or interdependencies were accepted before Corona and which meet one of the following four criteria, should now be produced domestically or avoided altogether. Firstly, if they are pure luxury; secondly, if they cause great ecological damage; thirdly, if their production and distribution is accompanied by social disruption; and fourthly, if they are so essential that their external production leads to critical dependencies. According to Paech, agricultural work should become more attractive again. This would be flanked by more appropriate wages and a 20-hour working week, leaving room for other, among them knowledge-intensive, activities. In Paech's understanding, post-growth means making people less dependent on consumer needs; firstly, by more frugality and liberation from sensory overload (according to the maxim "All you need is less") and secondly, by fostering locally produced supply with more durable, frugal products (Paech, 2012).

As Eurac Research scholar Daria Habicher put it in the Global Studies journal *Global-E*, the Corona crisis could have helped particularly the degrowth debate to acquire a larger audience, at least as a thought model to be taken seriously and to be worked with, since Corona transformed degrowth from an idea to the factual reality on a global level. This could lead to a "rethinking of globalisation" from a degrowth standpoint. In Habicher's vision, degrowth does not mean to "Do nothing". It is the exact opposite: an economic activity but from a different viewpoint and with a different attitude. In Habicher's words:

> Over the past three decades, globalization – understood as a mainly neoliberal project of liberalization and integration of countries into a global trading network – has been viewed as a great opportunity for nations to *develop* and *grow* in order to reduce poverty and increase social prosperity. The underlying assumption is that economic growth presents the best available solution to overcoming both social and material inequality. Ever since, international organizations such as the World Trade Organization, the World Bank, and the United Nations have been at the forefront in promoting this idea ... While the world community still holds to the dogma of infinite and linear economic growth, more and more scholars and activists argue that it is time to give up this credo. Unlimited population expansion and unlimited GDP growth is untenable due to planetary resource constraints, negative environmental impacts, adverse outcomes for social groups, and additional stress on lifestyles and mental health ... Today, postgrowth seems to be no longer just an ideological or normative concept. It has become in many ways our reality, although forced by a catastrophe. After the corona outbreak at the end of 2019, the IMF forecasted that in 2020 advanced economies would expect a negative growth rate of 6.1 percent, and the emerging markets a rate of negative one percent. These numbers indicate the urgency for countries characterized by

THE POST-CORONA WORLD

negative or low growth rates to develop new strategies for dealing with this *postgrowth reality*. Whether this should also be the case for the poorest countries is a question requiring a different response ... Postgrowth is neither the opposite of growth, nor does it indicate the absence of growth at all: Certain things would still grow, such as the deployment of green technologies and the availability of healthcare. Furthermore, even whole economies of poorer countries of the Global South might still be growing in order to guarantee a worthy life for their citizens. At the same time, however, some countries, mostly located in the Global North, need to overcome the growth imperative and start seriously thinking about alternative economic systems that limit the human ecological footprint. Furthermore, humanity should continue to *develop*, but 'rather than boosting material consumption, it can grow artistically, culturally, intellectually, and technologically'.

HABICHER, 2020

And this leads Habicher to the conclusion that:

The postgrowth movement stimulates a discussion about possible alternatives of how to organize economies and how to build a sustainable society [after Corona] ... Postgrowth is neither the opposite of growth, nor does it indicate the absence of growth at all: Certain things would still grow, such as the deployment of green technologies and the availability of healthcare ... The postgrowth movement responds to some of the challenges [of Re-Globalization after Corona] in an interesting, although open manner, aiming to reframe current social and economic systems on a local as well as global level, making step by step revisions to globalization from the ground up. It provides powerful tools to facilitate the emergence of new social imaginaries and stimulates a new way of thinking about globalization in the Anthropocene. In the end, the big challenge regarding globalization will be to get millions of people thinking 'outside the box.' But in order to do so, humanity first needs to become critically conscious of basic thought and action patterns around such concepts as prosperity, democracy, freedom, equality, leisure, happiness, and the human-nature relationship (Ibid.).

Although post-growth remains highly contested and, as we could see, also inherently heterogeneous regarding the desirable degree of radicality, it can be regarded as a possible approach towards more multi-resilience in a post-Corona world, addressing various global challenges at the same time, including, for example, economic instability, decreasing planetary resources, and climate change. Thus, despite criticism, similarly to the universal basic-income model, post-growth is gaining increasing attention and should thus be seriously considered for further assessment, experimental testing and development.

PART 5

Post-Corona Policy Design

∴

CHAPTER 36

Chances and Limits of Resilience

The Development Paradox and the Increasing Danger of Man-made Disasters with Multi-sectoral Side Effects

The above-mentioned "alternative" systemic options for renewing aspects of the Pre-Corona global system towards re-globalisation and post-Corona in more green, sustainable and de-centred ways have been taken up and debated mainly by the European Union (EU) and its de facto government, the European Commission (EC), much less by other global protagonists and powers. Given that the EU is a major trade and economic protagonist but represents only 6–7 percent of the global population, with shares shrinking, it remains open as to to which extent a European lead in such innovation may change the international system. The question is the more legitimate given that these measures require, as a fundament, a working democratic system of participation and inclusion, which many other crucial global protagonists in the post-Corona world neither dispose of nor want to implement. Not completely in alignment with such reality, in the EU itself, highly idealistic – to some extent even radical – post-Corona voices blossom. In spring 2020, the newly funded think-tank ESIR, connected with the European Commission, wrote with great pathos, but probably overestimating the will of average Europeans to systemically implement "radical" green-leftist change, as well as psychologically over-responding to the historic "break" Corona caused:

> The European Commission seems increasingly aware of the need for forward-looking solutions, rather than quick fixes to outstanding emergencies. And it is aware that there is no turning back to the status quo ante, which was already far from sustainable in the long term. Citizens in many EU countries are in agreement. Going back to pre-COVID-19 models of growth is not an option – greater focus should be placed on valuing 'sufficiency' and 'essential job' creation. Creating greater resilience by design, not by disaster should be at the core of a coordinated EU recovery response to the COVID-19 outbreak. In the midst of a global health emergency and imminent economic recession, an integrated 'people, planet and prosperity' recovery model and a concerted investment in research and innovation-led transformation will enable us to

© ROLAND BENEDIKTER AND KARIM FATHI, 2022 | DOI:10.1163/9789004469686_037

emerge from this pandemic more resilient as a region, as countries and as localities.

EUROPEAN COMMISSION, DIRECTORATE-GENERAL FOR RESEARCH
AND INNOVATION, 2020

It was symptomatic, though, that this statement changed the maxim of the Social Finance and Social Banking sector: "People, planet and profit" without declaring it and eliminating the "profit" aspect (Benedikter 2011b; 2011a). Radical approaches in European mainstream stem mainly from the leftist and democratic socialist belief of being in possession of "the truth" regarding the right path to follow. In post-Corona times, these approaches increase their minority-pressure upon silent minorities, legitimating themselves with the Corona anxiety on the one hand and the post-Corona challenges on the other. Yet radical approaches have poor chances of succeeding on an international level, and they delineate both the limits of European outreach on the one hand and of the traditional "resilience" discourse as a constructive social option on the other hand.

In essence, although resilience brings about several improvements compared to the common concept of sustainability, we must still assume some limits, which should be considered in order to develop future preparedness in post-Corona times. Although resilience does include strategies responding to all phases of crisis manifestation – i.e., before the crisis (preparedness), during the crisis (reaction) and after the crisis (recovery) – we can criticise that it provides no answer as regards preventing undesired man-made side effects. It simply accepts them and, in a certain way, contributes to creating them. Multi-resilience, rather than pointing at radical perspectives, has to deal with such limits in a pragmatic and enhancement-oriented way. The limits of resilience are illustrated, for example, by the so-called "development paradox".

According to the British historian Ian Morris, the development paradox describes that the development of any society always produces precisely those forces that impede its further growth. In other words: Every achievement and every problem solution create new problems (I. Morris, 2010). This has been confirmed by resilience researchers Zolli and Healy (2013), who claim that every new resilience strategy per se would be accompanied by new vulnerabilities.

For example, the development of the Internet as the prerequisite of today's information societies provides a high level of protection against the loss of information as a result of physical events (such as a conventional war) because it is stored virtually and in principle cannot be destroyed like a library. At the same time, this very problem-solving technology opens up new vulnerabilities through new virtual threats, such as cyber viruses and attacks (Ibid.). Similarly,

CHANCES AND LIMITS OF RESILIENCE

with regard to the Corona crisis, we could observe that today's highly inter-connected infrastructure brought about considerably more effective and faster information transfer. What is certain is that each level of complexity generates new challenges that are man-made – and this is a crucial factor to consider. Resilience in this regard largely concentrates on enhancing collective intelli-gence which is crucial in order to develop technological and social innovations and to adapt to an increasingly complex environment. However, it so far did not sufficiently critically question that collective intelligence, as in principle empowered by the Internet, also contributes towards generating problems and vulnerabilities for which it has to find new solutions.

This ambiguous process has been described by the model of "risk societies" or "reflexive modernity" of social scientists such as Anthony Giddens, Niklas Luhmann and Ulrich Beck who identified man-made problems that society has to face as unintended side effects of complex solution patterns. Giddens used the image of the "Jagannath wagon", which originates from Hindu philos-ophy. Jagannath is a Hindi word and roughly means "Lord of the World", which is a title of the Hindu god Krishna. The Jagannath wagon is a huge vehicle that used to be driven through the streets of India once a year with an image of the god Krishna. It is said that some of his followers even threw themselves under this chariot out of reverence (Giddens, 1995).

Transferred to the present day, this image symbolises, according to Giddens, an "unbridled and enormously powerful machine that we as human beings can control collectively to a certain degree, but which at the same time is in danger of being urgently removed from our control and could destroy itself" (Ibid., p.173). The sociologist Ulrich Beck coined the term "risk society" in a similar context. The term describes the fact that at an advanced level of modernity, the social production of wealth systematically goes hand in hand with the produc-tion of social risk. According to this, it is not only a matter of distribution and conflicts of the society about scarcity, which, according to classical neoliberal theory, must be solved through economic growth, but also of "problems and conflicts arising from the production, definition and distribution of scientifi-cally and technically produced risks" (Beck, 1986).

A great number of extreme risks (see Figure 8) which could potentially seriously harm or even destroy humanity are man-made and called "existen-tial risks". An existential risk is defined as an event that is capable of extin-guishing intelligent life that has developed on earth or of drastically and permanently restricting its desirable development (Bostrom, 2013; Bostrom, 2002). Despite its enormous significance, the systematic analysis of existen-tial risks only began in the early 2000s (Bostrom, 2002). In the analysis of Nick Bostrom, the Director of Oxford's Future of Humanity Institute (FHI), who is considered a pioneer in this field, distinguishes the concept of "existential risk" from "global catastrophic risk". In comparison to all other types of risk, existential risk manifests itself in its greater spatial and temporal scope and in its lethality.

To date, existential risks are not likely to occur frequently. However, due to their critical impact, their potential occurrence remains significant. Corona was one expression of such potential. With increasing technological development in the areas of Artificial Intelligence (AI), nano- and biotechnology, it can be assumed that capacities to solve today's global problems will increase, but also the likelihood of man-made existential risks in post-Corona times. For example, strategic competition among nation-states is changing in response to emergent digital and AI-enabled technologies. Without doubt, this is creating new instabilities and flows ridden by uncertainty. Typical scenarios could be the emergence of a superior super-intelligent AI accidentally wiping out humanity or an earth-wide expansion of self-replicating nano-robots going out of control ("grey goo-scenario") (Bostrom, 2016), an intensified nuclear threat scenario (what analysts call "Wormhole escalation in the new nuclear age" (Hersman, 2020)) or maybe another super-lethal pandemic (Ibid.). Those who think Corona is over with Corona, are wrong.

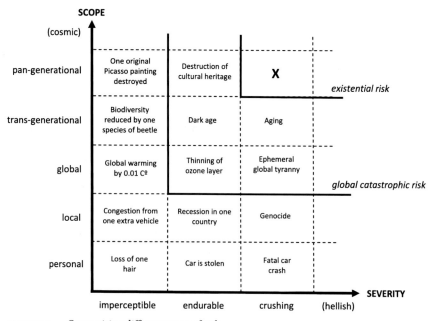

FIGURE 8   Categorising different types of risks
SOURCE: BOSTROM, 2013, P. 17

Although multi-resilience does not provide a concrete solution to these dilemmas of resilience, the practical implications remain to be addressed as well as can be in contextualised settings. According to Bostrom, this would mean to foster global interdisciplinary joint research and knowledge distribution, in order to maximise collective awareness towards future risk scenarios. Before Corona, despite some rhetoric this was widely neglected. This does not only imply enhancing collective intelligence – which is a major component of multi-resilience – but also "collective wisdom". This term has been coined by Bostrom himself (Bostrom 2016). "Collective wisdom" can be accessed by expanding the concept of multi-resilience further and by contrasting and integrating it with other contemporary concepts of social future preparedness.

CHAPTER 37

Towards a Broader and More Integrated Policy of Future Preparedness

Contributions from Selected Guiding Concepts

From a wider perspective, we can distinguish between at least three major discourses and respective guiding concepts of future preparedness which today's societies are more or less orienting themselves to: resilience, sustainability and development. Since each one of them – and, to a certain extent, even an integrated and expanded concept of multi-resilience – proves to be limited, we hold that all three should be politically and socially combined in post-Corona times.

37.1 A Brief Outline of Three Contemporary Coping Concepts: Development, Sustainability, Resilience

All of these three major discourses imply more or less concrete concepts for a "future-prepared" society, yet in different ways and with different accents (Fathi, 2019c):

1) The discourse and concept of *developed society* is the relatively oldest one. It has existed for as long as there has been modernity; some even hold since there have been settled communities. This may be explained by the fact that the development of a society is essentially linked to the most existential of all questions – that of inner cohesion that makes it able to co-develop. This cohesion is ensured above all by the fact that society must enable its population to meet its (basic) needs and develop its own creative potential. The issue of development contains many different facets, such as the "happy society" or the "economically effective" and/or "economically efficient" or the "conflict-preventing welfare" society which may all be drivers of productivity and wealth-generation. Given exponential progresses in key development technologies for the future such as in the areas of AI or microbiome research, it can be observed that the context of technological development is likely to dominate the further discourse of development in toto. To date, Western societies are (still) considered to be leading development-wise in global

© ROLAND BENEDIKTER AND KARIM FATHI, 2022 | DOI:10.1163/9789004469686_038

comparison, although observers state that the 21st century will be an "Asian century" (Khanna, 2019) or an "African century" (Benedikter, Tsedze & Unterkircher, 2019). The major contribution of the developed society concept is that it drives technological and economic progress and achievements which are necessary to enable socio-economic satisfaction and social cohesion and thus prevent social-conflict potential. With regard to the Corona crisis, the accent on development enables more efficient research on faster employment of new vaccines and technological protection solutions against pandemics. However, development also unavoidably drives the above-mentioned development paradox – in other words: more and more achievements bring along more complexity, and more complexity brings along more and more complex undesired side effects.

2) The concept of *sustainable society* extends the view of economic and social development to include the aspect of inter-generational equity. At the intersection of the ecological and economic pillars, representatives of this concept discuss whether "clean" or "green" growth is possible by means of technological and social innovations. Altogether, at least three schools of thought can be distinguished within the sustainability discourse, differing from each other with regard to the degree of transformation of the current paradigm of socio-economic growth as related to a finite planet. These are the schools of "green growth", "post-social market economy" and "post-growth economy" (Paech, 2012). An albeit often little-noticed characteristic of the sustainability discourse is its comparatively high normative orientation; and another special feature is its wide focus traditionally going beyond the society context, comprising the whole global environmental context. The core focus of the concept of sustainable society consists above all in its inbuilt holistic crisis-preventive measures, covering all ethical-human-social, ecological and economic pillars. The concept of sustainable society overlaps in the social-ethical field with the claim of the developed society to secure the needs of the citizens. However, the sustainability discourse has a much sharper eye on the ecological impact of economic growth and therefore criticises the "automatised" growth paradigm of the concept of developed society. In international comparison, Nordic and Continental European societies are currently leading the discourse on sustainable societies. With regard to Corona, this concepts privileges long-term solutions and prevention measures over short-term answers, even if these are against the immediate interests of the

population, such as free movement or the right to die, and it puts the analysis and solution search in a more holistic and inclusive picture that includes more facets than the developed society idea.

3) The concept of the *resilient society* is the comparatively newest one. It represents, to a certain extent, the continuation of the sustainability debate without replacing the model of the sustainable society, but aiming at taking it to a new level. If the motive of the sustainability debate existed in the question "How can we avoid humane, economic and ecological crises through inclusive and holistic foresighted actions (both in politics, the social sphere and economics)?", the resilience perspective is analogously characterised by the reflection: "How can societies be made more robust in the face of humane, economic and ecological crises, which are in any case inevitable and sooner or later will hit and be endured and mastered, in the ideal case triggering progress instead of regression?". Compared to a sustainable society, the resilient society is relatively free of ideology and the respective strands of ethics. Although it is also a matter of preventing social, ecological and economic crises in the best possible way, the basic motive of resilience is of purely pragmatic nature – it is simply a matter of "survival". As outlined above, the discourse about the resilient society is per se already very complex. On the one hand, it refers to all levels of a system (individuals, teams, organisations and societies); on the other hand it goes beyond the three pillars of sustainability and addresses any possible types of crises (e.g. also technological crises being not covered by the three pillars). Although we can outline at least five dimensions of resilience which together form the overarching advanced concept of multi-resilience, and which, in principle, can be applied to any country or system, it is not yet possible to determine which country and which political system in the world might be the most (multi-)resilient one. The reason is that resilience is not easy to measure, and the effectiveness of resilience capacities can only be clearly assessed in the face of concrete and direct crises. Hereby, resilience shows to be highly context-dependent. Even within the singular and to date unique context of pandemic-management during the Corona crisis, we could observe several very different countries with widely different strategies which were all defended by politicians as being particularly resilient and effective. Often-cited "success examples" include Sweden, which had a very open pandemics policy without confinement, but recommendations to keep only the risk-groups isolated on a voluntary basis.

As mentioned, after the first more accurate evaluations, this model proved much less successful than initially thought, producing one of the largest numbers of Corona victims pro capita in Europe and the by far largest among Scandinavian countries (Savage, 2020). Other examples are South Korea (Kim, 2020) or Taiwan (Griffiths, 2020b), similarly implementing a pandemics policy without lockdown, but with broad testing and highly elaborated contact-tracing management. On the other end of the spectrum, we had e.g. New Zealand (Gulley, 2020), with relatively strict confinement rules which could significantly reduce expansion of the pandemic, in combination with one of the worldwide most effective home-schooling approaches (Hasel, 2019).

Comparing these three concepts, we can derive several fault lines, but also common and mutually complementary points as being important to consider for future-preparedness policy design in multi-resilient directions. In essence, multi-resilient will mean to combine the best of all three approaches while getting rid, as much as possible, of their (unavoidable) negative sides.

37.2 Development versus Sustainability versus Resilience: Similarities, Fault Lines and Potential (Realistic) Complementarities

This is not easy in practice, though – for ideological reasons, for reasons of competition, and for aspects that are opposing each other and thus exclude each other. The most obvious *similarity* between all three guiding concepts lies in their orientation towards future preparedness. Hereby, an important overlap of all three concepts can be observed with regard to their focus on enhancing society's innovation capacity. The *capacity to innovate* is considered to be a core competence of a high-performance developed society, a forward-thinking sustainable society and a crisis-resistant and adaptive (multi-)resilient society.

In the sustainability and development discourse, for example, the technological innovation capacity is discussed primarily in connection with green growth. This is because green growth is not only seen as ecologically relevant but also as a lucrative economic sector of tomorrow, even if green growth is often at odds with the post-growth movement, and both can be found arguing with each other within the sustainability discourse. Social innovations are discussed primarily in the context of the principle of decentralisation and self-sufficient local units and are mainly part of the (multi-)resilience discourse. In the development discourse, in contrast, social innovation tends to be discussed almost exclusively in connection with technological and economic innovations; for example, the e-democracy topic would be a social innovation of the Smart City. Given the fact that the Corona crisis has been significantly pushing further digital transformation, digital surveillance and AI automatisation, the concept of pragmatic economic development through technological innovation, including AI and surveillance of different kinds, could remain of increasing relevance also in post-Corona times – obviously with all their pros and cons.

Nevertheless, there are several conflicts or fault lines *between* these three concepts:

– *Development versus Sustainability*. The most obvious point of friction is between the demand for ecological sustainability on the one hand and the demand of developed (and developing) societies for economic growth on the other. This results from a very different assessment of growth and technological innovation. The growth-optimistic representatives of the developed-society concept stress that progress and innovation could overcome the "scarcity paradox", leading to an increase in economic welfare for everyone. In their view, even exploitation of the planetary resources could be prevented or even reversed through new achievements in synthetic biology, nanotechnology, or exploration of resources in space and in deep water. In short: "Technology is the answer". In contrast, representatives from the sustainability discourse strongly question this credo and plead for more mindful political and economic practices (Fathi, 2019a). Within the context of the Coronavirus crisis, this fault line manifested particularly in the debate on where to focus the "restart" economic investments in order to boost the ailing economies: Should economic politics focus on supporting already established sectors such as the automotive industry, or should it use the Corona situation to boost new and sustainable sectors such as regenerative energies, etc. for a profoundly different post-Corona epoch?

– *Resilience versus Development*. Typical oppositions arising between (multi-)resilience and development concepts refer to two conflict issues: Firstly, the contradiction between economic efficiency and the need for redundancies; and secondly, avoiding new vulnerabilities resulting from (technological) innovations. The first opposition implies that (multi-)resilience management requires investments preparing for plausible (however, not necessarily immediate, close or likely) unpredictable problems of high impact. This may include establishing redundancies, i.e., security systems that remain unused for a long time and are only used when necessary. This contradicts the postulate of economic efficiency, which, in recent decades, has sought to streamline public administration and save unused resources. Ultimately, this contradiction may be decided by the question of "what price a society is prepared to pay for the establishment of security" (Perron, 2011). Moreover, as already mentioned, the (multi-) resilience concept has per se an ambivalent relationship to the trend towards technological innovation. It can be argued that technologisation, especially in the course of the spread of new information and communication technologies, contributes to the resilience of a society by strengthening its network, particularly through the enhanced ability of self-learning via Internet, and that it contributes to a democratisation of knowledge (as we could indeed also observe, to a certain extent, during the Corona crisis). However, it must be critically countered that technologisation also leads to new dependencies and vulnerabilities (Fathi, 2019c). With regard to the Corona crisis, as mentioned we can observe the worrying trend towards an infodemic, including expansion of fake news and conspiracy beliefs heating inter- and intranational conflicts.

- *Resilience versus Sustainability*. Between resilience and sustainability, at first glance there appear to be no direct points of friction, presumably because the narratives of both concepts have always been directly related to each other and therefore seem to complement each other (Dissen, Quaas & Baumgärtner, 2009). However, with regard to the teachings of the Corona crisis, there could be – as mentioned in a previous chapter – a relevant conflict line. The reason for this is that the concept of (multi-)resilience forwards no explicit ethical or normative implications, at least in principle. A criminal organisation or terrorist cell can just as well serve as an inspiring object of investigation regarding its best practices as a disease virus (yes, to a certain extent the Coronavirus has been an inspiration in terms of its high-degree resilience). As a result, resilience management can also lead to unethical consequences contradicting the claim of sustainability. As shown by various administrations in the geopolitical field of "re-globalisation", a national-egoistic approach can, to a certain extent, increase the resiliency of a society, for example by securing critical medical supply and infrastructure, and, as the intention went, even vaccine "only for the USA", "first of all for ourselves" or "as a priority for compatriots" (Chait, 2020). Another example was Germany's fiscal policy to support domestic companies being affected by the economic impact of the Corona crisis. Compared to most other EU member states, Germany proved to be economically much more resilient in the face of the crisis, being able to spend more than all EU member states together to keep its economy running. Until May 2020, the German Federal government spent more than 995 billion euros, comprising 51 percent of the overall amount of fiscal aids spent within the EU. On the supranational level, Germany's policy of economic resilience nevertheless had indirect negative effects on the other member states, leading to an outflow of capital and distortion of competition in favour of German domestic companies at the (albeit indirect) cost of indebted other EU member states (particularly in the South). Although this was not Germany's fault in principle, but due to structural inequivalence and the inactivity and inefficiency of Southern European states, this could lead to a new Euro crisis (Der Spiegel, 2020a). Simultaneously, the German Federal Monopoly Commission (*Monopol-Kommission*), dedicated to balancing private and state capitalism, criticised the governmental measures as (directly and indirectly) fostering a "Corona-Socialism" (Bockenheimer, 2020, p.2). In its view, excessive Corona economic-stimulus state measures undermine the independence and self-reliance of the private economic sector, leading to a lasting dependency of private enterprises, such as, for example, the airline Lufthansa and parts of the German industry, on the public sector and on public taxpayer's money in particular, which is, in the perspective of the Commission, in contrast to the principles of a balanced Social Market Economy and of the long-term interest of German open society (Ibid.). This means that "contextually right" resilience measures are not always *just and only* right. Both examples illustrate national resilience management leading to destructive consequences on the supranational level. Overcoming the contradiction between national resilience and sustainability means sensitising national politics to the needs of the overall joint international system and promoting overall global (multi-)resilience, as best as is possible under given contexts and conditions.

Yet the good news is that in addition to overlaps and frictions between these guiding concepts, we can also identify clear mutual complementarities, which are derived from very different core concerns of the three.

The *developed society* focuses on the exploitation of its own growth potential and thus also on securing the general welfare and satisfaction of the population's needs. The *sustainable society* also tries to expand this satisfaction for future generations and tries to politically prevent unintentional man-made

BROADER AND MORE INTEGRATED POLICY OF FUTURE PREPAREDNESS   239

side effects in the social, economic and ecological area. The *resilient society*, finally, prepares itself both for increasing complexity and its unintended side effects that could not be successfully prevented by sustainability policy. Transferred to the Corona crisis and similar challenges in the future, the core ideas of all three concepts come into play: the concept of the developed society particularly drives technological innovations, economic growth and capacity enhancement in order to enable e.g. healthcare, working from home, home-schooling, socio-economic support of companies, etc. Multi-resilience focusses on adequate strategies to reduce the expansion of an emergency by interrelating a variety of different tools and to effectively cope with resulting unintended side effects. Sustainability raises more awareness towards "soft" foresight and the durability of these measures.

37.3 *Collective Wisdom* as the Missing Connecting Principle towards Multi-Resilience?

As described in the previous chapters, we can assume that collective intelligence might be the most basic characteristic which a collective system, such as an organisation or society, needs in order to efficiently solve complex problems of all kinds, including those posited by a pandemic, and other emergencies. Thus, collective intelligence is an essential component of all three guiding concepts: the (multi-)resilient, the developed and the sustainable society. As described elsewhere, collective intelligence results from effective interaction and integration of perspectives within a social system. If the collective manages to ensure that all members affected by a problem can contribute their different analysis and solution perspectives, the resulting group opinion with a decision-making quality emerges that is "greater than the sum of its parts". The manifold achievements of a democratic society are the result of such collective efforts, which historically made democracies in principle superior to autocracies.

However, *collective intelligence* does not only bring new achievements (e.g. a rationed use of digital change), but also man-made unintended side effects (e.g. advanced cyber-hacking which, not by chance, is, in most cases, the work of groups and very rarely just of individuals). This is because collective intelligence is primarily a tool of functionality and efficiency, not necessarily of giving meaning and purpose. Therefore, it is the task of *collective wisdom* to weigh up these factors appropriately and come to optimal decisions by including meaning, sense and a stronger focus on ethics. In short, intelligence needs wisdom to gain a more human face. Collective wisdom thus represents a to date widely neglected complementary weight to collective intelligence. Yet what exactly is meant by this and what distinguishes collective wisdom? How can it be shaped and promoted in concrete terms? And why may it be particularly important for the coming years?

In general terms, wisdom usually refers to a deep understanding of life's interrelationships and the resulting ability to make the most pondered and reasonable decisions, including emotionally balanced decisions, when problems arise. Classical approaches to wisdom are found in philosophy (translated from the Greek: "love of wisdom") and in the so-called wisdom traditions of the religions. For example, Plato's famous allegory of the cave (which has influenced the history of philosophy and religion in equal measure) describes wisdom as a knowledge of the real world and a departure from the deceptions and errors of everyday knowledge, including contextually established or traditional prejudices. On an individual level, there is a significant connection between wisdom and mindfulness, which we can consider as an improved ability to deal with chaos and information diversity. In this context, the famous quote of the American psychologist and philosopher William James can be placed: "The art of being wise is the art of knowing what to overlook". The mindfulness researcher Ellen Langer describes this ability with the term "gentle openness":

> What you want is a soft openness – to be attentive to the things you're doing but not single-minded, because then you're missing other opportunities. [...] We have new data and analysis coming at us all the time. So, mindfulness becomes more important for navigating the chaos – but the chaos makes it a lot harder to be mindful. I think chaos is a perception. People say that there's too much information, and I would say that there's no more information now than there was before. The difference is that people believe they have to know it – that the more information they have, the better the product is going to be and the more money the company is going to make. I don't think it depends as much on the amount of information someone has as on the way it's taken in. And that needs to be mindfully.
>
> LANGER, 2014

This approach is, both in attitude and wording, very close to the UNESCO "Futures Literacy" approach that we are going to address a little later on as, in our view, one primordial and founding post-Corona pillar for multi-resilience.

On a collective level, we can describe collective wisdom compared to collective intelligence as follows: While collective intelligence is characterised as the ability to process as much information as possible, including information about the past and possible futures, collective wisdom is characterised by a fundamentally different perspective. Wisdom takes a step back and asks what really matters. It focuses less on what is possible and how new achievements can be invented and implemented in concrete terms, but rather on identifying what we really aspire to with our activities by asking: What is worth striving for? In doing so, collective wisdom questions the framework conditions that the collective intelligence approach would simply take for granted. What will become of the human "I" if we strive for boundless optimisation of the human body, in the sense of transhumanism? Does this actually lead to what we are really striving for, namely more happiness and well-being? What is the "I" anyway and what are we as a society? (Fathi, 2019a; Benedikter & Fathi, 2019). What do we really fear in the Corona crisis (individually and as a whole)?

These and other questions typically arise from the "wisdom" approach. Hereby, it is less a matter of active problem-solving, which is what the collective intelligence approach aims at, but rather of strategically and philosophically weighing up where the perceived problems are actually coming from, what new problems might result from the effort to solve them, and what, on this basis, might be the best decision in the long term from a philosophico-anthropological and humanistic perspective. This could even mean deciding not to pursue a certain developmental path. It could, for instance, mean deciding to stop any further efforts to develop certain high-risk technological innovations for a certain time (for example high-risk research on viruses such as Corona, advanced nanotechnologies or a super-intelligent AI), rationally speaking, as long as we cannot exclude unintended side effects with existential risk impact (Bostrom, 2012).

Of all three guiding principles, the concept of sustainable society is likely to have the largest share in the principle of collective wisdom. Today, it is above all the technological dimension, driven by the techno-economic and military-economic sectors, including high-risk research, which, in some areas, shows exponential leaps in development and can lead to man-made risks. In the private-sector context, isolated attempts to boycott dangerous technologies can be observed. For instance, the founders of Google-Deepmind, the company's AI division, and Tesla founder and investor Elon Musk have committed themselves to not participate in the development of autonomous, AI-based weapons, and to invest in the development of an ethical AI (Clifford, 2020). In the political context, better risk control could be achieved not only by means of bans or (unfortunately not very promising) voluntary commitments, but also, as a preventive measure, by regulating the allocation of support mechanisms. However, this is not likely to happen internationally or globally, for if a technology were feasible, it would be developed somewhere in the world by someone else. Collective wisdom in this context would be based on the "principle of non-simultaneous technological developments":

> Delay the development of dangerous and harmful technologies, especially those that could pose an existential risk, and accelerate the development of useful technologies, especially those that reduce natural or technological existential risks" (Bostrom, 2016, p. 323). A wise strategy could be measured by "how much time advantage it gives the desired technologies over the undesirable ones (Ibid.).

Without doubt, this applies also, and perhaps especially, for a post-Corona world.

In any case, future preparedness towards man-made unpredictable risks in a post-Corona world requires international, and, as far as possible, even global decision-making on the basis of *collective wisdom guiding collective intelligence*. Bostrom in this regard rightly opts for fostering worldwide interdisciplinary cooperation, particularly in the policy and science sectors (Bostrom, 2012; 2016).

Obstacles, but also chances towards such international cooperation and respective decision-making are illustrated in the so-called "prisoner's dilemma" (Axelrod, 1984) which we have already mentioned. Briefly explained, this model describes the scenario of two prisoners who are arrested and simultaneously interrogated in solitary confinement by the prosecutors, who offer each prisoner a bargain: each prisoner is given the opportunity to either cooperate with the other prisoner by remaining silent or to betray the other by testifying that the other committed the crime. The possible outcomes are: 1) If A betrays B, but B remains silent, A will be set free and B will serve four years in prison (and vice versa). 2) If both A and B betray each other, each of them serves two years in prison. 3) If A and B both remain silent, both of them will serve only one year in prison.

The structure of the prisoner's dilemma can be generalised from the prison setting and transferred to the collective level (Maughan, Thornhill & Maughan, 1996). An iterated prisoner's dilemma has an iterated dynamic of *mutually escalating actions*, for example the arms race during the Cold War between the USSR and the US, or the trade war between the USA and China. The example of the Cold War (1947–1991) shows an important insight of the prisoner's dilemma which, in the end, may lead to the destruction of the system itself. The respective overall dynamic of mutual escalation could be changed by fostering communication between the involved protagonists. Following this insight, the installation of the Moscow-Washington hotline directly after the

Cuban Missile Crisis in 1962 largely contributed towards reducing the escalation dynamic of that historic passage.

Referred to the teachings of the Coronavirus crisis, the necessary (and perhaps unavoidable) communicative effect of already existing inter- and supra-national institutions, such as the UN, the EU, the Belt and Road Initiative, and, in the context of the Corona crisis, particularly the WHO, might contribute to better communication and consciousness of interdependency. It could promote advanced international cooperation towards a truly shared global multi-resilience, at least in selected sectors, where pragmatically feasible, which have to be carefully identified and put at the centre of post-Corona diplomatic, political and economic efforts.

CHAPTER 38

Fostering Local, National and International Paths towards Multi-resilience

Leverage Points for Interrelated Social Change Bottom-up and Top-down

Based on the concept of multi-resilience, interpreted and practiced to some extent as integration of the three guiding concepts above, and relying on the positive teachings of the precautionary principle proven rather successful and, in most cases, without alternative during the Corona crisis, some leverage points for post-Corona social change can be derived. Learning from the Corona crisis can, in principle, mean to make societies more anticipation-aware, pro-reactive and problem-solving, capable of coping with differing, rapidly expanding, varying and interchanging crisis contexts. Considering its philosophical principles and its transdisciplinary references, any political or civil-society initiative proposing social multi-resilience should at least start at the following leverage points for a post-Corona society:

  - *Communication.* The Simplify tradition of transdisciplinary research (particularly Systems Thinking) illustrates which operation fundamentally holds social systems – such as societies – together: It is communication. It is communication that makes the networking of members into a "whole" possible. It enables the emergence of cultures, legal, informal and contextual norms, collective identities and visions, including features of civil religion, i.e., basic paradigmatic convictions and ideals felt and shared by larger parts of the populations; and it underpins both the efficiency and "flavour" to the public of institutions and infrastructures, and thus the acceptance of order structures. As we have seen during the Coronavirus crisis, non-acceptance of rules often resulted from poor communication, including, in particular, clarity of communication. In retrospect, successful communication is also an essential prerequisite for realising collective intelligence and collective wisdom. It is therefore the very basis of multi-resilience, so to say its "immaterial blood" (but also of the "sustainable society" and, to a certain extent, even of the "developed society"). A major implication is thus – as outlined earlier – that a post-Corona world must urgently and fundamentally improve communication and knowledge transfer within teams of influential decision-makers and between the elite and the broadest possible

© ROLAND BENEDIKTER AND KARIM FATHI, 2022 | DOI:10.1163/9789004469686_039

parts of the population *in* all society sectors, including e.g. politics, civil society, science and the private sector, but also *among* these society sectors.

- *Pluralism of dimensions*. From the Complexify tradition of transdisciplinary research (particularly Integrative Thinking) it can be deduced that social systems contain several dimensions that cannot be reduced to individual items. Distinguishing between an inner/subjective and an outer/objective reality dimension, as well as considering different system levels, i.e., the micro- (individuals), meso- (organisations) and macro- (societies) levels, results in an at least six-dimensional matrix. As we have seen in the previous parts of this book, all these dimensions would be potential windows of intervention to foster multi-resilience by means of structurally different yet, to some extent, converging initiatives. Difference can lead to unity without being annihilated ("United in diversity", or Latin: *In varietate concordia* is the motto of the EU, which is per se meant as a matter of resilience, i.e., aiming at adaptive stability in constant flux). Experience shows that initiatives at the macro level are likely to be relatively more complex than processes that are initiated on a small scale. Experience from international conflict research and peacebuilding also suggests that the dimension "culture" (i.e., the internal or subjective dimensions of the meso/macro system level) is located on a relatively deep "tectonic layer" and that processes of change in this dimension are correspondingly slower (Galtung, 1998). Pragmatically designed social interventions for the mere purpose of initiating change are likely to neglect this level and concentrate more on external interventions, especially at the micro- and, in particular, at the meso-level. These could include immediate implementation practices conducted by task forces, education programs to develop and enhance individual competencies, and, in the medium term, also the development of more plurality-prone, adaptive and flexible legislations and institutions.
- *Experiments*. Dealing with complex systems such as teams or societies requires accepting unknowns. The practical consequence is implementing an experimental approach by trial and error. As we have seen, this is particularly recommended when social systems (such as organisations, communities and societies) are so complex that the success of change processes cannot be predicted with the aid of a simple input-output model. Intelligent interventions consider inherent unknowns. They systematically run simulations and test

practices in a "protected space", making it possible to make mistakes and to develop alternative options. Simulations can strongly contribute to multi-resilience. However, what is needed in immediate and "close" crisis situations often goes beyond experimentation, because there is not time for it, as has been noted at various points. In concrete crises, (multi-)resilience manifests as immediate and strongly self-aware (re)action, not as a mere test run.

– *Simultaneous Top-Down and Bottom-Up.* There are various social subsectors that, during times of crises and non-crises alike, try to instil a variety of initiatives to promote social resilience and sustainability. Particularly in the context of multi-resilience, it is striking that these initiatives exist largely independently of one another, with spillover effects in two directions. Civil-society initiatives, for example, work "from the bottom up", while political initiatives typically work "from the top down". Both have to be integrated much more systemically for the sake of a stronger safety net that protects from risks and catches the solutions that are needed to go forward instead of just "bouncing back" to an (alleged) state of origin.

On the basis of these considerations, the following leverage points of crisis-intervention and post-crisis social change can be derived. These can contribute to fostering both collective intelligence and collective wisdom of modern societies and of the international community aiming at better (multi-)resilience.

38.1   Education Programs for Individual Resilience

Based on the motto "If you want to change the world, start with yourself", the educational leverage point is at the centre of a variety of social-change initiatives, most of which are civil-society initiatives. In many cases, training courses in individual resilience are offered (in some cases free of charge), increasingly also in the form of online courses. The initiators include the Center for Human Emergence (n.d) and Spiral Dynamics Integral (n.d.), as well as the programme "U.Lab: Transforming Business, Society and Self" provided and hosted by the "Presencing Institute"(n.d.) and its founders Peter Senge and Claus Otto Scharmer. Although most of them are labelled as "green" or even "alternative" and thus "naturally" close to the sustainability discourse, all of them present strong affinities to the multi-resilience concept. The U.Lab is, to date, the best-known and most representative example of educational resilience, offering since 2015 an annual six-week "social transformation" training for everyone via the digital learning platform edX (n.d). All of these offers are aimed at training multipliers, i.e., people who, in turn, should influence other people and drive social change towards a more sustainable *and* resilient society.

Regardless of the diversity of offers, there are indications that all these initiatives focus on the promotion of "universal" personal competencies being strongly associated with multi-resilience, because they can be applied to a wide range of problems. Typical universal personal competencies include Mindfulness (which is facilitated by regular meditation practice), Emotional Intelligence, and Learning to Learn approaches. Universal competences are deep-going and are usually accompanied by personal transformation.

As mentioned in previous chapters, the question of individual resilience arose with great prominence in several respects during the Coronavirus crisis. The most important one was the ability to deal with one's own stress and act calmly and in a longer view by keeping what we would call an "emotional rationality" as opposed to irrationality.

Whatever the other outcomes are, Corona has proven one thing in countless occasions that will be taken to fruition through individual and collective accounts and by action research over the coming years: Individual resilience can be learned and should be considered more systematically within traditional educational initiatives. There are numerous top-down and, above all, bottom-up initiatives aimed at fostering resilience of individuals and households. This includes, in the first instance, the promotion of universal personal competences. If everybody acquires them, the collective will work differently, including its responses to sudden, overwhelming and "universal" emergencies such as Corona. As the example of the above-mentioned U.Lab shows, the learning programmes are often provided as MOOCs (i.e., Massive Open Online Courses). On the top-down level, universal personal resilience competencies could be integrated in national education strategies and, to a certain extent, also in the derivation of multi-level policies.[1] Additionally, crisis prevention programmes prepare for specific post-Corona crisis scenarios, such as a longer-lasting power outage (e.g. as a result of natural hazards or a cyber-attack). Studies illustrate that only a few households in Germany would be prepared for such a scenario, although the German Federal Office for Civil Protection and Disaster Assistance explicitly recommends that all households stockpile sufficient water and food for at least ten days (Petermann et al., 2010). A similar situation is true for the whole of Europe, probably less for the U.S., but also reaching significant levels of concern, particularly with regard to the "post-modern"

---

1 Further aspects, including components for a curriculum to promote personal and social competences toward forming an interconnected and transdisciplinary multi-resilient society, can be found in Fathi (2019a).

coastlines East and West which, similar to Europe, usually "believe" less in the need for individual preparedness regarding risk and catastrophic scenarios.

On the international level, training and knowledge exchange about individualised (or, in the sense of the trend towards "precision medicine", contextually, socially and culturally "tailored") multi-resilience practices could be a constructive context for international cooperation. This could manifest in joint educational initiatives and programmes.

38.2 Bottom-up Transformational Impulses via Building Critical Masses for Positive Change

When the number of people who are willing to change in an organic developmental perspective towards a more sustainable future reaches a particular behaviour pattern, it approaches a "tipping point", as defined by the "Seneca Effect" (Bardi, 2017). In this case, change can be adopted by the community through the law of the "critical mass". This term, which originally goes back to epidemic research, in game theory means that it is sufficient to convince only a certain number of participants of a vision, belief or behaviour in order to influence the whole group. If a certain threshold of participant numbers is exceeded or the critical mass is reached, this vision will become self-supporting (Gladwell, 2000). In the Social Sciences, the concept of "critical mass" was influenced by the game theorist Thomas Schelling (1978) and the sociologist Mark Granovetter (1978). The concept became known at the turn of the millennium, mainly through Malcolm Gladwell's book "The tipping point – How Little Things Can Make A Big Difference" (Gladwell, 2000). In the book, Gladwell describes three communicative factors that are typical for the building of critical masses in social contexts:

1) *The Law of the Few.* Some individual members have more charisma, influence and power to instigate change than others. This is especially true for people with more far-reaching decision-making powers than others, like top-level politicians or managers.

2) *Stickiness.* The presentation (and presentability) of the vision is a key factor in determining whether the addressees can actually be motivated to act. Even small formal and communicational changes can have a big impact.

3) *The Power of Context.* Human actions are strongly influenced by environmental conditions. As an example, Gladwell cites the Broken Windows Theory, which has been dominating criminology and was successfully implemented in the 1990s by New York's then mayor

Rudolph Giuliani. New York City police focused on fighting seemingly minor crimes (including vandalism, such as broken windows), which, however, impaired the quality of life of New York's residents, thus setting an example of "zero tolerance" which then influenced most other sectors of crime "bottom-up". Giuliani's "micro"-policy led to a significant reduction in overall crime in New York (Ibid.).

Today, there is a wide range of initiatives, mainly at the intersection of academic and civil-society sub-sectors, which try to raise awareness and to provide competency development services on digital platforms, in some cases free of charge. The aim and purpose is to train multipliers, i.e., people who, in turn, trigger social-change impulses from below through numerous projects. The aforementioned MOOC "U.Lab: Transforming Business, Society and Self" teaches participants not only about methods for better self-reliance and how to apply them, but also to develop concrete projects in small groups of five people, which are designed to initiate social change and innovative practice (Scharmer & Käufer, 2008; Scharmer, 2009). According to Claus-Otto Scharmer and Kathrin Käufer, a critical mass of five people per group would be sufficient to achieve a significant impact on the overall system. Both quote Nick Hanauer, entrepreneur and long-time board member of Amazon:

> One of my guiding principles comes from Margaret Mead: 'Never doubt that a small group of committed citizens can change the world. On the contrary, it is the only way change has ever happened. That's a principle I completely believe in. You can do almost anything with just five people. With just one person it's difficult – but if you bring that one person together with four or five other people, you have incredible power. Suddenly there is a momentum of its own and almost everything that is immanent and possible can be achieved and realized.
> SCHARMER & KÄUFER, 2008

From the perspective of such a leverage point, change impulses towards a multi-resilient society could be induced by small-group projects with highly committed and creatively collaborating individuals. The projects can vary from non-profit civil-society sector initiatives to develop and test social innovations, to innovative entrepreneurship dedicated to promoting a more circular economy. Small-group projects could be systematically furthered by the public sector. Hackathons such as those that were successfully implemented during the Coronavirus crisis, e.g., as mentioned in Germany or Estonia, would be typical measures.

38.3 Experimental Prototyping Projects

Any initiative dealing with the integration of resilience and sustainability into multi-resilience – be it small-group projects or larger community-based civil-society projects – is usually implemented as a "real-world experiment" or "real-world laboratory" that tests social innovations through trial and error. The so-called "Transition Towns" initiatives are among the best known in this regard (Schneidewind & Singer-Brodowski, 2013; Schneidewind, 2011). Transition towns can be understood as grassroot community projects that seek to build social resilience in response – for example – to peak oil, climate destruction, and economic instability by creating local groups testing adaptive social practices of self-sufficiency, environmental balance and "production-consumption neutrality". The initiative first developed in 2006 in Britain. By September 2013, there were 1130 "Transition Town" initiatives registered in 43 countries, mostly in Western Europe and the USA (Transition Network, n.d.; Transparency International, 2019). "Real-world" learning labs in general, sometimes branded "Regulatory sandboxes" (as by the German Federal Ministry of Education and Research BMBF (2019)), and transition towns in particular remain influential concepts which are co-shaping the contemporary discussion on resilient societies.

An integrative experimental approach is also recommended for the more top-down oriented measures of politics. This includes, among others, systematic testing approaches to improve welfare policies, such as universal basic income or political governance – for example, "liquid democracy" or e-democracy. The basic insight here is that in view of increasing social complexity, there will be no simple or perfect solutions, but only approximations. What sets the right incentives, what sets the wrong incentives? What works? What does not work? Where can we learn how to do better? When, and why? These systematic questions enable early adjustments and pragmatical institutional learning.

In sum, it can be observed that notable pilot projects and real-world experiments are often not initiated by politics, but rather by other society sectors, particularly the civil society. The way towards societal multi-resilience is influenced from both: bottom-up and top-down initiatives. Sustainability researcher Derk Loorbach describes this process as a "governance panarchy" which is not to be confused with the aforementioned theoretical concept "panarchy of adaptive cycles". "Governance panarchy" is a more practical concept describing a multidimensional transitional order for shaping social change. The underlying idea is to transfer the market principle of free competition "laissez faire, laissez passer" to political systems. Thus, inside a society there could be a regulated co-existence of different governance systems, and any member could choose which system he/she would like to belong to (Loorbach 2007; 2014).

Similarly, bottom-up and top-down initiatives of resilience governance should coexist and could support each other based on their performance. However, it should be critically acknowledged that a mere focus on the competition principle remains dysfunctional and that both bottom-up and top-down governance cannot substitute one another. Multi-resilience emerges from synergies of perspectives and initiatives. Therefore, active collaborations instead of competitions between sub-sectors should be fostered. Respective steps can already be observed: The above-mentioned Transition Towns, for example, often involve cooperation between civil society and science. Collective learning-oriented social policy, as described above, can also involve cooperation between politics and the private sector. Both require communicative "bridges" between the subsystems.

38.4 Building Bridges between Subsystems

As we have seen, generating collective intelligence and collective wisdom within a social system, thus enhancing its multi-resilience, depends to a large extent on how the social protagonists are able to shape successful communication. In a modern society, this may involve nothing less than a "dialogue-based refoundation of science, business and politics" (Scharmer, 1995). Principally, any sector can act as a "bridge-builder" for cross-sectoral collaborations.

Traditionally, it is the *public sector* which has relatively vast resources for initiating cross-sectoral and transdisciplinary collaboration. Measures can imply funding programmes to support transdisciplinary research and problem-solving. The above-mentioned measure of the hackathons initiated by the German and Estonian governments during the Corona crisis are typical examples.

Cooperations between *the public and the private sector* have a long tradition within the context of so-called private-public partnerships. These are common in (however, often controversial) programmes to develop societies from the Third World. It is obvious that such cooperations are necessary to foster a "developed" modern society. A recent example was a team-up between the Estonian start-up community with Mistletoe Singapore, the European Commission and other local and international supporters to organise a 100-hour free online accelerator for start-ups with potentially strong impact on shaping the post-Coronavirus crisis world. The mentors included the Estonian President and the co-founders of the enterprises *Bolt, Skype, Pipedrive, Veriff,* and *Testlio* (Tambur, 2020).

In the *science sector*, it is particularly the debate on so-called "Mode 2" and "Mode 3" science. This approach deals with the role of science as a bridge-builder across disciplines and societal sectors. According to Schneidewind/Singer-Brodowski, this presupposes that science has a transdisciplinary orientation and a new self-understanding not only as a "neutral analytical observer" of society but also as a normatively oriented active co-designer of society (Schneidewind & Singer-Brodowski, 2013). The beginning of this debate was initiated by the concept of a "Mode 2" science, coined by Helga Nowotny and Michael Gibbons in the 1990s (Nowotny et al., 1994). In the meantime, since the second half of the 2000s, Schneidewind/Singer-Brodowski even refer to a "Mode 3" science (Schneidewind & Singer-Brodowski, 2013). Mode 1 science refers to conventional "normal science" with a strong reference to analytical observation and a mono-disciplinary and sometimes "weak" interdisciplinary orientation (Gibbons, 1994; Nowotny, Scott & Gibbons, 2001). Mode 2, on the other hand, stands for a "context-sensitive science", i.e., a science that is aware of the close feedback with society, is convinced about the need of developing a "reflexive modernity", and that concretely faces up to these developments (Nowotny, Scott & Gibbons, 2001). Mode 2 has a transdisciplinary knowledge orientation enabling the grasping and dealing with of complex problems that go beyond the specialised perceptions of the respective social subsystems (Gibbons, 1994; Nowotny, Scott & Gibbons, 2001). Beyond this, the concept of Mode 3 science goes even further by promoting institutional change (so-called "Third-Order Change"). In doing so, Mode 3 science is aware of its educational and mediating function and actively co-develops society (Schneidewind & Singer-Brodowski, 2013) as a "catalyst for processes of social change" (Wissenschaftlicher Beirat der Bundesregierung Globale Umweltveränderungen, 2011). Knowledge orientation in a fully developed "knowledge society" would therefore be not only transdisciplinary but also "transformative", based on cooperative organisational structures (Schneidewind & Singer-Brodowski, 2013). According to Schneidewind/Singer-Brodowski, there are different protagonists who have the potential to contribute to the development of Mode 3 science. These can span a wide range of organised civil society, including, for example, initiatives such as the German "Zivilgesellschaftliche Plattform Forschungswende" (Ibid.) ("Civil-Society Platform for Turning Research Around"), or foundations and even "alternative" science sponsors such as the Global Alliance for Banking on Values (GABV, n.d.), London or the International Association of Investors in the Social Economy (INAISE, n.d.).[2]

---

2 For more information about systematic investment on the basis of community values, as it unfolded after the last and, until then, biggest global emergency, the great economic and financial crisis of 2007–08, see Benedikter, 2011b; 2012a; 2014b.

Typical bridge-building impulses from the *private sector* are multi-stakeholder initiatives (MSI) and collaborative innovation networks (CoIN). Multi-stakeholder initiatives (MSI) are voluntary associations at the intersection between civil society, public and private protagonists with the aim of solving complex social problems in a cooperative manner. The board of directors of an MSI is the highest decision-making body and is usually made up of representatives of the various stakeholders (Both et al., 2012). Their focus is usually on promoting sustainable development by integrating Corporate Social Responsibility. Collaborative Innovation Networks (CoIN) are also characterised by trustful collaboration between organisations and external stakeholders. The focus here is on the development of product innovations, e.g. in the form of new services and business solutions. The term originally goes back to Peter Gloor from MIT Sloan's Center for Collective Intelligence (Gloor, 2006).

Transferred to multi-resilience, both approaches could be expanded to developing and monitoring technological innovations of potentially high impact, particularly in the areas of synthetic biology, nanotechnology and AI. CoINs would practice collective intelligence by systematically researching and developing technologically innovative problem solutions. Complementary to that and following the principle of collective wisdom, MSIs would rather monitor and supervise these processes with regard to potential man-made future (existential) threats resulting as side effects from these innovations.

In the end, each social sub-sector has the potential to promote cross-sectoral collaboration through appropriate initiatives – some of which are already being implemented today. And once again, successful collaboration requires successful communication – which, when all other factors are taken to a new level, must be elevated to a new quality, too.

38.5 Methods of Communicative Complexity Management

We have underscored it repeatedly since it is of crucial importance for multi-resilience to function: Any collaborative operation within and between social systems requires successful communication. Thus, communicative competencies and the systematic implementation of collaborative methods which enhance communication, be it as their main goal or as a side effect, can significantly promote the quality of knowledge transfer and collective intelligence and wisdom generation, thus increasing the quality of the overall social system. Regardless of how big social systems are – be it an organisation, a city or a society –, direct communication processes are behind almost every collective decision, both within sub-sectors and across sectors. Almost any situation of collective problem management results in settings of direct knowledge exchange between decision-makers from different disciplines, sub-sectors or fields of activity in order to jointly analyse and solve complex problems. Examples include agile development teams or quality circles, political, social and economic think tanks (such as, to mention just one example, the Institute for New Economic Thinking New York (n.d,)), MSIs or CoINs, committees with decision-makers, or interdisciplinary conferences and research initiatives. The objectives of these meetings may vary in detail, e.g. to create a complex product, to develop new insights or solutions to a complex problem, or to make joint decisions. Regardless of these different goals, though, all of these processes are based on the same criteria: They are jointly supported processes in which people with different backgrounds of experience communicate with each other and try to bring together their different perspectives in order to produce better results.

Direct communication, as Heidenreich et al. (2016) confirmed in their case studies, can be demonstrated as crucial in different types of governance (Heidenreich distinguishes between communities, networks, markets and hierarchical decisional structures). Direct communication makes it possible to agree on common procedures and standards for forms of cooperation that are difficult to control, such as communities or networks. It is also the most important means of resolving misunderstandings and solving problems that affect the bases of the communication process as such. As a further advantage, direct communication makes it possible to share implicit knowledge – i.e., knowledge in the form of personal experience or "tacit knowledge" (Alexander, 2018; Spacey, 2020) which cannot be effectively transferred as written knowledge (Heidenreich et al., 2016).

Designing direct communication in such a way that it enables an effective and time-efficient exchange of knowledge and, if necessary, leads to joint decisions, is not easy. Against the background of the relatively new "communicative complexity management" meta-framework, there are at least three dimensions of intervention to consider, in order to pragmatically improve direct communication and thus collective intelligence and collective wisdom. Related to the quadrant model of the Complexify tradition, these three intervention dimensions include: decision-making, understanding, and generative communication.

- *Decision-making*. Decision-making is one of the most central operations in collaboration, the more in emergencies or during (both spatially and time-wise extended) catastrophes. It is behind every collective action of groups, organisations and societies. Be it politicians and their advisory bodies discussing draft legislation or concrete measures, or think tanks or

NGOs developing political recommendations for action – they ultimately must take decisions. In all these and other settings, jointly supported directions are taken which often prove inefficient in everyday practice. Meetings often end in endless discussions or in "lonely" decisions that are not supported by the community. From this perspective, the systematic use of efficient methods for joint decision-making could make an important contribution. Such methods include, for example, Systemic Consensing (Maiwald, 2018) and the so-called C-i-E Concept.[3] The systematic implementation of such methods contributes to more time-efficient decision-making processes, which are also of high quality because they are able to include the perspectives of all, or the vast majority of participants in a solution-oriented fashion.

– *Understanding*. Whenever people with different academic and practical experience backgrounds communicate with each other, the fundamental challenge of understanding arises due to the fact that these different backgrounds often contain different references to reality, terms, concepts, paradigms, intellectual and educational frameworks and, accordingly, definitions. This becomes obvious when we look, to take just one example, at an exemplary encounter between sociologists and engineers who are working on the topic of "City and Mobility": Engineers will mainly focus on the material and infrastructural aspects, whereas sociologists have a specialised view on norms, values, and advanced socio-technologies. To make matters worse, language often proves to be ambiguous. To this day, these challenges prove to be so serious that participants in interdisciplinary conferences lasting several days on a complex topic do not even manage to agree on common definitions. How can communication between different knowledge carriers be optimised? How can language skills between disciplines be increased? Here, too, the targeted application of appropriate methods, which can also be combined with each other, could contribute to an improvement. This could include the use of visualisation techniques, symbols, metaphors and storytelling. These methods have proven themselves, especially in the promotion of innovation, in marketing and increasingly also in corporate communication, in order to interact on complex issues in an understandable way (Fathi, 2019b). They could and should also be applied on a broader scale, e.g.,

---

3 "C-i-E" stands for Cognition – intuition – Emotion (German: Kognition – intuition – Emotion) and has been developed by the emotion scientist and agile consultant Richard Graf, being described in detail in Graf (2018).

in political bodies, think tanks, at interdisciplinary conferences and in multi-stakeholder dialogues.

– *Generative communication.* Direct communication also proves to be a source of innovation and of transformation processes that are necessary to cope with complex problems. Hereby, it is to consider that innovation results most often from a new combination of already existing knowledge (Schumpeter, 2006). This requires dialogical exchange between different knowledge carriers. From another perspective, almost every problem-solving method based on dialogue can be seen as a process for changing systems. Methodologically, the factor "quality of dialogue" proves to be particularly relevant for innovative problem-solving in a collaborative process. Claus Otto Scharmer, founder of the popular social-systems transformation tool "U Theory", distinguishes four quality levels of exchange. These depend on the extent to which the discussion participants are able to free themselves from their own ideas and prejudices and can engage in a "Here-and-now" state of consciousness (called "Presencing") and interact with each other – not only referring to the content of the other discussion participants' points of view but also to their own underlying needs and feelings. In terms of stages, a distinction can be made between so-called "downloading", "debate", "empathic dialogue" and "generative dialogue". The latter stage of interaction has particularly high innovation potential. The systematic use of methods, such as the U Theory, could, if properly applied, significantly contribute to a generative, i.e., creative orientation of communication.

38.6   Towards the Integration of Standards?

Given that even the relationship between sustainability and law remains an epochal challenge in many respects (Mauerhofer, Rupo, & Tarquinio, 2020), and since the integration of global governance, different economic systems and sustainability standards is a still widely open task despite decades of efforts both by single countries and the international community (Negi, Pérez-Pineda & Blankenbach, 2020), it can be expected that this is and will remain similar or the same, for the foreseeable future, with regard to the stable implementation of advanced multi-resilience. What is certain is that single-sector improvements still mostly rooted in the sustainability discourse such as, for example, the broader introduction of sustainable environmental-protection technologies (Baltrėnas & Baltrėnaitė, 2020) or the embedment of sustainability aspects into the socio-economic process of crucial everyday processes with wide ramifications both on social practices and mindsets such as, for example, the policies and practices of the housing market (Akinbogun et al., 2020), will per se not suffice. Instead, it is certain that disaster risk reduction and resilience, if applied to systemic emergencies such as a new pandemic or other crises, will have to go hand in hand, both in theory and practice, and that given the complexity and fundamental interrelatedness of today's social mechanisms they will, sooner or later, have to unavoidably lead to some level and strategic implementation of multi-resilience (Yokomatsu & Hochrainer-Stigler, 2020).

PART 6

Recommendations for a Multi-Resilient Post-Corona World

∵

CHAPTER 39

"Health Terror"? Towards an Adequate Framework for a Post-Corona Socio-political Philosophy
"Resistance" and Power Critique Will Not Suffice

As we have seen, as a consequence of the Corona crisis the decisive challenge is not to remain stuck in details or single-sector solutions, but to proceed towards an as much as possible overarching, encompassing and integrative post-Corona policy design. As the multi-dimensional and pluri-ramified phenomenology of the problem has shown, such design must integrate critical thought with practical action and a broader and more inclusive anticipation concept with a more encompassing prevention and foresight process. To draw the lessons and draft adequate outlines for better preparedness and resilience, as always in rea-soned settings, a framing socio-political philosophy is needed, as in any com-plex, changeable and highly interdisciplinary and interconnected innovation challenge which drives non-linear and not fully controllable transformation.

Most current attempts toward such a necessarily open, trans-systemic, flexi-ble and integrative philosophical-ideological framework remain stuck, though, in a critique of the measures taken by governments or are manifests for univer-sal freedom, civil rights and non-obedience. In addition, many of them operate from a strictly anti-hierarchical and "postmodern" open-society viewpoint not applicable to integrated and interactive policies on a global level, for example including (as much as possible) China's current authoritarian political reality, culture and practice. This requires a philosophy (or idealistic framework) able to combine ideas with pragmatism.

In contrast to this requirement, though, many European and Western approaches which carry forward a philosophically sharp but very open-society and Western-centred view do not fully realise their inherent limits, since they are departing from a subconscious Western- and Eurocentrism with strong roots in the 1968s movements and subsequent "deconstructive" philosophies which dominated the Western academies from the 1970s to the first 2000s and continue to shape the public paradigm of socio-political correctness in many liberal and cosmopolitan European democracies and on the U.S. coastlines.

There were poets such as Mario Vargas Llosa who underscored the "princi-ple of freedom as a main power source for the fight against the virus. Without freedom, nothing is worth anything, not even the most perfect lockdown" (Vargas Llosa, 2020). Exemplary for such radically critical and "deconstructive"

© ROLAND BENEDIKTER AND KARIM FATHI, 2022 | DOI:10.1163/9789004469686_040

approach, the Italian philosopher Giorgio Agamben in May 2020 exemplified a critique of the Corona lockdown measures in the tradition of French postmodern "critique of power" à la Michel Foucault, Jean-Francois Lyotard, Julia Kristeva and Jacques Derrida. In a long treatise about "Biosecurity and Politics" which many thought was justified in many aspects, but (such as many others) stood hard at the edge to conspiracy theories and of poorly constructive, i.e., forward-oriented value, he criticised the Coronavirus handling by governments and communities as an expression of the separative character of power. Besides the character of "social distancing" to revive animalistic instincts of territory marking as related to self-assertion, Agamben saw the rise of "biopolitics" to universal instrument of power mechanisms which, in his view, tend to de-liberalise societies and to categorise human beings unjustly. Agamben's only recipe against this was "resistance against suppression" – which nevertheless seems hardly sufficient for preparing for new crises to come. As with other avant-garde thinkers, Agamben's philosophical-political analysis of the Coronavirus measures remained negative to the core. In so doing, it exemplified the paradox of the "postmodern" maxim to "positively" liberate individualities through universal deconstruction and negation of power mechanisms which, at the same time, are declared to be "everything". As early as 17 March 2020, i.e., at the first peak of the Coronavirus outbreak in Italy, Agamben had written:

> It is clear that Italians are willing to sacrifice practically everything: normal living conditions, social relations, work, even friendships, affections and religious and political beliefs to the danger of falling ill. The naked biological life – and the fear of losing it – is not something that unites men but blinds them and separates them.
>
> AGAMBEN, 2020b

Building on this observation, Agamben elaborated his socio-political philosophy of the Corona crisis as follows. Again, we have to point out that most philosophers adhering to the postmodern-critical (and, in essence, leftist) narrative (which in Europe and on the U.S. coastlines are the majority) followed him to some extent, or issued similar analyses:

> What is striking in the reactions to the exceptional devices and mechanisms that have been put in place in Italy (and not only in this country) is the inability to observe them beyond the immediate context in which they seem to operate. Rare are those who try instead, as a serious political analysis would require, to interpret them as symptoms and signs of a

"HEALTH TERROR"? TOWARDS AN ADEQUATE FRAMEWORK

wider experiment, in which a new paradigm of governance of men and things is at stake. Already in a book published seven years ago, which is now worth re-reading carefully ["Tempêtes microbiennes"]), Patrick Zylberman described the process by which health security, until then on the margins of political calculations, was becoming an essential part of state logics and international political strategies. In question is nothing less than the creation of a kind of 'health terror' as a tool to govern what was defined as the worst-case scenario.

AGAMBEN, 2020a

To prove this, Agamben refers back to the predecessors of Corona:

It is according to this logic of worst-case scenarios that already in 2005 the World Health Organization announced, 'two to 150 million deaths from the coming avian influenza', suggesting a political strategy that nations as at then were not yet prepared to accept. Zylberman shows that the device that was suggested had three points: 1) the construction, on the basis of a possible risk, of a fictitious scenario, in which the data are presented in such a way as to favor behavior that makes it possible to govern an extreme situation; 2) the adoption of the 'logic of the worst' as a regime of political rationality; 3) the integral organization of the physical body of citizens in such a way as to strengthen as much as possible the adherence to the institutions of government, producing a sort of 'superlative civism' in which the obligations imposed are presented as evidence of altruism and the citizen no longer has a right to health (health safety), but becomes legally obliged to health (biosecurity) (Ibid.).

And Agamben goes even further in the universality of his critique in applying these teachings to the Corona crisis of 2020:

What Zylberman was describing in 2013 has now [in 2020] occurred. It is clear that, beyond the emergency situation linked to a certain virus that may in the future give way to another one [or more], what is at issue is the design of a paradigm of government whose effectiveness far exceeds that of all forms of government that the political history of the West has so far known. If already in the progressive decline of [democratic] ideologies and political beliefs security reasons had allowed citizens to accept restrictions on freedoms that they were previously unwilling to accept, biosecurity has proved capable of presenting the absolute cessation of all political activity and all social relations as the highest form of civic participation. In this way, it was possible to witness the paradox of leftist organizations, traditionally used to claim rights and denounce violations of the constitution, to accept without reservation limitations of freedoms decided by ministerial decrees without any legality which not even fascism had ever dreamed of being able to impose (Ibid.).

In the leftist "deconstructivist" philosopher's eyes such as Agamben's and his colleagues (who still dominate the academia in Europe and partly in the U.S.), the conclusions with regard to the coming years obviously range from negative to terrible:

> It is clear – and the government authorities themselves never cease to remind us of this – that the so-called 'social distancing' will become the model of the policy that awaits us and that (as the representatives of so-called task forces have announced, whose members are in blatant conflict of interest with the function they are supposed to perform) they will take advantage of this distancing to replace direct human relations in their physicality, which have become *as such* suspicious of contagion (including political contagion, of course) everywhere possible by digital technological devices. University lectures, as [ministries have] already recommended, will be done permanently online, you people may no longer recognize themselves as persons by looking directly at their faces, which can be covered by a health mask, but through digital devices that will recognize biological data that must be taken. And any 'gathering', whether it is done for political reasons or simply for friendship, may continue to be prohibited. In question is a whole conception of the destinies of human society in a perspective that in many ways seems to have taken on from waning religions the apocalyptic idea of an end of the world. After politics have been replaced by economics, the economic order will now have to be integrated with the new paradigm of biosecurity, to which all other requirements will have to be sacrificed in order to govern. It is legitimate to ask whether such a society can still be defined as human or whether the loss of sensitive relationships, of face, of friendship, of love, can be truly compensated for by abstract and presumably completely fictitious health security.
>
> ibid.; ESPOSITO 2016

In short, "deconstructivist" academic mainstream philosophy expects the worst: that the social may be lastingly damaged, or even transformed into

"HEALTH TERROR"? TOWARDS AN ADEQUATE FRAMEWORK

something "inhuman" by Corona due to the temptation of those in charge of governments to use it as a pretext for better maintaining and further centralising power, now also in open societies with the help of the "biosecurity" paradigm. Although most of these apocalyptic expectations may be exaggerated or even unrealistic, radical "social philosophers" such as Agamben infused them into the intellectual elites of the West, at the same time refusing themselves to acknowledge even the categorisation of citizens according to nation states, and refusing, in the case of Agamben, to be a citizen of any country in the world. Thus, as inspiring as these lines by critical "deconstructive" philosophy may have been perceived by many critical citizens, foremost in the liberal and leftist socio-ideological spectrum, as non-constructive and extremist they appear when it comes to constructing a sound post-Corona future. Far from being abolished by emergency measures, European and Western democracies could even be strengthened by the Coronavirus crisis discussions about freedom and its limits, where the boundaries of civic restrictions are, where power and healthcare overlap, and where they should and where they should not. Certain is: a pure "deconstructive" and "resistance" ideology against all measures in emergency situations driven by the suspicion of "health terror" in view of (more or less subtle, direct and indirect) suppression will not make much progress happen. Besides its justified concern and valuable watchdog function, it may rather be in constant peril to trigger a self-fulfilling prophecy – as in the case of Agamben's assertions, read and debated with creepy joy mainly by the educated upper bourgeoisie who were the safest during the crisis.

Similarly, during the pandemic, (allegedly) "supercharged" leftist philosophers such as Slavoij Žižek who play the anti-elitist and anti-conformist but, in reality, have themselves long been exactly the expression of the elites and of mainstream (leftist) academic fashion, shot fast analyses with lots of wit and taste for contradictions and paradoxes, which often made things more complicated than clearer, but without concrete and feasible policy recommendations or constructive framework drafts to (simply) improve things (Žižek, 2020). As Žižek asserted:

> We live in a moment when the greatest act of love is to stay distant from the object of your affection. When governments renowned for ruthless cuts in public spending can suddenly conjure up trillions. When toilet paper becomes a commodity as precious as diamonds. And when ... a new form of communism – the outlines of which can already be seen in the very heartlands of neoliberalism – may be the only way of averting a descent into global barbarism (Ibid.).

Again, as inspiring such reasoning may be, and as sophisticated it may appear to many at first glance, it requires much less sophistication and work of the mind to point out contradictions, inconsistencies and errors than draft a concrete map of a better system to deal in more adequate ways with emergencies for the benefit of a "post-Corona world". In other words: Instead of just deconstructive, ironic, or cynical approaches all directed, in one way or the other, towards an attitude of "resistance" or critique, a more positive sketch of multiresilience is needed in reality – one that can provide some additional value for building a better systemic approach than before a crisis, e.g. COVID-19.

In essence, Žižek's remarks were apparently put onto paper rather fast and light-handedly which, in the first instance, are without doubt assets proving the inter- and trans-disciplinary reactivity, awareness and originality of an up-to-date social-science sector fed by informed and timely academic philosophy, as it should be. Yet besides its many valuable aspects, it at the same time also manifested the limits of "postmodern" "deconstructivist" critique: deconstructing "everything" by asking many questions, but not creating much. If Corona showed anything about the state of the institutionalised social sciences, including perhaps fashionable philosophy, it demonstrated that its mainstream and its primordial habits were paradigmatically constrained before the crisis and, in the crisis, manifested an inability of the current academic business to be policy-relevant, but also a certain bigotry in criticising everybody else except oneself, one's own favourites and "paradigm preferences". It also manifested its alliteration-based and associative style which all too often takes terms, notions and concepts and connects them according to their formal rather than to their inherent meanings, showing a superficiality partly due to the "nominalistic turn" since the 1980s which, in essence, took words for more real than the reality they co-create.

With Corona, this approach of what is sold as "intellectual" philosophy, but often is not very intellectual since it lacks substance, has manifested both its advantages and limits, partly also uncovering exaggerations and a trend to the apocalyptic and bizarre as the new normal in today's "fashionable" elitist academia dedicated to "universal and total critique" – a critique that, at least in the view of its proponents, simultaneously liberates its authors from any responsibility for the concrete processes underway. Yet such combinations of "total" critique with little or no (direct) responsibility belong to the pre-Corona world; after Corona, the sectors of philosophy, the academia, the Social Sciences and "postmodern" fashion-thinking should take their lessons and reasonably change, too, by searching for more appropriate and pondered ways of attitude and contribution.

CHAPTER 40

Seven Strategic Recommendations for Pro-positive Multi-resilient Policymaking in the Post-Corona World of Open Societies

So what would be more concrete, more pro-positive and more pro-active political recommendations for fostering and implementing multi-resilience in the post-Corona world? In light of the above-mentioned leverage points and first lessons learnt from the Coronavirus crisis, there at least five recommendations which can be derived.

40.1 Recommendation 1: Include Competency Development to Become a Crucial Part of the Education System

Multi-resilience of a society is not only based on the individual resilience of the society members (as outlined in previous chapters), but, as we have seen, also on enhancing social competencies (such as empathy and communication). According to multiple studies, an average of about ten percent of community projects trying to establish social innovations like "Transition Towns" would not survive the first five years. Iris Kunze argues that the reason would be a lack of community spirit and of rituals and competencies of conflict management. Thus, emotional intelligence, communication skills and related competencies are, in her view, crucial factors for the success of social innovations (Kunze, 2010) and in the widest sense of social resilience. Thus, fostering multi-resilience requires an even more advanced development of the aforementioned universal personal competencies, including Mindfulness and Emotional Intelligence. According to MIT and Harvard Fellow Gretchen Greene, this is also the case with regard to the (present and future) interconnection between AI and Emotional Intelligence. According to Greene, their growing post-Corona interconnection will need a new ethics of connecting emotional intelligence to (intelligent) machines (Greene, 2020).

Moreover, as we have also seen, the development of specific methodological competencies remains crucial to successfully implement specific tools, e.g. in the context of collective decision-making or in simulating best practices. This prominently includes, as mentioned, "Futures Literacy" which is, for example, already incorporated in the curriculum for Master's students at the

© ROLAND BENEDIKTER AND KARIM FATHI, 2022 | DOI:10.1163/9789004469686_041

Hanze University of Applied Sciences in Groningen, Netherlands, under the leadership of Loes Damhof, UNESCO Chair in Futures Literacy. In this context, students and teachers not only learn the capability of working about possible and probable futures, but also on how to design and facilitate them in order to apply their anticipated values and benefits in their studies and work (Larsen, Mortensen & Miller, 2020).

The first teaching is therefore simple. The development of universal (social and personal) competencies and of specific (methodological) competencies could and should be integrated in national education policies. On the one hand, they should be a systemic part of adult education, particularly in any area which employs and comprises influential decision-makers. On the other hand, competency development could also be implemented in the form of new school classes, courses and subjects, preferably by the introduction of a new school discipline "(Multi-)Resilience" in primary, middle and/or high schools. In general, a respective systemic simulation training should cover the full spectrum across different educational levels of all types, and in so doing could create bridges between them and among different schooling generations.

40.2 Recommendation 2: Strengthen European-Western Simulation Methodology and Strategic Foresight

In dealing with the Corona crisis, the measures taken by the pandemic-experienced states of South East and East Asia (in which the last international and global infectious diseases originated) proved to be relatively effective in containing the virus. The European states lacked comparable experience, and the measures were often characterised by political actionism and national egoisms. In order to learn more quickly and effectively from past experience and to be prepared for comparable crises in the future, the entire course of the crisis and the national and international measures taken could and should be systematically evaluated. Which practices of pandemic control (preventive and reactive) and for cushioning the social, economic and psychological side effects have proven themselves under which conditions? What should be done differently in the future?

An inter- and transdisciplinary task force could be set up for this purpose. The aim would be to further develop existing pandemic plans and more far-reaching contingency plans, and to make them ready for political decision-making as contextual option scenarios. This approach aimed at strategically establishing and standardising best practices by assessing past experiences nation- and worldwide, and learning from them, should be implemented in and after any crises.

Additionally, complex crises such as the Corona situation demand innovative practices. The Corona crisis has brought about huge – if not unprecedented – socio-economic impacts; therefore, as mentioned, some debates on formerly "utopian" concepts were gaining momentum. These included, as mentioned, the universal basic income respectively the negative income tax, or the concept of post-growth economy (Paech, 2012). Practicing "transformative resilience" implies being open and aware of chances and new opportunities which make it possible to further develop the social system and to emerge stronger from the crisis. A recommended measure for any crisis situation would therefore be to establish inter- and transdisciplinary forms of simulation and foresight collaboration composed of representatives from politics, the private sector, civil society and scientists from different disciplines. As mentioned previously, learning from the Corona crisis, this also means that it should not only be virology and nature sciences but also the social sciences and the humanities.

Such collaborations could and should systematically reflect on "new paths" and test and further develop social and technological innovations in appropriately provided laboratories. The benefit of innovation promotion is based above all on the fact that new crisis events require correspondingly new responses. As described in previous chapters, there were several promising approaches to systematically exploiting collective problem-solving capabilities being implemented within the first half of 2020. These included e.g. the hackathons, as implemented in Germany and Estonia, and a team-up between the Estonian start-up community, Mistletoe Singapore, the European Commission and other local and international supporters, in order to prepare the Estonian start-up sector for the imminent Post-Crisis world. An important next step will be to develop and initiate comparable forms and forums of collective-intelligent problem-solving development on a vast variety of levels of public-private partnerships.

For this purpose, a public-private crisis institution could be created that is politically empowered, independent, and active over a longer period of time. This institution would be concerned with implementing local and contextual inter- and transdisciplinary initiatives of innovative solution development, collecting the information gained from these initiatives, processing it into publicly available knowledge, and testing and further developing decision-ready measures and strategies for policymakers.

270   CHAPTER 40

40.3 Recommendation 3: Strengthen Future Anticipation Capacities and (Potentially) Their Integration. From the Futures Cone and the Futures Diamond to Futures Literacy

The Coronavirus crisis hit almost everyone unexpectedly. As repeatedly underscored, more, possibly even more dangerous, complex and equally unforeseeable crisis scenarios are possible in the future. A way to increase societies' ability to learn and react to unforeseeable extreme events will be to increase the general future anticipation capacities and to integrate them. This includes the systematic implementation and, where possible, integration of the three basic simulation and foresight methods of the "Futures Cone", the "Futures Diamond" and applied "Futures Literacy" in the widest sense. Following the precautionary principle of preventive multi-resilience, the strength of these measures lies in preparing for the unpredictable future, say: before the crisis occurs. Strategic foresight correlates, to a certain extent, with the aforementioned strategy of systematically developing best and innovative practices which come into play during the crisis (reactive resilience) and after the crisis (recovery resilience).

Foresight comprises a broad variety of tools preparing societies "to meet the needs and opportunities of the future" (Cuhls, 2003). Hereby, it does not assume "a future" or "one future", but rather "multiple futures", since the very nature of "the future" is to be non-determined by the present and the past, and not fixed. The notion of "multiple futures" includes: Probable, plausible and possible futures, preferable futures, undesirable futures, and preposterous futures (Figure 9). Additionally, there are "future potentials" or "weak signals" which can be found in the present and which might help us to anticipate the future, for example through methods such as "Horizon Scanning". All these different concepts of future are summarised in the so-called "futures cone", which has been popularised by future scientist Joseph Voros (2003; 2017).

Considering these different future trajectories which vary the more the more they are in the future, foresight implies a broad variety of practical tools which are summarised in the so-called "Futures Diamond" (n.d.; R. Popper, 2008a, b) – a practical framework including 44 methods (Figure 10). The "Futures Diamond" was developed by Rafael Popper in the "The Handbook of Technology Foresight" (Georghiou et al., 2008).

Of these 44 methods, "Simulation" and "Scenario" belong to the most important ones in terms of developing preventive resilience. They can be briefly outlined as follows:

Simulation. Advanced simulation methodology is a classical tool to develop behavioural routines on the basis of best or good practices in the face of

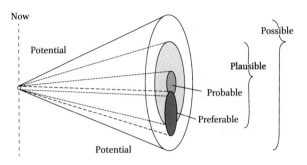

FIGURE 9   The futures cone
SOURCE: VOROS, 2003

unexpected, but to some extent structurally anticipated events. Typically, so-called "High Reliability Organizations" (HROs), such as firemen or special forces tactical units, strongly base their activities on this tool (Weick & Sutcliffe, 2001). However, the simulation tool comes to its limits in view of unknown or completely new events. These would require tools which are designed to explore possibilities which no one has thought of before, like in the scenario planning method. Also, such events require a higher degree of openness, flexibility and faster adaptability than most simulation models provide. Furthermore, simulations should be concrete and thus usually can be only related to one crisis type at a time. For instance, a simulation training on the next pandemic would significantly differ from a simulation regarding a – potential, expected or actual – natural disaster, or (in the rather improbable, but possible case) of the combination of both. Multi-resilience hereby means a resilience practice of life-long learning by the population. This could lead to regular simulation trainings of affected or steering groups about different crisis topics and contribute to further establishing best practices.

Scenario is rooted, among other influences and predecessors, in the strategic war-gaming practice of the empires of the 19th and 20th centuries. It was, to some extent, perfected during the Cold War 1947–1991. It has since been adopted by organisations to enhance their reactivity in the face of new VUCA threats, i.e., the increasing combination of Volatility, Uncertainty, Complexity, and Ambiguity.

Scenario Planning usually does not have a predictive claim. The strength of this tool lies much more in providing the opportunity to reflect even unlikely future events by comparing options and consequences, and to develop respective positive and counter strategies. This would enable a "learning from the future" process (a notion which is also used in the aforementioned "U Theory" tool to foster "out-of-the-box" thinking). Moreover, the tool itself implies

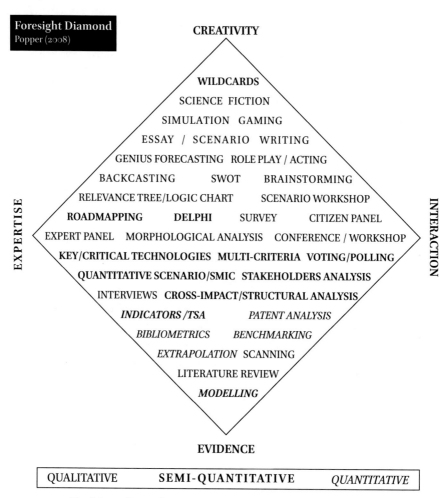

FIGURE 10 The futures diamond
SOURCE: POPPER N.D., 2008A

moderation techniques to integrate the knowledge of the perspectives of very different participants.

A typical scenario-planning workshop today varies between two and five days. Usually, it focuses on a specific topic or question, e.g.: "How will post-Corona societies develop in 2030 in Africa?". The principal weakness of scenario planning is its limitation to an excerpt of an expected situation in a precise moment in time, i.e., in a context-time combination, rather than on complex, changeable and intertwined processes in time. Also, most scenario-planning practices still neglect the methodologies related to "history gaming" (as related, for example, to the "World Systems Theory" of Wallerstein (2004) and others), i.e., to thinking about developments possible if certain events in history had been differently decided or enacted – which can be an important tool of "thought flexibilisation" and thus of "thought enhancement" with regard to multi-resilience related to futures preparedness.

Related to forecasting, but not identical with it, the previously mentioned approach of UNESCO *Futures Literacy* can be regarded as a meta-approach integrating different tools, methods and models which enable management of the future by "working actively with it". An important axiom is hereby that "anticipation" is the basic operation of any future reflection. The long-time head of UNESCO Futures Literacy and one of its inventors, main theorists and mentors, Riel Miller, defines Futures Literacy as:

> the capacity of an organism to incorporate the later-than-now into its functioning in ways that are relevant.
> R. MILLER, 2018

Building on that, Futures Literacy in his view means the:

> ability to imagine outside predefined paradigms, or to sense and make sense of phenomena that may not belong to pre-existing models. Imagined futures that do not arise from efforts to address what is currently deemed probable or desirable have no place in mainstream thinking. As a result, given the power that images of the future have over what we perceive and do, most novel phenomena remain invisible, bereft of meaning, because they are excluded from our images of the future (Ibid.).

In other words, Futures Literacy is the ability to overcome this "present bias" (which perhaps may even include some kinds of "presencing bias") in order to:

> combin[e] a broad palette of planning horizons and methods with what might appear to be a surreal or absurdist imagination, detached from deterministic purposes and methods (Ibid.).

The inherent discipline is called by Miller the "Discipline of Anticipation (DoA)". With this term, Miller delineates the ability:

> to become aware of assumptions about the future. Mastering it allows us to view uncertainty as a resource, rather than an enemy of planning. By imagining different futures, individuals can become aware of their capacity to shape and invent new *Anticipatory Assumptions* (*AA*), and the act

274   CHAPTER 40

of shifting this ability to anticipate from an unconscious to a conscious state (Ibid.).

Hereby, Futures Literacy distinguishes between two types of anticipation: Anticipation-for-the-Future (AfF) versus Anticipation-for-Emergence (AfE). AfF regards the future as a goal, in terms of a planned or desired future that people bet on. By contrast, AfE is, in a sense, a "non-future", "a use of the future to sense and make sense of aspects of the present, particularly novelty, which tends to be obscured by AfF" (Ibid., p.22). This would also allow for a "new strategic approach to resilience by leveraging complexity and the diversification of novelty affords" (Ibid.).

According to UNESCO's Riel Miller, almost all the theoretical and practical knowledge that to date is making up fields like "Future Studies" or foresight is about AfF. Thus, Futures Literacy could enrich mainstream Strategic Foresight and Future Studies in several regards. This includes mapping the tools (as in the sense of the Futures Diamond above), but also in a more integrative fashion. In the latter regard, Futures Literacy (see Figure 11) would not only provide a clearer view on the boundaries of contemporary tools (nearly all approaches of Strategic Foresight and Future Studies neglect concept related to AfE), it would also provide a better understanding of how to match specific (future) tools for specific (future) tasks. All the respective theories and methods can be attributed to different clusters of Anticipatory Assumptions (AA). These are integrated in the so-called "Futures Literacy Framework".

Briefly outlined, the different clusters in this schedule imply the following tools and processes (Ibid., p. 32):

- AA1 Closed/AfF and General-Scalable: 'forecasting': This cluster includes a conception of predictable (closed) and (through quantitative means) generalisable future(s). Typical tools are point forecasts with risk calculation, actuarial tables, trends and mega-trends, deterministic utopias versus dystopias, fortune-telling and expert prognostication, which are all part of imagining generalisable probable or desired futures.
- AA2 Closed/AfF and Specific-Unique: 'destiny': In this cluster, specific-unique aspects of imaginary futures are generated and assimilated on the basis of existing fatalistic or deterministic stories. Imaginary futures are hereby foretold. Indicators include affirmation of religious or ideologically pre-determined ("closed") futures.
- AA3 Semi-open/AfF and General-Scalable: Imaginary futures are developed to solve known problems in innovative ways. Creativity methods can be used to seek generalisable solutions "from within"

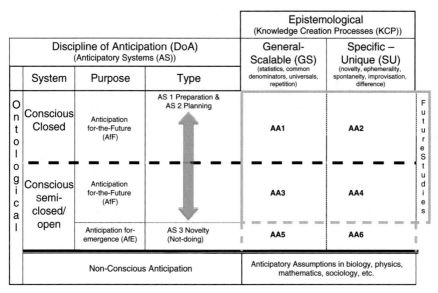

FIGURE 11   Futures literacy framework
SOURCE: MILLER 2018, P. 24

(endogenous), but within the confines of AfF-type goals. Thus, typical methods include (endogenous) reform within system, and plurifold approaches to foster resilience as adaptive continuity.

- AA4 Semi-open/AfF and Specific-Unique: 'self-improvement'. In this cluster, imaginary futures are often inward or consciousness-oriented, but in the service of attaining pre-determined normative futures (AfF). Consequently, the underlying motto of these interventions is "Consciousness raising" focusing on adaptation at personal or organisational culture levels through experience.
- AA5 Semi-open/AfE and General-Scalable: 'strategic thinking'. Methods in this cluster focus on sensing and making sense of emergence in the present (AfE) on the basis of identifiably general-scalable attributes. Applicants seek to detect and invent "novelty with reference to phenomena that repeat". This includes variation, in terms of a given variable that increases or decreases. Approaches imply e.g. identifying the parameters of paradigms – including existing paradigms which were previously invisible or partially hidden, or the invention of new notions to describe future(s).
- AA6 Semi-open/AfE and Specific-Unique: 'wisdom–Tao–being'. In this cluster, anticipation focusses on locally specific-unique attributes

of the present. Indicators can include "discovery or invention of novelty", resulting in the coining of new words and identifying missing words, or establishing relationships at specific or ephemeral process levels (Ibid.).

These clusters or their intersection, which at first glance may appear complex and difficult to handle but, in reality, is rather simple and not too complicated, can provide the bases for the design of tailored "Futures Literacy Labs". These vary strongly regarding the local contexts to which they are practically implemented.

Typically, a collaborative process with local participants includes first, identifying and describing one's own existing Anticipatory Assumptions (AA), and second, reassessing these perceptions of the past, present, and aspirations for the future. Third, to engage in a process of joint Action-Learning and Collective Intelligent Knowledge Creation (CIKR) to design and shape future(s).

Overall, Futures literacy has been pioneered and developed since 2012 by the United Nations Educational, Scientific and Cultural Organization (UNESCO), acting as:

> a global laboratory of ideas where the latest advances in the theory and practice of using the future are discussed and prototyped.
>
> R. MILLER & FEUKEU, n.d.

In the end, it is recommended that interdisciplinary teams are established, both from research and practice, simulating and describing different, possibly imminent crisis scenarios and designing appropriate, preferably innovative coping strategies and desired futures that are self- and process-learning. This could be implemented through decision-making processes on local and on federal levels. Additionally, based on the respective principles, it should be recommended that an independent crisis institution is established on federal levels, being responsible for permanently monitoring risk potentials both on its sub-levels and in the world; developing plausible worst-case and desired future scenarios with the help of interdisciplinary teams; developing and testing new strategies in laboratories; and, as a result, developing complexity-adequate decision-ready measures and strategies for policymakers.

On a global level, an inspiring starting point could indeed be the UNESCO Global Futures Literacy Network, serving as a platform to globally co-creating Futures Literacy with local participants in over 20 countries. To date, UNESCO has initiated Futures Literacy Chairs in Finland, Greece, Italy, Malaysia, Netherlands, Tunisia, United Kingdom, and Uruguay. These chairs are regarded as "catalysts for the development of Futures Literacy Centres" and as "key nodes in the emerging Global Futures Literacy Network" (Ibid.), working closely with partners in civil society, governments and the private sector (Larsen, Mortensen & Miller, 2020). After Corona and as a teaching of it, the Global Futures Literacy Network should be strengthened. It should not only be implemented in the Developing World within the context of development politics, but in all countries in order to foster local and global multi-resilience and future-related interconnection.

40.4 Recommendation 4: Improve Communication through "Complexity Workers"

It can be argued that the systematic use of methods such as strategic foresight, Futures Literacy or other methods is apt to improve communication. Nevertheless, critics remark that this requires already high methodological competencies which, in turn, would need a lot of education and training time. However, a high level of competence of all discussion participants is not a strict prerequisite. More important is the role of specially trained facilitators who could act as "complexity workers"[1] fostering dialogue and collaboration between participants of different societal sectors, classes and stripes and thus enhance the potential of overall collective intelligence. The post-Corona "complexity worker" could fulfil three roles: the role of a cross-sectoral knowledge broker, of a facilitator, and of a mediator.

As a *knowledge broker*, the complexity worker could foster cross-sectoral relationships and knowledge distribution by arranging contacts and networking between participants from all sectors. This approach is not new and can already be observed in lobbying and "strategic communication" professions involving contacting legislators and decision-makers from various sectors, trying to convince them to support or reject a given policy.

In the role of *facilitator*, the complexity worker could moderate dialogue processes between decision-makers making use of advanced complexity management methods. These include workshop tools such as Open Space, World Café, Team Syntegrity, scenario planning, or frameworks such as Design Thinking, Agile Thinking, or U Theory. The advantage would be to support discussion participants who are not trained in these methods and frameworks. This approach has been applied by the UNESCO in several countries within the framework of Futures Literacy via so-called "Futures Literacy Labs" (or FL

---

1 This term was coined by complexity expert Monia Ben Larbi.

Labs, R. Miller, 2018), including collaborative processes with partners from civil society, government and the private sector (R. Miller & Feukeu, n.d.).

As societal *mediators*, complexity workers would facilitate empathy and perspective-integration, particularly in the context of conflict lines cutting through societal rifts and polarisation and the resulting emotionally loaded debates. This was the case during the refugee crisis of 2015–16 and could be observed in 2020 with regard to the debate on "pandemic populism". Similar to a shuttle mediator, complexity workers would support the "translation" of knowledge content, the mediation of resources between the participants, and the provision of language to those who have none, in order to foster dialogue processes among those who are in conflict with each other.

40.5 Recommendation 5: Refine Multi-level Governance

Successful management of complex crises depends largely on how decision-making and implementation are structured. As outlined in previous chapters, the Corona crisis demonstrated the advantages of both centralised and decentralised coordination mechanisms (Hörr, 2020) and offered an opportunity to expand corresponding structures. Referring to the principles of the *Viable Systems Model* (vsm) discussed above, coping with future global challenges in a post-Corona world requires an appropriate balance between decentralised and overarching decision-making and implementation.

As a resulting recommendation, the public sector should strengthen local decision-making efficiency and capacities for crisis response. This includes promoting civil-society initiatives which contribute to sustainability and resilience, as well as supporting local governance institutions in their autonomy of decision-making and responding to crises. On the federal level, it will be necessary to weigh up from what point the higher system level does not only make recommendations but may also intervene in a regulatory fashion. Principally, according to the vsm, the federal level should, firstly, support the local units with resources and information; secondly, bundle information extracted from them; and thirdly, coordinate local units in a way that their resilience politics do not cannibalise each other. The federal governance level should set and communicate the overall direction; the local units should, however, be able to decide how they want to implement measures considering the particularities, demands and capacities of the local context.

Overall, the teaching of Corona is that existing forms of multi-level crisis coordination should be improved. The next step for the public sector would be to initiate an according legislation process. From a pragmatic perspective, the transition towards better coordinated multi-level governance could be accompanied by systematically supporting those initiatives of civil society and the private sector which are already operating top-down *and* bottom-up. The result could be a new coexistence of different initiatives and governance concepts. Referring to the competition principle among the building stones of multilevel governance, it would be important to assess and test this regarding its success in contributing to multi-resilience. Additionally, referring to the synergy principle, different initiatives on different levels should be assessed regarding their complementary points and their complementarity bonus. These tasks of assessment, testing, coordination and further development could be operated by an independent interdisciplinary institution which had already been requested by prior recommendations.

40.6 Recommendation 6: Expand and Improve International Cooperation

All previously mentioned recommendations and their inherent considerations also apply to the international context. These include: joint development of best and innovative practices, joint foresight and simulations, joint competency development via resilience education, joint fostering of effective communication with complexity workers, and interconnected expanding of multi-level governance. All of these activities do not only foster national multi-resilience, but could, applied on the international level, also contribute to better regional and global multi-resilience. As mentioned in previous chapters, the motivation to jointly develop multi-resiliency could enforce international cooperation and thus contribute to "Globalisation 2.0". International cooperation is widely established with regard to military security (take, for example, NATO). However, security concerns in the future will largely require multi-threat responses. Thus, the aforementioned initiatives must be slotted into international cooperation and within it should become routine.

Various topics of international cooperation to foster regional or global multi-resilience are possible. Knowledge transfer about collective and individual best practices would be likely to occur on a mutual basis, often enacted in bilateral relations (as pushed again by the current global political climate). Postmodern and relatively rich societies from the global North could contribute knowledge about hi-technological innovations, touching any aspects from energy efficiency to earthquake-resistant architectures or microbiome medicine, to the global South. By contrast, societies from the global South have much more experience in coping with situations of broken critical infrastructures. Globalised societies in both areas are much more dependent on increasingly complex "multimodal energy distribution systems" than ever before. These are characterised by the coupling and interdependence of energy sectors (electricity, heat, mobility) which are monitored and controlled through digital information and communication technology (ICT). As a result, these intelligent infrastructures and their mutual coupling make entire systems much more energy efficient and effective, but also more vulnerable due to their susceptibility to faults in the case of cyber-attacks or natural hazards (Deutsche Forschungsgemeinschaft, 2017). In the case of power outages, increasingly high-tech-driven information societies of the global North would suddenly lose all their functionality.[2] By contrast, societies from the global South with comparably less-complex energy infrastructures would prove to be less efficient, but at the same time more experienced in dealing with no or scarce energy resources. The question is who loses control when.

India could be an inspiring example in this case. In the face of short electricity supply, people try to make ends meet with batteries. This solution improves independence of the consumers but also proves to be very inefficient. In the end, both approaches from the South and North should be combined.

Today, experts from science and practice are testing the idea of equipping every household with a small box. This box could control which appliances should continue to run in the event of a power shortage and which not. It should be easy to program, so that each consumer can do this himself. Resilience from the "consumer's perspective" would mean that each person has the freedom to decide which system should be supplied with electricity according to which priority (Universität Passau, n.d.). Further contributions from the global South are so-called "frugal innovations", based on low-tech products which are robust, easy to repair, durable and in any regard resource efficient. Among the emerging countries, India remains an important pioneer in this area. For example, the start-up "First Energy" has launched a cheap and simple wood stove. Another example is "Little Cool" – a refrigerator for 70 US$, which lasts for a long time even during a power failure, developed by the industrial company Godrej & Boyce Manufacturing. Currently, frugal innovations are estimated to become an increasingly lucrative market due to the tripling of the global middle class to 4.8 billion potential consumers by 2030, driven mainly by developing countries (Tshidimba, Lateur & Sneyers, 2015). In the post-Corona world, they are expected to become increasingly attractive for Western consumers as well. On the one hand, frugal products will become better designed; on the

---

2   See, for example, the popular novel "Blackout" by Elsberg, M. (2012).

other hand, they systemically break with the typical growth paradigm "always more, always better". Thus, frugal goods could become the ideal product type in a more diversified socio-economic system, maybe including contributions to a post-growth economy.

These and other examples illustrate that multi-resilience for the post-Corona world comprises various sub-topics to foster international knowledge exchange, diversification and cooperation for the greater good of being prepared against further global challenges. Nevertheless, effective global crisis management will require further political integration, which, however, should not dissolve nation-state sovereignty and transfer it to a centralised supranational structure, but must rather preserve nation-state sovereignty and integrate it into a multi-level system.

What could be the first pragmatic steps? From a nation-state perspective, a first important starting point for the promotion of global cooperation could be implemented through trust-building Corona solidarity initiatives among nation states. Before and during the Corona crisis, China successfully took this informal approach to consolidate its "New Silk Road" or Belt and Road Initiative (BRI) by interconnecting the international, regional and local levels (Pechlaner et al., 2020). This could also be an inspiration for Western states. From a supra-national perspective, fostering, expanding and using the already existing UNESCO Global Futures Literacy Network (as mentioned in Recommendation 4) could also contribute to better globally coordinated resilience management. From a civil-society perspective, initiatives such as Simpol (n.d.) could contribute to improving international cooperation through resilience policies, too. Simpol, translated as "Simultaneous Policy", is an international citizens' campaign addressing a range of policies to solve global problems at the same time and on the same date, driving governments to implement them (Ibid.). To conclude, there are already existing leverage points and initiatives, at least on national, supra-national, and NGO level, contributing to global multi-resilience management which could be systematically sustained and expanded.

40.7 Recommendation 7: Sharpen Global "Crisis Automatisms" and Interconnected Responsibility Patterns on the Way to Global Governance

Resulting from increasingly interconnected crisis-management cooperation, a further important step would be to actively initiate cross-national mechanisms of global crisis coordination at the formal level of existing supranational institutions (e.g. at the UN or EU levels). This step, too, could be preceded by informal bilateral preliminary talks among states. In this regard, the Corona crisis should be the trigger for efforts to formalise active bilateral anticipated offers of support during upcoming crises, which would mean a new "crisis automatism" where possible under the umbrella of international organisations.

An important aspect in this direction would be to systemically strengthen responsibility patterns and to hold governments, officials and participants accountable. The minimum consequence on the political and juridical level with regard to Corona would be to implement an independent global enquiry commission, given that the virus had global consequences. The next potential step could be a multi-year recompensation plan of the world with that virus-originating nation which – if so – neglected basic security measures, as other countries such as, for example, Germany (but not only) had been forced to in the past for other reasons of guilt and behaviour.

In the long term, it should be the aim to achieve and establish real global governance in order to better manage global crises, although such an option may be still far away and currently unrealistic. The term "global governance" describes the entirety of coordination processes among different partici-pants in order to be able to cope with simultaneous, complex global chal-lenges (Messner, 2000). In this regard, this concept can be understood as a political programme to cooperatively and multilaterally shape globalisation (Hauff, 1987). Transferred to today, it would mean a joint mechanism to gov-ern re-globalisation. In contrast to the concept of a "global government", the "global governance" concept does not presuppose a centralised hierarchy or a global super-state. Rather, it emphasises collective regulation of complemen-tary social activities, which could be subsequently expanded. Such forms of regional or global regulation include markets (e.g. in the context of free-trade zones), networks (e.g. in the context of international and interdisciplinary science cooperation to develop and monitor universal technology progress including its inherent risks), or jointly developed communities, as is currently the case in the context of regional cooperation projects to develop Charter Cities or Smart Cities.

Aside from these reflections, the concrete picture of an international gover-nance system remains highly debated. Any viable solution to date means that the nation states retain the greatest possible sovereignty and, at the same time, are integrated into a supranational structure with more far-reaching rights and obligations. The EU can be seen as a process-open experiment for this in the economic and political integration of different nation states, perhaps currently the most advanced in the world. Despite all reasonable criticism against the EU, the fact that a relatively stable peace order between formerly conflicting European member states has been achieved that has remained stable since the end of wwii speaks in favour of this project. In this regard, the EU has strong potentials to co-initiate the discussion on re-globalisation and to inspire the world to develop a more explicit global governance. China's BRI initiative represents, to a certain extent, a pragmatic alternative towards multilateral regulation. In contrast to the EU, BRI is not conceived as a community of values but as a set of simultaneous parallel arrangements, including multilateral mechanisms and bilateral relations based on alleged win-win-cooperation (Godehardt, 2016). From a bottom-up perspective, global civil-society initiatives like the aforementioned Simpol could also contribute not only towards fostering global cooperation (as in Recommendation 6) but also towards influencing nation states to initiate and shape better global mechanisms.

CHAPTER 41

Recommendations for Global Post-Corona Policymaking in an Increasingly Multipolar World

41.1 Five Policy Trajectories Proposed by the University of the United Nations – Leading to the Key Concept of "Futures Literacy"

Most of these aspects make clear that international cooperation will be a crucial impetus for developing a multi-resilient world after Corona. Yet instead of the EU playing a UN substitute by collecting, together with some other countries, public and private charity money from the whole world to develop a vaccine (EC, 2020a; 2020b), thus once again confirming its over-idealistic and rather mono-lateral cosmopolitanism that is making some laugh and others nervous, in order to maintain both domestic coherence (in the sense of "European sovereignty") and international solidarity, the European Union should not conceive itself as a model student for the globe or act as an outstanding good-will benefactor. It should instead work by the means of global cooperation agreements on an equal basis side by side with the United Nations and other global bodies such as the World Trade Organization (WTO) and the World Bank. The University of the United Nations (UNU) made it clear at the peak of the crisis that in order to foster a forward-oriented post-Corona world, a global joint plan towards a more multi-resilient system is needed that goes beyond the European experiment, including its self-overestimation. According to UNU, this plan has to consider, evaluate, implement and integrate four socio-economic measures in particular:

1) Instilling a global debt suspension;
2) lending out more money to poor countries through coordinated and well-planned global mechanisms according to a stage-by-stage plan;
3) coordinating the post-Coronavirus response by establishing a global cooperation point;
4) forming a joint medical and prevention task force for future pandemics and other upcoming emergencies.

To this would have to be added:

5) founding new global cooperation institutions with regard to futures, foresight and anticipation, as already existent in a nutshell in the

above-mentioned UNESCO's "Futures Literacy" (R. Miller & Feukeu, n.d.; UNESCO, 2019; R. Miller, 2010) approach headed and coordinated by Riel Miller in Paris (R. Miller, 2018; 2019; 2017). This approach should be strongly further developed and obtain international funding in order to lead to more effect on international prevention, risk and futures exploration and coordination patterns, among others by the institution of more interacting UNESCO Chairs for Futures Literacy in an inter- and trans-disciplinary post-Corona perspective (R. Miller, n.d.; University of Trento, 2019).

As James Cockayne, Director of the United Nations University Centre for Policy Research (UNCPR) New York, pointed out in early April 2020:

> COVID-19 is a truly global crisis ..., the greatest challenge the United Nations has ever faced. No country can escape either the health dimension of this crisis, or the economic dimension, on its own ... Exit from the crisis will require intergovernmental and public-private coordination on testing and vaccination, travel regimes, economic safety nets, and, eventually, a synchronized rebooting of global trade and markets. ...
>
> COCKAYNE, 2020

In fact, such a policy is not just an idea, but was officially requested by the United Nations General Assembly in April 2020. It could lead to more lasting cooperation structures with regard to preventing the next global pandemic:

> On April 2, 2020, the UN General Assembly called unanimously for the United Nations system under the leadership of the United Nations Secretary-General to work with all relevant protagonists in order to mobilize a coordinated global response. The mandate was included in the first Resolution the [U.N.] General Assembly has ever adopted virtually, titled 'Global Solidarity to fight the coronavirus disease' ... (Ibid.).

On this basis, Cockayne sketched the "four steps" which he believes can make a difference and draft a productive post-Corona world on the inter- and transnational level:

> 1. *Broker a global debt holiday.* Developed countries have taken unheard steps ... to put their own economies into 'hibernation', including measures that effectively nationalize payrolls, corporate debt and in some cases childcare services. G20 leaders announced that these unilateral efforts

would, together, amount to some USD $5 trillion in domestic stimulus. Going further, the G20 also committed 'to do whatever it takes' to minimize the economic damage. So what *will* it take? The [U.N.] Secretary-General could start by brokering a temporary global debt holiday – a moratorium on debt repayments and interest – not just for developing countries, but for specific classes of debt globally ... The debt threat is not limited to developing countries. It also poses a growing test of social and political solidarity between and even within developed countries ... The Secretary-General should put the global financial sector to that test by challenging them to back a global debt holiday. This should start within the UN family, with relief from the World Bank and International Monetary Fund (IMF) (Ibid.).

Going further, Cockayne suggested even more drastic measures to incentivise the global economy that could last longer and have a medium- to long-term effect on the international trade and development sectors and serve perhaps as a model for future crises:

2. *Cut a deal on Special Drawing Rights (SDRs)*. There is more to the economic side of an exit plan than just debt relief. Developing countries are now staring into a far larger financing abyss. They need not only a debt holiday in order to be able to use the resources they already have available, but also a massive injection of *new* resources, especially because their traditional sources of revenue are collapsing. Developing countries stand to lose around USD $800 billion in trade. Many emerging economies face significant downturns in commodity and tourism revenues and in remittance income, as well as steep currency pressures and capital flight. Portfolio outflows from developing countries have been twice as great in the month since the virus went global as in the first month of the 2008 global financial crisis. Poor countries, especially in sub-Saharan Africa, have shrinking fiscal space to pay for public health responses, let alone the kind of economic life-support policies adopted in OECD countries in recent weeks. IMF managing director Kristalina Georgieva has warned that emerging economies would need USD $700 billion in funding even if they used all their foreign exchange reserves. And many of them cannot access international capital markets (Ibid.).

As a consequence, at the start of April 2020:

U.N. Secretary-General Guterres released a report on the socioeconomic impacts of the crisis, which his PR team billed, unambitiously, a plan that could "defeat the virus and build a better world". The report calls for 'a large-scale, coordinated and comprehensive multilateral response amounting to at least 10 per cent of global GDP' – roughly USD $8 trillion (Ibid.).

As a third point to foster the internationalisation of the post-Corona world, Cockayne urged a better coordination of cooperation and relief:

"3. *Create a global response clearinghouse.* An effective global public health response will require coordination going beyond the remit of the World Health Organization (WHO) ... This will require careful sharing and, as far as possible, coordination of national policies affecting operational response across interlocking policy domains. These would include:
– The movement of response-critical personnel and goods;
– Export restrictions on high-demand medical equipment;
– Lowering tariffs on essential medical equipment such as disinfectants and sanitization products; and,
– Soon, addressing sanitary, phytosanitary and labor migration disruptions of global agricultural markets and food security.
   A UN-convened policy clearinghouse could compile and maintain an up-to-date data set of policies affecting global response coordination across these domains. Clearinghouse mechanisms are springing up organically online, such as the IMF Policy Tracker and the Oxford University Government Response Tracker. Having such a mechanism centrally coordinated by the UN would help ensure transparency, certainty and trust for all governments" (Ibid.).

Fourth and last, Cockayne suggested co-creating a better international health task force, indirectly criticising the World Health Organization (WHO):

4. *Form a global COVID-19 diagnostics, vaccine and therapeutics task force.* Finally, the Secretary-General could convene a Global Task Force on COVID-19 diagnostics, vaccines and therapeutic treatments ... The Task Force would bring together key research, industry, financing and regulatory protagonists, to coordinate and accelerate the process of discovering, financing, manufacturing and distributing these medicines ... International efforts to develop a vaccine are currently highly fragmented and even competitive ... Regulators have a key role to play in unblocking barriers to effective cross-border information-sharing and cooperation. The Task Force could begin by agreeing to a set of principles to govern

the process of Research & Development for the vaccine and therapeutics, including ensuring commitment to equitable access (Ibid.).

As a fifth – and perhaps even indispensable – essential additional point, we would add:

> 5. *Upgrade, involve and expand the* UNESCO *"Futures Literacy" approach into all activities related to the points above, and make it, as far as possible, a methodological driver of innovation among and in-between countries, sectors and disciplines.* The Corona crisis has shown with unprecedented emphasis that the anticipation of potential futures has become a fundamental need of the international sphere partly neglected by the global community over the past decades of "exuberant globalisation"; and it has proven that to anticipate potential futures is not only about thinking about risks, but also, perhaps more importantly, about the capacities to imagine future situations and happenings, and to act flexibly according to options of innovative and out-of-the-box imagination able to deal with both the expected and the unexpected.

In short: COVID-19 has shown that to master potential future crises is not just about preparing physically and organisation-wise for emergencies ahead, but also to prepare one's mind here and now to "work with different futures" in the present, in order to be prepared in more encompassing ways. Futures Literacy is about preparing actual and future decision-makers on all levels, from civil society to the economy and politics, for "wicked problems", i.e., problems that are hyper-complex and interactive, and thus not solvable with just one approach, let alone with simple linear projections. If there was a "wicked problem" in recent times, it was without doubt the Corona crisis. In this sense, "Futures Literacy" could be a – if not *the* – key to a more sustainable post-Corona world. This is also because according to UNESCO's Riel Miller, who developed the concept, "Futures Literacy" is about recognising that:

> The world is not more complicated or complex today than yesterday; when it comes to seeing and acting in any specific situation it is capacity that makes the difference, not the absolute number of permutations or even unfamiliarity. What seems complicated to a child may seem like child's play to an adult. In particular, what matters is the sophistication of our sense-making: our ability to discover, invent and construct the world around us. To date, considerable effort has been made to improve sense-making capabilities. Policymakers call on familiar and intuitive methods

of everyday experience (preparation and planning), as well as techniques (such as forecasting, horizon scanning, scenarios, expert opinions) considered adequate based on past perceptions of our needs and capacities. Nevertheless, the perceived proliferation of so-called 'wicked problems' in recent times has added to a mounting sense of uncertainty and called into question both the decision-making value of these business-as-usual approaches as well as their sufficiency in accounting for complexity in practice. Recent advances in understanding complexity, uncertainty and emergence have opened up new ways of defining and using the future. The question is therefore not how to cope with a universe that seems to be getting more complex, but how to improve our ability to take advantage of the novel emergence that has always surrounded us.

R. MILLER, 2010

41.2 The Forgotten Perspective: Instilling a More Encompassing and Trans-systemic Concept of Health and Healing?

A last point has to be recommended: to expand the concept of healing to become a carrier of inter- and trans-disciplinary internationalisation of medicine. According to Marlen and Hartmut Schröder, experts in globalised "cultural medicine" located in Berlin, any path forward towards a sustainable multi-resilience system after Corona indeed includes a new, more encompassing concept of "healing":

The further course and possible outcome of the Corona crisis is not least connected to what we identify as a disease and understand by cure. Conventional (e.g. pharmacology oriented) medicine claims the sovereignty of interpretation and spreads the narrative of the virus threatening us on the one hand and of a saving vaccine on the other hand. This is supported by politics and the media by the means of an almost aggressive war rhetoric, which both stirs up fear (of infection with the virus) and awakens hope (for 'healing' through a vaccine). In this narrative, the term 'healing' is narrowed down in its meaning. It is reduced to an external act of heroically fighting virologists. The latter are staged in the media as experts 'who know' and proclaim 'salvation', which then has to be implemented by politics under the 'primacy of science'. A critical view, however, reveals that this narrative is fed by a mechanistic and reductionist image of mankind as well as by an almost naive image of science (as a neutral instance of the factual and the truth) that has long since the start of Corona become obsolete ... Viruses are *per se* neither 'good' nor 'bad': it is the milieu and the health conditions under which an infection occurs that determine the outcome. In an interview on Corona, virologist Karin Mölling noted: 'When major epidemics occur, we humans are usually at least partly to blame. I will only mention the keywords overpopulation, poor hygienic conditions and animal markets. (...) Only we humans create the conditions for diseases or deadly epidemics'.

SCHRÖDER & SCHRÖDER 2020; SCHRÖDER, 2020a

In this view, as a result of the Corona crisis, the Schröders pleaded for a more "holistic" approach to future pandemics and to the "healing" of similarly encompassing systemic crises more generally:

Any holistic concept of healing must aim at healing a sick society and economy as well as sick culture, science and politics ... In a global world in which everything is connected to everything else, health and healing are no longer divisible. They are the result of international processes and ecological developments. A solution can only be found together by different strands of society. In times of the Corona crisis not only those suffering from COVID-19 need healing. Nature, our culture, society and politics also need it. In essence, a more encompassing concept of healing is needed by the circumstances that have favoured ... the outbreak of the COVID-19 pandemic. If we want to learn something from this crisis, the first priority should be to replace a narrative that exaggerates vaccination as a *panacea* but neglects to strengthen the immune system in a more encompassing sense. Reducing healing to vaccination is an expression of the interests of a medical-industrial complex that ultimately may amplify the problems it claims to solve. In such context perhaps the Corona crisis will provide an opportunity for a new understanding of healing. In this new understanding, healing will no longer be something 'done' from the outside and by experts. Rather, it will be understood as an internal *and* external process of self-healing, in which the immune system of each individual can fully develop in the context of a resilient society and of a global immune system – an immune system of the globe (Ibid.).

PART 7

Outlook. The Coronavirus Legacy: A "New World" Ahead – or Back to Business as Usual?

CHAPTER 42

The (Productively) Ambiguous Post-Corona Vision

A "New World" Ahead?

Such a "new immune system" has unavoidably to rely on newly built trust and confidence – which together form the immune system of a society (Cook, 2001; Cook, Harden & Levi, 2005). In July 2020, Italian President Sergio Mattarella in his traditional summer speech to the Italians living abroad in view of the effects of the crisis solemnly declared that it was time "to relaunch trust in the future":

> Now the commitment is directed to the reconstruction of a tissue, able to face the risks that arise and to revive confidence in the future. The virus has crossed continental frontiers and distances. It has challenged consolidated paths and ways of life ... Only shared knowledge and effective choral action in defence of health by all countries can enable the disease to be defeated.
>
> ANTONINI, 2020

Indeed, trust will be the prerequisite to create any new social tissue after Corona (Cook, 2001). This is not going to be easy, since the psychological effects will have a lasting impact in the minds and hearts of many. In the end, from a "higher", perhaps even "post-" or "meta"-materialistic point of view, to try to "do everything" or to "do anything" in the midst of a profound, inter- and trans-disciplinary and trans-border interconnected crisis may still not be the same as to "Do nothing", but it may sometimes resemble it closely amid personal exhaustion in view of the relation of what can be personally done and what would be globally needed. To some who lived through the Corona crisis, both "to do" and "to do not" appeared, from a certain point on, to be equivalent – at least to personal experience in the midst of the "nothingness" of uncertainty, disorientation, and social chaos. The difference, though, for an (existing and upcoming) *community pattern*, be it regional, national or international, is quite obvious: it is pro-active cooperation and joint action.

In a Delphi study conducted by the German Ministry of Education and Research (BMBF) over five months during the Coronavirus crisis, 35 theses about the post-Corona world were formulated by international experts. They

© ROLAND BENEDIKTER AND KARIM FATHI, 2022 | DOI:10.1163/9789004469686_043

tried to envisage a potential "new world" after the Corona crisis, both in positive and negative ways. Among them, the *least likely* future scenarios chosen were:

> Thesis 13: In the aftermath of the crisis, there will be a temporary (at least for a few years) decrease in the willingness of the population to address other issues (such as climate or migration). Thesis 33: The digitisation of schools, teaching and work will lead to an educational explosion that will enable (educational) structural deficits to be overcome sustainably against the impermeable social barriers of education policy. Thesis 27: The awareness of the fragility and limitation of human existence will become socially much more relevant during and after the Corona crisis. The previous social marginalisation and tabooing of weakness, suffering, dying and death, on the other hand, will decrease. Viewed positively, the [Coronavirus emergency] experience could contribute to bringing back into the collective consciousness an image of humanity that is not characterised by perfection or by the ability to function and perform, but rather by being precarious, fragile and fluid.
>
> GLOCKNER ET AL., 2020

In contrast, the *most likely* post-Corona scenarios according to the experts were:

> Thesis 29: The interaction of monetary and fiscal policy will help to limit the economic damage ... The price, however, will be a permanently high level of public debt, which will continue to place a permanent burden on the younger generation and our children in particular. Hypothesis 10: The European Union will emerge stronger from the crisis, since the corona crisis opens the window of opportunity for comprehensive reform. Hypothesis 30: The enormous economic consequences of the corona pandemic could encourage new approaches in economic theory (e.g. modern monetary theory) and lead to new financial instruments. A global debt cut is being made for the first time. Hypothesis 11: As a result of the crisis, international cooperation will become more difficult, supranational organisations will come under further pressure. Hypothesis 9: Nation states will gain in importance at the expense of supranational and international institutions. Hypothesis 6: As a result of the corona crisis, it will be possible to re-think the health, economic and climate crises together and find an overarching approach to action. Hypothesis 3: The collective experience of the vulnerability of our economic and social system will accelerate (digital) innovations after the initial crisis. Hypothesis 21: Scientific findings and researchers will experience a social

revaluation, which will also benefit climate research – and subsequently lead to a higher acceptance of strict climate protection measures. Thesis 15: A new understanding of the social infrastructure that is to be provided in the sense of a service of general interest will be achieved – beyond economic logics in categories of profit and short-term efficiency. Thesis 33: The digitisation of schools, teaching and work will lead to an educational explosion that will enable (educational) structural deficits to be overcome sustainably against the impermeable social barriers of education policy (Ibid.).

It is interesting that thesis 33 about a positive "revolution" in educational policy and inequality was evaluated as both the least and the most likely in Germany and Europe.

Yet even in such a constructive and positive perspective, the visions for a post-Corona world varied starkly. They reached from "don't look back" to partly or pluri-innovative to a "new dream world", and then again back to apocalyptic. Like the mood of the citizens, they changed frequently. These differing visions will have to be remembered long after the crisis is over in order to prepare for new crises and emergencies, – learning the lesson that views and scenarios are volatile and often do not necessarily represent reality in stable and enduring ways. The views and expectations were indeed many.

First of all, some rightly asked if the post-Corona world, besides a fundamental educational overhaul, needs a new understanding of "world heritage" (Holtorf & Brolin, 2020) by re-valuating the fundamental resilience factor of culture, i.e., by elevating culture to a decisive global resilience factor, as promoted for example by the United Nation's cultural and educational branch UNESCO. As Cornelius Holtorf and Annalisa Brolin exemplarily put it:

Education, research, culture, and communication are important ... These are the realms of the United Nations Educational, Scientific and Cultural Organization, better known by the acronym UNESCO. Since its start after the end of World War II, UNESCO has been aiming to foster the building of peace, the eradication of poverty, sustainable development and intercultural dialogue. Of particular importance has been the ambition to increase mutual understanding and collaboration among the 193 member states and their populations ... Today, UNESCO's aims are as significant as ever, but the corona crisis could have detrimental consequences for the ability to achieve them in the future. We should therefore not forget that all the measures we take today to mitigate the crisis and its impact, the way in which we communicate on social media about the events as they unfold, and all the calls regarding what needs to be done, or must cease to be done once the crisis is over, have a bearing on our future ability to work globally for the building of peace, the eradication of poverty, sustainable development, and intercultural dialogue. We need a vision of the future that appreciates the full potential of culture to address global crises. In the COVID-19 context, UNESCO's Assistant Director General for Culture, Ernesto Ottone, argues that 'in moments of crisis, people need culture.' He reminds us of two important things about culture. Firstly, culture 'provides comfort, inspiration and hope at a time of enormous anxiety and uncertainty.' The proliferation and popularity of online tours allowing us to virtually visit museums around the world indicate the appetite for culture in these times. But secondly, Ottone adds, despite what culture gives us in the context of the pandemic, a serious financial crisis in the cultural and creative sectors has left many practitioners and institutions in serious hardship. Budget cuts, layoffs, lost contracts, and uncertainty are imperiling the survival of the cultural sector. What UNESCO has not been emphasizing enough, however, is the way in which global cultural values are affected when national strategies are prioritized over international collaboration. When Ottone suggests that 'Culture makes us resilient. It gives us hope. It reminds us that we are not alone,' he appears to refer to the diversity of cultures (in the plural) practiced in UNESCO's member states. Yet he does not highlight the core idea on which UNESCO was established: What makes us all most resilient, as human beings on this planet, is a culture (in the singular) of global peace, open dialogue, mutual understanding, and continuous collaboration (Ibid.).

From all this, Holtdorf and Brolin drew some basic long-term conclusions:

> In the light of the global spread and impact of the COVID-19 pandemic, it is time to remind ourselves once more of the interdependences between all the people and communities on this planet. We are all part of an interconnected humanity. The pandemic has demonstrated a strong need for global solidarity and cooperation. As the virus spreads across the world's societies, many have realized the benefits of a speedy global exchange of accurate information, of mutual support and solidarity between people to address everybody's needs, and not the least of joint strategies of medical research and the development of a safe vaccine. Over the years and decades to come, we can expect many other kinds of crises when similar collaboration will be important. The greatest crisis facing *Homo sapiens* as a collective – the climate crisis – is already here and demanding

THE (PRODUCTIVELY) AMBIGUOUS POST-CORONA VISION 297

extensive global cooperation in response ... In this respect, perhaps the demands of the response to COVID-19 can provide us with a roadmap for responding to even larger challenges: the need for collaboration and viewing all of our fates as intertwined, at the very least; the establishment of new routes for cooperation and information sharing; and openness to drastic but effective methodologies for mitigating large risks. The corona pandemic intersects with ongoing challenges to which we have not yet developed adequate responses. The likely origin of the virus in close human contact with animals, for example, should spur us to reassess our relationship with the animal world. We have long known that profound challenges arise from our current interactions with animals: antibiotic resistance, in part because of the widespread and indiscriminate use of antibiotics in industrial meat production, is a known problem. So too is the climate impact of such production, including the deforestation of fragile environments to satisfy global rates of meat consumption. In this sense, the coronavirus is simply another data point demonstrating the dangers of our current model of interaction with and exploitation of the natural world. What all of these issues, from coronavirus to the climate crisis, share is the need for global responses to global challenges (Ibid.).

Most observers and opinion-makers agreed with this, but some, in contrast, underscored the uncertainty factor. Disputed investor and finance guru George Soros called Corona the "crisis of a lifetime" (Soros, 2020) (yet speaking probably not for the younger generations), claiming that "only one thing is certain about the post-pandemic world: there is no way back to the globalised economy that preceded it. Everything else is up for grabs, including the rise of China, the fate of the United States, and the survival of the European Union" (Ibid.).

Nevertheless, many others were of the surprisingly optimistic opinion that "COVID-19 offers a chance to build a better world. We must seize it" (Metzl, 2020). Some researchers in particular hoped for a push in scientific-medical innovation, using this virus crisis to innovate mass testing for diseases in general and new pandemics to come:

How do you find out where a new Corona infection is spreading – and as quickly as possible, even before the affected persons are tested? Scientists from the Helmholtz Centre for Environmental Research (UFZ) in Leipzig, Germany, have asked themselves this question. They hope to find the answer in wastewater. For weeks they have been working on a sewage treatment plant method, and now the test phase is starting at around

20 locations nationwide. The basic idea: If you look for traces of Sars-CoV-2 in sewage treatment plants, you can detect an outbreak even if no infected persons are suffering from symptoms at that location.

BILD ONLINE, 2020S

Yet in reality, the Corona crisis showed that to focus on one crisis challenge may cause other problems and lead to new vulnerabilities and failures, which was clearly shown by the healthcare sector:

> The corona pandemic severely affected the care of people suffering from other diseases worldwide. This is the result of a survey conducted by the World Health Organization (WHO) in May 2020 in 155 countries ... According to the survey, 31 percent of the countries had to restrict or completely interrupt care in the event of acute cardiovascular problems. 42 percent cut back on care for cancer patients, 49 percent for diabetes patients and more than half were unable to maintain the usual care for people with high blood pressure. Rehabilitation programs were cut back in 63 percent of countries. Prevention programmes, for example for the detection of breast cancer, were also affected. The cuts were particularly severe in low-income countries. In most cases, appointments were cancelled because staff was withdrawn to treat COVID-19 patients, or because people could not attend appointments due to restrictions on going out. Non-transmittable diseases kill 41 million people every year, according to WHO estimates. That is 71 percent of the deaths worldwide

REDAKTIONSNETZWERK DEUTSCHLAND, 2020

In March 2020, German futurist

> Matthias Horx (65) published the text 'The post-Corona World' (Horx, 2020a) on the Internet. His thoughts about the post-virus world went viral, five million clicked on it. Horx's highlight: He put himself into the future after the crisis and asked himself the question how we could have mastered it the best way possible. His result was a wonderment about how Corona could have made the world a better place. Horx says: 'The virus can be an evolutionary accelerator for our society. The future is when we rise above ourselves in times of crisis and reinvent ourselves'.

HORX, 2020C

It was heavily criticised, though, that Horx stated that Corona was a "system reset" (Horx, 2020a) and "this is how the future works" (Ibid.). This – at least indirectly – seemed to suggest that as the main teaching of Corona, the world should see crises mainly positively – as if it were desirable for there to be more, in the end. This was perceived as cynical in face of 100,000 deaths in the crisis. Also, Horx's naively positivistic concept of "societal evolution" which proceeds with the help of catastrophes appeared to be rather one-dimensional, one-sidedly idealistic, if not dangerously suggestive in the eyes of moderate realists acquainted with the 20th century history of Europe.

Similarly (productively) ambiguous, Oxford scholar Timothy Garton Ash asserted in a long elaborate answering of his own question, "What kind of post-Corona world do Europeans want?":

> The corona crisis could lead us to the best of times. It could lead us to the worst of times. The corona crisis seems to be encouraging belief in radical change. An astonishing 71 percent of Europeans are now in favour of introducing a universal basic income, according to an opinion poll (Garton Ash & Zimmermann, 2020) designed by my research team at Oxford University. In Britain, the figure is 68 percent. Less encouraging, at least to anyone who believes in liberal democracy, is another startling finding in our survey: no less than 53 percent of young Europeans place more confidence in authoritarian states than in democracies to tackle the climate crisis … It would be fascinating now to ask Europeans which political system they think has proved better at combating a pandemic, as the United States and China, the world's leading democracy and the world's leading dictatorship, spray viral accusations at each other. Those two contrasting but equally striking survey results show how high the stakes will be as we emerge from the immediate medical emergency and face the subsequent economic pandemic and its political fallout. What kind of historical moment will this turn out to be, for Europe and the world?
>
> GARTON ASH, 2020

Garton Ash explained the most important aspects of a new, positive post-Corona "dream world" arising in his vision in a way not dissimilar to that sketched successfully and received by a broad audience by Horx (2020a; 2020b). As Ash asserted:

> The proposal for a universal basic income was, until recently, often dismissed as far-out and utopian. But during the anti-pandemic lockdowns, many developed countries have introduced something close to it, not for everyone, to be sure, but certainly for large parts of the population.

Spain's economy minister has said that its 'minimum vital income' could become a permanent instrument in the country's system. Hardly a day passes now when I do not read another article suggesting that universal basic income, or some variant of it, is an idea whose time has come. This would be one ingredient of a possible future in which we manage to turn one of the greatest crises of the post-war world into one of its greatest opportunities.

GARTON ASH, 2020

Departing from this lesson learned in the crisis, Garton Ash imagined golden times ahead:

We address the soaring inequality, both economic and cultural, that has been eroding the foundations even of established liberal democracies such as Britain and the US. Having learned during the lockdown to work in different ways, more from home and with less unnecessary travel, we turn this into a new life-work model. Having appreciated the cleaner air and clearer skies, the sounds of birdsong not drowned out by traffic and the slow changes of nature that we had previously been too busy to notice, we will get serious about taking the radical steps needed both to address climate change and to give us a better quality of life. After turning out on our balconies and rooftops, all across Europe, to applaud the doctors, nurses, and social care and other essential workers who have been risking their lives to save our own, we do not forget them once the medical danger has passed. Not only do they get a better deal socially and economically – the post-war slogan 'homes fit for heroes' comes to mind – but there is also what Polish populists slyly call a 'redistribution of respect'. And in making that necessary redistribution, we also deprive the nationalist populists of their electoral appeal ... At the same time, we recognise that a planet stalked by genuinely global threats such as this virus and climate change requires more international cooperation, not less. And the European Union, which convened an international meeting to raise funds for fighting COVID-19, becomes a prime mover of global collective action. That's the dream (Ibid.).

But according to Garton Ash, there will also be a flip side which may be an equally possible trajectory:

But then there's the nightmare. This may be a post-war moment, but it turns out more like the years after the First World War than post-1945 liberal and social democratic reconstruction. The nationalist impulses we see in Donald Trump and Xi Jinping become even more pronounced. With beggar-my-neighbour policies, the post-coronavirus recession descends into a great depression. Inequality soars, rather than being diminished, both within our societies and between different countries. In Europe, wealthy north European countries such as Germany and the Netherlands simply don't show the necessary degree of solidarity with the battered economies of South European Eurozone members. Instead, they use the EU's crisis-justified suspension of limits on state aid to pump public funds into their key industries, and the gulf between northern and southern eurozone states grows wider. In a couple of years' time, a populist ... gains power in an Italy, where public debt is now about 160 percent of GDP, and blames all the country's woes on a lack of north European solidarity ... And so, [countries] turn to authoritarian solutions. Europe looks ever less to the US, ever more to China. Come 2030, we probably won't have either this hell or that heaven, just some version of our usual human purgatory. But which variant we come closer to is entirely up to us (Ibid.).

CHAPTER 43

"Corona Positivism"

The Global Pandemic as an Unprecedented "Chance" for Radical Transformation – Or Even as the Epochal Example for What (Social) Art Should Achieve?

As mentioned, there were many surprisingly positive voices and views regarding the effects, teachings and the outlook. Some saw "the Corona turnaround" as an unprecedented chance for radical short-term transformation of the main mechanisms of today's world in a systemic manner towards the better. Others even praised the Coronavirus as the "real artist" of the 21st century who should be envied and imitated by every human artist.

To mention just one rather striking example, among the surprisingly positive voices who interpreted Corona as an unequalled "chance" was a policy study by the Wegener Center for Climate and Global Change of the University of Graz. The study pointed out that there was a broad variety of chances opened up by Corona for integrative forward transformation – as if such catastrophes would indeed indirectly also pave the way to a "new world ahead" and, to some extent, as a matter of principle. In fact, the nine authors literally spoke of the "innovation chance Coronavirus", not least with regard to what they considered the most important long-term challenge, i.e., the interrelated climate change and environmental crises. As the authors pointed out, compared to the Pre-Corona world, the post-Corona world could offer the unique opportunity for a radical turnaround towards a more balanced policy-making, including five points in particular: a higher CO_2 pricing, improved climate risk management, better climate information, a reform of contra-productive public funding and a more accentuated public-spending focus on research & development. As the authors summarised their findings:

> Due to the Corona crisis, the topic of non-action in climate policy and its economic consequences has again become particularly explosive, as the political directions that have now been set [to overcome the fallout of Corona] are also decisive for overcoming the climate crisis ... The [main points are the] costs of failure to implement climate policy in the course of economic reconstruction after the Corona lockdown, the direct and indirect social costs of climate damage, the effects of failure to implement climate policy on the national budget, domestic value added and

© ROLAND BENEDIKTER AND KARIM FATHI, 2022 | DOI:10.1163/9789004469686_044

"CORONA POSITIVISM"

the financial sector, and the social costs of climate-damaging support measures and a lack of innovation ... Many significant consequences, such as the effects of climate change on biodiversity or a number of health consequences, cannot yet be quantified – although they are no less important ... The economic slump resulting from the Corona lockdown was stronger than expected. It is undisputed that stimulation of demand by the public sector is necessary, and failure to act would have enormous social costs. However, public spending and investment, especially at such a high level, are only justified from an economic point of view if they are also geared towards sustainable structures in order to generate a permanently healthy economic structure. Figuratively speaking: A crisis patient can perhaps be relieved in the short term with drugs in increased doses, but he can only be helped in the long term with a recovery program.

STEININGER ET AL., 2020, p. 1–2

According to the authors, a perhaps historically unique chance was presented in particular by the many post-Corona lockdown economic stimulus programmes issued by governments around the world:

Using the Corona economic stimulus package as such a recovery program means that the infrastructure in the areas of mobility, buildings, energy and industrial production is being rebuilt in such a way that it enables an economic system that is robust in terms of climate change and provides long-term support for a circular economy of short distances. This can be achieved on the one hand directly through public investment, and on the other hand by reforming the regulatory framework to provide incentives for the private sector and households. The COVID-19 crisis [has] create[d] a unique opportunity to set state policy in favor of sustainably healthy structures, and to do so at lower financial, social and political costs than would otherwise have been possible. Fossil energy prices at the lowest possible level facilitate the reduction of environmentally harmful subsidies, but also the introduction of the planned CO_2 pricing at an earlier stage. For the time being, the latter could also help to rehabilitate public budgets, which are heavily burdened by the Corona support measures. Although the potential damage associated with a further increase in climate change manifests itself more slowly than that of this pandemic, it is more massive and permanent in the medium term. Large sections of the population have hardly ever been as open-minded as they are at present to preventing this potentially much more severe climate crisis. The longer [we wait] to contribute to 'keeping *this* curve flat', the greater the follow-up costs will be (Ibid.).

Not far from such fundamental "positivity", others, in an interestingly unconventional view, compared the Coronavirus (pro-actively) with art – just that the virus of 2019–20 had achieved, in their opinion, much more than art could ever achieve – and within a very short time. In this sense, the virus should be envied and imitated by artists:

> Learning from Corona ... is the best thing that artists can do. If Corona were not a virus but an artist, [s]he would certainly be the most famous artist in the world – and in many ways the best. She would be everything that artists always wanted to be, and what art itself should be: cosmopolitan, radical, changing, moving and unprejudiced.
>
> ANJA ES, 2020

As the – allegedly anonymous – author "Anja Es" ("Anja It", i.e., a name denoting a [potential] meta-gender persona speaking from the *chiaroscuro* of typical postmodern consciously ambiguous discourse) continued in a hilariously ironic, but at the same time clearly semi-serious tone which was as much entertaining as profound:

> Her stage name alone! CORONA! Crowning oneself with the name alone shows where the journey is heading. The lady knows what she can do and makes no secret of her intention: world domination. If she had sought a lover during the conquest of the planet, her choice would surely have been [German conceptual artist] Jonathan Meese, whose trend-setting maxim: 'A.R.T. is world domination' would surely sound like a declaration of love to her ears. What she is still working on has made it a reality in no time at all. Corona is omnipresent. She is around us, she is part of us; sometimes quite physical, and she makes us rethink our lives completely. And like any good artist, she is a true radical. Meese would certainly like that, too. 'A.R.T. is the destruction of the dominant, always has been.' For those affected, of course, this destruction is tragic, but nowhere is it written that you can't ruin yourself for art ... Corona knows this and consistently demands this willingness. History, literature and poetry provide countless examples ... But she is also fully committed to this. One cannot blame her for inactivity, success does not fall into her lap. And as so often with art, one does not know whether it is more of a pleasure or a burden.

"CORONA POSITIVISM"

And then, to provoke even further with a winking eye, Anja Es went into a more unexplored realm as far as concerns global virus pandemics and their potential of changing societies in the future – the realm of (societal, or social) *libido* as the allegedly driving force of change, and of Corona alike:

> I would, however, rather bet on lust, in view of the spectacular reproduction success [of Corona]. Speaking of reproduction ... I don't think a woman like Corona would leave it to just one lover. In Germany alone, Joseph Beuys could theoretically be considered. I suspect he would worship her, if only for the implementation of what he already defined in the [19]70s: Society as a social sculpture. A society that changes and reshapes itself through creative action and thinking, with creative people who have a shaping influence on the community worldwide. Every person is an artist! Unbelievable, what amount of creativity Corona releases in dusty heads! The unthinkable is suddenly not only possible, but feasible. New thoughts, crazy ideas and artistic concepts sprout from the driest cranial convolutions and sprout the strangest blossoms – and these blossoms do not only spread in the heads. Like climbing plants, they overgrow the foundations of our previous, state-bearing pillars, bringing down holy cows and depriving politicians of power. In short: Corona does exactly what Beuys always longed for: she understands democracy as a work of art. Otherwise, a queen like her thinks nothing at all of democracy. What artist asks the people what kind of art she is allowed to create? That would be the end of art, if not the end of the world (Ibid.).

Last, but not least, for "Anja Es", Corona was and remains to some extent the paradoxical embodiment of "human rights" of the 21st century – understood, of course, in an explicitly "artistic" way that may appeal even to China:

> In doing so, she [Corona] herself follows human rights as a regent. For her, all people are equal. There is also no vaccine against art. Whether one is rich or poor, uneducated or educated – every person can be infected by art. Whether [s]he falls ill or recovers from it is a question of perspective. Once you are infected by Corona and her work, there is no medicine to help. You have to go through it, and if it were a walk in the park, Corona would not be an artist but an interior decorator. Some hope for herd immunity. How short-sighted! Everyone knows that art is always changing. But the human race is a frightened little creature. It may have the courage to destroy the whole planet, including itself, with all available means, but it has that in its own hands. Corona scares them because

306　　　　　　　　　　　　　　　　　　　　　　　　　　　CHAPTER 43

they feel powerless. Corona and her art are ungovernable and free. There is nothing worse (for the powerless) to be powerful. This could be the great hour of religions, but Corona doesn't have much to do with that either, especially not as a woman. She also visits the places of worship, but never puts much in the collection bag. But not less either. Instead of folding their hands, people all over the world put on masks. WHAT a performance! (Ibid.).

And this, according to "Anja Es" or "Anja It", ultimately means that:

No artist has ever succeeded in staging a global art action of this magnitude, in which not only the hip, urban scene participates, but also the granny next door as well as the chancellor, Heidi Klum, [designer] Harald Glööckler or whoever else wears lipstick that nobody sees anymore. Nobody would have thought it possible that *haute couture* would one day find its expression in face masks. But Corona also seems to incorporate other concepts and stylistic devices of art into her work, and if you take a closer look, a whole lot comes together. In many places, one hears of a surreal-looking attitude to life with Corona. Plans and predictions remain abstract for the time being, political speeches sound like Dada, the self-cut hairstyles look like naive art, the look at the account seems like hyperrealism. The world as Corona found it is first declared readymade, then decisively changed, and reappears as constructivism. Corona has helped the *expanded concept of art* to grow exponentially. Fortunately for Corona, all attempts to return to A.R.T.-poor normality are nipped in the bud by the people. As soon as they see the possibility of escaping the exhausting creative work on social sculpture by shopping, eating *bratwurst* and renouncing artistic thinking, they open the borders (of good taste) and souvenir shops. In the hotel beds and cosy restaurants, Corona could then meet anarchic artists and passionate collectors for a rendezvous. 'Be fruitful and multiply and subdue the world' is the toast, and Corona moans with pleasure. Unfortunately, Corona is just a small, nasty virus that kills far too many people. Wouldn't it be nice if it were different [if Corona were art]?(Ibid.).

But – in a slightly more serious way – what about all the feared second or third infection waves? Are they then to be considered – in principle – "positive", too?

According to German virologists such as Hendrik Streeck, Director of the Institute of Virology of the University Hospital in Bonn, there may not be second or third waves in the strict sense, but rather a "continuous wave": a

"CORONA POSITIVISM" 307

Dauerwelle, which, in German, literally taken, is a hilarious term with the double meaning of a permanent wave, but also for a hairstyle made of artificially created tresses. The coming years may be a kind of ongoing cycle of ups and downs of infection numbers but no definitive "miraculous disappearance", as predicted famously by U.S. President Donald Trump. Therefore, Streeck, in a more normative perspective, proposed a "National Task Force" and a "National Association for Infectious Diseases" for Germany (*Nationale Eingreiftruppe und Nationaler Verband zur Bekämpfung von Infektionskrankheiten*), to be later perhaps fused with other national task forces and associations and expanded to the whole of the EU (Streeck, 2020):

> The feared second wave of the Coronavirus is being debated again and again ... Now virologist Hendrik Streeck (42), Director of the Institute of Virology at the University Hospital in Bonn, has made it clear that he does not believe in a second or even third wave. 'I don't believe that we will have a second or third wave. I think we are in a continuous wave. A continuous wave that goes up and down again and again,' Streeck explained. However, he said that the rate of infection probably depended on the weather, which is why more infections had to be expected in autumn. The schools were closed for weeks because of corona. The switch to learning at home led to serious side effects. Streeck also demanded an international intervention force and a corresponding national federation at the federal level to fight infectious diseases ... There must be 'an Emergency Response Team of the WHO' – a unit 'that can contain infections worldwide'. He would also like to see something like that for Germany. 'A rapid reaction force for infectious diseases. An association that operates nationally, not just at the federal states level' (Ibid.).

CHAPTER 44

Corona as a Driver of Re-globalisation towards Post-Corona Globalisation

As mentioned on various occasions in this book, the Coronavirus crisis was taken by many politicians both at the highest international and national, but also at regional levels as a precedent and hopeful trigger for renewal. Among the renewal hopes for global politics were, in particular, internationalism and *re-globalisation*, i.e., the rethinking, revision and reform of globalisation as we knew it before the Coronavirus crisis. Corona has accelerated the reform debate about globalisation (Benedikter, 2020b; Deutsches Bundesministerium für Bildung und Forschung, 2020), but also about post-politics (Kenis & Mathijs, 2014; Wilson & Swyngedouw, 2014; Meyer,2019) and future politics (Meyer, 2019), and it has interrelated these discourses like no other crisis before. And it has to some extent co-coined and pushed the notion of a "new globalisation" (Benedikter, 2020a).

The intriguing interface between the era of re-globalisation and the Coronavirus crisis of 2020 was perhaps best pointed out by U.N. Secretary-General António Guterres in June 2020 in his speech on the occasion of the 75th founding anniversary of the United Nations:

> Guterres for multilateralism. UN Secretary-General Guterres has spoken out in favour of reinventing multilateralism on the 75th anniversary of the founding of the United Nations. The current cooperation of the international community of states lacks 'significance, ambition and bite', said Guterres. It is difficult to achieve meaningful change in the mechanisms of global governance without the active participation of world powers, Guterres admitted, whose relations with each other 'have never been more dysfunctional'. He hoped that the Corona crisis was a wake-up call for a new multilateralism, the UN Secretary-General said
>
> APA, 2020j

In July 2020, Guterres renewed this claim, pledging for a "new global order" by asserting that:

> those nations which won the second World War seventy years ago have so far rejected thinking about reforms [of the global system]. Now, a new

global agreement is needed to share power, wealth and opportunities on the globe more justly

APA, 2020r

Not only Guterres but also many other politicians in Europe saw the Coronavirus crisis as a driver of re-globalisation. For example, in July 2020, Germany's President of the parliament (*Präsident des Bundestages*) and former Finance and Interior Minister as well as former Chief of the Federal Chancellery and Minister for Special Affairs, Wolfgang Schäuble (Christian Democratic Union, CDU), declared the Coronavirus crisis to be a test for re-globalisation – i.e., for what he called "the excesses of globalisation which must be corrected". Under the impression of Corona, Schäuble set three main priorities for re-globalisation: health, monetary union and migration, which, in his view, were all intertwined in the COVID-19 crisis:

> According to Wolfgang Schäuble, President of the German Bundestag, Europe should learn lessons from the corona pandemic and reduce its global dependencies. 'We now have the opportunity to critically review our entire economic model and to correct the excesses of globalization where they have contributed to the dramatic effects of the pandemic'. Schäuble pointed out, for example, the lack of even simple medical products such as protective masks for the mouth and nose. The European Union must take better precautions in order to be more resistant and sovereign in crises, warned the President of [the German] Parliament. To do so, it must be given 'greater strategic autonomy, for example by developing alternative supply chains with several low-cost production sites to diversify geographical risk'. In addition, [according to Schäuble] it is important to extend European sovereignty, especially in the health sector.
>
> BILD ONLINE, 2020h

Such new need for autonomy from "excess globalisation" was also ventilated by other national representatives in various countries around the world. On a more strictly European note, which was nevertheless meant as exemplary, Schäuble advocated that:

> Under the impression of the Corona pandemic we should expand the [European Union] monetary union started in 1999 into an economic union. It would need 'the courage we did not have during the 2010 crisis to finally achieve more integration in the eurozone', Schäuble said. 'We

must not miss the opportunity again'. The current discussion 'falls far short of the mark because it focuses primarily on aspects of financing, such as whether the planned aid will be provided in the form of grants or loans ... We should, however, focus it much more on the question of what we want to do in concrete terms to move Europe forward together.' The CDU politician also commented on the topic of migration, arguing in the debate for 'rescue and asylum centres outside the EU'. Human living conditions must be guaranteed in these centres, and they must also be protected, 'for example, under the umbrella of the United Nations, but also through the civil and military commitment of the EU,' said Schäuble.

BILD ONLINE, 2020h

Indeed, post-Corona according to Schäuble also means re-globalising the international refugee and migration system:

According to Schäuble, such a mission would 'certainly also involve those states that have so far refused to distribute migrants'. According to the President of the Bundestag, the issue of migration has lost none of its explosive power during the Corona crisis. In view of the internal security and stability of the EU and its credibility as a community of values, a common European asylum law with uniform standards and practicable recognition procedures is needed. The conflicts in the EU over migration policy could not be resolved by legal means. On the contrary: 'The attempt to force binding admission quotas through a majority decision in the Council has not pacified the conflict, but rather intensified it,' Schäuble said. Community initiatives were, however, indispensable for the protection of Europe's external borders and the people on both sides of these borders, 'above all for the dilemma of the rescue at sea in the Mediterranean, to which we have a humanitarian obligation, knowing that we are thereby encouraging a cynical smuggling of human beings' (Ibid.).

Similarly, Germany's Federal President Frank-Walter Steinmeier asked for medical equipment to again be produced by Europe itself in order to reform and reduce global dependencies, not least under a strategic viewpoint:

[German] Federal President Frank-Walter Steinmeier has spoken out in favour of producing more medical protective equipment in Europe again. The corona pandemic has shown how susceptible international supply chains can be to disruption, Steinmeier said during a visit to a medical-technology manufacturer in Lübeck.

KÖLNISCHE RUNDSCHAU, 2020

The respective claims included Federal Health Minister Jens Spahn:

> Pharmaceuticals: EU to become more independent. The German Minister of Health, Mr. Spahn, wants ... to advocate more independence for the EU in the supply of pharmaceuticals and protective equipment. 'It should not be up to China to decide whether we have enough protective masks and medicines,' said Spahn. In addition, Spahn wants to strengthen the European Centre for Disease Prevention and Control (ECDC).
>
> APA, 2020a

Other politicians tied the Coronavirus handling capacity in principle to the capacity of *leading* nations and the international community, thus de facto tying the strategic inclination to multi-resilience to "chancellorship ability" – such as Germany's chancellor-hopeful Friedrich Merz. Merz under the effect of the Coronavirus crisis measures said that "chancellor can be 'who can crisis'" (Bild Online, 2020r). As with other politicians in Europe and in countries around the world, Merz with such words de facto elevated the Coronavirus management to benchmark and scale of leadership capability – thus not least indirectly also elevating multi-resilience strategies and applications to the highest priority of political leadership of the post-Corona world.

Yet Corona was a driver of re-politicisation versus (post-)politics and of political in-depth debate by no means confined to positive connotations, discoveries or future visions. In some cases, it uncovered all too real and existing malfunctions and flaws in political systems and practices. It also unveiled sometimes shocking mismanagement and even misuse inbuilt in certain political cultures even in open systems. In India, for example, similarly as in Turkey and other democratically regressive, populist-led or (neo-) authoritarian societies, secrets abounded about probable misuse and rumours about corruption surrounded (Post-)Coronavirus crisis funds and stimulus programmes:

> A fund set up by Indian Prime Minister Narendra Modi to fight COVID-19 is now mired in controversy and concern over an alleged lack of transparency. On 27 March, just days after India began a country-wide lockdown to halt the spread of the coronavirus, Narendra Modi set up the Prime Minister's Citizen Assistance and Relief in Emergency Situations

Fund. The PM Cares Fund, for short. A day later, Mr Modi appealed to 'all Indians' to donate. 'It is my appeal to my fellow Indians, kindly contribute to the PM-Cares Fund,' he tweeted, telling the nation that their donations would strengthen India's fight against COVID-19 and 'similar distressing situations' in future. 'This will go a long way in creating a healthier India,' he wrote. Donations poured in – from industrialists, celebrities, companies and the common man. Within a week, reports said, donations had reached 65bn rupees ($858m; £689m). The fund is believed to have exceeded 100 billion rupees. But PM Cares has been controversial from the start. Many questioned the need for a new fund when a similar one – PM National Relief Fund or PMNRF – has existed in the country since 1948. Sonia Gandhi, the leader of the opposition Congress Party, suggested that the money raised should be transferred to PMNRF. Congress also suggested that the fund be used for the welfare of migrants. ...

BBC NEWS, 2020ff

But the problems did not end there:

Since the fund was set up, questions have also been asked about how it is constituted and managed, how much money has been collected, from whom, and how it is being put to use? There are no answers to any of these queries on the PM Cares website, and the prime minister's office (PMO), which is managing the fund, has refused to provide any information. Now opposition politicians, independent activists and journalists are asking whether the government has anything to hide? Petitions have been filed under the Right to Information (RTI) Act and in the courts, seeking more transparency. But so far, the fund has avoided any public scrutiny by insisting that PM Cares is not a 'public authority', which means it's not controlled or substantially financed by the government and so does not come under the RTI Act. It also means that it cannot be scrutinized by government auditors. 'It's absurd to say the PM Cares is not a public authority,' Kandukuri Sri Harsh, a law student, told the BBC. 'Millions of people did not donate to the fund thinking it's a private trust. The money has been collected upon the strength of the prime minister's name' (Ibid.).

To which extent such brawls about alleged misuse of the Coronavirus crisis by institutionalised politics even in the biggest democracy of the world – and beyond – may trigger a potential, concrete political renewal wave, including perhaps a forward transformation of existing parties and arrangements, a

CORONA AS A DRIVER OF RE-GLOBALISATION TOWARDS POST-CORONA 313

correction of practices and the coming-into-existence of potential new parties or popular movements, will have to be seen.

Perhaps most important, Corona in the leading democracy of the world, the United States, was seen as having the potential to rethink democratic politics at the federal-state interface and thus serve as a fundamental driver for both making democracy more efficient mechanism-wise and bringing politics closer to the people. In fact, in the eyes of policy experts such as, for example, New York University's David Stasavage, the Corona pandemic in the U.S., rather than strengthening national unity by cooperation and common nationwide standards, exposed the fundamental weakness of America's federal government (Stasavage, 2020) which, as an effect of such discovery, in his view had to be to some extent re-calibrated:

> For many, the COVID-19 pandemic has exposed the weakness of our federal government. The question is what could be done about it, and how it could be done in a way that strengthens democracy instead of undermining it. There are several paths that we could take in response to this crisis, and only one of them is desirable – strengthening the federal government by first making investments to reduce distrust among the citizenry. The United States has a form of government where a great deal of power rests with state and local authorities, even when compared to many other contemporary democracies such as France or the United Kingdom. That's a product of the way our country was first settled by Europeans, often in in small communities amidst a vast wilderness where strong central control, either from England or from capitals of the colonies, simply wasn't feasible. This helped pave the way not only for an American tradition of rugged individualism but also for an early form of democracy – for free White males – based on local control with a weak center ... (Ibid.).

But then came Corona und put the system to the test:

> Now, the big challenge for all democracies with such decentralized institutions is that sometimes central coordination and control is actually helpful, say to provide for external defense, or to facilitate economic development, or maybe even in the face of a pandemic to make sure that nurses don't have to wear garbage bags in place of standard protective equipment. It can actually be a good thing to have an effective central state. In the United States today we are in the process of learning how 40 years of an ideology bent on undercutting our government 'in Washington' has eroded central power just when we could have most used it to provide a

coordinated response to COVID-19. So, what does this mean for the future of our democracy? The potential risk with increased central control has always been that it will give way to the decline of democracy and the rise of autocracy. Throughout history, emergencies involving famine, pestilence and war have given a window to would-be autocrats to assert themselves, build strong central state institutions, and dispense with any need for consulting the people. Today, from Hungary to Cambodia, autocrats are hoping the current pandemic produces precisely this same outcome ... So, could we see a second, positive path for the United States where democracy is preserved, and central state institutions are strengthened in response to better deal with the next pandemic? Perhaps. But there's also a risk of a third, less positive trajectory: Our democracy will survive, but it will also keep failing to do what we want ... One idea here is to draw directly on early 19th-century experience and invest anew in civic education, a subject that has been given short shrift of late. (Ibid.).

Interestingly, the fundamental – and often partisan and neo-ideological – Coronavirus crisis divide over which system works better to fight (transnational) emergencies: a federal or a centralised system, touched upon the principles of various open-society models as well as upon their history. More importantly, it relied on two factors long neglected in best practices theory: size and scale. And to the reality of democracy as a practice closely tied to both. As, for example, Stasavage again put it, democracy in principle works best in small units, and much less so over too large territories (Ibid.). This is what the Coronavirus crisis has pointed out by experience. Or, in his own words:

It has actually been decades now – through presidential administrations of both parties – that there has been substantially lower trust in the federal government compared to state and local governments. The evidence on trust at different levels of government suggests that ... the United States have not escaped a fundamental constraint; across the broad sweep of human history, democratic governance has been most successful as a small-scale affair. Contrary to what James Madison told us ..., the US Constitution did not solve the problem of maintaining democracy over such a large territory. The big problem for large republics is to avoid having their citizens become distrustful of a distant center, a phenomenon that goes hand in hand with polarization ... Members of Congress set about trying to address this threat through investments such as the subsidized distribution of newspapers – so that people would have better information – and state governments began to provide funding for common schools where people could be educated to participate in democratic governance. The lesson from the early republic is clear: Large scale is a challenge for a democracy, but this obstacle can be overcome. If we are to hope to strengthen our institutions to deal with the next pandemic, or the next emergency, then we need to first think about how we can invest anew in connecting citizens to government (Ibid.).

So, what are the fundamental teachings of the Corona crisis with regard to the size and scale of open societies and their relation to re-globalisation? Although both factors are relatively less important to authoritarian societies, they are becoming crucial measurements of the effectiveness of participatory and multi-level governance alike; both size and scale will decide upon the future of democracy as compared with – on some occasions – highly efficient centralised and non-participatory top-down governments and administrative styles. If the *per naturam* trans-border crisis of Corona has proven something, then it is that well-confined small-scale democratic participatory and capillary structures must be reconciled with centralised coordinative powers in order to achieve the best results in resiliency.

CHAPTER 45

A Post-Corona Core Task

Re-positioning the Open Systems of Europe and the West by the Means of Multi-resilience

The positioning manoeuvres have been taking on various forms. With regard to the Hercules task of post-Corona economic recovery and stimulus programmes, the Austrian Society for European Politics directed a particular focus on the European Union (EU) post-Corona reconstruction fund launched in summer 2020 with around 750 billion euros. To some extent meant as exemplary, not only for internal solidarity but also for other global areas featuring a strong interconnection of nations across regions and borders, in the framework of the EU funds detailed-distribution debate, Thomas Leoni and Atanas Pekanov provided the following recommendations for post-Corona action:

1. "Overcoming the crisis requires joint solutions at the European level, which not only promote immediate economic recovery, but also provide answers to the long-standing unresolved questions surrounding the further development of the European monetary union. Institutional reforms of the Euro (€) architecture are just as necessary for this as measures to strengthen the political foundations of the euro.
2. The continuation of the European integration project is in the self-interest of all EU member states, especially the economically strong 'core countries' of the euro area. The question is not whether risks should be shared within the EU, but in what form a sensible, economically effective and politically acceptable risk sharing should take place.
3. With regard to the EU reconstruction fund ..., various options and possible arrangements are conceivable, which must, however, meet certain criteria, irrespective of the specific form they take. The European Commission's proposal for a reconstruction fund with a volume of € 750 billion meets these criteria".

   LEONI & PEKANOV, 2020

Summarising their findings, the authors point out that one core teaching of the Coronavirus crisis for Europe and the European Union in particular, and

A POST-CORONA CORE TASK   317

perhaps also for other areas in the world, is greater unity, which presupposes a stronger formal, juridical, economic and financial integration among the member countries of the European Union:

> The Corona crisis could become a turning point in the process of European integration. The economic constraints within the euro area and the political tensions associated with them are not the only challenge in this context, but the biggest. The deep [Coronavirus-triggered] recession of 2020 and the uncertainties of crisis management aggravate the structural weaknesses of the euro architecture and give a strong boost to centrifugal forces within the currency area. Politicians are not only faced with the task of leading the economy out of recession, but also of restarting the engine of European integration. The various options for a European response to the crisis must therefore not be discussed and assessed in isolation from the long-standing discussions surrounding the further development of the common currency architecture (Ibid.).

Yet as right as such strategic integration of post-Corona solution patterns into long-standing, Pre-Corona EU integration challenges is, the same as with other post-Corona recommendations that we have listed in this book may be true here: Without an encompassing and integrative *multi-resilience* framework, many or even the majority of these efforts may remain once again patchwork and doomed to coexist widely uncoordinated with other area-specific, national, trans-European and global policy construction sites.

In other words: measures of trans-sectoral aspiration like these rightly point at making (more) sense when they are integrated into a long-term coordinated resilience strategy for both the EU and their global interconnectedness for the years and decades to come, and much less as just another short-term handling of crucial crisis passages.

Here, a fundamental matter of principle for the imminent and long-term future surfaces. Steering through a crisis as best as possible and to then see what may be possible afterwards was all too often the usual practice in the politics of European and Western liberal democracies who, over the past decades (in essence, after the fall of the Berlin wall in 1989, the collapse of communism in 1991 and overall since the start of the 1990s), came to think that "liberty" and "openness" meant to renounce the long-term plans in order to not pre-empt or burden the decision of newly-elected future democratic leaders. This implied being ready to respond quickly and in short-term reaction times to emerging crises, but to refrain from developing long-term integrative strategies, since these would possibly restrain the options of future electorates and generations and make the decision spectrum reacting to possible futures more inflexible and less participatory. This was, to mention just one example, one of the complex and multi-faceted reasonings behind the fact that the European Union never developed its own global long-term development strategy, contrary to most other world powers and contrary to its own insights, as expressed, for example, as a core point in the farewell speech of EU Commission President José Manuel Barroso in October 2014 (The Sofia Globe, 2014; Barroso, 2010).

Yet this practice – which in reality was more a silent consensus than a written social contract, rooted in ill-positioned ultra-liberalism and self-overestimation – has proven to be wrong, already before the Coronavirus crisis of 2020 hit and then unmistakably and definitely with it. Such misconception must be urgently corrected by the development of an encompassing long-term EU multi-resilience strategy, perhaps to be developed jointly with other Western powers and allies so that open societies do not fall behind illiberal, closed and authoritarian systems (such as China), which all celebrate their long-term plans as one of their decisive advantages over multi- and short-term election and participatory systems. Ironically, Barroso in his farewell speech had pointed out that "the EU is 'now better prepared than we were before to face a crisis, if a crisis like the ones we have seen before should come in the future'" (Nitoiu, 2014). Barroso also said, "that we have shown great resilience" (The Sofia Globe, 2014).

Corona has proven that this was an illusion. Europe's (and perhaps also the U.S.') resilience strategy was insufficient, like so many other alleged securities and guarantees the EU and the Western open societies have maintained over the past decades.

Overall, the future of open-society systems will decisively depend on the extent to which they will be able to implement multi-resilience strategies to protect themselves from being too easily penetrable, and to withstand the competition of closed and authoritarian societies on the rise which claim that their resilience mechanisms are more effective *exactly because* they are authoritarian and top-down, and therefore do not need many debates to implement rapid and encompassing systemic measures to limit the fallout of emergencies.

CHAPTER 46

An End to Geopolitical Rivalry? Not Likely –
Despite Some Positive Signals

Simultaneously on the geopolitical front, many observers asked themselves if cooperation was not just one rather superficial layer, behind which the "real" geopolitics of competition and espionage were ruthlessly carried out not least with regard to the Coronavirus vaccine – with no mercy and no refrain, revealing the double bottom of international politics between idealism and realism:

> US and China both claim their research into a COVID-19 vaccine and treatments have been subject to cyberattacks. High-level cyberattacks on facilities researching COVID-19 vaccines have alarmed Australia and the United States, with defense strategists urging them to confront China, the nation widely believed to be responsible for them. The United States Studies Center at the University of Sydney, which receives part of its funding from the Australian government, said on June 23 that the US and Australia should jointly protect vulnerable medical sectors. Health research and vaccines 'are things that are almost universally considered off-limits for geopolitical rivalry,' warned Ashley Townshend, director of foreign policy and defense studies at the respected think tank. 'While all countries engage in underhanded activities in their national interest – this is one domain which I think the world really wants to see international progress on,' said the researcher.
>
> BOYD, 2020

The background was complex:

> Australian Prime Minister Scott Morrison revealed on June 19 [2020] that multiple tiers of government, business and academia had been targeted in a series of cyber incidents, including hospitals and education facilities. Security agencies in the US also warned that China was attempting to steal American research to develop COVID-19 vaccine and treatments. Beijing has made it clear that China wants to produce and distribute the first coronavirus vaccine. At least a dozen research centers are helping to develop or test potential COVID-19 treatments and vaccines in Australia, as well as pharmaceutical firms and academic faculties ... Morrison did

© ROLAND BENEDIKTER AND KARIM FATHI, 2022 | DOI:10.1163/9789004469686_047

not say why the medical sector had been targeted, or who was behind the attacks, but said it involved a 'state-based protagonist with very significant capabilities.' Analysts said China, Russia, Iran, North Korea and Israel and the Five Eyes intelligence-sharing network comprised of the US, Australia, United Kingdom, Canada and New Zealand were the only countries with this high-level of capability. Cybersecurity firms have tagged increased spying activity by a suspected Chinese group since late January, when COVID-19 cases were first reported. FireEye said there were 'multiple possible explanations' for the upsurge in cyber-attacks, including clashes between China and Western countries over the virus. Its report said the attacks were 'one of the broadest campaigns by a Chinese cyber espionage protagonist we have observed in recent years.' The company believed that Chinese government contractors were to blame (Ibid.).

As early as May 2020, the US and UK decried that "cyber-spies hunt COVID-19 research" in a joint warning that:

> Cyber-spies are targeting the health sector. Hackers linked to foreign states have been hunting for information, including COVID-19 data and vaccine research, they say. UK sources say they have seen extensive activity but do not believe there has been any data theft so far. Those behind the activity are not named in the alert but are thought to include China, Russia and Iran. The three countries have all seen major outbreaks of the virus but have denied previous claims of involvement in such activity. The joint advisory says the UK and US are currently investigating a number of incidents in which other states are targeting pharmaceutical companies, medical-research organisations, and universities, looking for intelligence and sensitive data, including research on the virus (National Cyber Security Centre, 2020) ... Meanwhile, Western spies will be focusing hard on China as they seek to understand what Beijing may know of the virus's origins (Corera, 2020c)- with the US administration pushing the theory it may have escaped from a lab – as well as looking for any data on the true extent of the outbreak in the country
>
> CORERA, 2020a; NATIONAL CYBER SECURITY CENTRE, 2020

Another aspect of continuing, if not re-invigorated geopolitical rivalry as an effect of the Corona crisis was what scholars called the new "vaccine nationalism". As Thomas J. Bollyky and Chad P. Bown wrote in *Foreign Affairs*:

AN END TO GEOPOLITICAL RIVALRY? 321

Trump administration officials have compared the global allocation of vaccines against the coronavirus that causes COVID-19 to oxygen masks dropping inside a depressurizing airplane. 'You put on your own first, and then we want to help others as quickly as possible,' Peter Marks, a senior official at the U.S. Food and Drug Administration who oversaw the initial phases of vaccine development for the U.S. government, said during a panel discussion in June [2020]. The major difference, of course, is that airplane oxygen masks do not drop only in first class – which is the equivalent of what will happen when vaccines eventually become available if governments delay providing access to them to people in other countries ... Absent an international, enforceable commitment to distribute vaccines globally in an equitable and rational way, leaders will instead prioritize taking care of their own populations over slowing the spread of COVID-19 elsewhere or helping protect essential health-care workers and highly vulnerable populations in other countries. That sort of 'vaccine nationalism,' or a 'my country first' approach to allocation, will have profound and far-reaching consequences. Without global coordination, countries may bid against one another, driving up the price of vaccines and related materials. Supplies of proven vaccines will be limited initially even in some rich countries, but the greatest suffering will be in low- and middle-income countries. ...

BOLLYKY & BOWN, 2020

And that, according to the authors, may lead to dramatic consequences in the medium and long term:

In their quest to obtain vaccines, countries without access to the initial stock will search for any form of leverage they can find, including blocking exports of critical vaccine components, which will lead to the breakdown of supply chains for raw ingredients, syringes, and vials. Desperate governments may also strike short-term deals for vaccines with adverse consequences for their long-term economic, diplomatic, and strategic interests. The result will be not only needless economic and humanitarian hardship but also intense resentment against vaccine-hoarding countries, which will imperil the kind of international cooperation that will be necessary to tackle future outbreaks – not to mention other pressing challenges, such as climate change and nuclear proliferation ...(Ibid.).

Yet despite such new competition – which some branded as the new immorality of "real politics" – reaching new levels of bigotry that came out of the shockwaves of Corona, Bollyky and Bown held that:

It is not too late for global cooperation to prevail over global dysfunction, but it will require states and their political leaders to change course. What the world needs is an enforceable COVID-19 vaccine trade and investment agreement that would alleviate the fears of leaders in vaccine-producing countries ... Such an agreement could be forged and fostered by existing institutions and systems. And it would not require any novel enforcement mechanisms: the dynamics of vaccine manufacturing and global trade generally create layers of interdependence, which would encourage participants to live up to their commitments. What it would require, however, is leadership on the part of a majority of vaccine-manufacturing countries – including, ideally, the United States (Ibid.).

The conclusion and outlook of the authors is nevertheless mixed:

When the oxygen masks drop in a depressurizing plane, they drop at the same time in every part of the plane because time is of the essence and because that is the best way to ensure the safety of all onboard. The same is true of the global, equitable allocation of safe and effective vaccines against COVID-19. Vaccine nationalism is not just morally and ethically reprehensible: it is contrary to every country's economic, strategic, and health interests. If rich, powerful countries choose that path, there will be no winners – ultimately, every country will be a loser. The world is not doomed to learn this the hard way, however. All the necessary tools exist to forge an agreement that would encourage cooperation and limit the appeal of shortsighted "my country first" approaches ... As a first step, a coalition of political leaders from countries representing at least 50 percent of global vaccine-manufacturing capacity must get together and instruct their public health officials and trade ministers to get out of their silos and work together. Combining forces, they should hammer out a short-term agreement that articulates the conditions for sharing, including with the legions of poorer, nonmanufacturing countries, and makes clear what would happen to participants who subsequently reneged and undertook vaccine nationalism. Such a step would get the ball rolling and convince even more of the manufacturing countries to sign on. The fear of missing out on vaccine access, in the event their countries' own vaccine candidates fail, may be what it takes to pressure even today's most reluctant leaders to cooperate (Ibid.).

Debates like these are likely to also apply to future pandemics and other upcoming global emergencies. What happened in Corona times might

AN END TO GEOPOLITICAL RIVALRY?

inspire protagonists in new crises. Not only the good teachings of crises are remembered, and reapplied – on the contrary. The hacking, espionage and "vaccine nationalism" debates clearly showed that behind the curtains of diplomacy and good will, pre-Corona mindsets are still all too active in a rising post-Corona world, and this is unlikely to change abruptly. Thus, when the U.N. in February 2020 on the occasion of its 75th founding anniversary immediately prior to the full outbreak of the Coronavirus crisis declared that there was a "new era of conflict and violence" (United Nations, 2020), this prediction may have been confirmed or even further strengthened by the Corona crisis. The question as to whether this might fundamentally change over time once the crisis is defeated as an in-depth learning effect of Corona which takes time and energy, and whether political realism and idealism due to its "universal" shock may be better reconcilable than before it, as some predicted or hoped, including by the way of new agreements, remains of insecure prospect.

In July 2020, the powerful but little unified, on the contrary often competing if not arguing G20 countries, as a first step towards more systemic cooperation at least considered jointly extending a debt moratorium for the poorest countries because of Corona:

> The G20 countries are considering extending the debt moratorium for the world's poorest countries because of the coronavirus pandemic. A possible extension would be discussed in the second half of 2020, the finance ministers and central bank heads of the G20 group declared after a virtual meeting. In April, the G20 countries had agreed to a 12-month debt moratorium for the poorest countries because of the corona pandemic. This should help developing countries to have the necessary financial resources to fight the pandemic. The World Bank and several aid organisations are calling for the initiative to be extended. According to the G20 countries, 42 countries have so far applied for debt relief and asked for the postponement of debt repayments totalling 5.3 billion dollars (4.6 billion euros). A possible extension of the initiative would depend on the development of the pandemic and the recommendations of the International Monetary Fund (IMF) and the World Bank … Germany pledged another three billion euros in the form of a long-term loan for an IMF aid program for low-income countries. With the funds from the programme, low-income countries can receive strongly discounted loans and bridge liquidity bottlenecks. 'With the additional funds, we are sending a strong signal of solidarity and helping those who are particularly suffering from the consequences of the pandemic,' said

German Finance Minister Olaf Scholz after the G20 meeting. The G20 group includes the seven most important industrial nations as well as numerous emerging countries such as Russia, China, India, Brazil and South Africa. Saudi Arabia currently holds the G20 presidency.

SÜDTIROL ONLINE, 2020

CHAPTER 47

Back to Business as Usual – Systemic Improvements at the "Evo-devo" Interface?

According to futurist Tristan Horx (von Stefanelli, 2020), apart from international competition or cooperation, the main twofold trend resulting from the Coronavirus crisis will be *regionalisation* and *ecologisation* – including a higher degree of their systemic interrelation, policy connection and integration.

- *Regionalisation*, because despite some revivals of nationalisms (or perhaps precisely because of them), regional identities were factually strengthened by the collective solidarity necessary to master the crisis less in theory, but certainly in practice. While nationalism is more theoretical and thus can span great ranges of territory even if they do not feature substantial interconnections with each other, solidarity in encompassing emergencies is experienced as more practical and immediate: it is in the first instance concretely related to those who are there and who can help, and who understand the situation as it is on the ground. The (self-)isolation of municipalities and provinces during the lockdown of boroughs, quarters and sometimes even only blocks due to Corona brought about a re-thinking of "far" and "close", including multi-layered patterns of belonging to groups, environments and geographical areas.
- *Ecologisation*, because the (in the meantime already iconic) images of rare fish swimming again in the crystal-clear waters of Venice and other formerly strongly polluted places transformed for the better (or more precisely: to some extent restored) during the Coronavirus crisis may not completely vanish from the public and private imagination. Given that the economy at the regional-national-international intersection has to be rebuilt after the lockdown, it now has the chance to be rebuilt in ecological manners – something that the European Union is actively sustaining with its post-Corona multi-billion economic stimulus programme for the member countries hardest hit, such as, for example, Italy and Spain .

  EUROPEAN PARLIAMENT, 2020

© ROLAND BENEDIKTER AND KARIM FATHI, 2022 | DOI:10.1163/9789004469686_048

According to Horx, an example for "good" regionalisation is the Autonomous Province of South Tyrol, in Northern Italy, the border region between Austria and Italy, with its high degree of self-administration, "hyper-regionalisation" and special pluri-cultural identity tied to a territory rather than to a nation state or a partisan sense of ethnic belonging (Autonomous Province of South Tyrol, n.d.). "Small is beautiful" allows for better handling of emergencies and crises such as corona, since solidarity is high, common sense for the environment widespread and the responsibility for each other given since people in most cases know each other personally or feel that they belong together in a special setting. Horx expects that the nation states will lose in importance over the coming 50 years to give more room to federalisation among smaller entities, as well as to a further gain in importance of supranational instances and big cities. This combination can be seen as a factor of multi-resilience, or at least it can be actively developed as such. Horx is convinced that "an era is beginning which will actively combine regionalisation with globalisation, and this will be no contradiction anymore" (Von Stefenelli, 2020). Corona may have accelerated the rise of this era: "The important thing will be to strengthen regional identity and solidarity patterns without isolating oneself from the world" (Ibid.).

Last, but not least, according to Horx, the personal and public "introspection" imposed by the Coronavirus lockdown may have the rather lasting effect of a greater receptibility for the climate change and environmental emergencies. Given that people now know from their own direct experience and on a personal basis how a real global crisis feels, they may put more attention and more serious care into the environmental question, which is perhaps the even bigger systemic global crisis that will decisively co-mould the globe over the coming decades. In the eyes of Horx, the respective sensitivity has increased because of Corona, and the old patterns of behaviour may not fully return to business as usual (Ibid.). This remains to be seen, though. It was also said after the global financial and economic crisis of 2007–08 and, before that, after 9/11, without tangible results after either of the two crises.

Not dissimilar to Horx, the Director of the "Ethos observatory" of LUISS University Rome's Business School (n.d.), Sebastiano Maffettone, asserted that the Coronavirus crisis may eventually have paved the way for a rethinking of the "evo-devo" interface, i.e., of the intersection where evolution and development meet. This may lead to new definitions and applications of "civil society" connected to a future-oriented "theory of values":

> Prior to the Coronavirus crisis, there had been too much economic and technological development with regard to nature and society. I propose

a thesis that I have not invented, it is called 'evo-devo', evolution-development. How can we, in the future, better think together evolution and development – better than we did prior to the crisis? It is said that the times of evolution are very long, millions of years; and the times of development are relatively short, years and decades. To join them both is difficult and has been even more so for the forms of capitalism we had over the past decades. We could say that the Coronavirus crisis was a sort of cosmic sign of this mismatch between evolution and development. We have to join them in the aftermath of the crisis, and this is the core of what we should think about: to reconcile evolution and development, i.e., the short- and long-term visions of our ways to produce wealth in more sustainable ways.

MAFFETTONE, 2020

In order to do so, Maffettone is convinced that "civil-society ethics" will play a greater, if not crucial role in post-Corona times, because without them, true innovation is impossible in open societies which want to retain their democratic and participatory core and, at the same time, advance to even better implemented and lived solidarity:

Public ethics in essence means to have a society that does internalise the common norms by their own will. My father was an entrepreneur and said if the customer did not want to pay there was nothing to be done, not even the police could help in the end. Luckily, 97 percent want to pay and the judicial system and the police serves for the remaining the 3 percent that cannot pay or do not want to pay. But if it were the opposite, society would fail, with or without police and laws. So before the imposition of rules always comes the conviction of the public to cling to common basic ethics of understanding, sharing, taking care of each other, including respect for the rules. I believe that the pandemic makes us think of ourselves in a more critical way, also from the points of view of sustainable policies, which are closely related to a common consciousness. The value of an organic unit has more value than the sum of its constituent parts. I always think back to the origins of the football championship won by the team of Napoli with Diego Armando Maradona. Now there is no doubt he was a great football player, but without the team he would not have won. So the functionality of the organic unit sometimes gives you a value greater than the sum of the parts. This could be true for a football team, a large symphony orchestra, a society, a family or a company: all work better if things are created jointly. The ultimate value, in the end, is to be together with others to feel good creatively. This is obviously easy to say but difficult to practice, but after Corona we are well advised to try it even harder. Otherwise we can end up with a clash of civilisations. No man is an island. Every theory about values eventually tells us that the other self is an integral part of ourselves. The economy as we had it is a terrible mess from the point of view of evolution. Thus, we have to change it. Only history can tell us ex post, as Hegel said, if we have managed to treasure what we have understood out of this crisis. What I am sure about is that we have to change direction in terms of equality and environment. Hic rhodus hic salta (Αὐτοῦ γὰρ καὶ ̔Ρόδος καὶ πήδημα [Prove what you can do, here and now]) (Ibid.).

In this sense of "evolutionary development" at the "evo-devo" interface, multi-resilience in essence reinforces the old saying, in the words of Albert Einstein: "It's not that I am so smart, it's only that I stay with problems longer" (Einstein, 2016). And the many flaws and failures in policy, mindset and preparedness from such a long-term view remind us only once again of Henry Ford's "Failure is only the opportunity to begin again, this time more intelligently" (Ibid.). It reminds us that during the Coronavirus challenge, many countries – willingly or unwillingly – developed their own resilience patterns which went beyond the old mono-layered meaning of resilience as "bouncing back and restart". Some of the best multi-layered and pluri-resilience-oriented reasonings were mirrored in the official rankings showing which country had best mastered the crisis published by specialised research units. In June 2020, a ranking of countries was published by British weekly statistical publication "The Economist Intelligence Unit (EIU)" which analysed the performance of the most developed countries in comparative ways (The Economist Intelligence Unit, 2020):

> A study by the British research group Economist Intelligence Unit (EIU) has compared the reactions to the Corona crisis of 21 OECD countries in a ranking. In it, Austria takes second place behind New Zealand. Surprisingly, the USA is ahead of South Korea and Japan, with Belgium and Great Britain at the very bottom. Decisive factors for the results are the number of tests, Corona-related deaths and the maintenance of healthcare. With 3.56 points, Austria is ex aequo with Germany. Only New Zealand performed better with 3.67 points
>
> APA, 2020b

Although these rankings were (as in most cases) disputed, they indicated that development helps with coping with crises, that smaller countries fared on average better, and that federal states and those with a high sense of belonging to special or vulnerable or historically or geographically highly interdependent areas had a higher performance than others.

The question as to which extent the crisis-mastering performance was concretely dependent on socio-political systems, ideology and leadership styles remained open. While some asserted that an authoritarian system with strong dictatorial and suppressive features such as communist China's is more effective in imposing restrictions such as a total lockdown and thus able to better master virus outbreaks by isolating people – which is a common feature of authoritarian systems even in "normal times", no crisis needed –, others held that open-society systems may be better equipped to include people and to share knowledge more rapidly and in equal ways and to produce "collective intelligence" and "collective wisdom" so as to be more effective in ending a crisis sooner than authoritarian systems after a comparatively necessarily longer period of incubation. The question as to whether countries with "populist" leaders – a term both useful and over-used in the meantime, so that many question its remaining effectiveness when analysing different policy choices (University of Aberdeen, Centre for Citizenship, Civil Society & Rule of Law, 2020) – have fared better or worse than those without populism (e.g. Brazil, the UK, or Hungary as compared with Germany or Canada) remains highly disputed, although it may present an interesting research topic for the coming years in order to learn for the future (Gruber, 2020b). In this regard, the teachings of the Coronavirus crisis could provide additional knowledge with regard to the differentiation of the pros and cons of political, governmental, constitutional and administrative systems.

A third pillar parallel to a boost to regionalisation and ecologisation proposed by many open-society think-tanks in Europe (and beyond) was the *homogenisation of healthcare systems*. This could lead to a higher degree of integration and quality in provision and prevention, as well as to building a system of complimentary assistance, replenishment and completion. This is, in essence, a matter of securitisation, communication, mutual alignment and cooperation, methodologically and politically not dissimilar to other crucial European challenges such as securing the EU's outer borders against illegal migration or better protecting Europe from terrorism, hacker attacks and cyber-espionage. As the Austrian Society for European Politics asserted (Marzi, 2020), a "European Health Security System" would make sense, not only to prevent and address future pandemics, but also to serve as a vehicle for further European integration:

> "From February [2020] onwards, the European health systems were suddenly confronted with a new type of virus and, as a consequence,

with the global COVID 19 pandemic. Since responsibility for health systems is reserved for EU member states, it quickly became clear that the lack of uniform standards to combat a pandemic was a shortcoming in European cooperation. Against this background, [we must] examine what health measures – taking into account legal aspects – could be taken by the EU and its member states to be better prepared in the future. Recommendations for action are:

1. In times of crisis, national health systems must be supported on a supra-regional and supra-national basis, and the necessary measures must be coordinated across borders.

2. Uniform EU-wide standards are needed for the provision and storage of medicines, medical devices, protective clothing etc. to combat an upcoming [next] pandemic. A joint EU authority for safety in the healthcare sector, which is yet to be established, should efficiently monitor compliance with these standards, be active in matters of prevention, constantly monitor, analyse and define strategies, advise EU decision-makers and coordinate the action of the member states in an emergency.

3. In order to establish the competence of the European Union to combat pandemics in a legally sound manner, the treaty on the functioning of the EU must be extended by an Article ... so that in the event of a crisis, supra-regional measures can be implemented quickly by the competent EU authority" (Ibid.).

Last, but not least, there were, fourth, interesting intellectual contributions mostly related again to the environmental-sustainability nexus and to the term "Anthropocene" in the broader sense, such as by "alternative forward-thinker" Charles Eisenstein and leading German futurist Werner Mittelstaedt. Indeed, another popular (and, admittedly, partly populist) text much read on both sides of the Atlantic came from Eisenstein, the "alternative economy" and New Age-leaning author of "Sacred Economics" (2011) ideologically close to the strongly leftist Occupy and New Economics movements. His text was titled "The Coronation" (Eisenstein, 2020), a typical Eisenstein title. Among other things, in his usual solemn tone, the 13-page document declared:

For years, normality has been stretched nearly to its breaking point, a rope pulled tighter and tighter, waiting for a nip of the black swan's beak to snap it in two. Now that the rope has snapped, do we tie its ends back together, or shall we undo its dangling braids still further, to see what we might weave from them? Covid-19 is showing us that when humanity is

SYSTEMIC IMPROVEMENTS AT THE "EVO-DEVO" INTERFACE? 331

united in common cause, phenomenally rapid change is possible. None of the world's problems are technically difficult to solve; they originate in human disagreement. In coherency, humanity's creative powers are boundless. A few months ago, a proposal to halt commercial air travel would have seemed preposterous. Likewise, for the radical changes we are making in our social behavior, economy, and the role of government in our lives. Covid demonstrates the power of our collective will when we agree on what is important. What else might we achieve, in coherency? What do we want to achieve, and what world shall we create? That is always the next question when anyone awakens to their power (Ibid.).

And even more solemn, albeit highly speculative, Eisenstein concluded his monologue with:

Covid-19 is like a rehab intervention that breaks the addictive hold of normality. To interrupt a habit is to make it visible; it is to turn it from a compulsion to a choice. When the crisis subsides, we might have occasion to ask whether we want to return to normal, or whether there might be something we've seen during this break in the routines that we want to bring into the future. We might ask, after so many have lost their jobs, whether all of them are the jobs the world most needs, and whether our labor and creativity would be better applied elsewhere. We might ask, having done without it for a while, whether we really need so much air travel, Disneyworld vacations, or trade shows. What parts of the economy will we want to restore, and what parts might we choose to let go of? [...] Perhaps the great diseases of civilization have quickened our biological and cultural evolution, bestowing key genetic information and offering both individual and collective initiation. Could the current pandemic be just that? Novel RNA codes are spreading from human to human, imbuing us with new genetic information; at the same time, we are receiving other, esoteric, 'codes' that ride the back of the biological ones, disrupting our narratives and systems in the same way that an illness disrupts bodily physiology. The phenomenon follows the template of initiation: separation from normality, followed by a dilemma, breakdown, or ordeal, followed (if it is to be complete) by reintegration and celebration (Ibid.).

Yet, as Eisenstein himself remarks, this has to be further clarified:

Now the question arises: Initiation into what? What is the specific nature and purpose of this initiation? The popular name for the pandemic offers a clue: coronavirus. A corona is a crown. 'Novel coronavirus pandemic' means 'a new coronation for all.' Already we can feel the power of who we might become. A true sovereign does not run in fear from life or from death. A true sovereign does not dominate and conquer (that is a shadow archetype, the Tyrant). The true sovereign serves the people, serves life, and respects the sovereignty of all people. The coronation marks the emergence of the unconscious into consciousness, the crystallization of chaos into order, the transcendence of compulsion into choice. We become the rulers of that which had ruled us. The New World Order that the conspiracy theorists fear is a shadow of the glorious possibility available to sovereign beings. No longer the vassals of fear, we can bring order to the kingdom and build an intentional society on the love already shining through the cracks of the world of separation (Ibid.).

In a more pondered, scientific, centrist and practical tone, German Post-1968 and "green" Futurist Werner Mittelstaedt published a post-Corona book on "The Anthropocene and sustainability" (Mittelstaedt, 2020a), which he explicitly collocated in the context of the Coronavirus crisis and its potential aftermath:

Before the Coronavirus pandemic, the level of quantitative socio-economic growth was at its highest level in the history of the global society. Most oil was produced, most cars were built, never before have more people in airplanes been in the air at the same time, most surfaces were sealed, most meat was eaten, most goods were produced and transported, and so on and so forth. The socio-economic activities have gravitational negative consequences for the Earth system and reduce its capacity to restore and secure its great diversity of life (humans, animals, plants), because the reactivity of the Earth's biosphere and atmosphere has been exceeded for decades. The pattern of progress shaped by the countries of the North, which has now been adopted by practically all the emerging countries and the countries of the South, was not sustainable. Then came the Coronavirus pandemic. It led to the greatest deceleration of global socio-economic activities since the start of the Anthropocene. The measures that have been taken worldwide to combat it surpass everything that has been undertaken so far in the many crises and catastrophes of the Anthropocene. Neither the large-scale demonstrations against the climate crisis and for more climate protection, which the global movement 'Fridays for Future' and other climate activists have brought about worldwide, nor the uncountable actions for nature and environmental

SYSTEMIC IMPROVEMENTS AT THE "EVO-DEVO" INTERFACE? 333

protection, the regular warnings of scientists and non-governmental organisations from the fields of environmental protection and science, neither the words of the Pope in his encyclic *Laudato si* published in 2015 nor those of countless intellectuals were as consequential as the urgently necessary measures against the coronavirus pandemic. The reason for this is the collective fear of the Coronavirus and its extremely serious consequences. The immediate fear of it clearly surpasses the fear of the long-term consequences of climate change and the progressive destruction of the earth's bases of life.

MITTELSTAEDT, 2020b

And this fear, asserts Mittelstaedt, may also have some forward and progressive power, after all, as a consequence of Corona:

A tiny 'event' in the form of a new virus spreading to pandemic has led to this interruption. There is talk of a 'war' against the new Sars CoV-2 virus ... But epidemics and pandemics are nothing new. They accompanied mankind for thousands of years and they also accompany today's globalised society. In the 20th century they have claimed many million lives. But in the global society of the 21st century with currently 7.78 billion people and a highly interconnected economy as well as 'an inherent migration trend of peoples' through global tourism every pandemic spreads even faster than in earlier times, so that the medical capacities come under enormous pressure. They are often not able to care for and treat all the people who are ill. Is the coronavirus pandemic striking back at nature because we are continually endangering and destroying it through our unsustainable socio-economic model of progress? [...] The Corona crisis has advanced learning processes at almost all levels of human activity, which we should also use in the fight against the many crises of the Anthropocene (Ibid.).

As a result, Mittelstaedt and colleagues:

[issue] the call to press ahead with a 'second enlightenment'. It is necessary to use the remaining window of a few decades to make the Anthropocene sustainable. The Coronavirus came also into existence because we humans ruthlessly manipulate, exploit and destroy the flora and fauna. The coronavirus pandemic has dramatically confirmed [one] core message: If we do not take massive action against the climate crisis and enforce truly sustainable action, then we endanger all life on Earth

– including the life of Homo sapiens. Now is the time to rethink. The Corona crisis is both a warning and an opportunity. If lessons are learned from the measures taken against the Coronavirus crisis, the individual measures proposed by civil society and leaders around the world against the climate crisis and for sustainable action would, compared to those taken against the Coronavirus pandemic, have almost no impact on normal everyday life. But the gain in sustainability and quality of life would be enormous!.

MITTELSTAEDT, 2020a, p. 110

CHAPTER 48

Integrating the Obvious

Post-Corona, Multi-Resilience and "Futures Literacy": "Bring Together What Belongs Together"

Against the background of one of the first guiding question of this book: "How can societies prepare for unpredictable bundle crises and crisis bundles?", we argued that more collective intelligence and collective wisdom based on cross-national, cross-sectoral, and cross-disciplinary knowledge creation will be needed. Against this background, multi-resilience can serve as useful concept to increase future preparedness. As we have argued, multi-resilience is not meant to replace the many already existing approaches of mono-resilience, but to integrate them on a transdisciplinary and systemic level. Moreover, it makes us aware of man-made new vulnerabilities and undesired rebound effects which could result from innovations. Furthermore, the motto of multi-resilience could also serve as another incentive for cross-sectoral and cross-national cooperation against the background of a new vision of Globalisation 2.0 to be achieved by re-globalisation.

We have also learned that multi-resilience may not be the only meta-concept to bear in mind. As outlined in previous chapters, it could be summarised that multi-resilience will not and cannot replace the meta-concepts of a "sustainable society" and a "developed society" but is instead complementary to them and, in the ideal case, integrates them into a tandem of options.

When referring to our second guiding question: "What are the chances for progress in the aftermath of the Coronavirus crisis?", other meta-concepts such as Future Studies or Foresight and Futures Literacy came into place. We have learned that Future Studies and Foresight contribute a broad variety of methods to analyse, imagine, describe and manage futures. Referring to this, it will be important for decision-makers to open not only towards one, but multiple futures, as outlined in the "Futures Cone" (figure 9). These futures include at least the concepts of probable (likely to happen), plausible (might happen based on our current knowledge) and possible futures (might happen, but based on future knowledge we still do not possess), preferable futures (based on value judgements on what we think should happen), undesirable futures (what we want to avoid), preposterous futures (what we think is impossible, showing us the boundaries of our thinking), as well as "future potentials" or "weak signals" which can be found in the present. As we have underscored,

© ROLAND BENEDIKTER AND KARIM FATHI, 2022 | DOI:10.1163/9789004469686_049

any of these trajectories is worthy of thoughtful reflection in cross-disciplinary teams. Such teams should "bring together what belongs together": different futures which have to be taken seriously on the bases of their own inherent logics and options.

Overall, in terms of multi-resilience, it will be decisive to anticipate and prepare for different possible futures. These could and should also include existential threats and man-made disasters; however (and this might still be a blind spot of the nascent multi-resilience paradigm), they should also sensitise for best-case "preposterous" scenarios. In this specific regard, the post-Corona strategy discussion should reflect scenarios such as the following:

- *Decline or collapse through natural disasters.* In this scenario, the world would collapse under a bundle of disastrous events such as the next super-pandemic, bad weather events, or climate wars and corresponding migrations. This can also include non-man-made disasters such as a meteorite impact.
- *Machine takeover.* In this ambivalent scenario, the world would be the result of increased breakthroughs in digital and AI technology going out of control. Global economic growth might have highly increased; however, negative side effects to prepare for could include overexploitation of raw materials, and shorter product lifecycles which cannot be balanced even by a relatively efficient recycling industry. In this scenario, the world would be flooded with waste.
- *Pragmatic global development and joint solution-finding.* This "better case" scenario could be influenced by the concept of the "developed society" leading to the realisation of a global governance world order, with a world parliament that finds solutions to most solvable world problems. Cross-national synergies would result in further technological breakthroughs and a highly mobilised world. Since new habitats in space are explored, and the resource and energy problem are solved, the sustainable discourse might lose importance.
- *Limits and self-discipline through Post-Growth.* In this scenario, the post-Corona world would be characterised by the impacts of resource scarcity and simultaneous climate change. As a result, concepts of sustainability and adaptive multi-resilience could prevail and would become part of any social, political and cultural practice. Populations would learn to adapt to growing internal and environmental limits. This could result into a "slower", de-globalised world, maybe based on zero-growth with communities of increased "local resiliency" in terms of more self-sufficiency and less top-down dependency.

INTEGRATING THE OBVIOUS

These are just a few of the manifold possible post-Corona futures based on different variables and with different implications for future preparedness. All, though, make it important not only to consider multi-resilience, but also other concepts.

Taken together, future preparedness in a post-Corona world will not only imply strategically considering multiple perspectives on the future; it also requires becoming aware of inherent anticipatory assumptions and cognitive biases (which is often neglected in mainstream Foresight). In this regard, the future we imagine and create is largely dependent on perceptions of our past and present, and on what we are anticipating (or not) about the future. As can be derived from the Futures Literacy Framework, this does not only refer to futures we are planning or preparing for (Miller calls it "Anticipation-for-the-Future", short AfF), but then also to a "non-future" in terms of unknown novelties and potentials unfolding (Miller's term for it is "Anticipation-for-Emergence", short AfE). As an integrative approach, the Futures Literacy Framework (FLF) provides orientation for locally customised interventions of foresight and for "using-the-future", i.e., to constantly think about different futures and their implications in order to be prepared for them, by considering different types of Anticipatory Assumptions (AA), as described in previous chapters.

Figure 12 provides an example of how different Futures Literacy Labs (FLL) for a post-Corona world could look within this framework.

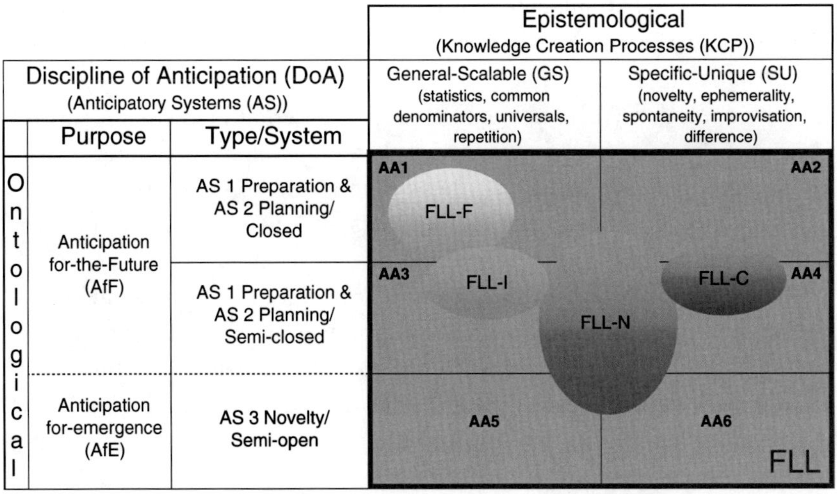

FIGURE 12   Mapping futures literacy labs within the futures literacy framework
SOURCE: MILLER 2018, P. 40

- FLL-F is a lab targeting the Anticipatory Assumptions (AA) of forecasting, as conducted, for example, in Thailand in 2010. In this case example, the aim of the intervention was to develop scenarios in order to prepare for climate change. Methods included a "Delphi" survey involving not only experts but also the whole population, and a scenario-planning process envisaging the risk of higher water levels and flooding. The result was that the scenario was considered unrealistic, so that no decisions and resilience programs were implemented. Months later a strong rainfall killed many people and the chaos generated turmoil (Cuhls, 2015). Considering critical AA reflection within the context of Futures Literacy would have prevented being unprepared for this scenario.
- FLL-I relates to AfF innovation and is designed to discover the according inherent assumptions. Typical interventions in this cluster include design or innovation labs, such as the Corona-crisis Hackathons mentioned previously.
- FLL-C are, by contrast, locally tailored processes of action-learning and "Collective Intelligence Knowledge Creation" (CIKC) that assist participants in becoming aware of the AA related to their 'consciousness'. According to Miller, this is sometimes the target of work in the "Integral Futures field" (R. Miller, 2018). A recent case example, covering aspects of the FLL-I and FLL-C clusters, can be found in the "Innovation 25" programme of Japan (Prime Minister of Japan and his Cabinet, n.d.), a country which can be regarded as one of the most experienced countries of systematic foresight activity, going back to 1972.[1] "Innovation 25" was a national strategy programme, launched by the Japanese governmental bureau. Its aim was to increase innovation in the country. Similar to Thailand, Japan used a broad participatory model of protagonists in the population (thus, not only experts) and combined Delphi surveys with scenario development. As a result, 25 key Delphi theses and scenarios were developed and distributed among the population in the form of *mangas*. The feedback was incorporated into a national innovation strategy.
- FLL-N are approaches where N stands for Novelty. This again includes FLL that have been custom designed for a project, with, however, a broader combination of methods and at least three design elements: action learning and research, CIKC and reframing. In their ground-breaking book, Riel Miller and colleagues describe 14 different country cases (R. Miller, 2018),

---

1   In comparison, the first scenario process by the company Royal Dutch Shell, which is internationally renowned as a pioneer in business foresight, was conducted in 1973. See: Shell, 2017.

often conducted in three phases including: 1) "Revealing" by inviting participants to expose their values, aspirations and hopes, as well as their expectations and predictions; 2) "Reframing" by exploring discontinuous futures based on alternative Anticipatory Assumptions. Participants were invited to imagine a societal context which was fundamentally different from their current paradigms; and 3) "Initiating the exploration" of new strategic questions arising from a review of the assumptions that influenced the participants' understanding of the present.

It appears to be obvious that multi-resilience and Futures Literacy have various connection and complementary points which have to be carefully considered for a successful post-Corona policy. There are various ways of how to do so.

Firstly, making use of both concepts can imply integrating the one into the other. That means taking Futures Literacy as an essential strategical part to foster national and global multi-resilience in terms of enhancing individual competencies of the population and concretely applying methods of future anticipation. In turn, multi-resilience can also be integrated into a Futures Literacy Lab, e.g. by the motto "How could our society or community become more multi-resilient in a post-Corona future?". Futures Literacy could hereby also serve as a bridge between multi-resilience and other societal concepts of future preparedness, for example by running Future Labs under different mottos, such as "How could our society become more sustainable in the future?" or "How could our society develop further?".

Secondly, it appears obvious that both concepts complement each other by focussing on different time-foci. While Futures Literacy has a clear orientation to the present and future, multi-resilience appears to address a more balanced attention to past (post-crisis), present (during the crisis) and future (preparedness).

Thirdly, both multi-resilience and Futures Literacy have a strong and explicit aim to foster and design cross-sectoral Collective Intelligent Knowledge Creation (CIKC).

Both, nevertheless, as highlighted throughout this book, should not neglect the pillar of collective wisdom which questions the deeper sense of our collective motivations (for example: "Does transhumanism really make us happier?"). Collective wisdom also makes us aware of potentials of man-made future side effects (e.g. what happens to our concept of "I" with the development of brain-computer interfaces and mind-uploading?). Here, too, we can assume useful and necessary synergies between Futures Literacy (application of forecast and anticipation technologies), sustainability studies (sensitising for cross-generational needs-satisfaction), and multi-resilience (strategies for preparedness and responsiveness across crisis context).

The necessity to combine multi-resilience with other meta-concepts such as Futures Literacy becomes more obvious in view of expected "global challenges" which do not only include annually changing "likely" and "impactful risks" as highlighted e.g. in the above-mentioned "Global Risk Reports". The notion of "global challenges" implies much more concrete problem-solving questions, potentially requiring all of the world population's collective intelligence and collective-wisdom future-imagination capacities. The respective questions include, but are not limited to the following (The Millennium Project, 1996):

1. How can sustainable development be achieved for all while addressing global climate change?
2. How can everyone have sufficient clean water without conflict?
3. How can population growth and resources be brought into balance?
4. How can genuine democracy emerge from authoritarian regimes?
5. How can decision-making be enhanced by integrating improved global foresight during unprecedented accelerating change?
6. How can the global convergence of information and communications technologies work for everyone?
7. How can ethical market economies be encouraged to help reduce the gap between rich and poor?
8. How can the threat of new and re-emerging diseases and immune micro-organisms be reduced?
9. How can education make humanity more intelligent, knowledgeable, and wise enough to address its global challenges?
10. How can shared values and new security strategies reduce ethnic conflicts, terrorism, and the use of weapons of mass destruction?
11. How can the changing status of women help improve the human condition?
12. How can transnational organised crime networks be stopped from becoming more powerful and sophisticated global enterprises?
13. How can growing energy demands be met safely and efficiently?
14. How can scientific and technological breakthroughs be accelerated to improve the human condition?
15. How can ethical considerations become more routinely incorporated into global decisions?

All these questions remain crucial for a post-Corona world, whatever it may look like in detail. These questions offer a first orientation for national and international post-Corona "future-preparedness" policies. Multi-resilience, in fruitful combination with other meta-concepts such as Futures Literacy, could provide impulses towards necessary changes and developments to answer these questions.

CHAPTER 49

Corona and Emerging New Responsibility Patterns

What will the future bring? And what will the post-Corona world look like?

While the virus may never be fully defeated and humanity may have to coexist with it to a certain extent, as was the case with previous infectious diseases, a "post-Corona" world would denote a situation where COVID-19 has been pushed back to a tolerable or at least co-liveable dimension that can be dealt with and that allows for a certain "normality". Yet although an astoundingly vast variety of treatments were developed in rather short timeframes, partly relying upon antibodies of animals such as llamas (Gill, 2020), "normality" is and will remain a disputed term. This is more the case, as research by King's College London suggested that Coronavirus immunity may be short-lived and last only for months (BBC News, 2020zz; Regan et al., 2020; S.M. Knight, 2020); as new pandemics may arise; and, perhaps more important, as other global threats of even more encompassing size and effect may hit in unknown moments.

The threat of a return of the virus was and is destined to remain real. This was elucidated by the fact that exactly at the moment when most countries had eased or totally revoked lockdowns and other restrictions and many thought the worst was over, it was as late as in the second half of August 2020 when the peak of daily infections was reached globally with 294,237 cases in 24 hours on August 15–16 (BBC News, 2020c). As COVID-19 reappeared in New Zealand after the nation thought it had defeated it, its Deputy Prime Minister called for an election delay (Ibid.). At that same time, South Korea, another country which had done very well in containing the virus, recorded the biggest outbreak of new cases in five months (Ibid.). Such ups and downs might persist in principle indefinitely.

This is why the WHO Secretary-General Tedros Ghebreyesus on 30 July 2020 asserted on the future outlook of the crisis that "the new normal" was most probably to "live with the virus". He also announced the new insertion of a Social Sciences branch into a more inter- and trans-disciplinary research pattern and long-term oriented action task force on this and other viruses, also with regard to potential future pandemics:

> Countries can and must take ... measures to adapt to the new normal. It's not easy, but it can be done. The pandemic does not mean life has to stop. We must all learn to live with the virus, and to take the steps necessary

to live our lives, while protecting ourselves and others – especially those at highest risk of COVID-19. Although older people are at a higher risk of severe disease, younger people are at risk too. One of the challenges we face is convincing younger people of this risk. Evidence suggests that spikes of cases in some countries are being driven in part by younger people letting down their guard during the northern hemisphere summer. We have said it before, and we'll say it again: young people are not invincible. Young people can be infected; young people can die; and young people can transmit the virus to others. That's why young people must take the same precautions to protect themselves and protect others as everyone else. They can be leaders – they should be leaders and drivers of change ...

Then Tedros Ghebreyesus announced a new scientific initiative by enlarging and strengthening the pool of involved sciences by interdisciplinary behavioural sciences:

People make decisions based on a wide range of factors to do with their culture, beliefs, values, economic circumstances and more. They make decisions under unprecedented financial and social pressure, high levels of anxiety and with ill-equipped health systems. Countries have been asking their citizens to understand their risk; to adapt; to engage; to give up to things they value and that define them. In the face of the COVID-19 pandemic, countries are using a range of tools to influence behaviour: information campaigns are one tool, but so are laws, regulations, guidelines and even fines. We are learning what works, and what doesn't. That's why behavioural science is so important – it helps us to understand how people make decisions, so we can support them to make the best decisions for their health. Today I'm proud to announce that WHO has created a Technical Advisory Group on Behavioural Insights and Sciences for Health. This broadens and deepens WHO's existing work on behavioural science and will support our work to offer health advice that is not only stronger, but more effective. The technical advisory group consists of 22 outside experts from 16 countries, with expertise in areas including psychology, anthropology, health promotion, neuroscience, behavioural economics, social marketing and more. This new group will advise WHO on how to increase and improve the use of behavioral and social sciences in a range of health areas, including COVID-19.

WHO, 2020e

344   CHAPTER 49

The WHO had previously already developed other tools for anticipating pandemics and similar global emergencies, such as in 2017 PISA, the "Pandemic Influenza Severity Assessment" (WHO, 2017), and in 2016 TIPRA, "the Tool for Influenza Pandemic Risk Assessment [which]is used to assess the pandemic risk of influenza viruses with pandemic potential" (WHO, n.d.). Interestingly, both were developed shortly before Corona, in a sign that the WHO had their sensors out, was aware of increasing pandemic risks and tried to prevent them with the help of systematic and applied scientific anticipation measures. To which extent this was, at least indirectly, an anticipation of the potential fact that Corona will not be the last pandemic but that the risk of new such events remains high and may actually increase even after a potential defeat of this specific virus, remains open.

Most probably, a "post-Corona" world will remain more unstable and prone to radical and encompassing upheaval than the world before. This thesis has some legitimacy, since the Coronavirus crisis only exemplified the unpreparedness of the globe for crises specific to the globalised 21st century, let alone for planetary ones such as the climate and environmental crisis which is due to show its full effects only over the coming decades. If the crisis has brought us more awareness of this precarious situation, not only on a national but also on a global dimension, and if it has thus strengthened the self-perception of a global community where, in the face of "universal" crises, everybody is in the same boat, then it has furthered some progress that may be useful for "re-globalisation".

Without doubt, the solution bundles presented in the midst of the crisis and shortly afterwards were manifold. And there was as much solidarity as distrust. Nevertheless, the World Health Organization (WHO) in June 2020:

> asked for more solidarity. The WHO identified a 'lack of global solidarity and leadership'. These are bigger dangers than the virus itself, said WHO chief Tedros Adhanom. He fears decade-long effects of the pandemic, which could even increase. A non-solidary world in his view could not be victorious against the virus: 'None of us is safe as long as not all of us are safe'
>
> APA, 2020e

Could, in such situation, a "healthcare NATO" (or even "health NATO", which would, without doubt, be something greatly different from the first-mentioned term in mechanisms, order structures, hierarchies and focus) be the solution – and, in the medium term, an adequate trans-national preparatory instrument for future crises, at least among the Western-European alliance of democracies? This is what German Minister of Health Jens Spahn proposed in June 2020:

> Europe needs a better mechanism for health crises, just as we have found one for financial crises: The EU as the core of an alliance for mutual assistance in the case of a pandemic, a kind of health [care] NATO.
>
> BILD ONLINE, 2020C

Many of such per se good ideas were poorly interconnected, though. This is nothing new, but is the repetition of century-old habits and coping mechanisms which seem not to have changed much over time.

According to Stanford's Walter Scheidel, throughout history, pandemics were often chaotic and self-organising catalysts of social and economic change, often levelling social and economic differences between the social strata of populations within and across countries (Scheidel, 2020). Moreover, pandemics were always as much about politics as about science. For example:

> the inability of 14th-century medicine to stop the plague from destroying societies throughout Europe and Asia helped advance scientific discovery and transformed politics and health policy.
>
> FINDLEN, 2020

The rise of new viruses also depends on the destruction of the natural world and the encroachment of human settlements into natural environments. According to most researchers from different disciplines, globalisation is and remains a decisive factor for present and future pandemics:

> Humanity has engineered a world ripe for pandemics. Emerging infectious diseases have become more likely – and more likely to be consequential – partly as a result of how people move around the planet and relate to the natural world.
>
> GARTHWAITE, 2020

On a global level, the Corona crisis has brought back a renaissance of "grand narratives" and systematic propaganda which goes against the trend towards the "deconstruction" of grand narratives and collective mythologies in open societies (Molter, 2020). In particular, fake news had a massive blossom during the Corona crisis:

As people increasingly social distance themselves to prevent the spread of the novel coronavirus, social media is an appealing way to stay in contact with friends, family and colleagues. But it can also be a source of misinformation and bad advice – some of it even dangerously wrong", said Jeff Hancock (2020). "People's uncertainty about the coronavirus can lead them to believe misinformation.

Certain is, as Matthew Jackson pointed out, that:

> failing to coordinate against the coronavirus pandemic may be very costly for the world. Without coordination within and across countries, the coronavirus will endlessly reemerge, with devastating consequences for public health and the global economy.
>
> M.O. JACKSON, 2020

Overall, what will be most important as the heritage of Corona is that we have to renew both our thinking and practice regarding basic concepts of resilience as we knew them towards more complexity-adequate patterns that have to guide us into the future. As the head of the National Commission on Global Change of the Austrian Academy of Sciences, Roland Psenner, put it, "resilience is not enough":

> We need a better definition of resilience that is not just based on past conditions. We will only be resilient as a community if resilience does not mean a return to business as usual, but if we firstly consider the permanent social, economic, technological and ecological changes and secondly look to the future, i.e., to the management of imminent global challenges. There is no going back.
>
> PSENNER, 2020

CHAPTER 50

Outlook: A Post-Corona World in the Making

Towards Difficult, but Feasible Innovation – For the Sake of a More Pro-positive Re-globalisation

What is it, then, to go forward?

First, as a result of the Corona crisis there may (and hopefully will) be corrections on how we have conceived globalisation in principle up to here. Such corrections have, in essence, been long overdue. Globalisation was already in crisis well before the Coronavirus emergency. And for years people have been thinking about how to transform its patterns in order to better "re-globalise" the world. The pandemic has only sped up and intensified the reframing and reform processes already underway.

Second, the global community is in fact called by the Corona crisis to rethink the whole system of domestic and globalised interaction from the bottom up. We must begin to implement more balanced, rational and better contextualised processes of less global and more "glocal" character. The Corona crisis showed that it is practically possible, and useful, to return to the "local" not as a universal measure but where it makes sense: to shop near one's homes, to trust the people in the shop around the corner more than far-away companies or multinational chains as the advertising industry suggested to us all the time, and to choose regional products, where available, instead of those imported from around the world for dumping prices which harmed their producers, accentuated inequality, fostered unnecessary waste, and destroyed the environment. Sustainability and "glocalisation" are trends that are becoming stronger in the aftermath of the crisis and as crucial parts of multi-resilience, and they are phenomena that affect not only single areas but most open societies around the world. They involve not only the production but also the investment sector, which will both be at least in part "re-shored", that is, more will be produced, consumed and invested locally, not least for the increased need for security in increasingly risky times. What is closest to us, we consider more secure – despite the fact that sometimes it is also more expensive. This is, overall, a positive development, since it strengthens local economic circuits and, more generally, patterns of a future "circle economy" which must complement globalised transfer mechanisms and is environmentally more reasonable than the often unnecessarily overstretched globalised production and consumption chains.

© ROLAND BENEDIKTER AND KARIM FATHI, 2022 | DOI:10.1163/9789004469686_051

Third, the outcome of the crisis can strengthen what the sustainability sector has always tried to favour: to reconcile work and community. Companies large and small will think twice before relocating production abroad. In terms of medicine, civil protection, the military, but also patents and copyright, Europe and the West have outsourced and then neglected entire sectors, including critical areas of anticipation and foresight. Now we are paying the consequences. Nevertheless, the creation of new production ecosystems in Europe and the West will create new opportunities, including economic ones. Through economic change, the Coronavirus crisis will have repercussions for the whole of societies, and this can turn out to be a good thing in the longer perspective. As German Federal Development Minister Gerd Müller summed it up at the start of May 2020 with an explicit hint towards the need for re-globalisation:

> the Corona crisis can be the start for a fundamental rethinking. Development Minister Gerd Müller pleads for a mind shift because of the Corona crisis. 'The ever-faster-more capitalism of the last 30 years must stop', he said. He described the Corona crisis as 'a wake-up call to mankind to deal with nature and the environment in different ways. One of the triggers of the pandemic is the over-exploitation of nature, the clearing of the rainforests. That is why we have to shift our minds and cannot simply return to the normality of globalisation as we knew it'.
> SWR, 2020

A fourth point is the necessary simplification of systems. The Corona crisis of 2020 has shown that current societal systems, particularly in open societies, with highly complex taxation and redistribution mechanisms complexly interwoven with anticipatory elements, for example in the mutually interdependent forms of lending, debt, income expectation and social security, are too vulnerable for crises, since when one cog falls out, the whole system collapses immediately. The "societal machine" works only if every element operates at maximum level, including people and persons who have to be hyper-active collectively, i.e., as a society, to keep things going at the very edge of possibilities and feasibilities to maintain the system. Simplification here means an increase in resilience, for example in the income-revenue-taxation nexus.

Related to this, the Corona crisis has shown, perhaps for the first time in such clarity in recent history, that the current socio-economic system is adjusted to the very edge, or peak of running modus: taxation and redistribution are working only for a society in which there is hysteric activity by more or less everyone. They are implemented in such a way that a sectoral change in behaviour towards less frenetic patterns immediately brings the whole system down, since there are no margins given that the system operates on the very edge of the razor's blade, exploiting every single drop of activity to produce ever-increasing growth and, from there, to constantly re-finance the working of the machine. The breakdown of the economy and the social chaos created by two months of virus-imposed inactivity of the larger part of the population showed that the socio-economic system of Western societies needs more reserves for the unexpected and sudden change; that there must be a margin between constantly operating on the peak or maximum level of capacity and speed, and a reasoned, more moderate pace and style to which the system has to be re-calibrated; and that there must be more flexibility for change phases in principle. This implies less dependency on "growth at any price".

Overall, the teaching of the Corona crisis is that open-society systems operating at the very limit of their possibilities work only if the largest portions of populations take part in frenetic activity, and that such a system is so vulnerable to partial inactivity due to over-complexity and anticipatory (debt!) growth orientation that it is not sustainable. If Western open societies learn these teachings, reduce their growth dependency, and enlarge the margins to manoeuvre in order to be better prepared for fluctuations and variability, the Corona crisis may also have instilled some benefit for the common good in the service of safeguarding modernity and the modern lifestyle.

Fifth, the Corona crisis has proven that for all this, multi-resilience is a concept that strongly matters in the future. Multi-resilience could be a resource for decision-makers from the political, but maybe also the private, civil-society and science sector, to give a necessary push to strongly required re-globalisation. Although multi-resilience will be strongly required by the international community, it does not by itself guarantee proper, balanced and shared re-globalisation. However, since the international community is still lacking an appealing vision of the future of globalisation, the concept of multi-resilience could be used as a chance to jointly develop a respective vision in multilateral ways. Such a process has to be carefully pondered and moderated by "neutral" international institutions such as the U.N. and its sub-organisations. As the Corona crisis showed all too clearly, both the tendencies towards national egoism or global cooperation are subject to confirmation biases, but also to credible global leadership, and the resulting willingness of international protagonists to cooperate.

Against this backdrop it was – and remains – worth trying to use pandemics such as Corona to show the benefits of interconnected democracies on the example of the transnational cooperation patterns within the "civic power" Europe and "to bring the EU closer to its citizens" (Hopkins & Fleming, 2020) by "inviting members of national parliaments, local authorities and civil-society groups to participate" (Ibid.) in solving the crisis, as French President Emanuel Macron pushed at the height of the pandemic as a more institutionalised inner-European health cooperation which could become a future practical pillar of EU cooperation and visibility.

In July 2020, a European parliament poll found:

> that Europeans want a stronger European Union (EU) role in the [Post-] Corona crisis. More than two thirds of EU citizens want the EU to play a greater role in tackling the Corona crisis, according to a survey commissioned by the European Parliament. More than half of respondents say the EU needs more money to do so, the EU Parliament said in Brussels. The main aim is to cushion the impact of the epidemic on public health and the economy. Also, more than half of the respondents remained dissatisfied with the level of mutual solidarity shown by EU member states during the Corona crisis. According to the survey, 68 percent of respondents wanted the EU to have more powers to deal with crises such as the Corona pandemic. [...] In addition to healthcare and economic recovery, [to shape the post-Corona world] respondents also wanted the EU to invest more in employment and social affairs and in combating climate change.
>
> MEDINLIVE, 2020

In contrast, it is – as mentioned – hardly a credible solution if one geopolitical player, i.e., in the Coronavirus crisis the European Union, in compensation for its loss of global influence played the substitute for global institutions like the U.N. by organising, under the leadership of German EU Commission President Ursula von der Leyen, a donor conference in May 2020 for the whole world, public and private. The conference included "countries and organisations" (Euobserver, 2020) to collect "around US\$ 8 billion" for a Coronavirus vaccine and paying, as usual, itself the lion's share in demonstration of its allegedly "outstanding" cooperative, cosmopolitan, universally generous and peaceful role. Besides the fact that this suggests that the priority is not the search for those politically responsible but to "peacefully solve the problem", which once again profiles Europe as a toothless tiger, such moves are not popular among a European citizenry already polarised over the all too exuberant and one-way cosmopolitanism of its elite globalisation leadership. In a multipolar world, the EU's role is not and cannot be, as one of many powers in a global concert, itself hard hit and with its own interests as all other powers, to be the host of global charity events, nor – as a global power among others – to collect the money of others to give it to the U.N. To do this either signals that the

EU is no global power – which is unnecessarily self-depreciative and factually wrong, although the EU has no global strategy as the only major player –, that it is the only cosmopolitan power and thus "overarching" the interests of others – which is neither the case nor credible in the eyes of others –, or that it practices an "inverse Eurocentrism", i.e., the unconscious belief in being something "better" than the rest of the world, now not by conquering the world as in times of colonialism, but by signalling indirectly "to be in charge of it". This is inappropriate and a sign of a perduring lack of realism in the EU's leadership, worsened by the loss of pragmatism that goes along with Brexit and which was necessary to balance German (compensatory) over-idealism and French complacent and self-ascribed "superior" rationalism. It would be rightly seen as critical if China or the U.S. tried to play such an in essence inappropriate, over-idealistic and bordering on kitsch role with international money involved. The EU must instead normalise and play its role as a serious power in a concert of powers, which may try to provide an example, not play once again the "civil leader" of the world, which is not the role ascribed to it by or agreed with others and is therefore not sustainable in creating enduring and shared multi-resilience.

Also, it seems to be a rather bad idea of the European Union to introduce new taxes and debts in Europe, given that European citizens and enterprises are already among the highest taxed in the world by their nation states:

> New taxes could finance EU corona aid. The EU Commission wants to finance the billions in aid foreseen for states and economic sectors particularly affected by the corona crisis through new levies and taxes. One of the proposals to be proposed to the EU member states is to ask digital companies and users of plastic to pay more. In addition, the proceeds from the trade in emission certificates could in future flow into EU coffers. Ursula von der Leyen's EU Commission intends to present a new draft for EU finances for 2021 until the end of 2027, which is to include a reconstruction plan for the economy badly hit by the Corona pandemic. The ... market-financed instrument for reconstruction ... is to be called the 'Next Generation EU' and, according to Germany and France, will make corona aid of 500 billion euros possible.
>
> FINANZEN.CH, 2020; TELEBASEL SCHWEIZ & WELT, 2020; FOCUS ONLINE, 2020a

In this situation, the presentation of rather radical and one-sided programmes by the EU, which seem to be not sufficiently evidence-based but rather leftist-ideological and partly directed in toto against the European economy in polemic ways, can hardly be the right path to follow (European Commission. Directorate General for Research and Innovation, 2020).

The more general and deeper-reaching question as to whether in deeply polarised European and Western societies the virus crisis has favoured the left or the right of the political spectrum, including some of their extremist factions, remains open. It will need particularly thorough investigation which may have to continue for years – well-spent years, certainly! – to come to relevant and plausible conclusions that can be accepted by all factions and stripes of the open societies' socio-political range.

The effort towards multi-resilience as the central task of the post-Corona world will have a crucial role in any rethinking of globalisation and the development of a pragmatic and functional multilateral safety net, including a necessary underlying mind shift by single global protagonists. It may coincide with a new, more prominent role for methodological approaches in working with anticipation and the future (Poli, 2019b) in inter-, trans- and multi-disciplinary ways such as UNESCO's Riel Miller's "Futures Literacy" (R. Miller & Feukeu, n.d.) or Roberto Poli's "Science of Anticipation" (Poli, 2019a), which must be implemented on a much broader level in research and teaching globally in order to prepare the new generations for dealing with uncertain futures and new crises. In contrast, the option pushed by "transhumanists": to increasingly delegate decision-making to machines (Johnson, 2020), e.g., Artificial Intelligence (AI), in order to "avoid errors", may not be the optimal nor the more sustainable nor the most secure path for dealing better with similar future crises.

Last, but not least, a better encompassing multi-resilience of globalised (and globalising) societies must also include a new international system of responsibility, accountability and, where necessary, recompensation mechanisms which ensure that mistakes, negligence and misbehaviour in high-risk sectors are sanctioned by the global community. A respective court of justice including non-traditional responsibilities, as well as a binding common ethics of how to deal with high-risk biotechnological research, in particular in order to deal with interconnected dangers, are highly recommended. The latter could be implemented through new "Geneva declarations" on bioethics, or similar.

Exemplarily, a joint historical enquiry commission is needed to uncover the whole truth about the origins of the virus, in order to avoid similar cases in the future. This should include, in this and potential future cases, close cooperation with the assumed geographical host, encouraging it to fully collaborate on a broad level and also considering best-practice cases in its own interest as well. For example, besides obstructing initial information (Gardner, 2020), rejecting independent investigations into the origin of the crisis (BBC News, 2020l; Page & Khan, 2020) and even putting restrictions on the publication of academic research on the origins of the virus (Gan, Hu & Watson, 2020), the communist Chinese government tried to hinder Taiwan in participating as an observer in international Coronavirus conferences, although Taiwan was one of the best countries as regards dealing with the virus outbreak (Asher, 2020). The world will have to draw its conclusions and deal with all this consequently.

Indeed, almost all experts agree that uncovering the origins of the virus is critical for the post-Corona future in many respects. Although the WHO in August 2020 declared that the origins of the Coronavirus were still unclear, and that it could have originated in Wuhan (Sudworth. 2020; BBC News, 202000) where the WHO therefore installed an investigation group (WHO, 2020f), but could have also come from somewhere else, there were many indications that China's totalitarian regime did not only delay information but used and misused the Corona crisis for its own purposes. In April 2020, China's government censored and restricted even its own scientific publications about the virus (Gan, Hu & Watson, 2020), and later it used the crisis for suppressing and potentially ending democracy in Hong Kong, violating all agreements with the UK and the international community about the autonomy zone's 50-year status. Some in Hong Kong may indeed have been reminded, on this occasion in a double sense, of the famous word of Richard Nixon who, after his China visit of 1972, stated that he feared that by interconnecting the – until then, isolated – Chinese communist regime with the world, he had created a "Frankenstein" power (Bild Online, 2020w). At the same time, hacker espionage about a vaccine was advanced prominently and intensely by the Chinese regime against societies around the world according to all Western intelligence services throughout the crisis, leading to public prosecution in several countries long before the end of the global peak of Corona (Bild Online, 2020b). Critics also observed that China had directly or indirectly "corrupted" the WHO, thus undermining its credibility and contributing to the epochal crisis of global bodies, such as the U.N. (Bild Online, 2020a). Whether this was the case or not, the best-documented critique of China's response to the Corona crisis came from pro-democracy China initiatives – i.e., by civil-society groups such as "Citizen Power Initiatives for China":

> Citizen Power Initiatives for China released a comprehensive report on August 24, 2020, documenting how the global COVID-19 pandemic, which has killed over 800 thousand people, including more than 176,000 Americans, could have been avoided had the Chinese Communist Party acted in an honest and responsible manner.
>
> J. YANG ET AL., 2020

The initiative called COVID-19 "the catastrophe that could have been avoided".

Those who do not see this last, more juridical and political – and probably more uncomfortable – aspect, or do not want to see it out of political correctness or boundless self-interest, ignore the fact that there is already an international community and a highly interconnected system in place where common rules based on the new level of fundamental interdependency the globe experienced in the Corona crisis must be expanded, protected, respected and implemented. This will have to be carried out against the resistance of authoritarian powers who allegedly gave origin to the virus and, at the same time, potentially took profit from it. The global Corona crisis of 2020 could turn out to leave exactly this insight into the paradoxes of re-globalisation, and what to do about them, as its main benefit and heritage for the generations to come.

Afterword

Globalisation is now at its most uneven and disjunctive phase in human history. The current global COVID-19 pandemic (GCP) has combined with the existing vulnerabilities of global capitalism to disrupt familiar social routines around the world. Many national borders have been closed to travellers other than those returning home. The value of stock-market fluctuations has exceeded those of the 2008 Global Financial Crisis and is overtaking those of the Great Depression. Supermarket shelves in the world's wealthiest cities, once carrying multiple competing brands of toilet paper and hand sanitisers, have been cleared daily by consumers apprehensively stockpiling essentials during long weeks of "lockdown". "Social distancing" has become a ubiquitous global term and government-mandated practice, while instances of "distant socialising" via such digital platforms as Zoom and Google Hangout have exploded.

The neoliberal shibboleths of financial management have, for a time, been discarded in favour of calls for massive government emergency bailouts, cheap money supplied by central banks, and old-fashioned Keynesian stimulus packages. Indeed, commentators have referred to the GCP as a "historic trigger event" that has not only left social life as we know it unrecognisable but cast a dark cloud of doubt on people's hope to return to "normal" anytime soon. Moreover, as a 2020 report of the Imperial College COVID-19 Response Team concludes, the social effects of the measures which are needed to achieve the global policy goal of epidemic suppression will be profound.

While it is important to acknowledge that the GCP has had negative impacts on the integrity of the globalisation system, it would be a mistake to refer to these tendencies as "deglobalisation". Rather, the current moment of crisis should be described as the latest and most intense phase of the "Great Unsettling" – shorthand for the intensifying conditions of instability, volatility, disintegration, insecurity, inequality, and degradation that are threatening familiar local lifeworlds and identities. On a systemic level, however, none of this is to suggest that globalisation-in-general is waning. What we are experiencing seems to point to the intensification of complex and uneven processes of global social mobility that require close scrutiny in order to spark new lines of enquiry leading to necessary alternative understandings. Indeed, more discerning academic analyses must approach globalisation in the context of our current crisis not as a single phenomenon primarily based on world trade and transnational financial flows, but a multi-braided and multidimensional set of processes of both conjuncture and disjuncture.

356   AFTERWORD

It is entirely fitting that Roland Benedikter – the European scholar who, some years ago, coined the term "global systemic shift" to describe the macro-dynamics of globalisation in our era of the Great Unsettling – has emerged as one of the first global-studies researchers to take up the challenge to forge such necessary new lines of enquiry. The outcome of his research efforts is the present volume that provides a comprehensive analysis of the 2020 global coronavirus pandemic (GCP) and its multiple catastrophic social impacts. As Benedikter and his co-author Karim Fathi point out in this remarkable volume, the GCP constitutes a "multi-systemic" crisis that requires new intellectual strategies to devise new, more comprehensive, strategies of "multi-resilience" that go beyond specialised and sectorial perspectives.

Much to their credit, the authors realise that any encompassing enquiry into the various aspects, implications, and effects of the GCP calls for the hard work of developing innovative transdisciplinary pathways. And this is precisely the methodological framework they utilise in their efforts to not only illuminate the complex *gestalt* and dynamics of the current global calamity, but also to give flesh to the concept of "multi-resilience" as a tool capable of bridging the theory-practice gap.

Indeed, multidimensional processes of globalisation and their associated global challenges such as pandemics, climate change, terrorism, digital tech-nologies, marketisation, migration, urbanisation, and human rights represent examples of transnational issues that both cut across and reach beyond con-ventional disciplinary boundaries. As Benedikter and Fathi remind us, the dynamics of the GCP add extra layers of complexity to contemporary social life that reveal that "real-world" problems in the twenty-first century conform less and less to the conventional disciplinary organisation of knowledge anchored in early twentieth-century Western contexts. Thus, this volume offers readers a more sophisticated and integrated "post-Corona" approach, designed to serve the twin objectives of conceptual development and public policy guidance in consistent transdisciplinary fashion.

Overall, then, this book contributes greatly to advancing our understand-ing of the GCP not as an isolated event, but a multidimensional crisis – or, as the authors characterise it, a "bundle of crises" – that should be analysed in its proper global context. COVID-19 has not put an end to globalisation but is actually the new and threatening face of worldwide interdependence and interconnectivity. Hence, globalisation still matters a lot – just not in the same way as it did two or three decades ago.

As Benedikter and Fathi emphasise, the flipside of what has been described as "deglobalisation" in some aspects of social life is really "reglobalisation", that is, a profound rearrangement of the global system's constituent formations that move at different speeds and at different levels of intensity. Thus, the present volume advances what should be main agenda of current and future research on the ever-changing global-local nexus: to describe and analyse the enduring significance of reconfigured globalisation dynamics by utilising the multiple methodological tools of cutting-edge transdisciplinary research.

Manfred B. Steger
Professor of Global and Transnational Sociology
University of Hawai'i at Manoa
Global Professorial Fellow
Western Sydney University

Bibliographic References

A Plus (2020). 'Ghanaian Brothers Create Solar-Powered Hand-Washing Basin', *Daily Motion*, June. Available at: https://www.dailymotion.com/video/x7uf37x.

Abdurasulov, A. (2020) 'Coronavirus: The strangers reaching out to Kyrgyzstan's lonely teenagers'. *BBC*, 26 May. Available at: https://www.bbc.com/news/world-asia-52587 000.

Abeysinghe, T., Hao, W.Y. (2014). 'Income inequality in Singapore: Do housing prices play a role?', *Department of Economics SCAPE Working Paper Series*, Paper No. 2014/ 01, May. Available at: https://www.semanticscholar.org/paper/Income-inequality -in-Singapore%3A-Do-housing-prices-a-Abeysinghe-Hao/fb6b52edeac47d838b986 0976199bcfoed5a8475.

Abraham, R. and Kavya, B. (2021). 'Global COVID-19 deaths hit 5 million as Delta variant sweeps the world', *Reuters*, 3 October. Available at: https://www.reuters.com/world/ global-covid-19-deaths-hit-5-million-delta-variant-sweeps-world-2021-10-02/.

Agamben, G. (2020a). 'Chiarimenti' [Clarifications], *Quodlibet*, 17 March. Available at: https://www.quodlibet.it/giorgio-agamben-chiarimenti.

Agamben, G. (2020b). 'Biosicurezza e politica' [Biosafety and policy], *Quodlibet*, 11 May. Available at: https://www.quodlibet.it/giorgio-agamben-biosicurezza.

Agence France-Presse (2020). 'Drones with heat sensors are used to spot people infected with coronavirus walking around during lockdown in Italy', *Daily Mail*, 10 April. Available at: https://www.dailymail.co.uk/news/article-8208549/Italian-pol ice-using-heat-sensor-drones-catch-people-coronavirus-lockdown.html.

Akinbogun, S.P., Aigbavboa, C., Gumbo, T., Thwala, W. (2020). *Modelling the Socio-Economic Implications of Sustainability Issues in the Housing Market*. Springer International Publishing. DOI: 10.1007/978-3-030-48954-0.

Alber, E., Zwilling, C. (2016). 'South Tyrol', *Autonomy Arrangements in the World*, January. Available at: http://www.world-autonomies.info/tas/styrol/Documents/ South%20Tyrol__2016-01-15.pdf.

Alexander, R. (2018). 'Implicit, Tacit, or Explicit: All Knowledge Is Valuable', *Bloomfire*, 16 January. Available at: https://bloomfire.com/blog/implicit-tacit-explicit-knowle dge/.

Aljazeera (2020). 'WHO: Coronavirus pandemic is a 'once-in-a-century' health crisis', *Aljazeera*, 31 July. Available at: https://www.aljazeera.com/news/2020/07/31/who -coronavirus-pandemic-is-a-once-in-a-century-health-crisis/.

Allen, J., Burns, N., Garrett, L., Haass, R.N., Ikenberry, J.O., Mahbubani, K., Menon, S., Niblett, R., Nye, J.R., O'Neil, S.K., Schake, K., Walt, S.M. (2020). 'How the World Will Look After the Coronavirus Pandemic', *Foreign Policy*, 20 March. Available at: https:// foreignpolicy.com/2020/03/20/world-order-after-coroanvirus-pandemic/.

Allotey, P., Schwalbe, N., Reidpath, D.D. (2020). 'Are Men Really That Much More Likely to Die from Coronavirus? We Need Better Data to Be Certain', *Our World*, 22 September. Available at: https://ourworld.unu.edu/en/are-men-really-that-much-more-likely-to-die-from-coronavirus-we-need-better-data-to-be-certain.

Allum, F., Bolchini, D. (2020). 'Can a Virus (Re)Shape Organised Crime?', *Australian Institute of International Affairs*, 3 June. Available at: http://www.internationalaffairs.org.au/australianoutlook/can-a-virus-reshape-organised-crime/.

Alon, T., Doepke, M., Olmstead-Rumsey, J., Tertilt, M. (2020). *The Impact of COVID-19 on Gender Equality*, National Bureau of Economic Research Working Paper Series, No. 26947 (April). DOI:10.3386/w26947. Available at: http://www.nber.org/papers/w26947.

Amadeu Antonio Foundation (n.d). *About Us, Advocacy. Training. Funding.* Available at: https://www.amadeu-antonio-stiftung.de/en/about-us/.

Amnesty International (2020). 'COVID-19, surveillance and the threat to your rights', *Amnesty International*, 3 April. Available at: https://www.amnesty.org/en/latest/news/2020/04/COVID-19-surveillance-threat-to-your-rights/.

Amos, O. (2020). 'Ten countries kept out COVID. But did they win?', *BBC News*, 24 August. Available at: https://www.bbc.com/news/world-asia-53831063.

Anderson, J., Bergamini, E., Brekelmans, S., Cameron, A., Darvas, Z., Domínguez Jíménez, M., Lenaerts, K., Midões, C. (2020). 'The fiscal response to the economic fallout from the coronavirus', *Brugel*, 24 September. Available at: https://www.bruegel.org/publications/datasets/COVID-national-dataset/.

Angell, J. (2020). 'Seven building blocks for a post-corona world', *OpenDemocracy*, 19 April. Available at: https://www.opendemocracy.net/en/transformation/seven-building-blocks-post-corona-world/.

Anger, H. (2020). 'Die Coronakrise erschwert die ohnehin geringe Gleichstellung' [The corona crisis complicates the already low equality], *Handelsblatt*, May 01. Available at: https://www.handelsblatt.com/unternehmen/beruf-und-buero/the_shift/frauen-in-fuehrung-die-coronakrise-erschwert-die-ohnehin-geringe-gleichstellung/25792352.html.

Anja Es (2020). 'Anja Es: Statement. Von Corona lernen ...' [Anja Es: Statement. Learning from Corona ...]', *Stayinart* (2, June). Zurich-Innsbruck-Vienna: Cosmopolitan, p.142. Also available at: https://www.stayinart.com/anja-es-statement-6/.

Antonini, R. (2020). 'Coronavirus, Mattarella: "Ricostruire il tessuto, rilanciare la fiducia nel futuro"' [Coronavirus, Mattarella: "Reconstructing the fabric, reviving confidence in the future"], *Dire*, 25 luglio. Available at: https://www.dire.it/25-07-2020/488527-coronavirus-mattarella-ricostruire-il-tessuto-rilanciare-la-fiducia-nel-futuro/.

Arana, M. (2019). Latin Americans Are Souring on Democracy. That's Not So Surprising Considering the Region's History, *Time*, 27 August. Available at: https://time.com/5662653/democracy-history-latin-america/.

Ashby, W. R. (1956). *An introduction to cybernetics.* London: Chapman & Hall Ltd.

BIBLIOGRAPHIC REFERENCES

Asher, S. (2020). 'Coronavirus: Why Taiwan won't have a seat at the virus talks', *BBC*, 16 May. Available at: https://www.bbc.com/news/world-asia-52661181.

ASTAT – Landesinstitut für Statistik (2020). 'COVID-19-Lockdown', *Astatinfo*, No. 40 (July). Available at: https://astat.provinz.bz.it/de/aktuelles-publikationen-info.asp?news_action=4&news_article_id=641709.

Austrian Press Agency (2020a). 'Arzneien: EU soll unabhängiger werden' [Pharmaceuticals: EU to become more independent], *APA*, 13 July.

Austrian Press Agency (2020b). 'Bestnoten für Krisenbewältigung' [Best marks for crisis resilience], *APA*, 19 June.

Austrian Press Agency (2020c). 'Corona hat psychische Folgen' [Corona has psychological consequences], *APA*, 14 July.

Austrian Press Agency (2020d). 'Corona Krise verstärkt die Sorgen' [Corona crisis increases worries], *APA*, 22 June.

Austrian Press Agency (2020e). 'Corona: WHO fordert mehr Solidarität' [Corona: WHO asks for more solidarity], *APA*, 22 June.

Austrian Press Agency (2020f). 'Erde lebt nur noch "auf Kredit"' [Earth now lives solely "on credit"], *APA*, 22 August.

Austrian Press Agency (2020g). 'Experte: Fliegen wird teurer' [Flying will become more expensive], *APA*, 23 May.

Austrian Press Agency (2020h). 'Experten warnen vor "Bio-Anschlägen"' [Experts warn about "bio-attacks"], *APA*, 25 May.

Austrian Press Agency (2020i). 'Forderung nach mehr Psychotherapie' [Call for more psychotherapy], *APA*, 22 May.

Austrian Press Agency (2020j). 'Guterres für Multilateralismus' [Guterres for multilateralism], *APA*, 26 June.

Austrian Press Agency (2020k). 'Hotels von Krise schwer getroffen' [Hotels hit hard by crisis], *APA*, 13 July.

Austrian Press Agency (2020l). 'Iran vergleicht Israel mit Corona' [Iran compares Israel to Corona], *APA*, 22 May.

Austrian Press Agency (2020m). 'Jugendarbeitslosigkeit wächst' [Youth unemployment grows], *APA*, 12 August.

Austrian Press Agency (2020n). 'Mehr psychische Probleme durch Corona' [More psychological problems because of Corona], *APA*, 5 May.

Austrian Press Agency (2020o). 'Sharon Stone lobt Männer in der Krise' [Sharon Stone praises men in crisis], *APA*, 11 May.

Austrian Press Agency (2020p). 'Studie: ÖsterreicherInnen legen mehr Wert auf Umweltschutz seit Corona' [Study: Austrians place more emphasis on environmental protection since Corona], *APA*, 11 August. Available at: https://www.ots.at/press eaussendung/OTS_20200811_OTS0046/studie-oesterreicherinnen-legen-mehr -wert-auf-umweltschutz-seit-corona.

Austrian Press Agency (2020q). 'Super-Reiche werden noch reicher' [The super-rich are becoming even richer], *APA*, 23 May.

Austrian Press Agency (2020r). 'UNO-Chef Guterres für neue Weltordnung' [U.N. chief Guterres for new global order], *APA*, 18 July.

Austrian Press Agency (2020s). 'Über 300.000 Corona-Tote in Europa' [Over 300,000 Corona deaths in Europe], *APA*, 11 November.

Austrian Press Agency (2020t). 'Viel weniger Krankenstände im April' [Much less sick leave in April], *APA*, 26 May.

Autonomous Province of South Tyrol (n.d.). *Home Page*. Available at: http://www.prov inz.bz.it/this-is-south-tyrol/default.asp.

Axelrod, R. (1984). *The Evolution of Cooperation*. New York: Basic Books.

Backhaus, A. (2020). 'Battling Virulent Coronavirus Rumors in Africa', *Der Spiegel*, 19 March. Available at: https://www.spiegel.de/international/world/deadly-fake -news-battling-virulent-coronavirus-rumors-in-africa-a-56aff54e-29cb-4f79-9839 -a8ba0598063f.

Baltrėnas, P., Baltrėnaitė, E. (2020). *Sustainable Environmental Protection Technologies*. Cham: Springer International Publishing. DOI: 10.1007/978-3-030-47725-7.

Banner, T. (2020). 'Symptome: Corona oder Grippe? Diese Symptome deuten auf COVID-19 hin' [Symptoms: Corona or flu? These symptoms indicate COVID-19], *Frankfurter Rundschau*, 23 November. Available at: https://www.fr.de/wissen/cor ona-symptome-COVID-19-grippe-coronavirus-sars-cov-2-krankheit-verlust-geru chssinn-geschmackssinn-90082236.html.

Bardi, U. (2017). *The Seneca Effect*. Cham: Springer International Publishing. DOI: 10.1007/978-3-319-57207-9.

Barkham, R., Brown, K., Parpa, C., Breen, C., Hooton, C., Carver, S. (2014). *Resilient Cities: A Grosvenor Research Report*. Available at: https://www.researchgate.net/ publication/283320811_Resilient_Cities_A_Grosvenor_Research_Report.

Barnes, O. (2020). 'Coronavirus: Vietnam coma pilot warns people 'not to be blasé'', *BBC*, 27 July. Available at: https://www.bbc.com/news/uk-scotland-53544345.

Barnes, O., Thu, B. (2020). 'Patient 91: How Vietnam saved a British pilot and kept a clean COVID-19 sheet', *BBC*, 26 June. Available at: https://www.bbc.com/news/ world-asia-53196009.

Barroso, J.M. (2010). 'Europe's rising global role', *The Guardian*, 3 January. Available at: https://www.theguardian.com/commentisfree/2010/jan/03/europe-global-role.

Basrur, R., Kliem, F. (2020). 'COVID-19 and international cooperation: IR paradigms at odds', *SN Social Sciences*, 1 (7, 2021). DOI: https://doi.org/10.1007/s43545-020-00006-4.

Bateman, J. (2020). 'Solidarity knows no borders': Germany treating dozens of corona-virus patients from Italy and France', *The Independent*, 1 April. Available at: https:// www.independent.co.uk/news/world/europe/coronavirus-germany-italy-france -hospital-treatment-COVID-19-a9440906.html.

BIBLIOGRAPHIC REFERENCES

Bauer, W. (2020). 'Freiheit auf Koreanisch' [Freedom in Korean], *Die Zeit*, No. 22/2020, 20 May, pp. 13–15. Also available at: https://www.zeit.de/2020/22/suedkorea-coro navirus-lockerungen-freiheit-neuinfektion/komplettansicht.

BBC News (2020a). 'Africa 'needs \$1.2tn' to recover coronavirus losses', *BBC*, 10 October. Available at: https://www.bbc.com/news/world-africa-54491053.

BBC News (2020b). 'Andrea Bocelli 'humiliated' by Italy's COVID rules', *BBC*, 28 July. Available at: https://www.bbc.com/news/entertainment-arts-53564949.

BBC News (2020c). 'As it happened: New daily infection record reported by WHO', *BBC*, 16 August. Available at: https://www.bbc.com/news/live/world-53797129.

BBC News (2020d). 'As it happened: UK reports highest death toll in Europe. Raab insists virus death tolls shouldn't be compared', *BBC*, 5 May. Available at: https:// www.bbc.com/news/live/world-52539905.

BBC News (2020e). 'Baltimore to use planes to patrol city from the sky', *BBC*, 1 May. Available at: https://www.bbc.com/news/world-us-canada-52505486.

BBC News (2020f). 'China coronavirus: 'Wartime state' declared for Urumqi in Xinjiang', *BBC*, 18 July. Available at: https://www.bbc.com/news/world-asia-china-53458412.

BBC News (2020g). 'Coronavirus au Sénégal: des étudiants créent un robot pour réduire le risqué de contamination du COVID-19' [Coronavirus in Senegal: students create robot to reduce COVID-19 contamination risk], *BBC*, 16 May. Available at: https:// www.bbc.com/afrique/media-52642805.

BBC News (2020h). 'Coronavirus by Air: The spread of COVID-19 in the Middle East', *BBC*, 5 May. Available at: https://www.bbc.com/news/av/world-middle-east -52537663.

BBC News (2020i). 'Coronavirus was already in Italy by December, waste water study finds', *BBC*, 19 June. Available at: https://www.bbc.com/news/world-europe -53106444.

BBC News (2020j). 'Coronavirus will be with us forever, Sage scientist warns', *BBC*, 22 August. Available at: https://www.bbc.com/news/uk-53875189.

BBC News (2020k). 'Coronavirus: Brazil passes 100,000 deaths as outbreak shows no sign of easing', *BBC*, 9 August. Available at: https://www.bbc.com/news/world-latin -america-53712087.

BBC News (2020l). 'Coronavirus: China rejects call for probe into origins of disease', *BBC*, 24 April. Available at: https://www.bbc.com/news/world-asia-china-52420536.

BBC News (2020m). 'Coronavirus: Chinese state media take aim at US 'lab theory'', *BBC*, 5 May. Available at: https://www.bbc.com/news/world-asia-52540737.

BBC News (2020n). 'COVID: Donald Trump and Melania test positive', *BBC*, 2 October. Available at: https://www.bbc.com/news/world-us-canada-54381848.

BBC News (2020o). 'Coronavirus: Donald Trump vows not to order Americans to wear masks', *BBC*, 18 July. Available at: https://www.bbc.com/news/world-us-canada -53453468.

BBC News (2020p). 'Coronavirus: First US deaths weeks earlier than thought', BBC, 22 April. Available at: https://www.bbc.com/news/world-us-canada-52385558.

BBC News (2020q). 'Coronavirus: Four out of five people's jobs hit by pandemic', BBC, 7 April. Available at: https://www.bbc.com/news/business-52199888.

BBC News (2020r). 'Coronavirus: France's first known case 'was in December'', BBC, 5 May. Available at: https://www.bbc.com/news/world-europe-52526554.

BBC News (2020s). 'Coronavirus: Germany hails couch potatoes in new videos', BBC, 16 November. Available at: https://www.bbc.com/news/world-europe-54959871.

BBC News (2020t). 'Coronavirus: Germany puts on crowded concerts to study risks', BBC, 22 August. Available at: https://www.bbc.com/news/world-europe -53875370.

BBC News (2020u). 'Coronavirus: Greatest test since World War Two, says UN chief', BBC, 1 April. Available at: https://www.bbc.com/news/world-52114829.

BBC News (2020v). 'Coronavirus: Hong Kong on verge of 'large-scale' outbreak, says Carrie Lam', BBC, 29 July. Available at: https://www.bbc.com/news/world-asia -china-53575875-.

BBC News (2020w). 'Coronavirus: Hospitality industry 'faces thousands of closures'', BBC, 17 March. Available at: https://www.bbc.com/news/business-51923804.

BBC News (2020x). 'Coronavirus: Israel marks Jewish New Year with second lockdown', BBC, 19 September. Available at: https://www.bbc.com/news/world-middle-east -54201834.

BBC News (2020y). 'Coronavirus: Kenyan boy who made hand-washing machine awarded', BBC, 2 June. Available at: https://www.bbc.com/news/world-africa -52898797.

BBC News (2020z). 'Coronavirus: Melbourne police 'assaulted and baited' over lockdown rules', BBC, 4 August. Available at: https://www.bbc.com/news/world-austra lia-53645759.

BBC News (2020aa). 'Coronavirus: Missing school is worse than virus for children – Whitty', BBC, 23 August. Available at: https://www.bbc.com/news/uk-53875410.

BBC News (2020bb). 'Coronavirus: Money worries in pandemic drive surge in anxiety', BBC, 4 May. Available at: https://www.bbc.com/news/uk-52527135.

BBC News (2020cc). 'Coronavirus: most severe health emergency WHO has faced', BBC, 21 July. Available at: https://www.bbc.com/news/world-53557577.

BBC News (2020dd). 'Coronavirus: New Zealand claims no community cases as lockdown eases', BBC, 27 April. Available at: *https://www.bbc.com/news/world-asia-52436658.*

BBC News (2020ee). 'Coronavirus: Risk of death is higher for ethnic minorities', BBC, 2 June. Available at: https://www.bbc.com/news/health-52889106.

BIBLIOGRAPHIC REFERENCES

BBC News (2020ff). 'Coronavirus: Secrecy surrounds India PM Narendra Modi's '$1bn' COVID-19 fund', *BBC*, 30 June. Available at: https://www.bbc.com/news/world-asia -india-53151308.

BBC News (2020gg). 'Coronavirus: See how students for dis African kontris dey help fight coronvirus' [Coronavirus: See how students in this African country help fight coronavirus], *BBC*, 8 May. Available at: https://www.bbc.com/pidgin/world -52577948.

BBC News (2020hh). 'Coronavirus: South Korea confirms second wave of infections', *BBC*, 22 June. Available at: https://www.bbc.com/news/world-asia-53135626.

BBC News (2020ii). 'Coronavirus: Spain set for basic income to ease crisis pain', *BBC*, 18 May. Available at: https://www.bbc.com/news/world-europe-52707551.

BBC News (2020jj). 'Coronavirus: Ten African innovations to help tackle COVID-19', *BBC*, 15 August. Available at: https://www.bbc.com/news/world-africa-53776027.

BBC News (2020kk). 'Coronavirus: Two million deaths 'very likely' even with vaccine, WHO warns', *BBC*, 25 September. Available at: https://www.bbc.com/news/world -54303628.

BBC News (2020ll). 'Coronavirus: Victoria declares state of disaster after spike in cases', *BBC*, 2 August. Available at: https://www.bbc.com/news/world-australia-53627038.

BBC News (2020mm). 'Coronavirus: What does 'from Russia with love' really mean?', *BBC*, 3 April. Available at: https://www.bbc.com/news/world-europe-52137908.

BBC News (2020nn). 'COVID-19 pandemic: Where are the global coronavirus hotspots?', *BBC*, 23 September. Available at: https://www.bbc.com/news/world-51235105.

BBC News (2020oo). 'COVID-19 pandemic: Tracking the global coronavirus outbreak', *BBC*. Available at: https://www.bbc.com/news/world-51235105.

BBC News (2020pp). 'COVID-19: tighter national rules considered for England by government', *BBC*, 18 September. Available at: https://www.bbc.com/news/uk-54199 642.

BBC News (2020qq). 'Dalai Lama: Seven billion people 'need a sense of oneness'', *BBC*, June 12. Available at: https://www.bbc.com/news/stories-53028343.

BBC News (2020rr). 'Ex-Colombia spy chief Maria del Pilar Hurtado jailed for 14 years', *BBC*, 1 May. Available at: https://www.bbc.com/news/world-latin-america-32544248.

BBC News (2020ss). 'Hong Kong bars 12 opposition candidates from election', *BBC*, 30 July. Available at: https://www.bbc.com/news/world-asia-china-53593187.

BBC News (2020tt). 'Hong Kong postpones elections for a year 'over virus concerns'', *BBC*, 31 July. Available at: https://www.bbc.com/news/world-asia-china-53563 090.

BBC News (2020uu). 'In pictures: How coronavirus swept through Brazil', *BBC*, 16 July. Available at: https://www.bbc.com/news/world-latin-america-53429430.

BBC News (2020vv). 'India coronavirus: 14-year-old sexually assaulted at Dehli COVID-19 centre', *BBC*, 24 July. Available at: https://www.bbc.com/news/world-asia-india-53522998.

BBC News (2020ww). 'India's COVID crisis sees rise in child marriage and trafficking', *BBC*, 17 September. Available at: https://www.bbc.com/news/world-asia-india-54186709.

BBC News (2020xx). 'Koroonaavaayiras: Kalaqa mana rifeensaatti tamsa'ina COVID-19 hir'isuuf kaayyeffate', *BBC*, 12 April. Available at: https://www.bbc.com/afaanoromoo/oduu-52613923.

BBC News (2020yy). 'Singapore offers 'pandemic baby bonus' to boost births', *BBC*, 6 October. Available at: https://www.bbc.com/news/business-54429706.

BBC News (2020zz). 'Too many countries headed in wrong direction – WHO', *BBC*, 13 July. Available at: https://www.bbc.com/news/live/world-53386093/page/3.

BBC News (2020aaa). 'Trans Mountain pipeline: Protest ban is 'great time' to build, says minister', *BBC*, 26 May. Available at: https://www.bbc.com/news/world-us-canada-52804344.

BBC News (2020bbb). 'US charges Chinese COVID-19 research "cyber-spies"', *BBC*, 21 July. Available at: https://www.bbc.com/news/world-us-canada-53493028.

BBC News (2020ccc). 'Vietnam records first COVID-19 deaths', *BBC*, 31 July. Available at: https://www.bbc.com/news/world-asia-53606917.

BBC News (2020ddd). 'What India's lockdown did to domestic abuse victims', *BBC*, 2 June. Available at: https://www.bbc.com/news/world-asia-india-52846304.

BBC News (2020eee). 'Zindzi Mandela's family praised for revealing she had COVID-19', *BBC*, 17 July. Available at: https://www.bbc.com/news/world-africa-53442504.

BBC *News Radio World* (2020). 28 July.

BBC Sport (2020). 'Neymar: Barcelona president says it is 'unfeasible' to sign Brazilian during COVID-19 pandemic', *BBC*, 2 August. Available at: https://www.bbc.com/sport/football/53627309.

Beck, U. (1986). *Risikogesellschaft. Auf dem Weg in eine andere Moderne* [Risk society. Towards a New Modernity]. Frankfurt: Suhrkamp.

Beer, S. (1974). *Designing freedom*. Toronto: CBC Learning Systems.

Belwe, A. (1999). *Ungesellige Geselligkeit. Kant: Warum die Menschen einander 'nicht wohl leiden', aber auch 'nicht voneinander lassen' können*. [Unsociable socialising. Kant: Why people 'do not like' each other, but also 'cannot leave each other']. Würzburg: Königshausen & Neumann.

Benedikter, R. (1999). 'Mille Plateaux. Capitalisme et schizophrénie II / Tausend Plateaus. Kapitalismus und Schizophrenie II' [Mille plateaux. Capitalisme et schizophrénie II / A thousand plateaus. Capitalism and Schizophrenia II] in Volpi, F. (ed) *Großes Werklexikon der Philosophie* [Large dictionary of works of philosophy], Volume 1. Munich: Kröner Verlag, pp. 358–359. Reprinted in: Ders. (Ed.) *Großes*

BIBLIOGRAPHIC REFERENCES

Werklexikon der Philosophie. 2nd edn. Munich: Kröner Verlag 2004. Reprint of a translation into Spanish in Volpi, F., Martínez-Riu A. (ed.) *Enciclopedia de obras de filosofía*. Barcelona: Herder Editorial. 2005. Vol. 1, pp. 522–528.

Benedikter, R. (2011a). *Social Banking and Social Finance: Answers to the Economic Crisis*. New York: Springer-Verlag. DOI: 10.1007/978-1-4419-7774-8.

Benedikter, R. (2011b). 'European Answers to the Financial Crisis: Social Banking and Social Finance', *Stanford Program on International and Cross-Cultural Education SPICE Digest Series* (Spring). Available at: https://spice.fsi.stanford.edu/docs/european_answers_to_the_financial_crisis_social_banking_and_social_finance.

Benedikter, R. (2012a). 'Social Banking and Social Finance: Building Stones Towards A Sustainable Post-Crisis Financial System?', *The European Financial Review*, 12 February. Available at: https://www.europeanfinancialreview.com/social-banking-and-social-finance-building-stones-towards-a-sustainable-post-crisis-financial-system/.

Benedikter, R. (2012b). 'The Enlightenment', in Anheier, H. K., Jurgensmeyer, M. (eds.) *Encyclopedia of Global Studies*, 1. Thousand Oaks, CA: SAGE Publications, Inc., pp. 484–488. DOI: http://dx.doi.org/10.4135/9781452218557.

Benedikter, R. (2014a). 'Pro und contra: Braucht Europa eine Zivilreligion?' [Pros and cons: does Europe need a civil religion?], *Philosophie InDebate*, 14 March. Available at: https://philosophie-indebate.de/.

Benedikter, R. (2014b). 'Social finance and global development: Questions and challenges', *Global Social Policy*, 14 (2, July), pp. 277–279. DOI: https://doi.org/10.1177/1468018114539864e. Reprint of a reworked version under the title: 'The State of Social Banking in A Changing World: Transitions and Trends' In: Held, D., Nag, E.-V., Rodrik, D. (Eds.) *Global Policy Journal*, Durham University, London: Wiley & Sons Publishers, August 13, 2015.

Benedikter, R. (2018). 'Citizen Robot. Rights in A Post-Human World', *Cato Unbound*, 9 April. Available at: https://www.cato-unbound.org/node/2342.

Benedikter, R. (2019). 'Suicide Terrorism: A Trope of Our Time', *Challenge*, 5 (62, August), pp. 322–353. DOI: https://doi.org/10.1080/05775132.2019.1638093.

Benedikter, R. (2020a). 'Benvenuti nell'era della nuova globalizzazione' [Welcome to the era of the new globalisation] interviewed by Elmar Burchia for *NOI Magazine*, 21 April. Available at: https://noi.bz.it/it/magazine-innovazione/intervista-roland-benedikter-reglobalizzazione-eurac-research.

Benedikter, R. (2020b). 'Corona beschleunigt die Reformdebatte zur Globalisierung', *Statement der Mitglieder der Zukunftskreises: Die Coronakrise* [Corona accelerates the reform debate on globalisation', Statement by the members of the Zukunftskreis: The corona crisis]. Berlin: Deutsches Bundesministerium für Bildung und Forschung (BMBF) [Federal Ministry of Education and Research]. Available at: https://www.vorausschau.de/files/BMBF_Foresight_Benedikter.pdf.

Benedikter, R., Fathi, K. (2017). 'What is a Resilient Society?', *International Policy Digest*. September 17, pp. 1–8. Available at: https://intpolicydigest.org/2017/09/17/what-is-a-resilient-society/. Reprinted under the title: 'What is a Resilient Society? Toward Integrated Resilient Communities: A View From Germany', in *Localities, International Journal for Humanities and Locality Studies of the Korean Studies Institute Seoul (KSI), Pusan University and the National Research Foundation of Korea*, 7 (November, 2017). Seoul: 2017, pp. 209–222. DOI: 10.15299/local.2017.11.7.209.

Benedikter, R., Fathi, K. (2019). 'The Future of the Human Mind: Techno-Anthropological Hybridization?', *Challenge*, 62 (1, March), pp. 77–95. DOI: https://doi.org/10.1080/05775132.2018.1560943.

Benedikter, R., Göschl, G. (2014). 'Zur Überwindung der Krise: Europa braucht eine Zivilreligion' [To overcome the crisis: Europe needs a civil religion], *POP*, 3 (1, Mar). DOI: https://doi.org/10.14361/pop-2014-0118.

Benedikter, R., Gruber, M. (2019). 'The Technological Retro-Revolution of Gender. In a Rising Post-Human and Post-Western World, It is Time to Rediscuss the Politics of the Female Body' in Coeckelbergh, M., Loh, J. (eds.) *Feminist Philosophy of Technology*. Book series: Techno:Phil – Aktuelle Herausforderungen der Technikphilosophie [Phil – Current challenges in the philosophy of technology], Volume 2, pp. 187–205. Stuttgart: J. B. Metzler Publishers / Springer International.

Benedikter, R., Kofler, I. (2019a). 'Globalization's Current Transition Phase: The 5 R's', *Global-e' series: Re-Globalization,*12 (36, 29 August). Available at: https://www.21global.ucsb.edu/global-e/august-2019/globalization-s-current-transition-phase-5-r-s.

Benedikter, R., Kofler, I. (2019b). 'Re-Globalization: Globalism's New Frontiers (2019–20)' *Global-e series: Re-Globalization*. Available at: https://www.21global.ucsb.edu/global-e/global-e-series/re-globalization.

Benedikter, R., Siepmann, K. (2016). '"Transhumanism": A New Global Political Trend?', *Challenge*, 59 (28 January), pp. 47–59. DOI: https://doi.org/10.1080/05775132.2015.1123574.

Benedikter, R., Tsedze, W.M., Unterkircher, K. (2019). 'Africa, Go Green! A New Initiative for the Continent's Youth to Become Leaders in the Global Environment Needs to Combine Activism with Knowledge, Research and Policy', *New Global Studies,* 14 (1, November). DOI: https://doi.org/10.1515/ngs-2019-0026.

Berman, R. (2020). 'What the 'Liberate' Protests Really Mean for Republicans', *The Atlantic*, 23 April. Available at: https://www.theatlantic.com/politics/archive/2020/04/coronavirus-protests/610363/.

Bien (2017). *BIEN affiliated organisations and their definitions of Basic Income*. Available at: https://basicincome.org/news/2017/01/bien-affiliated-organisations-definitions-basic-income/.

Biermann, T., Haentjes, W., Wilke, P. (2020). '20 000 Protestieren Gegen Corona-Regeln: Impfgegner, Regenbogen-Flaggen, Profi-Sportler' [20 000 protest against

BIBLIOGRAPHIC REFERENCES

Corona rules: Vaccination opponents, rainbow flags, professional athletes], *Bild*, 2 August. Available at: https://www.bild.de/politik/inland/politik-inland/corona -demo-in-berlin-von-impfgegnern-bis-neo-nazis-eine-irre-mischung-72180844 .bild.html.

Bild Live (2020). 'Corona-Experiment Macht Hoffnung. So wären Konzerte wieder möglich!' [Corona Experiment Gives Hope. So concerts would be possible again!], *Bild*, 30 October. Available at: https://www.bild.de/video/clip/leipzig-regional/cor ona-experiment-macht-hoffnung-so-waeren-konzerte-wieder-moeglich-73669614 -73671462.bild.html.

Bild Online (2020a). 'Angst vor der Zweiten Welle – China feiert, die Welt leidet' [Fear of the second wave – China celebrates, the world suffers], *Bild*, 3 August. Available at: https://www.bild.de/politik/ausland/politik-ausland/coronavirus-china-feiert -die-welt-leidet-72205394.bild.html.

Bild Online (2020b). 'Anklage in den USA: China-Hacker spionierten Corona-Forschung aus!' [Indictment in the USA: China hackers spied on Corona research!], *Bild*, 22 July. Available at: https://www.bild.de/geld/wirtschaft/wirtschaft/corona-china -hacker-spionierten-corona-forschung-aus-anklage-in-den-usa-72008916.bild.html.

Bild Online (2020c). 'ANTI-RASSISMUS-PROTESTE Spahn warnt vor Massen-Demos ohne Corona-Abstand' [ANTI-RACISM PROTESTS Spahn warns against mass demos without Corona distancing], *Bild*, 7 June. Available at: https://www.bild.de/ politik/inland/politik-inland/anti-rassismus-demos-spahn-besorgt-wegen-corona -71110430.bild.html.

Bild Online (2020d). 'Attacke auf Berliner Museumsinsel. Täter spritzten ölige Flüssigkeit auf 63 Exponate' [Attack on Museumsinsel Berlin. Perpetrators sprayed oily liquid on 63 exhibits], *Bild*, 21 October. Available at: https://www.bild.de/regio nal/berlin/berlin-aktuell/berlin-oel-anschlag-auf-museumsinsel-warum-wurden -museen-zur-zielscheibe-73513838.bild.html.

Bild Online (2020e). 'Australische Corona-Studie: Das Virus überlebt bis zu 4 Wochen auf Oberflächen' [Australian study on Corona: the virus survives up to 4 weeks on surfaces], *Bild*, 12 October. Available at: https://www.bild.de/ratgeber/2020/ratge ber/australische-corona-studie-das-virus-ueberlebt-bis-zu-4wochen-auf-oberflaec hen-73369186.bild.html.

Bild Online (2020f). 'Bei 78 Prozent der Genesenen bleiben Herzschäden zurück' [In 78 percent of the recovered heart damage remains], *Bild*, 30 July. Available at: https://m.bild.de/ratgeber/2020/ratgeber/corona-studie-aus-frankfurt-bei-78 -prozent-der-genesenen-bleiben-herzschaeden-72117198.bildMobile.html.

Bild Online (2020g). 'Bundesregierung bestätigt Einflussversuche aus China' [Federal government confirms attempts of influence by China], *Bild*, 24 April. Available at: https://www.bild.de/politik/ausland/politik-ausland/coronavirus-bundesregier ung-bestaetigt-einflussversuche-aus-china-70275498.bild.html.

Bild Online (2020h). 'Bundestagspräsident Wolfgang Schäuble „Exzesse der Globalisierung" müssen korrigiert werden' ['Bundestag President Wolfgang Schäuble "excesses of globalisation" must be corrected'], *Bild*, 6 July. Available at: https://www.bild.de/politik/inland/politik-inland/wolfgang-schaeuble-exzesse -der-globalisierung-muessen-korrigiert-werden-71713028.bild.html.

Bild Online (2020i). 'Wegen der Corona-Pandemie: 150 Millionen Kinder zusätzlich in Armut' [Because of the Corona pandemic: 150 million children additionally in poverty], *Bild*, 19 September. Available at: Corona: 150 Millionen Kinder wegen Pandemie zusätzlich in Armut – Politik Ausland – Bild.de.

Bild Online (2020j). 'Einflussreicher Franzose fordert wegen Corona 'Verkaufen wir die Mona Lisa für 50 Milliarden an Bezos!"' [Influential Frenchman demands we sell the Mona Lisa to Bezos for 50 billion because of Corona!], *Bild*, 13 May. Available at: https://www.bild.de/politik/ausland/politik-ausland/wegen-corona-franzose -will-mona-lisa-fuer-50-milliarden-an-bezos-verkaufen-70625124.bild.html.

Bild Online (2020k). 'Erster Flughafen bekämpft Corona mit Robotern. UV-licht Gegen das Virus' [First airport fights Corona with robots. UV-light against the virus], *Bild*, 8 May. Available at: https://www.bild.de/digital/multimedia/multimedia/corona-ers ter-flughafen-bekaempft-das-virus-mit-robotern-70530318.bild.html.

Bild Online (2020l). 'Folge der Corona-Pandemie: Jeder Fünfte ist häufiger nieder- geschlagen' [Consequence of the corona pandemic: one in five is more frequently depressed], *Bild*, 9 October. Available at: https://www.bild.de/ratgeber/2020/ratge ber/corona-jeder-fuenfte-ist-durch-die-pandemie-laut-umfrage-haeufiger-nieder geschla-73334300.bild.html.

Bild Online (2020m). 'Gegen Parteiausschluss: Grüne stellen sich hinter Boris Palmer' [Against party exclusion: Greens stand behind Boris Palmer], *Bild*, 12 May. Available at: https://www.bild.de/regional/stuttgart/stuttgart-aktuell/gruene-unterstuetz ung-fuer-tuebinger-ob-palmer-gehoert-zum-urgestein-70593884.bild.html.

Bild Online (2020n). 'Junge Männer, die Integration nicht wollen' ['Young men who do not want Integration', *Bild*, 20 July. Available at: https://www.bild.de/regional/frankf urt/frankfurt-aktuell/polizei-gewerkschafter-junge-maenner-die-integration-nicht -wollen-71977316.bild.html.

Bild Online (2020o). 'Krimi um Impfstoff: Warum ein weltweites Impf-Chaos droht' [Crime story around vaccine: Why there is the threat of a global vaccination chaos], *Bild*, 5 May. https://www.bild.de/bild-plus/politik/ausland/politik-ausland/coro nakrise-warum-ein-weltweites-chaos-beim-impfstoff-droht-70452074,view=conver sionToLogin.bild.html.

Bild Online (2020p). 'Limburger (36) verübt Anschlag auf Belgiens Parlament' [Limburger (36) carries out attack on Belgium's Parliament], *Bild*, 30 July. Available at: https://www.bild.de/regional/frankfurt/frankfurt-aktuell/molotow-cocktail -limburger-veruebt-anschlag-auf-belgiens-parlament-72105332.bild.html.

BIBLIOGRAPHIC REFERENCES   371

Bild Online (2020q). 'Mai Thi Nguyen-Kim: Die Youtuberin, die es in Merkels Corona-Rede schafft' [Mai Thi Nguyen-Kim: the YouTuber who makes it into Merkel's Corona speech], *Bild*, 20 October. Available at: https://www.bild.de/politik/inland/ politik-inland/corona-mai-thi-nguyen-kim-die-youtuberin-die-es-in-merkels-rede -schaffte-73652352.bild.html.

Bild Online (2020r). 'Merz feuert K-Frage in der Union an: "Kanzler kann werden, wer Krise kann"' [Merz fires K-question in the union 'Chancellor can become, who can crisis'], *Bild*, 7 July. Available at: https://www.bild.de/politik/inland/politik-inland/merz -zur-k-frage-bei-cdu-csu-kanzler-kann-werden-wer-krise-kann-71738940.bild.html.

Bild Online (2020s). 'Neues Frühwarnsystem startet Testphase: Klärwerke geben Corona-Alarm' [New early warning system starts test phase: Sewage treatment plants issue Corona Alarm], *Bild*, 18 May. Available at: https://www.bild.de/news/inl and/news-inland/coronavirus-klaerwerke-geben-covid-19-alarm-neues-fruehwar nsystem-70725222.bild.html.

Bild Online (2020t). 'Neugeborenes mit Coronavirus infiziert' [Newborn infected with Coronavirus], *Bild*, 15 September Available at: https://www.bild.de/ratgeber/ gesundheit/gesundheit/coronavirus-waehrend-schwangerschaft-auf-ungeborenes -baby-uebertragen-71900726.bild.html.

Bild Online (2020u). 'Studie: Lockdown rettete 3,1 Millionen Leben in Europa' [Study: Lockdown saved 3.1 million lives in Europe], *Bild*, 9 June. Available at: https://www.bild.de/ratgeber/wissenschaft/ratgeber/coronavirus-studie-lockd own-rettete-3-1-millionen-leben-in-europa-71154878.bild.html.

Bild Online (2020v). 'Umfrage Zeigt Anstieg Scheidungsgrund: Corona' [Survey Shows Rise In Reason For Divorce: Corona], *Bild*, 18 June. Available at: https://www.bild .de/ratgeber/leben-und-wissen-verbraucherportal/verbraucherportal/scheidungsgr und-corona-scheidungsrate-koennte-durch-pandemie-stark-ansteigen-71350544 .bild.html.

Bild Online (2020w). 'US-Aussenminister Mike Pompeo: China ist zum „Frankenstein" geworden' [US Secretary of State Mike Pompeo: China has become "Frankenstein"], *Bild*, 24 July. Available at: https://www.bild.de/politik/ausland/politik-ausland/us -aussenminister-mike-pompeo-china-ist-zum-frankenstein-geworden-72040570 .bild.html.

Bild Online (2020x). 'US-Forscher Fanden Die Drei Haupttreiber der Pandemie: Wo stecken wir uns hauptsächlich mit Corona an?' [US researchers found the three main drivers of the pandemic: Where do we mainly contract Corona?], *Bild*, 22 October. Available at: https://www.bild.de/bild-plus/ratgeber/2020/ratgeber/us -forscher-wo-stecken-wir-uns-hauptsaechlich-mit-corona-an-73541838,view=con versionToLogin.bild.html.

Bild Online (2020y). 'Virus-Mutation! Dänemark riegelt 7 Kommunen ab. Es Wird Von Nerzen Übertragen'[Virus Mutation! Denmark seals off 7 municipalities. It Is

Transmitted By Mink], *Bild*, 6 November. Available at: https://www.bild.de/news/inland/news-inland/corona-virus-mutation-daenemark-riegelt-7-kommunen-ab-es-wird-von-nerzen-uebertr-73787102.bild.html.

Bild Online (2020z). 'Wie Superreiche sich jetzt überall einkaufen'. [How the super-rich are now shopping everywhere], *Bild*, 23 May. Available at: https://www.bild.de/geld/wirtschaft/politik-inland/coronavirus-die-gewinner-der-krise-wie-superreiche-sich-jetzt-ueberall-einkaufen-70780926.bild.html.

Bild Online (2020aa). 'Wirkung der Mehrwertsteuer-Senkung – Konsum-Boom nach Corona-Krise' [Effect of the VAT reduction – Consumption boom after the corona crisis], *Bild*, 24 July. Available at: https://www.bild.de/geld/wirtschaft/wirtschaft/corona-und-mehrwertsteuer-senkung-konsum-boom-nach-der-krise-72026466.bild.html.

Bild Zeitung, (2020). 'Weiter Streit um Demo' [Further dispute over demo], *Bild*, 4 August, p.2.

Bischof D. (2020). 'Gericht kippt Corona-strafe' [Court overturns corona penalty], *Wiener Zeitung*, 15 May. Available at: https://www.wienerzeitung.at/nachrichten/politik/oesterreich/2060786-Gericht-kippt-Corona-Strafe.html.

Blanke, S. (2020). 'Globale Zwangsquarantäne' [Global forced quarantine], *Internationale Politik und Gesellschaft*, 17 March. Available at: https://www.ipg-journal.de/regionen/global/artikel/globale-zwangsquarantaene-4161/.

Blatter, J. (2013). 'Glocalization', *Encyclopædia Britannica*, 21 May. Available at: https://www.britannica.com/topic/glocalization.

Bloom, J. (2020). 'Will coronavirus reverse globalisation?', BBC, 2 April. Available at: https://www.bbc.com/news/business-52104978.

Bloomberg (2021). 'The Covid Resilience Ranking. The Best And Worst Places to Be as Reopening, Variants Collide', 28 July. Available at: https://www.bloomberg.com/graphics/covid-resilience-ranking/.

Blume, G. (2020). 'Endlich wieder Liebe' [Finally love again], *Die Zeit Online*, 18 May. Available at: https://www.zeit.de/politik/ausland/2020-05/eu-wiederaufbauplan-angela-merkel-emmanuel-macron-coronavirus.

Bockenheimer, J.C. (2020). 'Monopol-Kommission warnt vor Corona-Sozialismus' [Monopoly Commission warns of corona socialism], *Bild Zeitung*, 18 June, p.2.

Boffey, D. (2018). 'Amsterdam to embrace 'doughnut' model to mend post-coronavirus economy', *The Guardian*, 8 April. Available at: https://www.theguardian.com/world/2020/apr/08/amsterdam-doughnut-model-mend-post-coronavirus-economy.

Bollyky, T.J., Bown, C.P. (2020). 'The Tragedy of Vaccine Nationalism', *Foreign Affairs*, Essay No. 2 (September/October). Available at: https://www.foreignaffairs.com/articles/united-states/2020-07-27/vaccine-nationalism-pandemic.

Bond, P. (2018). 'The BRICS, global governance, accumulation, class struggle and resource extractivism', CADTM, 25 April. Available at: https://www.cadtm.org/The-BRICS-global-governance-accumulation-class-struggle-and-resource.

BIBLIOGRAPHIC REFERENCES

Bonds, M.H. Keenan, D.C., Rohani, P. Sachs J.D. (2009). 'Poverty trap formed by the ecology of infectious diseases', *The Royal Society*, 9 December. This article was also published in *Proceeding of The Royal Soviet*, 277 (1685, April 2010). DOI: https://doi.org/10.1098/rspb.2009.1778.

Boone, L. (2020). 'Coronavirus: The world economy at risk. OECD Interim Economic Outlook', *OECD*, 16 September. Available at: https://www.oecd.org/economic-outlook/.

Borghese, L., Iddiois, R. (2020). 'Several Italian mafia bosses released from prison over coronavirus fears', *CNN*, 26 April. Available at: https://edition.cnn.com/2020/04/25/europe/mafia-bosses-italy-coronavirus-trnd/index.html.

Borrell, J. (2020). The post-coronavirus world is already here. *European Council on Foreign Relations*. 30 April. Available at: https://www.ecfr.eu/publications/summary/the_post_coronavirus_world_is_already_here.

Bostrom, N. (2002). 'Existential Risks: Analyzing Human Extinction Scenarios and Related Hazards', *Journal of Evolution and Technology*, 9 (1, March). Yale: Yale University.

Bostrom, N. (2013). 'Existential Risk Prevention as Global Priority', *Global Policy*, 4 (1, February), pp. 15–31. DOI: https://doi.org/10.1111/1758-5899.12002.

Bostrom, N. (2016). *Superintelligenz – Szenarien einer kommenden Revolution* [Superintelligence: Paths, Dangers, Strategies]. Frankfurt: Suhrkamp.

Both, I., Domic, K., Eimers, J., Flath, V., Keuler, K., Krings, C., Noltemeyer, O., Reinke, Y., Steckelbruck, L., Weidental, R. (2012). *Multi-Stakeholder-Initiative – eine methodische Einführung* [Multi-stakeholder initiative – a methodical introduction]. Mönchengladbach: Global Workers Protection (GWP). Available at: https://d-nb.info/1044211555/34.

Bottici, C. (2011). 'Imaginal politics', *Thesis Eleven*, 106 (1, August), pp. 56–72. DOI: 10.1177/0725513611407446.

Boyd, A. (2020). 'Cyberattacks plague COVID-19 vaccine race', *Asia Times*, 23 June. Available at: https://asiatimes.com/2020/06/cyberattacks-plague-COVID-19-vaccine-race/.

Brady, K. (2020). 'Scapegoats: Virologists face death threats during coronavirus crisis', *Deutsche Welle*, May 29. Available at: https://www.dw.com/en/scapegoats-virologists-face-death-threats-during-coronavirus-crisis/a-53613193.

Brauer, M. (2020). 'Corona lässt Scheidungszahlen explodieren' [Corona explodes divorce rates], *Stuttgarter Zeitung*, 22 June. Available at: https://www.stuttgarter-zeitung.de/inhalt.ehen-in-zeiten-der-pandemie-corona-laesst-scheidungszahlen-explodieren.ff495f6f-c83a-4f2f-a9e4-bfd6aa078bdc.html.

Bremmer, I., Roubini, N. (2011). 'A G-Zero World – The New Economic Club Will Produce Conflict, Not Cooperation', *Foreign Affairs*, March. Available at: https://www.foreignaffairs.com/articles/2011-01-31/g-zero-world.

Briggs, H. (2020a). "Billions of years of evolutionary history' under threat', *BBC,* 26 May. Available at: https://www.bbc.com/news/science-environment-52808103.

Briggs, H. (2020b). 'Mutated coronavirus may 'jump back and forth' between animals', *BBC*, 13 November. Available at: https://www.bbc.com/news/science-environment -54918267.

Broom, D. (2020a). '11,000 deaths avoided during lockdown in Europe – thanks to cleaner air', *World Economic Forum*, 11 May. Available at: https://www.weforum.org/ agenda/2020/05/coronavirus-lockdown-cuts-air-pollution-deaths-avoided/.

Broom, D. (2020b). 'This country came up with 5 novel ideas to tackle the pandemic', *World Economic Forum*, 27 July 2020. Available at: https://www.weforum.org/age nda/2020/07/estonia-hackathon-pandemic-covid19-technology/.

Brown, R. (2020). 'China: victory over coronavirus will be heralded as boost for Xi Jinping's brand of Marxism', *The Conversation*, 27 May. Available at: https://thec onversation.com/china-victory-over-coronavirus-will-be-heralded-as-boost-for-xi -jinpings-brand-of-marxism-136347.

Bufacchi, V. (2020). 'Is Coronavirus Bad for Populism?', *Global-e Series: Covid-19 and Populism*, 13 (25, 27 April). Available at: https://www.21global.ucsb.edu/global-e/ april-2020/coronavirus-bad-populism.

Bundesministerium für Bildung und Forschung (BMBF) [Federal Ministry of Education and Research](2014). 'Bekanntmachung'[Announcement], 15 July. Available at: https://www.bmbf.de/foerderungen/bekanntmachung-950.html.

Bundesministerium für Bildung und Forschung [Federal Ministry of Education and Research] (2019). *Regulatory Sandboxes – Testing Environments for Innovation and Regulation*. Available at: https://www.bmwi.de/Redaktion/EN/Dossier/regulatory -test-beds-testing-environments-for-innovation-and-regulation.html.

Bundesministerium für Bildung und Forschung [Federal Ministry of Education and Research] (2020). 'A New Impetus for Vocational Education and Training in Europe', 15 September. Available at: https://www.bmbf.de/en/a-new-impetus-for-vocatio nal-education-and-training-in-europe-12496.html.

Bundesregierung [Cabinet of Germany] (2019). '*Deutsch-Französische Erklärung von Toulouse*' [Franco-German declaration of Toulouse] [Announcement], 16 October. Available at: https://www.bundesregierung.de/breg-de/aktuelles/deutsch-franzo esische-erklaerung-von-toulouse-16-oktober-2019-1682252.

Bundesregierung [Cabinet of Germany] (2020). *#WirvsVirus – Der Hackathon der Bundesregierung* [We vs. Virus – The Hackathon of the Cabinet of Germany]. Available at: https://wirvsvirus.org/.

Buras, P. (2020). 'Resilience before reinvention: The EU's role in the COVID-19 crisis', *European Council on Foreign Relations*, 24 March. Available at: https://www.ecfr.eu/arti cle/commentary_resilience_before_reinvention_the_eus_role_in_the_COVID_19_crisi.

Burgers, T., Romaniuk, S. N. (2020). 'Can the Coronavirus Strengthen China's Authoritarian Regime?', *The Diplomat*, 10 March. Available at: https://thediplomat .com/2020/03/can-the-coronavirus-strengthen-chinas-authoritarian-regime/.

BIBLIOGRAPHIC REFERENCES 375

Bush, G.W. (2020). 'A Message from President George W. Bush – The Call to Unite', *George W. Bush Presidential Center*, 1 May. https://www.bushcenter.org/about-the -center/newsroom/press-releases/2020/05/president-bush-call-to-unite.

Cabestan, J.-P. (2020). 'China's Battle with Coronavirus: Possible Geopolitical Gains and Real Challenges', *Aljazeera Centre for Studies*, 19 April. Available at: https:// studies.aljazeera.net/en/reports/china%E2%80%99s-battle-coronavirus-possible -geopolitical-gains-and-real-challenges.

Campbell, K. M., Doshi, R. (2020). 'The Coronavirus Could Reshape Global Order', *Foreign Affairs*, 18 March. Available at: https://www.foreignaffairs.com/articles/ china/2020-03-18/coronavirus-could-reshape-global-order.

Carlà, A. (2020). 'Minoranze e nazionalismi 'virati', *Eurac Research – Blog: COVID-19 and beyond*. 2 July. Available at: https://blogs.eurac.edu/COVID-19/nazionalismo/.

Castle, S. (2020). 'To Enforce Coronavirus Rules, U.K. Police Use Drones, Shaming and Easter Egg Bans', *The New York Times*, 7 April. Available at: https://www.nytimes .com/2020/04/01/world/europe/uk-police-coronavirus.html.

Center for Disease Control and Prevention (CDC) (2018). '1918 Pandemic influenza: three waves. Centers for Disease Control and Prevention', *CDC*, 11 May. Available at: https:// www.cdc.gov/flu/pandemic-resources/1918-commemoration/three-waves.htm.

Center for Human Emergence (n.d.). *Courses and Trainings*. Available at: http://hum anemergence.de/en/courses/.

Center for Security Studies (2009). *Resilienz: Konzept zur Krisen- und Katastrophenbewältigung* [Resilience: Concept for crisis and disaster management]. Paperwork, No. 60 (September). CSS Analysen zur Sicherheitspolitik, ETH Zürich. Available at: https://css.ethz.ch/content/dam/ethz/special-interest/gess/ cis/center-for-securities-studies/pdfs/CSS-Analysen-60.pdf.

Chait, J. (2020). 'Report: Trump Tried to Deny Coronavirus Vaccine to Foreign Countries', *Intelligencer*, 16 March. Available at: https://nymag.com/intelligencer/ 2020/03/trump-coronavirus-vaccine-germany-united-states-only.html.

Chan, S. P. (2020). 'Coronavirus: 'World faces worst recession since Great Depression'. *BBC*, 14 April. Available at: https://www.bbc.com/news/business-52273988.

Checkland, P.B. (1981). *Systems Thinking, Systems Practice*. Chichester: John Wiley & Sons Ltd.

Cheung, H. (2020). 'COVID-19: Why Hong Kong's 'third way' is a warning', *BBC*, 31 July. Available at: https://www.bbc.com/news/world-asia-china-53596299.

Christmann, G., Ibert, O., Kilper, H., Moss, T. (2011). *Vulnerabilität und Resilienz in sozio-räumlicher Perspektive – Begriffliche Klärungen und theoretischer Rahmen* [Vulnerability and resilience from a socio-spatial perspective – Conceptual clarifications and theoretical framework]. Working paper, 44. Erkner: IRS Leibniz-Institut für Regionalentwicklung und Strukturplanung. Available at: http://www.irs-net.de/ aktuelles/meldungen-detail.php?id=206.

Christoph, M. (2020). 'Corona vs. Gleichberechtigung -Wie sich Corona auf Gender Equality auswirken könnte' [Corona vs. Equality – How Corona could affect gender equality], *Plus*, 20 April. Available at: https://www.br.de/puls/themen/leben/cor ona-vs-gleichberechtigung-100.html.

Clayton, J. (2020). 'Tech giants Facebook, Google, Apple and Amazon to face Congress', BBC, 29 July. Available at: https://www.bbc.com/news/technology-53571562.

Clifford, C. (2020). 'Elon Musk, Google's DeepMind co-founders promise never to make killer robots', CNBC, 20 July. Available at: https://www.cnbc.com/2018/07/20/elon -musk-google-deepmind-co-founders-pledge-no-killer-robots.html.

Clinton, D. (2003). 'Deleuze, Gilles and Felix Guattari. "Rhizome", in *A Thousand Plateaus*. annotation by Dan Clinton', *University of Chicago*. http://csmt.uchicago. edu/annotations/deleuzerhizome.htm.

CNA Daily News (2020). 'Pope Francis to sign a new encyclical on human fraternity on Oct. 3', *The Catholic World Report*, 5 September. https://www.catholicworldreport .com/2020/09/05/pope-francis-to-sign-a-new-encyclical-on-human-fraternity-on -oct-3/.

CNN (2020a). 'Don Lemon to Trump: What is it about Obama that gets under your skin?', CNN, 4 May. Available at: https://edition.cnn.com/videos/politics/2020/05/ 04/don-lemon-trump-obama-obsession-ctn-vpx.cnn.

CNN (2020b). 'Inmates appear to purposely infect themselves with virus', CNN, 12 May. Available at: https://www.cnn.com/videos/us/2020/05/12/california-inmates-jail -coronavirus-spread-eg-orig.cnn.

CNN (2020c). 'These coronavirus job losses will be permanent', *Fox News 55*, 5 May. Available at: https://www.wfft.com/content/news/570217212.html.

Cockayne, J. (2020). 'States Back a UN-led International Response to COVID-19: Now What?', *United Nation University, Centre for Policy Research*, 3 April. Available at: http://cpr.unu.edu/fourstepsforthesg.html.

Cohen, B. (2011). 'Global Ranking of Top 10 Resilient Cities', *Triple Pundit*, 28 June. Available at: http://www.triplepundit.com/2011/06/top-10-globally-resilient-cities/.

Cohen, J., Kupfershmidt, K. (2020). 'NIH-halted study unveils its massive analysis of bat coronaviruses', *Science*, 1 June. Available at: https://www.sciencemag.org/news/ 2020/06/nih-halted-study-unveils-its-massive-analysis-bat-coronaviruses.

Coleman, C. (2020). 'Teraanga: the word that defines Senegal', BBC, 16 November. Available at: http://www.bbc.com/travel/story/20201115-teraanga-the-word-that -defines-senegal.

Collerton, S. (2020). 'WHO urges caution over Russian vaccine claims', BBC, 4 August. Available at: https://www.bbc.com/news/live/world-53591031.

Connolly, K. (2020). 'Coronavirus: How to tell which countries are coping best with COVID', BBC, 5 October. Available at: https://www.bbc.com/news/world-europe -54391482.

BIBLIOGRAPHIC REFERENCES

Cook, K. (2001). *Trust in Society*. New York: Russell Sage Foundation.

Cook, K., Harden, R., Levi, M. (2005). *Cooperation Without Trust?*. New York: Russell Sage Foundation.

Cooley, B. (2020). 'COVID-19 immunity certificates: What could go wrong?', CNET, 7 May. Available at: https://www.cnet.com/health/COVID-19-immunity-certificates -what-could-go-wrong/.

Corera, G. (2016). 'CIA taps huge potential of digital technology', BBC, June 29. Available at: https://www.bbc.com/news/world-us-canada-36462056.

Corera, G. (2020a). 'Coronavirus: Cyber-spies hunt COVID-19 research, US and UK warn', BBC, 5 May. Available at: https://www.bbc.com/news/technology-52551023.

Corera, G. (2020b). 'Coronavirus: How will it change national security and spying?', BBC, 2 April. Available at: https://www.bbc.com/news/uk-52122991.

Corera, G. (2020c). 'Coronavirus: US allies tread lightly around Trump lab claims', BBC, 5 May. Available at: https://www.bbc.com/news/world-52546542.

Corporación Latinobarómetro (2018). *Informe 2018* [Report 2018]. Santiago: Corporación Latinobarómetro. Available at: https://www.latinobarometro.org/lat.jsp.

Corum, J., Zimmer, C. (2020). 'How Coronavirus Mutates and Spreads', *The New York Times*, 30 April. Available at: https://www.nytimes.com/interactive/2020/04/30/ science/coronavirus-mutations.html.

COVID-19 Scenario (2020). *Germany*. Available at: https://COVID19-scenarios.org/.

Crowcroft, O. (2020). 'Coronavirus is biggest challenge for Germany since WW2, says Angela Merkel', *Euronews,* 19 March. Available at: https://www.euronews.com/2020/ 03/19/coronavirus-is-biggest-challenge-for-germany-since-ww2-says-angela-merkel.

CSSE – Center for Systems Science and Engineering (2020). *COVID-19 Dashboard*. Available at: https://gisanddata.maps.arcgis.com/apps/opsdashboard/index.html#/ bda7594740fd40299423467b48e9ecf6.

Cuhls, K. (2003). 'From forecasting to foresight processes–new participative foresight activities in Germany', *Journal of Forecasting*, 22 (2–3, March-April), pp. 93–111. DOI: https://doi.org/10.1002/for.848.

Cuhls, K. (2015). *Bringing Foresight to decision-making – lessons for Policy-making from selected non-European countries*. European Commission. Luxembourg: Publications Office of the European Union. Also Available at: https://ec.europa.eu/research/inn ovation-union/pdf/expert-groups/rise/cuhls-foresight_into_decisions.pdf.

Cutuli, J.J., Herbers, J.E., Lafavor, T.L., Masten, A.S. (2008). Promoting competence and resilience in the school context. *Professional School Counseling,* 12(2), 76–84. DOI: https://doi.org/10.5330/PSC.n.2010-12.76.

Cutway, A. (2020). 'Don't do this: Woman films herself licking toilet seat on flight to Miami for 'coronavirus challenge'', *ClickOrlando*, 19 March. https://www.clickorla ndo.com/news/local/2020/03/19/dont-do-this-woman-films-herself-licking-toilet -seat-on-flight-to-miami-for-coronavirus-challenge/.

Daily Nation (2020). *Mpesa agent from Mwea, Kirinyaga County creates wooden cash sanitiser*. Available at: https://www.youtube.com/watch?v=DMr64RXZFOE&feature=youtu.be.

Dale, B., Stylianou, N. (2020). Coronavirus: What is the true death toll of the pandemic?, *BBC*, 18 June. Available at: https://www.bbc.com/news/world-53073046.

Dallison, P. (2016). 'Germany the 'best country in the world'. New rankings look at global perception', *Politico*, 20 January. Available at: https://www.politico.eu/article/germany-the-best-country-in-the-world-top-where-to-live-best-place-davos/.

Danaher, K. (2001). 'People's globalization vs. elite globalization', *ISR – International Socialist Review* (19, July-August). Available at: https://isreview.org/issues/19/Kevin Danaher.shtml.

Darüber spricht Bayern (2020). 'Giffey fürchtet Rückschritte bei der Gleichberechtigung' [Giffey fears regression in terms of equality], *Bayern 2 Nachrichten*, 6 May. Available at: https://www.br.de/nachrichten/meldung/giffey-fuerchtet-rueckschritte-bei-der-gleichberechtigung,3002c3bb9.

Davidson, H. (2020). 'Coronavirus chaos could strengthen China's debt hold on struggling nations', *The Guardian*, 12 April. Available at: https://www.theguardian.com/world/2020/apr/12/coronavirus-chaos-could-strengthen-chinas-debt-hold-on-struggling-nations.

De Schutter, H., Tinnevelt, R. (eds.) (2011). *Nationalism and Global Justice: David Miller and his critics*. Oxon/New York: Routledge.

Deleuze, G., Guattari, F. (1980). *Mille Plateaux* [A Thousand Plateaus]. Paris: Minuit.

Dennison, S., Dworkin, A., Shapiro, J. (2020). 'Pulling through the coronavirus together: European and international solutions to the pandemic', *European Council on Foreign Relations*, 27 March. Available at: https://www.ecfr.eu/article/commentary_pulling_through_the_coronavirus_together_european_and_internatio.

Der Spiegel (2020a). 'Corona-Wirtschaft: EU-Staaten fordern mehr Solidarität von Deutschland' [Corona economy: EU states are demanding more solidarity from Germany], *Der Spiegel*, 15 May. Available at: https://www.spiegel.de/wirtschaft/coronakrise-eu-staaten-fordern-mehr-solidaritaet-von-deutschland-a-97475cd4-a42a-4014-8a69-98a2091b4a88.

Der Spiegel (2020b). 'Merkel sieht Coronakrise als größte Herausforderung seit dem Zweiten Weltkrieg' [Merkel sees the corona crisis as the greatest challenge since the Second World War], *Der Spiegel*, 18 March. Available at: https://www.spiegel.de/politik/deutschland/angela-merkel-sieht-corona-krise-als-groesste-herausforderung-seit-dem-zweiten-weltkrieg-a-bd56dc3f-2436-4a03-b2cf-5e44e06ffb49.

Der Spiegel (2020c). 'Rund 50.000 Krebsoperationen verschoben'[Around 50,000 cancer operations cancelled], *Der Spiegel*, 13 July. Available at: https://www.spiegel.de/wirtschaft/service/wegen-coronavirus-rund-50-000-krebs-operationen-in-deutschland-verschoben-a-d327e5ea-6552-4f9b-9adb-0b95b9001f36.

BIBLIOGRAPHIC REFERENCES

Der Spiegel (2020d). 'Veränderte Lebensgewohnheiten – Handelsexperten sagen großes Ladensterben voraus' [Changed lifestyles – retail experts predict extensive shop deaths], *Der Spiegel*, 20 March. Available at: https://www.spiegel.de/wirtsch aft/institut-sagt-grosses-ladensterben-voraus-a-a0f90f84-8602-4dfe-9bd6-247f9 211e02a.

Deutsche Forschungsgemeinschaft (2017). *Multi-Resilienz – Resilienz in multimodalen Energiesystemen mit starker Durchdringung von IKT im Verteilnetz* [Multi-Resilience – Resilience in ICT-based Multimodal Energy Distribution Systems]. GEPRIS. Available at: https://gepris.dfg.de/gepris/projekt/360352892?language=de.

Deutsche Welle (2020). 'World risks permanent surveillance with coronavirus controls', *DW – Deutsche Welle*, 2 April. Available at: https://www.dw.com/en/world -risks-permanent-surveillance-with-coronavirus-controls/a-53000886.

Deutsches Bundesministerium für Bildung und Forschung (2020). *VOR AUS:schau – Orientierung für die Welt von morgen* [OUT:look – Orientation for the world of tomorrow]. Available at: https://www.vorausschau.de/.

Diamond, L. (2019). 'The Global Crisis of Democracy', *The Wall Street Journal*, 17 May. Available at: https://www.wsj.com/articles/the-global-crisis-of-democracy-11558105 463.Dignös, E. (2020). 'Overtourism ist durch Corona nicht vorbei – im Gegenteil' 'Corona does not end over-tourism – on the contrary', *Süddeutsche Zeitung*, 31 July. Available at: https://www.sueddeutsche.de/reise/tourismus-overtourism-corona -1.4978149.

Dissen, S., Quaas, M., Baumgärtner, S. (2009). *The relationship between resilience and sustainability in ecological-economic systems.* University of Lüneburg Working Paper Series in Economics No. 146. Lüneburg: Leuphana Universität Lüneburg Institut für Volkswirtschaftslehre. Also Available at: https://core.ac.uk/download/pdf/6271 725.pdf.

Djuve, A.B. (2016). *Refugee migration – a crisis for the Nordic model?.* Bonn: Friedrich Ebert Stiftung.

Dorling, D. (2020). 'Coronavirus: Is the cure worse than the disease? The most divisive question of 2020', *The conversation.* 06 October. Available at: https://theconversat ion.com/coronavirus-is-the-cure-worse-than-the-disease-the-most-divisive-quest ion-of-2020-147343.

Drinkard, A. (2020). 'Conspiracy beliefs could increase fringe political engagement, shows new study', *Eurekalert*, 28 February. Available at: https://www.eurekalert.org/ pub_releases/2020-02/sfpa-cbc022520.php.

Drosten, C. (2020). 'Wir müssen jetzt die Fälle senken. Sonst schaffen wir es nicht' [We have to lower the cases now. Otherwise we will not make it]. Interviewed by Florian Schumann for *Zeit Online*, 20 March. Available at: https://www.zeit.de/wissen/ges undheit/2020-03/christian-drosten-coronavirus-pandemie-deutschland-virologe -charite/komplettansicht.

Duff-Brown, B. (2020). 'Federalism Meets the Covid-19 Pandemic: Thinking Globally, Acting Locally', *Stanford Health Policy*, 2 April. Available at: https://healthpolicy.fsi .stanford.edu/news/federalism-meets-covid-19-pandemic-thinking-globally-act ing-locally.

Dugyala, R. (2020). 'Gov. DeWine: My face mask order went 'too far'', *Politico*, 5 May. Available at: https://www.politico.com/news/2020/05/03/dewine-ohio-face-masks -coronavirus-231175.

Durach, F., Greil, A., Haase, K., Kettenbach, M., Lanzinger, J., Wolfsperger, N. (2020). 'Coronavirus weltweit: Hilfsorganisationen warnen vor "Massensterben in Syrien"- Keine Neu-Infektionen in China' [Coronavirus worldwide: aid organisations warn of "mass deaths in Syria" – no new infections in China], *Merkur*, 8 August. Available at: https://www.merkur.de/welt/coronavirus-china-russland-iran-suedkorea-putin -bosnien-infizierte-tote-sars-cov-2-pandemie-who-COVID-19-news-zr-13587400 .html.

Eadicicco, E. (2020). 'A man used a drone to take his dog for a walk while he was in lock-down because of the coronavirus', *Business Insider*, 20 March. Available at: https:// www.businessinsider.com/video-dog-being-walked-by-drone-cyprus-coronavirus -lockdown-2020-3?r=DE&IR=T.

Economist Intelligence Unit (EIU) (2020). 'Quality of OECD countries' response to the pandemic', *EIU*, 17 June. Available at: https://www.eiu.com/n/quality-of-oecd -countries-response-to-the-pandemic/.

Edel, C. (2019). 'Democracy Is Fighting for Its Life', *Foreign Policy*, 10 September. Available at: https://foreignpolicy.com/2019/09/10/democracy-is-fighting-for-its -life/.

EdX (n.d.). *U.lab: Leading From the Emerging Future*. Available at: https://www.edx.org/ course/ulab-leading-from-the-emerging-future.

Egan, M. (2020). 'GE is cutting up to 13,000 jobs at its jet engine division because of pandemic', *CNN*, 4 May. Available at: https://edition.cnn.com/2020/05/04/business/ ge-aviation-job-cuts/index.html.

Einstein, A. (2016). '30 Albert Einstein Quotes That Will Make You Question EVERYTHING', *Your Tango*, 12 April. Available at: https://www.yourtango.com/201 6286101/30-albert-einstein-quotes-that-will-make-you-question-life.

Eisentstein, C. (2011). *Sacred Economics: Money, Gift and Society in the Age of Transition.* North Atlantic Books.

Eisenstein, C. (2020). 'The Coronation', *Charles Eisenstein*, March. https://charleseis enstein.org/essays/the-coronation/.

Eliassen, I., Pena, P. (2020). 'Real 5G issues overshadowed by Covid-19 conspiracy the-ories', *Investigate Europe*, 12 June. Available at: https://www.investigate-europe.eu/ en/2020/5g-covid-conspiracy/.

Elsberg, M. (2012). *Blackout.* Munich: Blanvalet.

BIBLIOGRAPHIC REFERENCES 381

Esping-Andersen, G. (1990). *Three Worlds of Welfare Capitalism*. Cambridge: Polity Press.

Esposito, R. (2016). *Biopolitik* [Bio politics], pp. 97–115, in Benedikter, R. (ed.). *Italienische Politikphilosophie* [Italian philosophy of politics], Wiesbaden: Springer.

Euobserver (2020). 'EU to host online donor vaccine conference', *Euobserver*, 16 April. Available at: https://euobserver.com/tickers/148074.

Eurac Research (2020a). 'Minorities and Covid-19: A webinar series of the Institute for Minority Rights', Eurac Research, 13 May – 10 June. http://www.eurac.edu/en/resea rch/autonomies/minrig/services/Pages/default.aspx.

Eurac Research (2020b). 'Nicht nur das Gesundheitswesen, auch unser Rechtssystem wurde unvorbereitet getroffen' [Not only the health system but also our legal system was taken unawares], *Eurac Research*. Available at: http://www.eurac.edu/en/pages/newsdetails.aspx?entryid=135118.

Euractiv & AFP (2020). 'Studie: Corona-Sterblichkeitsrate bei Kindern unter einem Prozent' [Study: Coronavirus Child Death Rate Below One Percent], *Euractiv*, 26 June. Available at: https://www.euractiv.de/section/gesundheit-und-verbrauche rschutz/news/studie-corona-sterblichkeitsrate-bei-kindern-unter-einem-prozent/.

Euronews (2020) 'How is Tunisia developing MedTech to fight Covid-19 with limited resources?', *Euronews*, 17 July. Available at: https://www.euronews.com/2020/07/17/how-is-tunisia-developing-medtech-to-fight-covid19-with-limited-resources.

European Centre for Disease Prevention and Control (ECDC) (2020). *Prevention and control of Covid-19*. Available at:https://www.ecdc.europa.eu/en/all-topics-z/coro navirus/threats-and-outbreaks/covid-19/prevention-and-control-covid-19.

European Commission (2019). *EU-China – A strategic outlook*. Strasbourg. Available at: https://ec.europa.eu/commission/sites/beta-political/files/communication-eu -china-a-strategic-outlook.pdf.

European Commission (2020a). *Coronavirus Global Response: €7.4 billion raised for universal access to vaccines* [Press release]. 4 May. Available at: https://libguides.ioe .ac.uk/c.php?g=482485&p=3299834.

European Commission (2020b). *Coronavirus Global Response: EU launches pledging effort* [Press release]. 24 April. Available at: https://ec.europa.eu/commission/pres scorner/detail/en/ip_20_710.

European Commission. Directorate-General for Research and Innovation (2020). *Protect, prepare and transform Europe: Recovery and resilience post COVID-19*, ESIR Policy Brief No. 1 (May). Luxembourg: Publications Office of the European Union. Available at: https://ec.europa.eu/info/sites/info/files/research_and_innovation/groups/esir/ec_rtd_esir-recovery-resilience-COVID19.pdf.

European Council on Foreign Relations (2020). *ECFR Quarantinmes #3 – with Arancha González, ECFR*, 30 April. Available at: https://ecfr.eu/video/quarantimes_arancha _gonzalez/.

European Council on Foreign Relations (n.d.). *Homepage*. https://www.ecfr.eu/.

European Parliament (2020). COVID-19: the EU plan for the economic recovery, *News European Parliament*, 28 May. Available at: https://www.europarl.europa.eu/news/en/headlines/economy/20200513STO79012/COVID-19-the-eu-plan-for-the-econo mic-recovery.

Ewing, J. (2020). 'Some Countries Are Better Armored for Epidemics Than Others', *The New York Times*, 19 March. Available at: https://www.nytimes.com/2020/03/19/business/europe-economies-coronavirus-winners.html.

Farrington, R. (2020). 'As Harvard Goes Online, Will Students Pay Top Dollar For Higher Education?', *Forbes*, 8 June. Available at: https://www.forbes.com/sites/robertfar rington/2020/06/08/as-harvard-goes-online-will-students-pay-top-dollar-for-hig her-education/#5ef9fc2e65e7.

Fathi, K. (2013). 'Conflict potentials of different welfare regimes – a metatheoretical perspective' in Karolewski, I. P., Suszyki, A. M. (eds.) *Identity, Citizenship and Welfare: National and International Perspectives*. Osnabrück: Fibre, pp. 41–74.

Fathi, K. (2019a). *Das Empathietraining – Konflikte lösen für ein besseres Miteinander* [Empathy training – resolving conflicts for better collaboration]. Paderborn: Junfermann.

Fathi, K. (2019b). *Kommunikative Komplexitätsbewältigung – Grundzüge eines integrier-ten Methodenpluralismus zur Optimierung disziplinübergreifender Kommunikation* [Communicative Complexity Management – Basic features of an integrated meth-odological pluralism to optimise interdisciplinary communication]. Wiesbaden: Springer Nature.

Fathi, K. (2019c). *Resilienz im Spannungsfeld zwischen Entwicklung und Nachhaltigkeit – Anforderungen an gesellschaftliche Zukunftssicherung im 21. Jahrhundert* [2022: Multi-Resilience on the edge between Development and Sustainability – Requirements for securing the future of societies in the 21st century. Wiesbaden: Springer Nature]. Wiesbaden: Springer Nature.

Fathi, K. (2020). 'Gesellschaftliche Resilienz in der Coronakrise und darüber hinaus' [Societal resilience in the corona crisis and beyond], *Eurac Research Blog: COVID-19 and Beyond*, 2 April. Available at: https://blogs.eurac.edu/covid-19/gesellschaftli che-resilienz-fathi/.

Finanzen.ch (2020). 'Neue Steuern könnten Corona-Hilfen der EU finanzieren' [New taxes could finance corona aid from the EU], *Finanzen.ch*, 26 May. Available at: https://www.finanzen.ch/nachrichten/konjunktur/neue-steuern-koennten-cor ona-hilfen-der-eu-finanzieren-1029234250.

Findlen, P. (2020). 'For Renaissance Italians, combating black plague was as much about politics as it was science, according to Stanford scholar'. Interviewed by Melissa de Witte for *Stanford News*, 12 May. Available at: https://news.stanford.edu/2020/05/12/combating-black-plague-just-much-politics-science/.

BIBLIOGRAPHIC REFERENCES   383

Fisher, M., Bubola, E. (2020). 'As Coronavirus Deepens Inequality, Inequality Worsens Its Spread', *The New York Times*, 15 March. Available at: https://www.nytimes.com/2020/03/15/world/europe/coronavirus-inequality.html.

Fitch Ratings (2020). 'Deep Global Recession in 2020 as Global Corona crisis Escalates', *Fitch Ratings*, 2 April. Available at: https://www.fitchratings.com/research/sovereigns/deep-global-recession-in-2020-as-coronavirus-crisis-escalates-02-04-2020.

Fock, R., Bergmann, H., Bußmann, H., Fell, G., Finke, E.-J., Koch, U., Niedrig, M., Peters, M. Scholz, D., Wirtz, A. (2001). 'Management und Kontrolle einer Influenzapandemie. Konzeptionelle Überlegungen für einen Deutschen Influenzapandemieplan' [Management and Control of an Influenza Pandemic. Conceptual Considerations for a German Influenza Pandemic Plan], *Bundesgesundheitsblatt – Gesundheitsforschung – Gesundheitsschutz* [Federal Health Gazette – Health Research – Health Protection], 44 (10, October). Berlin: Springer-Verlag, pp. 969–980. DOI: 10.1007/s001030100267.

Focus Online (2020a). 'EU will milliardenschwere Corona-Hilfen mit neuen Steuern finanzieren' [EU wants to finance billions in Corona aid with new taxes], *Focus Online*, 26 May. Available at: https://www.focus.de/finanzen/steuern/information-aus-bruesseler-kreisen-eu-will-milliardenschwere-corona-hilfen-mit-neuen-steuern-finanzieren_id_12033976.html.

Focus Online (2020b). 'Kubicki, Nida-Rümelin, Papier: So begründen Prominente ihre Corona-Kritik' [Kubicki, Nida-Rümelin, Papier: This is how prominent figures justify their Corona criticism], *Focus Online*, 11 May. Available at: https://www.focus.de/politik/deutschland/konstruktive-corona-kritik-kubicki-nida-ruemelin-papier-so-begruenden-prominente-ihre-corona-kritik_id_11978184.html.

Fogarty, P., Frantz, S., Hirschfeld, J., Keating, S., Lafont, E., Lufkin, B., Mishael, R., Ponnavolu, V., Savage, M., Turits, M. (2020). 'Coronavirus: Will our day-to-day ever be the same?', *BBC*. Available at: https://www.bbc.com/worklife/article/20201109-coronavirus-how-cities-travel-and-family-life-will-change.

Fona (2019). *Home page*. Available at: https://www.fona.de/en/.

Foreign Policy (2020). 'The Covid-19 Global Response Index', *Foreign Policy*, 6 August. Available at: https://foreignpolicy.com/2020/08/06/the-covid-19-global-response-index/.

Fottrell, Q. (2020). '"The 1918 Spanish flu's second wave was even more devastating": WHO advises caution to avoid 'immediate second peak"', *Market Watch*, 31 May. Available at: https://www.marketwatch.com/story/we-will-not-have-a-vaccine-by-next-winter-what-happens-when-coronavirus-returns-2020-04-22.

Fox, C., Kelion, L. (2020). 'Coronavirus: Russian spies target Covid-19 vaccine research', *BBC*, 16 July. Available at: https://www.bbc.com/news/technology-53429506.

Fox, M. (2020). 'More than 1 million US children have been diagnosed with Covid-19, pediatricians say', *CNN*, 16 November. Available at: https://edition.cnn.com/webv iew/world/live-news/coronavirus-pandemic-11-16-20-intl/h_35e53f6ad92ace2fo b6faecod37oca8a.

Frantzman, S.J. (2020). 'Israel and Iran agree: The struggle against coronavirus is a war effort', *The Jerusalem Post*, 18 March. Available at: https://www.jpost.com/middle -east/israel-and-iran-agree-the-struggle-against-coronavirus-is-a-war-effort-621447.

Frederico, G. (2020). 'Achieving More Resiliency Against Covid-19 Outbreak', *Supply Chain Management Review*, 6 April. Available at: https://www.scmr.com/article/in _times_of_coronavirus_maturity_in_supply_chain_management_really_mat.

Frey, R. (2020). 'Corona und Gender – ein geschlechtsbezogener Blick auf die Pandemie und ihre (möglichen) Folgen' [Corona and Gender – a gender-related look at the pandemic and its (possible) consequences], Georg-August-Universität Göttingen. Available at: https://www.uni-goettingen.de/de/document/download/5of9c1fd6 b35b6423398266622bae424.pdf/gender_corona.pdf.pdf.

Friebe, R., Karberg, S. & Rövekamp, M. (2020). Welche gesundheitlichen Schäden der Lockdown verursacht. [What damage the lockdown causes to health], *Der Tagesspiegel*. 27 April. Available at: https://www.tagesspiegel.de/wissen/risiken -und-nebenwirkungen-der-coronakrise-welche-gesundheitlichen-schaeden-der -lockdown-verursacht/25778410.html

Futures Diamond (n.d.). *The Diamond – About Futures Diamond: The Framework*. Available at: https://www.futuresdiamond.com/the-diamond.

Gabriel, M. (2020). 'Virologie als neue Religion' [Virology as a new religion] [Podcast]. Deutschlandfunk Kultur. 18 May. Available at: https://www.deutschlandfunkkultur .de/philosoph-markus-gabriel-virologie-als-neue-religion.1008.de.html?dram:art icle_id=476866.

GABV (n.d.). *Home page*. Available at: http://www.gabv.org/.

Gallagher, J. (2020). 'Coronavirus came to UK 'on at least 1,300 separate occasions', *BBC*, 10 June. Available at: https://www.bbc.com/news/health-52993734.

Gallagher, J. (2020b). 'Covid: Antibodies 'fall rapidly after infection'', *BBC*, 27 October. Available at: https://www.bbc.com/news/health-54696873.

Gallagher, J. (2020c). 'Covid reinfection: Man gets Covid twice and second hit 'more severe'', *BBC*, 12 October. Available at: https://www.bbc.com/news/health-54512034.

Gallagher, J. (2020d). 'Long Covid: Who is more likely to get it?', *BBC*, 21 October. Available at: https://www.bbc.com/news/health-54622059.

Galtung, J. (1998). *Frieden mit friedlichen Mitteln. Friede und Konflikt, Entwicklung und Kultur* [Peace by peaceful means. Peace and Conflict, Development and Culture]. Opladen: Lecke + Budrich.

Galtung, J. (2008). *50 Years: 100 Peace and Conflict Perspectives*. Bergen: Transcend University.

BIBLIOGRAPHIC REFERENCES

Gan, N., Hu, C., Watson, I. (2020). 'Beijing tightens grip over coronavirus research, amid US-China row on virus origin', *CNN*, 16 April. Available at: https://edition.cnn.com/2020/04/12/asia/china-coronavirus-research-restrictions-intl-hnk/index.html.

Gardiner, B. (2020). 'Pollution made Covid-19 worse. Now, lockdowns are clearing the air', *National Geographic*, 8 April. Available at: https://www.nationalgeographic.com/science/2020/04/pollution-made-the-pandemic-worse-but-lockdowns-clean-the-sky/.

Gardner, P. (2020). 'China's coronavirus cover-up: how censorship and propaganda obstructed the truth', *The Conversation*, 6 March. Available at: https://theconversation.com/chinas-coronavirus-cover-up-how-censorship-and-propaganda-obstructed-the-truth-133095.

Garton Ash, T. (2020). 'What kind of post-corona world do Europeans want?', *European Council on Foreign Relations*, 11 May. Available at: https://www.ecfr.eu/article/commentary_what_kind_of_post_corona_world_do_europeans_want.

Garton Ash, T., Zimmermann, A. (2020). 'In Crisis, Europeans Support Radical Positions', *Europinions*, 6 May. Available at: https://eupinions.eu/de/text/in-crisis-europeans-support-radical-positions.

Gartwhwaite, J. (2020). 'Stanford researchers explain how humanity has 'engineered a world ripe for pandemics'', *Stanford News*, 25 March. Available at: https://news.stanford.edu/2020/03/25/covid-19-world-made-ripe-pandemics/.

Gazzetta dello Sport (2020). 'Valente: "Il calcio va salvato, vale il 7% del Pil". E Rossi (Pd): "Si può ripartire" [Valente: "Football must be saved, it is worth 7% of GDP". And Rossi (Pd): "We can start again"], *Gazzetta dello Sport*, 5 May. Available at: https://www.gazzetta.it/Calcio/Serie-A/05-05-2020/valente-calcio-sport-base-uniti-campionato-riparta-370731915882.shtml.

Gelfeld, B. (2020). 'Between Enemies and Adversaries: Winning the Battle against Covid-19 and the War for a Liberal World Order', *International Policy Digest*, 6 May. Available at: https://intpolicydigest.org/2020/05/06/between-enemies-and-adversaries-winning-the-battle-against-covid-19-and-the-war-for-a-liberal-world-order/.

Georghiou, L., Cassingena Harper, J., Keenan, M., Miles, I., Popper, R. (2008). *The Handbook of Technology Foresight*. Cheltenham: Edward Elgar Publishing.

Gessen, M. (2020). 'Why Estonia Was Poised to Handle How a Pandemic Would Change Everything', *The New Yorker*, 24 March. Available at: https://www.newyorker.com/news/our-columnists/why-estonia-was-poised-to-handle-how-a-pandemic-would-change-everything.

Gholipour, H., Nguyen, J., Farzanegan, M.R. (2016). 'Higher property prices linked to income inequality: study', *The Conversation*, 21 November. Available at: https://theconversation.com/higher-property-prices-linked-to-income-inequality-study-68664.

Gibbons, M. (1994): *The New Production of Knowledge. The Dynamics of Science and Research in Contemporary Societies*. London: Sage.

Gibson, R., Singh, J. P. (2018). *China RX: Exposing the risks of America's dependence on China for medicine*. New York: Prometheus Books.

Gidari, A., Driscoll, S. (2020). 'Privacy and New Google-Apple Covid-19 Tracing Technology'. *Stanford Law School*, 7 May. Available at: https://law.stanford.edu/2020/05/07/privacy-and-new-google-apple-covid-19-tracing-technology/.

Giddens, A. (1995). *Konsequenzen der Moderne* [Consequences of Modernity]. Frankfurt: Suhrkamp.

Gill, V. (2020). 'Coronavirus: Llamas provide key to immune therapy', BBC *News*, 13 July. Available at: https://www.bbc.com/news/science-environment-53369103.

Gills, B. (2018). Globalizations Journal. Taylor & Francis Online. Available at: https://www.tandfonline.com/toc/rglo20/current.

Gillett, F. (2020). 'Coronavirus: What's the future for the office?', BBC, 26 May. Available at: https://www.bbc.com/news/uk-52720007.

Gladwell, M. (2000). *The Tipping Point – How Little Things Can Make A Big Difference*. New York/Boston/London: Little, Brown and Company.

Globalization 101 (2016). *Global Education as Business*. Available at: http://www.globalization101.org/global-education-as-business/.

Globetrenderer (2020). 'These are the only ten countries in the world that are covid-free', *Globetrenderer*, 8 September. Available at: https://globetrender.com/2020/09/08/these-are-only-ten-countries-in-world-that-are-coronavirus-free/.

Glockner, H., Grünwald, C., Bonin, D., Irmer, M., Astor, M., Klaus, C., Hornik, A., Spalthoff, F. (2020). Langfristige Chancen und Herausforderungen infolge der Corona-Pandemie [Long-term opportunities and challenges as a result of the corona Pandemic]. Berlin: Prognos.

Gloor, P. A. (2006). *Swarm Creativity: Competitive Advantage through Collaborative Innovation Networks*. Oxford: Oxford University Press.

Godehardt, N. (2016). *No End of History: A Chinese Alternative Concept of International Order?*. SWP Research Paper, RP 2 (January). Berlin: SWP. Available at: https://www.swp-berlin.org/en/publication/no-end-of-history/.

Godehardt, N., Kohlenberg, P. J. (2017). 'Die Neue Seidenstraße: Wie China internationale Diskursmacht erlangt' [The New Silk Road: How China Gains International Discourse Power], *Stiftung Wissenschaft und Politik*, 18 May. Available at: https://www.swp-berlin.org/kurz-gesagt/die-neue-seidenstrasse-wie-china-internationale-diskursmacht-erlangt/.

Goenaga, A (2016). 'Democracy in Latin America', *Oxford Bibliographies*. DOI: https://doi.org/10.1093/OBO/9780199756223-0189.

Goodin, R. E., Tilly, C. (2006). *The Oxford Handbook of Contextual Political Analysis*, Oxford Handbooks of Political Science, Vol. 5. Oxford: Oxford University Press. DOI: 10.1093/oxfordhb/9780199270439.001.0001.

Goodman, P.S. (2020). 'Why the Global Recession Could Last a Long Time', *The New York Times*, 1 April. Available at: https://www.nytimes.com/2020/04/01/busin ess/economy/coronavirus-recession.html.

Gophe, M. (2020) "UWC Alumnus Develop Swift Covid-19 Testing Kit", *University of the Western Cape*, 22 April. Available at: https://www.uwc.ac.za/News/Pages/UWC-Alumnus-Develop-Swift-Covid-19-Testing-Kit-.aspx.

Gopinath, G. (2020). 'The Great Lockdown: Worst Economic Downturn Since The Great Depression', *International Monetary Fund (IMF) blog*, 14 April. Available at: https://blogs.imf.org/2020/04/14/the-great-lockdown-worst-economic-downt urn-since-the-great-depression/.

Gorvett, Z. (2020). 'What we can learn from conspiracy theories', *BBC*, 25 May. Available at: https://www.bbc.com/future/article/20200522-what-we-can-learn-from-con spiracy-theories.

Goßner, C., Stam, C., Lawton, S., 'All eyes on Germany's 'crisis' presidency, expected to lead EU recovery', *Euractiv*, 28 May. Available at: .

Gould, E. (2020). 'Lack of paid sick days and large numbers of uninsured increase risks of spreading the coronavirus', *Economic Policy Institute*, 28 February. Available at: https://www.epi.org/blog/lack-of-paid-sick-days-and-large-numbers-of-uninsu red-increase-risks-of-spreading-the-coronavirus/.

Graf, R. (2018). *Die neue Entscheidungskultur – mit gemeinsam getragenen Entscheidungen zum Erfolg* [The new decision-making culture – with jointly sup-ported decisions to success]. Munich: Carl Hanser Verlag GmbH & Co.

Granovetter, M. (1978). 'Threshold Models of Collective Behavior', *American Journal of Sociology*, 83 (6, May), pp. 489–515. DOI: 1420.doi:10.1086/226707.

Great Britain. Department for Business, Innovation and Skills (2013). *International Education – Global Growth and Prosperity: An Accompanying Analytical Narrative*. Available at: https://assets.publishing.service.gov.uk/government/uploads/system/ uploads/attachment_data/file/340601/bis-13-1082-international-education-accom panying-analytical-narrative-revised.pdf.

Greene (2020). *The Ethics of AI and Emotional Intelligence* [Online]. Partnership on AI. Available at: https://www.partnershiponai.org/the-ethics-of-ai-and-emotional-intelligence/.

Griffiths, J. (2020). 'China's model of control has been blamed for the coronavirus crisis, but for some it's looking increasingly attractive', *CNN*, 29 April. Available at: https:// edition.cnn.com/2020/04/28/asia/china-coronavirus-model-democracy-intl-hnk/ index.html.

Griffiths, J. (2020). 'Taiwan's coronavirus response is among the best globally', *CNN*, 5 April. Available at: https://edition.cnn.com/2020/04/04/asia/taiwan-coronavirus -response-who-intl-hnk/index.html.

Grimm, I. (2020). 'Medienforscherin über inszenierte Corona-Konflikte: " 'Bild'-Chef Julian Reichelt schlägt um sich" ' [Media researcher on staged corona conflicts: " 'Bild' boss Julian Reichelt lashes out"], *Redaktionsnetzwerk Deutschland*, 10 June. Available at: https://www.rnd.de/medien/medienwissenschaftlerin-uber -bild-julian-reichelt-und-christian-drosten-LKY2IXJB3RBIXE36NRPE2W3AGY .html?utm_source=pocket-newtab-global-de-DE.

Gruber, M. (2020a). 'Rethinking Tech to Emancipate Women', *Global-e Series: Re-Globalization*, 13 (26, May). Available at: https://www.21global.ucsb.edu/global-e/ may-2020/rethinking-tech-emancipate-women.

Gruber, M. (2020b). 'Trust me, I'm a populist: Populismus in der Krise' [Trust me, I'm a populist: Populism in crisis], *Eurac Resarch Blog: Covid-19 And Beyond,* 16 April. Available at: https://blogs.eurac.edu/covid-19/populismus/.

Gulley, A. (2020). 'New Zealand has 'effectively eliminated' coronavirus. Here's what they did right', *National Geographic*, 30 April. Available at: https://www.nationalgeo graphic.com/travel/2020/04/what-new-zealand-did-right-in-battling-coronavirus/.

Gupta, S., Kane, A. (2020). 'Do some people have protection against the coronavirus?', *CNN*, 3 August. Available at: https://edition.cnn.com/2020/08/02/health/gupta-coronavirus-t-cell-cross-reactivity-immunity-wellness/index.html.

Guriev, S. (2015). 'Five questions about the BRICS nations' *World Economic Forum*, 8 July. Available at: https://www.weforum.org/agenda/2015/07/five-questions-about -the-brics-nations/.

Guterres, A. (2020). "The fury of the virus illustrates the folly of war", *United Nations*, 23 March. Available at: https://www.un.org/en/un-coronavirus-communications -team/fury-virus-illustrates-folly-war.

Habicher, D. (2020). 'Revise Globalization from a Postgrowth Perspective', *Global-e Series: Re-Globalization*, 13 (40, June). Available at: .

Hackenbroich, J. (2020). 'CureVac, covid-19, and economic statecraft: Lessons for Europe', *European Council on Foreign Relations*, 24 March. Available at: https://www .ecfr.eu/article/commentary_curevac_covid_19_and_economic_statecraft_lessons _for_europe.

Halinan, C. (2020). India & Coronavirus: Independent Press Fights Back, *International Policy Digest*, 14 April. Available at: https://intpolicydigest.org/2020/04/14/india -coronavirus-independent-press-fights-back/.

Hancock, J. (2020). 'People's uncertainty about the novel coronavirus can lead them to believe misinformation, says Stanford scholar'. Interviewed by Melissa De Witte for *Stanford News*, 16 March. Available at: https://news.stanford.edu/2020/03/16/fake -news-coronavirus-appealing-avoid/.

Harari, Y. N. (2020). 'Yuval Noah Harari: the world after coronavirus', *Financial Times*, 20 March. Available at: https://www.ft.com/content/19d90308-6858-11ea-a3c9-1fe6f edcca75.

Harrendorf, S., Heiskanen, M., Malby, S., HEUNI / UNODC (2010). *International Statistics on Crime and Justice*, Helsinki: HEUNI Publication Series No. 64. Available

BIBLIOGRAPHIC REFERENCES

at: https://www.heuni.fi/material/attachments/heuni/reports/6KHnYYyK7/Hakap aino_final_07042010.pdf.

Harvard University (2020). *Covid-19 – Moving Classes Online, Other Updates*. Available at: https://www.harvard.edu/covid-19-moving-classes-online-other-updates.

Harvey, F. (2020). 'UK's coronavirus recovery should have green focus, Johnson urged', *The Guardian*, 6 May. Available at: https://www.theguardian.com/environment/2020/may/06/uks-coronavirus-recovery-should-have-green-focus-johnson-urged.

Hasel, V. F. (2019). 'Gebt den Kindern einen Grund zum Lernen' [Give the children a reason to learn], *Die Zeit* Online, 26 December. Available at: https://www.zeit.de/gesellschaft/schule/2019-12/bildung-neuseeland-schulen-lehrer-kinder-lernen.

Hauff, V. (1987). *Unsere Gemeinsame Zukunft. Der Brundtland-Bericht der Weltkommission für Umwelt und Entwicklung* [Our common future. The Brundtland Report of the World Commission on Environment and Development]. Greven: Eggenkamp Verlag.

Heidenreich, M., Kädtler, J., Mattes, J. (2016). *Die innerbetriebliche Nutzung externer Wissensbestände in vernetzten Entwicklungsprozessen – Endbericht zum Projekt „Kollaborative Innovationen"* [The internal use of external knowledge in networked development processes – final report on the project "Collaborative Innovations"], Oldenburger Studien zur Europäisierung und zur transnationalen Regulierung, No. 25. Available at: https://uol.de/f/1/inst/sowi/ag/cetro/download/25_2016_Heidenre ich_Kaedtler_Mattes.pdf.

Helfer, C. (2014). 'Roland Benedikter: "Europa braucht eine Zivilreligion um zusammenzuwachsen"' [Roland Benedikter: "Europe needs a civil religion to grow together"], *Salto*, 21 May. Available at: https://www.salto.bz/it/article/21052014/rol and-benedikter-europa-braucht-eine-zivilreligion-um-zusammenzuwachsen.

Herreros, R. (2020). 'Coronavirus: L'Union européenne sera-t-elle la prochainevictime?'[Coronavirus: Will the European Union be the next victim?], *The Huffington Post*, 26 March. Available at: https://www.huffingtonpost.fr/entry/lue-est-elle-lau tre-victime-du-coronavirus_fr_5e7a0b4ac5b6f5b7c54b47bc.

Herrero, A.V., Faiola, A. (2020). 'Venezuelan government says it stopped 'invasion' launched from Colombia', *CNN*, 5 May. Available at: https://edition.cnn.com/2020/05/05/americas/venezuela-maduro-americans-failed-invasion-intl/index.html.

Hergersberg, P., Hoffrogge, C., Beck, C. (2020). 'Strategien zur Eindämmung der Covid-19 Pandemie' [Strategies to contain the Covid-19 pandemic], *Max-Planck-Gesellschaft*, 29 April. Available at: https://www.mpg.de/14759871/corona-stellungnahme.

Hershock, P. D. (2020). *Inequality, Social Cohesion and the Post-Pandemic Acceleration of Intelligent Technology*, Human Artificial Intelligence: Working Paper Series No. 1. East-West Center. Available at: https://www.jstor.org/stable/resrep25513.

Hersman, R. (2020). 'Wormhole Escalation In the New Nuclear Age', *Texas National Security Review*, 3 (3, Autumn). Print: ISSN 2576-1021. Available at: https://tnsr.org/2020/07/wormhole-escalation-in-the-new-nuclear-age/.

BIBLIOGRAPHIC REFERENCES

Herszenhorn, D.M., Paun, C., Deutsch, J. (2020). 'Europe fails to help Italy in coronavirus fight', *Politico*, 3 May. Available at: https://www.politico.eu/article/eu-aims-better-control-coronavirus-responses/.

Herszenhorn, D.M., Wheaton, S. (2020). 'How Europe failed the coronavirus test. Contagion's spread is a story of complacency, overconfidence and lack of preparation', *Politico*, 7 April. Available at: https://www.politico.eu/article/coronavirus-europe-failed-the-test/.

Hildebrandt, A. (2020). '„Er hat dem Stier das rote Tuch vorgehalten"' [He held up the rag to the bull], *Cicero – Magazin Für Politische Kultur*, 27 May. Available at: https://www.cicero.de/innenpolitik/bild-zeitung-christian-drosten-lockdown-schulen-georg-streiter-twitter/plus.

Hilson, M. (2011). *The Nordic Model: Scandinavia Since 1945*. London: Reaktion Books Ltd.

Hodgson, A. (2009). *Transformative Resilience – A response to the adaptive imperative* for Carnegie UK Trust, Investigations of the International Futures Forum. Available at: https://www.academia.edu/5493454/Transformative_Resilience.

Holling, C., Gunderson, L., Peterson, G. (2002). 'Sustainability and Panarchies' in Gunderson, L., Holling, C. (eds.) *Panarchy: Understanding Transformations in Human and Natural Systems*. Washington: Island Press, pp. 63–102.

Holling, C., Gunderson, L. (2002). 'Resilience and Adaptive Cycles' in: Holling, C., Gunderson, L. (Eds.) *Panarchy. Understanding Transformations in Human and Natural Systems,* Washington: Covelo, pp. 25–62.

Holon IQ (2018). '$10 Trillion Global Education Market in 2030', *Holon IQ*, 3 June. Available at: https://www.holoniq.com/2030/10-trillion-global-education-market/.

Holtorf, C., Brolin, A. (2020). 'Corona crisis, UNESCO and the future: Do we need a new world heritage?', *Seeingthewoods.org – A blog by the Rachel Carson Center*, 25 May. Available at: https://seeingthewoods.org/2020/05/25/corona-crisis-unesco-and-the-future-do-we-need-a-new-world-heritage/.

Hopkins, V., Fleming, S. (2020). 'Coronavirus re-sets agenda for Conference on Future of Europe', *The Financial Times*, 13 April. Available at: https://www.ft.com/content/b7fd7f3c-e97b-4d96-870e-907cef8985d1.

Horowitz, J. (2020). 'These coronavirus job losses will be permanent', *CNN*, 5 May. Available at: https://edition.cnn.com/2020/05/05/investing/premarket-stocks-trading/index.html.

Hörr, C. (2020). 'Warum Spahn nicht hart durchgreifen kann'[Why Spahn cannot take tough action], *NTV*, 11 March. Available at: https://www.n-tv.de/politik/Warum-Spahn-nicht-hart-durchgreifen-kann-article21631911.html.

Horx, M. (2020a). '48 – The Post Corona World', *Zukunftsinstitut Horx GmbH*. Available at: https://www.horx.com/en/post.php/?page_id=5423.

BIBLIOGRAPHIC REFERENCES

Horx, M. (2020b). 'A Backwards Corona Forecast: Or how we will be surprised when the crisis is "over"', *diezukunftnachcorona.com*, 16 March. Available at: https://www.diezukunftnachcorona.com/en/the-post-corona-world/.

Horx, M. (2020c). 'Zukunftsexperte Matthias Horx sagt voraus – Wie die Welt nach der Corona-Krise aussehen könnte' [Future Expert Mathias Herz Predicts – What the world could look like after the Corona crisis]. Interviewed by Volker Weinl for *Bild*, 24 May. Available at: https://www.bild.de/bild-plus/ratgeber/2020/ratgeber/zukunfts-experte-kann-die-welt-nach-corona-wirklich-eine-bessere-werden-70808336,view=conversionToLogin.bild.html.

Hsiang, S., Allen, D., Annan-Phan, S., Bell, K., Bolliger, I., Chong, T., Druckenmiller, H., Huang, L. Y., Hultgren, A., Krasovich, E., Lau, P., Lee, J., Rolf, E., Tseng, J., Wu, T. (2020). 'The effect of large-scale anti-contagion policies on the Covid-19 pandemic', *Nature*, 584, pp. 262–267. DOI: https://doi.org/10.1038/s41586-020-2404-8.

Huang, S. (2020). '#TaiwanCanHelp: Riding vs. Confronting the Covid-19 Crisis in Taiwan', *21st Century Global Dynamics*, 2 June. Available at: https://www.21global.ucsb.edu/global-e/june-2020/taiwancanhelp-riding-vs-confronting-covid-19-crisis-taiwan.

Huggler, J. (2020). 'Coronavirus is Germany's biggest challenge 'since Second World War' Angela Merkel says', *The Telegraph,* 18 March. Available at: https://www.telegraph.co.uk/news/2020/03/18/coronavirus-germanys-biggest-challenge-since-second-world-war/.

Huld, S. (2020). 'Verschwörungstheorie QAnon: Horrormärchen der Kinderfolterer geht um'[Conspiracy theory QAnon: Horror tale of child torturers goes around], *NTV*, 12 May. Available at: https://www.n-tv.de/politik/Horrormaerchen-der-Kinderfolterer-geht-um-article21776816.html?utm_source=pocket-newtab-global-de-DE.

Hydropoint (2019). 'Resilience is the New Sustainability', *Hydropoint*, 25 March. Available at: https://www.hydropoint.com/blog/resilience-is-the-new-sustainability/.

Iati, M., Goff, S., Hawkins, D., Brice-Saddler, M., Sonmez, F., Itkowiz, C., Shepherd, K., Wagner, J., Armus, T., Berger, M. (2020). 'Experts say coronavirus might never go away as U.S. death toll reaches 100,000', *The Washington Post*, 28 May. Available at: https://www.washingtonpost.com/nation/2020/05/27/coronavirus-update-us/.

INAISE (n.d.). *Home page*. Available at: http://inaise.org/en/#.

Infante, C.C. (2020a). 'Covid-19 in Latin America: if the virus doesn't kill us, hunger will', *Eurac Research Blog: Covid-19 and Beyond*, 16 June. Available at: https://blogs.eurac.edu/covid-19/covid-19-in-latin-america/.

Infante, C.C. (2020b). 'Peeling back the curtain of Covid-19 in Latin America', *Eurac Research Blog: Covid-19 and Beyond*, 20 July. Available at: https://blogs.eurac.edu/covid-19/peeling-back-the-curtain-of-covid-19-in-latin-america/.

Institute for New Economic Thinking New York (n.d.). *Home page*. Available at: https://www.ineteconomics.org/.

Ischinger, B. (2020). 'Coronavirus Challenges in the Interconnected Health and Education Sectors', *Global-e, Series: Re-Globalization*, 13 (29, May). Available at: https://www.21global.ucsb.edu/global-e/may-2020/coronavirus-challenges-interconnected-health-and-education-sectors.

Isidore, C. (2020). 'Some retailers are too broke to go bankrupt', *CNN*, 4 May. Available at: https://edition.cnn.com/2020/05/04/business/retailers-lack-of-store-closing-sales-delaying-bankruptcy/index.html.

Italian Ministry of Health. Novel coronavirus (2020). *FAQ – Covid-19*. Available at: http://www.salute.gov.it/portale/nuovocoronavirus/dettaglioFaqNuovoCoronavirus.jsp?lingua=english&id=230#1.

Itskov, D., Kurzweil, R., Martin, J., Berger, T., Diamandins, P.H., Hanson, D, Goertzel, B., Vita-More, N., Koene, R., Sandberg, A., Hameroff, S., Hayworth, K., Dubrovsky, D., Dunin-Barkowski, W.L., Panov, A., Bushell, W., Puhalo, L., Maharaj, S.V.G.J., Brill, A., Ackland, N. (2013). 'Open Letter to UN Secretary-General Ban Ki-Moon', *GF2045*, 11 March. Available at: http://gf2045.com/read/208/.

Iyer, P. (2009). *The Open Road. The Global Journey of the Fourteenth Dalai Lama*. London/Berlin/New York: Bloomsbury Trade.

Jack, S. (2020). 'World faces staggering jobs challenge, says Microsoft president', *BBC News*, 18 July. Available at: https://www.bbc.com/news/business-53444823.

Jackson, M. (2020). 'As it happened: Pandemic cost tourism industry 'at least $320bn'', *BBC*, 28 July. Available at: https://www.bbc.com/news/live/world-53550540.

Jackson, M.C. (2003). *Systems Thinking: Creative Holism for Managers*. Chichester: John Wiley & Sons, Ltd.

Jackson, M.O. (2020). 'Failing to coordinate against the coronavirus pandemic may be very costly for the world, says Stanford scholar'. Interviewed by Melissa De Witte for *Stanford News*, 26 March. Available at: https://news.stanford.edu/2020/03/26/coordinated-response-needed-fight-coronavirus-pandemic/.

Jackson, T. (2009). *Prosperity Without Growth: Economics for a Finite Planet*. London: Earthscan.

Jacobs, L. (2020). 'Für die deutsche Arbeitskultur eine einmalige Chance' [A unique opportunity for the German work culture], *Die Zeit Online*, 16 March. Available at: https://www.zeit.de/arbeit/2020-03/coronavirus-folgen-homeoffice-vorgesetzte-arbeitsbedingungen.

Jaffe, J. (2020). '5 ways people are using drones during the coronavirus lockdown', *CNet*, 3 April. Available at: https://www.cnet.com/news/5-ways-people-are-using-drones-during-the-coronavirus-lockdown/.

Janetsky, M. (2020). 'How a Colombian market is using AI to combat Covid-19 outbreaks', *BBC News*, 18 July. Available at: https://www.bbc.com/news/world-latin-america-53388656.

BIBLIOGRAPHIC REFERENCES

JapanTimes (2020). 'Wuhan lab had three live bat coronaviruses, but none matched Covid-19', *JapanTimes*, 24 May. Available at: https://www.japantimes.co.jp/news/2020/05/24/asia-pacific/science-health-asia-pacific/wuhan-lab-three-bat-corona viruses-china/#.Xu-HNfLgo_U.

Jawad, R. (2020) 'Coronavirus: Tunisia deploys police robot on lockdown patrol', *BBC News*, 3 April. Available at: https://www.bbc.com/news/world-africa-52148 639.

Jefferson, T., Del Mar, C.B., Dooley, L., Ferroni, E., Al-Ansary, L.A., Bawazeer, G.A., Nair, N.S., Conly, J., Thorning, S., Van Driel, M., Jones, M.A. (2011). 'Physical interventions to interrupt or reduce the spread of respiratory viruses', *Cochrane Database of Systematic Reviews 2011* (7). New York: John Wiley & Sons Ltd, pp. 1465–1858. DOI: http://doi.wiley.com/10.1002/14651858.CD006207.pub4.

Jiang, M. (2020). 'A Future of Work for All Work(ers)', *Journal of Beautiful Business*, 1 April. Available at: https://journalofbeautifulbusiness.com/a-future-of-work-for -all-work-ers-44102d6ba3a1.

John Cabot University (2018). 'Professor Stefan Sorgner Recognized Internationally for work in Transhumanism', *John Cabot University*, 1 October. Available at: https:// news.johncabot.edu/2018/10/stefan-sorgner-transhumanism/.

Johnson, J. (2020). 'Delegating strategic decision-making to machines: Dr. Strangelove Redux?', *Journal of Strategic Studies* (April). DOI: 10.1080/01402390.2020.1759038.

Journal of Democracy (n.d.). *Subject: Democratic decline*. Available at: https://www.jou rnalofdemocracy.org/subjects/democratic-decline/.

Jung, A. (2018). 'Wir brauchen ein deutsch-französisches Zukunftswerk' [We need a Franco-German future project], *Main Post*, 12 August. Available at: https://www .mainpost.de/ueberregional/politik/zeitgeschehen/Wir-brauchen-ein-deutsch-fra nzoesisches-Zukunftswerk;art16698,10033725.

Kahana, A. (2020). 'Foreign Ministry prepares for a post-corona world', *Israel Hayom*, 14 March. Available at: https://www.israelhayom.com/2020/04/13/foreign-ministry -prepares-for-a-post-corona-world/.

Kant, I. (1784). 'Idea for a Universal History from a Cosmopolitan Point of View'. Translation by Lewis White Beck on *marxists.org*. Available at: https://www.marxi sts.org/reference/subject/ethics/kant/universal-history.htm.

Käppner, J. (2020). 'Die Corona-Krise entzaubert die Populisten' [The corona crisis disenchants the populists], *Sueddeutsche Zeitung*, 17 March. Available at: https://www .sueddeutsche.de/politik/coronavirus-populismus-covid-19-1.4848247.

Kelion, L. (2020a). 'Coronavirus: First Google/Apple-based contact-tracing app launched', *BBC News*, 26 May. Available at: https://www.bbc.com/news/technology -52807635.

Kelion, L. (2020b). 'Coronavirus: UK contact-tracing app is ready for Isle of Wight downloads', *BBC News*, 4 May. Available at: https://www.bbc.com/news/technology- 52532435.

Kelion, L. (2020c). 'NHS Covid-19 app to issue more self-isolate alerts', *BBC*, 29 October. Available at: https://www.bbc.com/news/technology-54733534.

Kenis, A., Mathijs, E. (2014). 'Climate change and post-politics: Repoliticizing the present by imagining the future?', *Geoforum*, 52 (March), pp. 148–56. DOI: https://doi.org/10.1016/j.geoforum.2014.01.009.

Khan, N. (2020). 'The post-corona world politics', *Daily Times*, 17 April. Available at: https://dailytimes.com.pk/596937/the-post-corona-world-politics/.

Khanna, P. (2019). *The Future is Asian*. London: Weidenfeld & Nicolson.

Kim, T.H. (2020). 'Why is South Korea beating coronavirus? Its citizens hold the state to account', *The Guardian*, 11 April. Available at: https://www.theguardian.com/commentisfree/2020/apr/11/south-korea-beating-coronavirus-citizens-state-testing.

Kingsley, P., Bautista, J. (2020). "Here we go again': a second virus wave grips Spain', *The New York Times*, 31 August. https://www.nytimes.com/2020/08/31/world/europe/coronavirus-covid-spain-second-wave.html.

Klein, J. T. (1990). *Interdisciplinarity: History, Theory and Practice*. Detroit: Wayne State University Press.

Klein, J. T., Newell, W.H. (1997). 'Advancing Interdisciplinary Studies' in Gaff, J. G., Ratcliff, J. L. (eds.) *Handbook of the Undergraduate Curriculum: A Comprehensive Guide to Purposes, Structures, Practices, and Change*. San Francisco: Jossey Bass, pp. 393–415.

Knight, C. (2011). 'In defence of cosmopolitanism', *Theoria*, 58 (129), pp.19–34. ISSN 0040-5817.

Knight, S.M. (2020). 'Coronavirus immunity: Can you catch it twice?', *Ethical Editor*, 13 July. Available at: .

Koch, M. (2020). 'Europas "Hamilton-Moment": Das Mega-Thema dieser Zeit' [Europe's "Hamilton Moment": The mega-topic of this time], *RedaktionsNetzwerk Deutschland*, 22 May. Available at: https://www.rnd.de/politik/europas-hamilton-moment-das-mega-thema-dieser-zeit-3ACNMNNEDZGA3GDXW42V3Y6IYE.html.

Kölnische Rundschau (2020). 'Produktion medizinischer Schutzausrüstung verstärken' [Strengthen the production of medical protective equipment], *Kölnische Rundschau*, 9 July. Available at: https://www.rundschau-online.de/produktion-medizinischer-schutzausruestung-verstaerken-36990508.

KonBriefing (2021). 'Cyberangriffe aktuell 2021. Hackerangriffe auf Unternehmen und Organisationen in Deutschland, Österreich, Schweiz & weltweit' 19 August. Available at: [Cyber attacks current 2021. Hacker attacks on companies and organisations in Germany, Austria, Switzerland & worldwide], https://konbriefing.com/de-topics/cyber-angriffe-2021.html.

Kramer, M. (2015). 'Resilience is the New Sustainability', *GreenBiz*, 20 February. Available at: https://www.greenbiz.com/article/resilience-new-sustainability.

BIBLIOGRAPHIC REFERENCES 395

Krastev, I. (2020a). 'Seven early lessons from the coronavirus', *European Council on Foreign Relations,* 18 March. Available at: https://www.ecfr.eu/article/commentary _seven_early_lessons_from_the_coronavirus.

Krastev, I. (2020b). 'Sieben Schlüsse aus der Coronavirus-Krise' [Seven conclusions from the coronavirus crisis], *Zeit Online,* 20 March. Available at: https://www.zeit .de/gesellschaft/2020-03/coronavirus-pandemie-auswirkungen-folgen-panik-wir tschaft-zukunft-europa.

Kretchmer, H. (2020). '3 reasons we can't compare countries' coronavirus responses', *World Economic Forum,* 5 May. Available at: https://www.weforum.org/agenda/ 2020/05/compare-coronavirus-reponse-excess-deaths-rates/.

Krupa, M. (2020). 'Vorsicht, doch bissig' [Careful, it bites after all], *Die Zeit Online,* 17 June. Available at: https://www.zeit.de/2020/26/europaeische-union-corona-krise -zusammenhalt-staerke/komplettansicht.

Krupa, M., Lau, J. (2020). 'Das Ende der Heuchelei' [The End of the Hypocrisy], *Die Zeit Online,* 9 June. Available at: https://www.zeit.de/2020/25/europaeische-union-ratsp raesidentschaft-deutschland-fuehrung-corona-krise/komplettansicht.

Kuhls, K. (2003). 'From forecasting to foresight processes – new participative foresight activities in Germany', *Journal of Forecasting,* 22 (2–3, March), pp. 93–111. Available at: https://onlinelibrary.wiley.com/doi/abs/10.1002/for.848.

Kunze, I. (2010). 'Gemeinschaftsprojekte als Experimente nachhaltiger Ökonomie' [Joint projects as experiments in sustainable economics], in Fein, E. (ed.) *Wirtschaft in der Zeitenwende – zur Vision einer Maßwirtschaft der Lebensfülle und Schritte zu ihrer Verwirklichung* [Economy at the turn of an era – to the vision of a eco-intelligent economy of abundance of life and steps to its realisation]. Freiburg: Institut für Integrale Studien (IFIS), pp. 86–95. Also available at: https://www.ifis-freiburg.de/sites/default/ files/2020-09/Wirtschaft in der Zeitenwende_DOKUMENTATION.pdf.

Laborde, D., Martin, W., Swinnen, J., Vos, R. (2020). 'Covid-19 risks to global food security', *Science,* 369 (6503, July), 500–502. DOI: 10.1126/science.abc4765. Available at: https://www.sciencemagazinedigital.org/sciencemagazine/31_july_2020/Mob ilePagedArticle.action?articleId=1604813&app=false#articleId1604813.

Lakritz, T. (2020). '12 innovative ways companies are helping people affected by the coronavirus', *Business Insider,* 23 March. Available at: https://www.businessinsider .com/coronavirus-companies-donations-helping-people?r=DE&IR=T.

Langer, E. (2014). 'Mindfulness in the Age of Complexity' interviewed by & for *Harvard Business Review,* March. Available at: https://hbr.org/2014/03/mindfulness-in-the -age-of-complexity.

Larsen, N., Mortensen, J.K., Miller, R. (2020). 'What Is 'Futures Literacy' and Why Is It Important?', *Medium,* 11 February. Available at: https://medium.com/copenha gen-institute-for-futures-studies/what-is-futures-literacy-and-why-is-it-important -a27f24b983d8.

Larsson, P. (2020). 'Anti-Asian racism during coronavirus: How the language of disease produces hate and violence', *The Conversation,* 31 March. Available at: https://thec onversation.com/anti-asian-racism-during-coronavirus-how-the-language-of-dise ase-produces-hate-and-violence-134496.

Laughland, O., Zanolli, L. (2020). 'Why is coronavirus taking such a deadly toll on black Americans?', *The Guardian,* 25 April. Available at: https://www.theguardian.com/ world/2020/apr/25/coronavirus-racial-disparities-african-americans.

Lauren, M., Sauer, M.S. (2020). 'What Is Coronavirus?', *John Hopkins Medicine.* Available at: https://www.hopkinsmedicine.org/health/conditions-and-diseases/coronavirus.

Laviola, E. (2018). 'QAnon Conspiracy: 5 Fast Facts You Need to Know', *Heavy,* 1 August. Available at: https://heavy.com/news/2018/08/qanon-conspiracy-trump/.

Layder, D. (1997). *Modern Social Theory: Key Debates and New Directions.* London/ Bristol: UCL Press.

Leberecht, T. (2020a). 'The Great Reset: What Will (Need to) Change after the Crisis?', *Journal of Beautiful Business,* 30 March. Available at: https://journalofbeautifulbusin ess.com/the-great-reset-what-will-need-to-change-after-the-crisis-a1a2aab6bc73.

Leberecht, T. (2020b). '6 Hopes for a Post-Corona World', *Psychology Today,* 5 April. Available at: https://www.psychologytoday.com/us/blog/the-romance-work/202 004/6-hopes-post-corona-world.

LeBlanc, P. (2020) 'GOP congressman says letting more Americans die of coronavirus is lesser of two evils compared to economy tanking', *CNN,* 15 April. Available at: https:// edition.cnn.com/2020/04/14/politics/trey-hollingsworth-coronavirus/index.html.

Lederach, J. P. (2003). "Conflict Transformation" in Burgess, G., Burgess, H. (Eds.) *Beyond Intractability.* Boulder: Conflict Information Consortium, University of Colorado. Available at: http://www.beyondintractability.org/essay/transformation.

Leggett, T. (2020). 'Why Covid could remove barriers for women in the car industry', *BBC,* 9 October. Available at: https://www.bbc.com/news/business-54479745.

Legrain, P. (2020). 'The Coronavirus Is Killing Globalization as We Know It', *Foreign Policy,* 12 March. Available at: https://foreignpolicy.com/2020/03/12/coronavirus -killing-globalization-nationalism-protectionism-trump/.

Leitmeyer, F. (2020). 'Kein Komplett-Lockdown, Kaum Tote, Wirtschaft Stabil: Darum ist Südkorea der Corona-Sieger' [No complete Lockdown, hardly any deaths, economy stable: That is why South Korea is the corona winner], *Bild,* 2 October. Available at: https://www.bild.de/bild-plus/politik/ausland/politik/suedkoreas-wir tschaft-floriert-trotz-corona-lockdown-gab-es-dort-nie-73138566,view=conversion ToLogin.bild.html.

Lemon, D. (2020). Don Lemon to Trump: What is it about Obama that gets under your skin?, *CNN.* https://edition.cnn.com/videos/politics/2020/05/04/don-lemon -trump-obama-obsession-ctn-vpx.cnn.

Leonard, M. (2020a). 'Corona Angst – How the virus puts the European Project and globalisation at risk', *Mark Leonard's World in 30 minutes* [podcast], 18 March. Available at: https://soundcloud.com/ecfr/corona-angst-how-the-virus-puts-the-european -project-and-globalisation-at-risk.

Leonard, M. (2020b). 'Geopolitics in the coronavirus era – who will be crowned winner?', *Mark Leonard's World in 30 minutes* [podcast]. 25 March. Available at: https:// soundcloud.com/ecfr/geopolitics-in-the-corona-era-who-will-be-crowned-win ner?in=ecfr/sets/coronavirus.

Leonard, M. (2020c). 'Salvaging globalization', *European Council on Foreign Relations*, 4 May. Available at: https://ecfr.eu/article/commentary_salvaging_globalisation/.

Leoni, T., Pekanov, A. (2020). *Die Corona-Krise – Ein Stresstest für den Euro* [The corona crisis – a stress test for the euro], ÖGfE Policy Brief No. 17. Wien: ÖSTERREICHISCHE GESELLSCHAFT FÜR EUROPAPOLITIK. Available at: https://oegfe.at/2020/07/cor ona-krise-stresstest-euro/.

Leven me twater (2020). *Homepage*. http://www.levenmetwater.nl/home/.

Levin-Waldman, O.M. (2020). 'Globalism and Inequality Are the Real Threats to Our Democracy', *Challenge*, 63 (2), pp. 77–89. DOI: 10.1080/05775132.2019.1709725.

Lewis, T. (2020). 'Business soaring for delivery drones during Covid-19 pandemic', *Fox 5*, 9 April. Available at: https://www.fox5dc.com/news/business-soaring-for-delivery -drones-during-covid-19-pandemic.

Lichtenberger, E., Pelinka, A. (2020). 'Demokratie in der Krise – Krise in der Demokratie' [Democracy in Crisis – Crisis in Democracy][discussion], *Universität Innsbruck*, 23 July. Available at: https://www.uibk.ac.at/events/2020/07/23/demokratie-in-der -krise-krise-in-der-demokratie.xml.

Limphaibool, W. (2020). 'Collective Mindfulness in Times of Crisis: Learning from Thailand's Fight Against the Covid-19 Pandemic', *Harvard International Review*, 14 October. Available at: https://hir.harvard.edu/learning-from-thailand-covid/.

Liu, L.S., Ran, G.J. (2020). 'Ethnic Solidarity in Combating the Covid-19 Threat in New Zealand', *Globale-e Series: Pandemic: Border-Crossing Caveats*, 13 (47, July). Available at: https://www.21global.ucsb.edu/global-e/july-2020/ethnic-solidarity-combating -covid-19-threat-new-zealand.

Loorbach, D. (2007). *Transition Management. New Mode of Governance for Sustainable Development*. Utrecht: International Book.

Loorbach, D. (2014). *To Transition! Governance Panarchy in the New Transformation*. Drift. Available at; https://drift.eur.nl/wp-content/uploads/2016/12/To_Transition -Loorbach-2014.pdf.

Lopez, J. (2020). 'The coronavirus: A geopolitical earthquake', *ECFR*, 2 April. Available at: https://www.ecfr.eu/article/commentary_the_coronavirus_a_geopolitical_ear thquake.

Love, D. (2020). 'The jury's still out on whether universal basic income will save us from job-stealing robots', *Business Insider*, 24 November. Available at: https://www .businessinsider.com/will-universal-basic-income-save-us-from-job-stealing-rob ots-2017-11?r=DE&IR=T.

Luft, S. (2020). 'The Corona summer certainly worked as catalyst', interviewed by Tobias Armbrüster for *Deutschlandfunk*, 20 July. Available at: https://www.deut schlandfunk.de/konfliktforscher-zu-krawallen-der-corona-sommer-hat-sicher.694 .de.html?dram:article_id=480870.

Luhmann, N. (1993). *Soziale Systeme – Grundriß einer allgemeinen Theorie* [Social Systems – Outline of a General Theory]. 4th edn. Frankfurt: Suhrkamp.

LUISS University Rome's Business School (n.d.). *Ethos Luiss Business School*. Available at: https://businessschool.luiss.it/osservatorio-ethos/.

Lyons, T. (2020). 'Antitrust hearing with CEOs of Facebook, Amazon, Google, and Apple rescheduled to Wednesday', *The Verge*, 25 July. Available at: https://www .theverge.com/2020/7/25/21338238/antitrust-hearing-ceos-facebook-amazon-goo gle-apple-rescheduled.

Lyotard, J.-F. (1988). *The Different: Phrases in Dispute*. Minneapolis: University of Minnesota Press.

Mäder, C. (2016). 'Der Philosophie steht eine neue grosse Zeit bevor' [A new great age is ahead for philosophy], *Neue Zürcher Zeitung*, 19 November. Available at: https:// www.nzz.ch/feuilleton/zeitgeschehen/richard-david-precht-ueber-die-gegenwart -der-philosophie-steht-eine-neue-grosse-zeit-bevor-ld.129311?reduced=true.

Maffettone, S. (2020). *Società Civile ed Etica* [Civil society and ethics]. Interview for *RAI 2 TG 2 Mizar*, 21 June. Available at: http://www.tg2.rai.it/dl/tg2/rubriche/Publ ishingBlock-4d179a82-04c1-4164-856b-2afc28c38206.html.

Maissen, T. (2020). 'Staaten nutzen Krisen, um sich immer wieder neu zu erfinden' [States use crises to keep reinventing themselves], *Neue Züricher Zeitung*, 29 March. p. 35.

Maiwald, J. (2018). *Smart decision-making: Systemic Consensing for Managers*. Holzkirchen: A-bis Publications.

Malik, F. (1992). *Strategie des Managements komplexer Systeme* [Strategy of the management of complex systems]. Wien/Stuttgart/Bern: Verlag Paul Haupt.

Markets and Markets (2020). *Higher Education Market*. Available at: https://www .marketsandmarkets.com/Market-Reports/higher-education-market-192416446.html.

Markson, S. (2020). 'Coronavirus NSW: Dossier lays out case against China bat virus program', *The Daily Telegraph*, 4 May. Available at: https://www.dailytelegraph.com. au/coronavirus/bombshell-dossier-lays-out-case-against-chinese-bat-virus-prog ram/news-story/55add857058731c9c71c0e96ad17da60.

Marr, B. (2020). '9 Future Predictions For A Post-Coronavirus World', *Forbes*, 3 April. Available at: https://www.forbes.com/sites/bernardmarr/2020/04/03/9-future-pred ictions-for-a-post-coronavirus-world/#4ac5ca9f5410.

Martos, C. (2020). 'Von der Leyen: 'We now need to build a resilient, green, and digital Europe'', *Euractiv*, 20 April. Available at: https://www.euractiv.com/section/future -eu/interview/von-der-leyen-we-now-need-to-build-resilient-green-digital-europe/.

BIBLIOGRAPHIC REFERENCES

Marzi, L.-M. (2020). *Vorschläge für eine effiziente, europäische Bekämpfung von Pandemien – Juristische Aspekte im Gesundheitsbereich* [Proposals for an efficient European fight against pandemics – Legal aspects in the health sector], *ÖGfE* Policy Brief, No 15. Wien: ÖSTERREICHISCHE GESELLSCHAFT FÜR EUROPAPOLITIK. Available at: https://oegfe.at/2020/06/eu-pandemie-bekaempfung/.

Mast, M., Schumann, F., Simmank, J. (2020). 'Skandal oder alles normal?' [Scandal or is everything normal?], *Zeit Online*, 26 May. Available at: https://www.zeit.de/wissen/gesundheit/2020-05/bild-artikel-christian-drosten-corona-studie-schuloeffnung#worum-geht-es-in-der-debatte.

Mauerhofer, V., Rupo, D. & Tarquinio, L. (2020). *Sustainability and Law*. Springer. DOI: https://doi.org/10.1007/978-3-030-42630-9.

Maughan, M., Thornhill, A., Maughan, C. (1996). 'Using the red-blue exercise to facilitate learning transfer: theory and practice'. *Journal of European Industrial Training*, 20 (8), pp. 18–21. MCB University Press. DOI: https://doi.org/10.1108/03090599610128845.

McAfee, A., Brynjolfsson, E. (2014). *The Second Machine Age: Work, Progress, and Prosperity in a Time of Brilliant Technologies*. London/New York: W. W. Norton & Company.

Medinlive (2020). 'Europäer wollen stärkere Rolle der EU in Corona-Krise' [Europeans want EU to play a stronger role in Corona crisis], *Medinlive*, 14 July. Available at: https://www.medinlive.at/gesellschaft/europaeer-wollen-staerkere-rolle-der-eu-corona-krise.

Medrano, J. (2012). Interpersonal Trust, Banco de datos ASEP/JDS. Available at: http://www.jdsurvey.net/jds/jdsurveyMaps.jsp?Idioma=I&SeccionTexto=0404&NOID=104

Membretti, A. (2020). 'A new compulsion to locality', *Eurac Research Blog: Covid-19 and Beyond*, 5 May. Available at: https://blogs.eurac.edu/covid-19/a-new-compulsion-to-locality/.

Merlot, J. (2020). 'Wir gehen davon aus, dass es ein Stresstest wird für unser Land' [We assume that it will be a stress test for our country], *Der Spiegel*, 13 March. Available at: https://www.spiegel.de/wissenschaft/medizin/coronavirus-wir-gehen-davon-aus-dass-es-ein-stresstest-wird-fuer-unser-land-sagt-rki-chef-lothar-wieler-a-86251a54-182c-4bfa-9d60-1dc6084b987d.

Messner, D. (2000). 'Globalisierung, Global governance und Perspektiven der Entwicklungszusammenarbeit' [Globalization, global governance and prospects for development cooperation] in Nuscheler F.(ed.) *Entwicklung und Frieden im 21* [Development and Peace in the 21st], Bonn: Dietz, 267–294.

Metzl, J. (2020). 'Covid-19 offers a chance to build a better world. We must seize it', *CNN*, 17 May. Available at: https://edition.cnn.com/2020/05/17/opinions/covid-19-worldwide-response-metzl/index.html.

Meyer, J.M, (2019). 'The politics of the "post-political" contesting the diagnosis', *Democratization*, 27 (3), pp. 408–425. DOI: https://doi.org/10.1080/13510 347.2019.1676737.

Meyerssohn, N. (2020). 'This is the most dangerous place in the grocery store', *CNN Business*, May 1. Available at: https://edition.cnn.com/2020/04/30/business/grocery-stores-coronavirus-cashiers/index.html.

Meyrowitz, J. (2005). 'The Rise of Glocality: New Senses of Place and Identity in the Global Village' in Nyíri, K. (Ed.) *A Sense of Place: The Global and the Local in Mobile Communication*. Vienna: Passagen Verlag, pp. 21–30.

Michaelson, J., Abdallah, S., Steuer, N., Thompson, S., Marks, N. (2009). *National Accounts of Well-being: bringing real wealth onto the balance sheet*. London: New Economics Foundation (NEF). Available at: https://neweconomics.org/uploads/files/2027fb05fed1554aea_uim6vd4c5.pdf.

Miller, C. (2020). 'Signs of depression during the Coronavirus crisis', *Child Mind Institute*. Available at: https://childmind.org/article/signs-of-depression-during-coronavirus-crisis/.

Miller, D. (2005). 'Reasonable Partiality Towards Compatriots', *Ethic Theory Moral Practice*, 8, pp. 63–81. https://doi.org/10.1007/s10677-005-3296-2.

Miller, D. (2008). *National Responsibility and Global Justice*. Oxford: Oxford Scholarship Online. DOI:10.1093/acprof:oso/9780199235056.001.0001.

Miller, D. (2018). 'COSMOPOLITISMO DEBOLE E "COMPATRIOT PARTIALITY"' Interviewed by Bertoncin, B., for *Una Città*, 252 (October). Available at: https://www.unacitta.it/newsite/intervista.asp?id=2657.

Miller, M.A., Viboud, C., Balinska, M., Simonsen, L. (2009). 'The Signature Features of Influenza Pandemics – Implications for Policy', *The New England Journal of Medicine*, 360 (25, June), 2595–2598. DOI: 10.1056/NEJMp0903906.

Miller, R. (2010). 'Futures Literacy – Embracing Complexity and Using the Future', *Ethos*, 10 (10, October), pp. 23–28.

Miller, R. (2017). 'Transforming the Future: Anticipation in the 21st Century' [PowerPoint presentation], *Network for Future Studies*, 17 October. Available at: https://pdfs.semanticscholar.org/6f5d/7483b2f34311d74d59dfaf13d50c169be467.pdf.

Miller, R. (2018). *Transforming the Future: Anticipation in the 21st Century*. Paris/New York: UNESCO/Routledge.

Miller, R. (2019). 'Interview about Futures Literacy with Riel Miller, Head of Foresight at UNESCO' interviewed by & for *Eit Climate-Kic*, 12 December. Available at: https://www.climate-kic.org/community/interview-with-riel-miller/.

Miller, R. (n.d.). 'My Reform Story – UNESCO Pioneers Futures Literacy', *UNESCO*. Available at: https://en.unesco.org/sites/default/files/myreformstory_riel-miller.pdf.

Miller, R., Feukeu, K.E. (n.d.). 'Futures Literacy: A Skill for the 21st Century', *UNESCO*. Available at: https://en.unesco.org/themes/futures-literacy.

BIBLIOGRAPHIC REFERENCES

Ministry of the Interior and Kingdom Relations (2009). 'Mega-Crises in the 21st Century', *National Safety & Security and Crisis Management Magazine*, special issue (October). Available at: https://www.patricklagadec.net/fr/pdf/Magazine%20Spec ial%20Mega-crises%20in%20the%2021st%20century.pdf.

Mitteldeutsche Zeitung (2018). 'Rückkehr der Krankheit durch den Klimawandel? Professor warnt vor neuer Pest-Epidemie' [Is the disease returning due to climate change? Professor warns of new plague epidemic], *Mitteldeutsche Zeitung*, October 22. Available at: https://www.mz-web.de/panorama/rueckkehr-der-krankheit -durch-den-klimawandel--professor-warnt-vor-neuer-pest-epidemie-31454946.

Mittelstaedt, W. (2020a). *Anthropozän und Nachhaltigkeit – Denkanstösse zur Klimakrise und für ein zukunftsfähiges Handeln* [Anthropocene and sustainability – Food for thought on the climate crisis and future-oriented action]. Berlin: Peter Lang Verlag.

Mittelstaedt, W. (2020b). 'Das Anthropozän, die Klimakrise, das Coronavirus und die Zukunft der Weltgesellschaft' [The Anthropocene, the climate crisis, the coronavirus and the future of global society], *Vereinigung Deutscher Wissenschaftler* (*VDW*), 10 May. Available at: https://vdw-ev.de/werner-mittelstaedt-anthropozaen-klimakr ise-coronavirus/.

Mohideen, R. (2010). 'Disaster management: New Zealand, Haiti and the 'Cuban way'', *Link – International Journal of socialist renewal*, 8 September. Available at: http:// links.org.au/node/1890.

Molter, V. (2020). 'Virality Project (China): Pandemics & Propaganda', *Stanford Cyber Policy Center Freeman Spogli Institute*, 19 March. Available at: https://cyber.fsi.stanf ord.edu/news/chinese-state-media-shapes-coronavirus-convo.Montgomery, F.U. (2020). 'Interview mit Weltärztepräsident Montgomery: „Ein Lockdown ist eine politische Verzweiflungsmaßnahme"' [Interview with World Medical Association Chairperson Montgomery: "A lockdown is a political desperation measure"], interviewed for *RP.Online*, 4 April. Available at: https://rp-online.de/politik/deutschland/ interview-mit-weltaerztepraesident-montgomery-pandemie-ist-chaos_aid-49596217.

Moore, C., Lipsitch, M., Barry, J., Osterholm, M. (2020). Covid-19: The CIDRAP Viewpoint, Part 1: The Future of the Covid-19 Pandemic: Lessons Learned from Pandemic Influenza, CIDRAP. Available at: https://www.cidrap.umn.edu/sites/defa ult/files/public/downloads/cidrap-covid19-viewpoint-part1_0.pdf.

Moorstedt, M. (2020). 'In der Krise boomt auch die Überwachung durch den Chef' [Supervision by the boss is also booming during the crisis], *Süddeutsche Zeitung*, 6 April. Available at: https://www.sueddeutsche.de/digital/home-office -ueberwachung-tracking-chef-zoom-1.4868739?fbclid=IwAR16dGC1zO1FhoqGI _IR8RyPWzMkbxB8fPiysz_30W6cM_slqThtaytcWSg.

Morlino, L. (2016). *The Quality of Democracy in Latin America*. Strömsborg: International IDEA. Available at: https://www.idea.int/sites/default/files/publications/the-qual ity-of-democracies-in-latin-america.pdf.

Morris, C., Reuben, A. (2020). 'Coronavirus: Why are international comparisons difficult?', *BBC*, 17 June. Available at: https://www.bbc.com/news/52311014.

Morris, I. (2010). *Why the West Rules – For Now: The Patterns of History, and What They Reveal About the Future*. New York: Farrar, Straus and Giroux.

Moss, L. (2020). 'Singing 'no riskier than talking' for virus spread', *BBC*, 20 August. Available at: https://www.bbc.com/news/health-53853961.

Mounk, Y (2018). "The Undemocratic Dilemma", in *Journal of Democracy* 29:2, April 2018, pp. 98–112.

Müller-Seitz, G. (2014). 'Von Risiko zu Resilienz – zum Umgang mit Unerwartetem aus Organisationsperspektive' [From risk to resilience – how to deal with the unexpected from an organisational perspective] in Kaiser, S. (Ed.) *Zukunftsfähige Unternehmensführung zwischen Stabilität und Wandel* [Sustainable corporate management between stability and change]. Düsseldorf: Handelsblatt Fachmedien GmbH. pp. 102–122.

Muller, R.T. (2020). 'Covid-19 Brings a Pandemic of Conspiracy Theories', *Psychology Today*, April 24. Available at: https://www.psychologytoday.com/us/blog/talking-about-trauma/202004/covid-19-brings-pandemic-conspiracy-theories.

Mundasad, S. (2020). 'Black people 'twice as likely to catch coronavirus'', *BBC*, 12 November. Available at: https://www.bbc.com/news/health-54907473.

Muntean, P. (2020). 'United Airlines COO says employees should 'seriously consider' voluntary separation for the airline', *CNN*, 5 May. Available at: https://edition.cnn.com/2020/05/04/business/united-voluntary-separation/index.html?bt_ee=DKobKzrj7G25ijHzvGdycuoZ28WE%2BdVVGF4%2FpSYvwKUkpgMiwuKmerqdW9EEhA%2FE&bt_ts=1588678973130.

Nachrichten.at, APA (2020). 46,4 Prozent weniger Kriminalität in der Corona-Krise [46.4 percent less criminality in the corona crisis], *nachrichten.at*, 19 May. Available at: https://www.nachrichten.at/panorama/chronik/kriminalitaet-in-der-corona-krise;art58,3259525.

National Cyber Security Centre (2020). 'Cyber warning issued for key healthcare organisations in UK and USA', *National Cyber Security Centre*, 5 May. Available at: https://www.ncsc.gov.uk/news/warning-issued-uk-usa-healthcare-organisations.

Nature Research (n.d.). 'What 5G means for our health', *Nature*. Available at: https://www.nature.com/articles/d42473-019-00009-7.

NDTV (2020). ' "Terrorists May See Window Of Opportunity": UN Chief Warns Amid Covid-19', *NDTV*, 11 April. Available at: https://www.ndtv.com/world-news/coronavirus-terrorists-may-use-covid-19-window-to-strike-un-security-council-2209307.

Negi, A., Pérez-Pineda, J.A., Blankenbach, J. (2020). *Sustainability Standards and Global Governance*. Singapore: Springer Singapore. DOI: 10.1007/978-981-15-3473-7.

New Economic Foundation (NEF) (2012). *National Accounts of Well-being*, http://www.nationalaccountsofwellbeing.org/explore/countries/gb.

News Wires (2020). 'New Zealand reports no new coronavirus cases', *France 24*, 4 May. Available at: https://www.france24.com/en/20200504-new-zealand-repo rts-no-new-covid-19-cases.

Nida-Rümelin, J., Weidenfeld, N. (2018). *Digitaler Humanismus. Eine Ethik für das Zeitalter der Künstlichen Intelligenz* [Digital humanism. An ethic for the age of arti-ficial intelligence]. Munich: Piper Verlag.

Nielsen, B.F., Eilersen, A., Sneppen, K. (2020). 'The strategy against Covid-19 spread-ing depends on mathematical modelling – but how?', *Niels Bohr Institute at the University of Copenhagen*, 8 May. Available at: https://www.nbi.ku.dk/ english/ news/news20/the-strategy-against-covid-19-spreading-depends-on-mathematical -modelling--but-how/.

Nitoiu, C. (2014). 'Barroso's farewell speech', *Open Democracy*, 4 November. Available at: https://www.opendemocracy.net/en/can-europe-make-it/barrosos-farewell-speech/.

Nordling, L. (2020) 'The pandemic appears to have spared Africa so far. Scientists are struggling to explain why', *Science*, 11 August. Available at: https://www.science mag.org/news/2020/08/pandemic-appears-have-spared-africa-so-far-scientists -are-struggling-explain-why?utm_campaign=news_daily_2020-08-11&et_rid= 49319877&et_cid=3443358.

Nowotny, H., Limoges, C., Schwartzman, S., Scott, P., Trow, M., Gibbons, M. (1994). *The New Production of Knowledge. The Dynamics of Science and Research in Contemporary Societies*. London: SAGE.

Nowotny, H., Scott, P., Gibbons, M. (2001). *Re-Thinking Science. Knowledge and the Public in an Age of Uncertainty*. Cambridge/Maiden: Polity Press and Blackwell Publishers.

Security, *Science*, 369 (6503, July), 500–502. DOI: 10.1126/science.abc4765.

NTV (2020). 'Wie um zehn Jahre gealtert. Studie: Geistiger Verfall durch Covid-19' [As if aged by ten years. Study: mental decline due to Covid-19], NTV, 27 October. Available at: https://www.n-tv.de/panorama/Studie-Geistiger-Verfall-durch-Covid-19-article22128492.html.

O'Dougherty Wright, M., Masten, A. S., Narayan, A. J. (2013). 'Resilience Processes in Development: Four Waves of Research on Positive Adaptation in the Context of Adversity', in Goldstein, S., Brooks, R. B. (Eds.) *Handbook of Resilience in Children*. Berlin: Springer Science + Business Media, pp. 15 – 37.

OECD (2011). *Society at a Glance 2011: OECD Social Indicators*. Paris: OECD Publishing, https://doi.org/10.1787/soc_glance-2011-en.

OECD et al. (2020) 'Latin American Economic Outlook 2020: Digital Transformation for Building Back Better', *OECD Publishing*, Paris. Available: https://doi.org/10.1787/ e6e864fb-en.

Olivier, B. (2015). 'What is a 'rhizome' in Deleuze and Guattari's thinking?', *Mail&Guardian Thought Leader*, 15 June. Available at: https://thoughtleader.co.za/ bertolivier/2015/06/15/what-is-a-rhizome-in-deleuze-and-guattaris-thinking/.

Olivier, C. (2019). 'Christchurch mosque shootings: Shootings prompt review of lockdown procedures', *NZ Herald*, 18 Mar. Available at: https://www.nzherald.co.nz/rotorua-daily-post/news/christchurch-mosque-shootings-shootings-prompt-review-of-lockdown-procedures/3CDA75RW7YLODCDGOSPO7575CA/.

Ortéga, A. (2020). 'The deglobalisation virus', European Council on Foreign Relations, 18 March. Available at: https://www.ecfr.eu/article/commentary_the_deglobalisation_virus.

OXFAM International (2020). The hunger virus: how Covid-19 is fuelling hunger in a hungry word, *OXFAM,* 9 July. Available at: https://www.oxfam.org/en/research/hunger-virus-how-covid-19-fuelling-hunger-hungry-world.

Oxford Economics (2019). *How Robots Change the World.* Oxford: Oxford Economics. Available at: https://cdn2.hubspot.net/hubfs/2240363/Report%20-%20How%20Robots%20Change%20the%20World.pdf.

Pace News (2020). 'Time to put armed conflict 'on lockdown'?', *Pace News*, 3 April. Available at: https://www.peacenews.com/single-post/2020/04/03/Time-to-put-armed-conflict-on-lockdown.

Paech, N. (2012). *Befreiung vom Überfluss – auf dem Weg in die Postwachstumsökonomie* [Liberation from abundance – on the way to the post-growth economy]. Munich: Oekom Verlag.

Paech, N. (2020). 'Niko Paech über Postwachstum und Corona "Nicht mehr zurück ins Hamsterrad"' [Niko Paech on post-growth and corona "No more back to the hamster wheel"]. interviewed by Jost Maurin for *Taz*, 17 April. Available at: https://taz.de/Niko-Paech-ueber-Postwachstum-und-Corona/!5680789/.

Page, J., Khan, N. (2020). 'On the Ground in Wuhan, Signs of China Stalling Probe of Coronavirus Origins', *The Wall Street Journal*, 12 May. Available at: https://www.wsj.com/articles/china-stalls-global-search-for-coronavirus-origins-wuhan-markets-investigation-11589300842.

Paul, E. (2020) '6 amazing African innovations against Covid-19: A cure from physics?', *Techpoint.africa*, 23 April. Available at: https://techpoint.africa/2020/04/23/african-innovations-covid-19/.

Paun, C. (2020). 'Populists seize on coronavirus to stoke immigration fear', *Politico*, 18 February. Available at: https://www.politico.eu/article/populists-cite-coronavirus-outbreak-to-advance-anti-immigration-agenda/.

Pauwels, A. (2020). 'How Europe's terrorists take advantage of the pandemic', *Euobserver*, 29 April. Available at: https://euobserver.com/opinion/148173.

Pearce, M. (2020). 'In fighting the coronavirus pandemic, the U.S. is going to live and die by its decentralized public health system', *Los Angeles Times*, 5 April. Available at: https://www.latimes.com/politics/story/2020-04-05/coronavirus-states-take-the-lead.

Pechlaner, H., Erschbamer, G., Thees, H., Gruber, M. (2020). *China and the New Silk Road.* Cham: Springer International. DOI: 10.1007/978-3-030-43399-4.

BIBLIOGRAPHIC REFERENCES

Pechlaner, H., Innerhofer, E., Erschbamer, G. (2019). *Overtourism. Tourism management solutions*. London: Routledge. DOI: 10.4324/9780429197987.

Pendall, R., Foster, K., Cowell, M. (2010). 'Resilience and regions: building understanding of the metaphor', *Cambridge Journal of Regions, Economy and Society*, 3(1, 22 July), pp. 71–84. Available at: https://doi.org/10.1093/cjres/rsp028.

Pennisi, E. (2020). 'How bats have outsmarted viruses – including coronaviruses – for 65 million years', *Science Magazine*, 22 July. Available at: https://www.sciencemag .org/news/2020/07/how-bats-have-outsmarted-viruses-including-coronaviruses -65-million-years.

Perron, W. (2011). 'Resilienz in der offenen Gesellschaft' [Resilience in an open society] in Just, H., Kind, H., Koch, H. (eds.) *Solidarität: Dem Einzelnen oder der Gesellschaft verpflichtet?* [Solidarity: Committed to the individual or to society?] Kolloquium 19, Schriftenreihe der Ethik – Kommission der Albert-Ludwigs-Universität, 6. Freiburg: Universität Freiburg.

Perthes, V. (2020). 'The Corona Crisis and International Relations: Open Questions, Tentative Assumptions', *Stiftung Wissenschaft und Politik*, 31 March. Available at: https://www.swp-berlin.org/en/publication/the-corona-crisis-and-internatio nal-relations-open-questions-tentative-assumptions/.

Peterlini, S.O. (2009). 'The South-Tyrol Autonomy in Italy' in Oliveira J.C., Cardinal P. (eds.) *One Country, Two Systems, Three Legal Orders – Perspectives of Evolution*. Berlin/Heidelberg: Springer. DOI: https://doi.org/10.1007/978-3-540-68572-2_8.

Petermann, T., Bradke, H., Lüllmann, A., Poetzsch, M., Riehm, U. (2010). *Gefährdung und Verletzbarkeit moderner Gesellschaften – am Beispiel eines großräumigen und langandauernden Ausfalls der Stromversorgung* [The endangerment and vulnerability of modern societies – using the example of a large-scale and long-lasting power outage]. Technology Assessment at the German Bundestag (TAB) report No. 141. Berlin: Office of TAB.

Peters, K.G. (2020). 'Südkoreas Strategie der radikalen Transparenz' [South Korea's strategy of radical transparency], *Der Spiegel*, 29 February. Available at: https:// www.spiegel.de/netzwelt/netzpolitik/covid-19-in-suedkorea-dem-virus-digital -auf-der-spur-a-50ef1096-ce69-465e-885c-bc77b3443feb.

Pfeifer, H. (2020). "'Pandemic populism': Germany sees rise in conspiracy theories', *Deutsche Welle*, 24 April. Available at: https://www.dw.com/en/pandemic-popul ism-germany-sees-rise-in-conspiracy-theories/a-53240063.

Pföstl, E. (2010). 'Tolerance Established by Law: The Autonomy of South Tyrol in Italy', *Libera Università S. Pio V*. Available at: https://www.semanticscholar.org/ paper/Tolerance-Established-by-Law%3A-The-Autonomy-of-South-Pf%C3%B6stl/ f665c59cdc5143d73aab12537f4de1c587437095.

Piatov, F. (2020a). 'Die Geheimen Regeln Fur Den Zweiten Lockdown: Merkel will Obergrenze für Corona-Infektionen' [The secret rules for the second lockdown: Merkel wants upper limit for corona infections], *Bild*, 5 May. Available at: https://www.bild.de/bild-plus/politik/inland/politik-inland/coronavirus-geheime-regeln-im-kanzleramt-fuer-moeglichen-neuen-lockdown-70453836,view=conversionToLogin.bild.html.

Piatov, F. (2020b). 'Fragwürdige Methoden – Drosten-Studie über ansteckende Kinder grob falsch' [Questionable Methods – Drosten Study of Infectious Children Grossly Wrong], *Bild*, 25 May. Available at: https://www.bild.de/ politik/inland/politik-inland/fragwuerdige-methoden-drosten-studie-ueber-ansteckende-kinder-grob-falsch-70862170.bild.html.

Piatov, F. (2020c). 'Was passiert, wenn Keine zweite Welle kommt?' [What will happen if there is no second wave?], *Bild*, 18 May. Available at: https://www.bild.de/politik/inland/wirtschaft/corona-was-passiert-wenn-keine-zweite-welle-kommt-70731640.bild.html.

Pierson, P. (2001). 'Post-Industrial Pressures on the Mature Welfare States' in Pierson, P. (ed.) *The new politics of the welfare state*, Oxford: Oxford University Press, pp. 80–105.

Poli, R. (2019a). *Handbook of Anticipation – Theoretical and Applied Aspects of the Use of Future in Decision Making*. Cham: Springer International. DOI: 10.1007/978-3-319-91554-8.

Poli, R. (2019b). *Working With the Future*. Milano: Bocconi University Press (BUP).

Politico (2020). 'How Europe is responding to the coronavirus pandemic', *Politico*, 13 March. Available at: https://www.politico.eu/article/how-europe-is-responding-to-the-coronavirus-pandemic/.

Popper, K. R. (2004). *Alles Leben ist Problemlösen – Über Erkenntnis, Geschichte und Politik* [All life is problem solving – about knowledge, history and politics]. 20th edn. Munich: Piper Taschenbuch.

Popper, R (n.d.). *Homepage*. Available at: https://rafaelpopper.wordpress.com/foresight-diamond/.

Popper, R. (2008a). 'Foresight Methodology' in Georghiou, L., Cassingena, J., Keenan, M., Miles, I., Popper, R. (eds.) *The Handbook of Technology Foresight*, Cheltenham: Edward Elgar, pp. 44–88.

Popper, R. (2008b). 'How are foresight methods selected?', *Foresight*, 10 (6), pp. 62–89. DOI: 10.1108/14636680810918586.

Post Growth Institute (n.d.). *About Post Growth*. Available at: http://postgrowth.org/learn/about-post-growth/.

Pouliakas, K. (2018). Automation risk in the EU labour market A skill-needs approach. Aberdeen: European Centre for the Development of Vocational Training (Cedefop). Available at: https://www.cedefop.europa.eu/files/automation_risk_in_the_eu_labour_market.pdf.

Presencing Institute (n.d.). *Home Page*. Available at: https://www.presencing.org/.

BIBLIOGRAPHIC REFERENCES

Press, C. (2020). 'The anatomy of a Pandemic – What have Scientists uncovered six months on?', *BBC*, 6 June. Available at: https://www.bbc.co.uk/news/extra/Qwh Ygq2Le3/anatomy-of-a-pandemic.

Prime Minister of Japan and his Cabinet (n.d.). *Innovation 25*. Available at: https://japan.kantei.go.jp/innovation/index_e.html.

Pring, C., Vrushi, J. (2019). *Global Corruption Barometer. Latin America and Caribbean 2019. Citizens' View and Experience of Corruption*. Berlin: Transparency International. https://www.transparency.org/en/gcb/latin-america/latin-america-and-the-caribb ean-x-edition-2019#.

Psnenner, R. (2020). 'Why resilience is not enough', *Eurac Research* Blog: Covid-19 *and Beyond*, 15 April. Available at: https://blogs.eurac.edu/covid-19/why-resilience-is -not-enough/.

Pueyo, T. (2020a). 'Coronavirus: the Hammer and the Dance', *Medium*, 19 March. Available at: https://medium.com/@tomaspueyo/coronavirus-the-hammer-and -the-dance-be9337092b56.

Pueyo, T. (2020b). To beat the Coronavirus, build a better fence', *The New York Times*, 14 September. https://www.nytimes.com/interactive/2020/09/14/opinion/politics/ coronavirus-close-borders-travel-quarantine.html.

Puglierin, J. (2020). 'Shared goals: How Germany's crisis response could strengthen Europe', *ECFR*, 28 April. Available at: https://ecfr.eu/article/commentary_shared _goals_how_germanys_crisis_response_could_strengthen_europ/.

Puntmann, V.O., Careri M. L., Wieters, I., Fahim, M., Arendt, C., Hoffmann, J., Shchendrygina, A., Escher, F., Vasa-Nicotera, M., Zeiher, A.M., Vehreschild, M., Nagel, E. (2020). 'Outcomes of Cardiovascular Magnetic Resonance Imaging in Patients Recently Recovered from Coronavirus Disease 2019 (Covid-19)'. *Jama Cardiol* (27 July). DOI: 10.1001/jamacardio.2020.3557.

Purdy, C. (2020). 'The Dutch want to make big economic reforms with a doughnut', *Quartz*, 9 April. Available at: https://qz.com/1835237/amsterdam-adopted-a-new -economic-model-for-life-after-covid-19/.

Qui Finanza (2020). 'Arrivano gli "Assistenti civici": chi sono e cosa faranno' ['The 'Civic Assistants' arrive: who they are and what they will do'], *Qui Finanza*, 24 May. Available at: https://quifinanza.it/info-utili/bando-assistenti-civici/386081/.

Raford, N. (2010). 'Drawing a better Panarchy Diagram', *Noah Raford – 21st Century Policy, Design*, 29 June. http://noahraford.com/?p=648.

RAI – Notizie Televideo (2020). 'OMS: La pandemia sarà 'molto lunga'', *Rai* 2 August.

Ralph, A. K. (2020). 'Religion as Private and Public Good', *Aspen Institute*, 14 April. Available at: https://www.aspeninstitute.org/blog-posts/religion-as-private-and -public-good/.

Rashid, H., Ridda, I., King, C., Begun, M., Tekin, H., Wood, J.G., Booy, R. (2015). 'Evidence compendium and advice on social distancing and other related measures for response to an influenza pandemic', *Paediatr. Respir Rev*, 16 (2, January), pp. 119–26. doi: 10.1016/j.prrv.2014.01.003.

Rauscher, H. (2020). 'Kurz: „Spitzfindigkeiten" oder Rechtsstaat?' [Kurz: "Quibbles" or the rule of law?], *Der Standard*, 8 April. Available at: https://www.derstandard.at/ story/2000116622381/kurz-spitzfindigkeiten-oder-rechtsstaat.

Raworth, K. (2018). *Doughnut Economics: Seven Ways to Think Like a 21st-Century Economist*. London: Random House Business Books.

Raworth, K. (n.d.): *What on Earth is the Doughnut?* ... https://www.monon.eu/en/engl ish-doughnut-economics/.

Redaktionsnetzwerk Deutschland (2020). 'Wegen Corona: Patienten mit anderen Krankheiten müssen sich häufig hinten anstellen' [Because of Corona: Patients with other diseases often have to wait in line], *Redaktionsnetzwerk Deutschland* (*RND*), 1 June. Available at: https://www.rnd.de/ gesundheit/wegen-corona -patienten-mit-anderen-krankheiten-mussen-sich-haufig-hinten-anstellen -BTVY3XWTS7U6D4R7DUWMZI7U6M.html.

Regan, H., George, S., Wagner, M., Macaya, M., Hayes, M., Rocha, V. & CNN (2020). 'July 13 coronavirus news', *CNN*, 13 July. Available at: https://edition.cnn.com/ world/live-news/coronavirus-pandemic-07-13-20-intl/h_a0d04b187f771ea035ef8b6d42d31ab5.

Reichelt, J. (2020). 'Sie gefährden die ganze Welt' [You are endangering the whole world], *Bild Online*, 16 April. Available at: https://m.bild.de/politik/ausland/politik -ausland/corona-krise-bild-chef-schreibt-an-chinas-staatschef-70087876.bildMob ile.html.

Reinhart, C., Reinhart, V. (2020). 'The Pandemic Depression. The Global Economy Will Never Be the Same'. *Foreign Affairs,* September/October 2020. Available at: https://www.foreignaffairs.com/ articles/united-states/2020-08-06/coronavirus -depression-global-economy?utm_medium=promo_email&utm_source=pre _release&utm_campaign=mktg_reguser_reinhart_pandemic_depression&utm _content=20200806&utm_term=registrant-prerelease.

Reiss, K. & Bhakdi, S. (2020). *Corona, False Alarm?: Facts and Figures*. Vermont: Chelsea Green Publishing Co.

Reivic, K. & Shatté, A. (2003). *The Resilience Factor – 7 Keys to Finding Your Inner Strength and Overcoming Life's Hurdles*. New York: Harmony Books.

Resalliance (n.d. a). *Adaptive Cycle*. https://www.resalliance.org/adaptive-cycle.

Resalliance (n.d. b). *Panarchy*. https://www.resalliance.org/panarchy.

Research and Markets (2020). 'Global Online Education Market Worth $319+ Billion by 2025 – North America Anticipated to Provide the Highest Revenue Generating Opportunities', *GlobeNewswire*, 16 April. Available at: https://www.globenewswire .com/news-release/2020/04/16/2017102/0/en/Global-Online-Education-Market -Worth-319-Billion-by-2025-North-America-Anticipated-to-Provide-the-Highest -Revenue-Generating-Opportunities.html.

BIBLIOGRAPHIC REFERENCES 409

Rettman, A. (2020). 'Nine EU states close borders due to virus', *Euobserver*, 16 March. Available at: https://euobserver.com/coronavirus/147742.

Reuters (2020). 'WHO – China hat Hunderttausende Infektionen verhindert' [China has prevented hundrets of thousands of infections], *Reuters*, 24 February. Available at: https://de.reuters.com/article/virus-who-idDEKCN20I1GH.

Reuters, Landau, N. (2020). 'After Iran's Khameini Compares Zionism to Coronavirus, Netanyahu and Gantz Issue Warnings', *Haaretz*, 22 May. Available at: https://www.haaretz.com/middle-east-news/iran/iran-s-khameini-compares-zionism-to-coronavirus-urges-palestinians-to-resist-1.8865343.

Richter, F., Hoffmann, B. (2020). 'Coronavirus: Warum die Aussagen von Wolfgang Wodarg wenig mit Wissenschaft zu tun haben' [Coronavirus: Why Wolfgang Wodarg's statements have little to do with science], *Correctiv*, 18 March. Available at: https://correctiv.org/faktencheck/hintergrund/2020/03/18/coronavirus-warum-die-aussagen-von-wolfgang-wodarg-wenig-mit-wissenschaft-zu-tun-haben.

Riker, W.J. (2011). 'Compatriot Partiality Thesis' in Chatterjee D.K. (Ed.) *Encyclopedia of Global Justice*. Dordrecht: Springer. DOI: //doi.org/10.1007/978-1-4020-9160-5.

Rinke, M. (2020). 'Am Ende müssen alle Experten in die Irrenanstalt – bis auf einen' [In the end, all experts have to go to the lunatic asylum – except for one], *Der Tagesspiegel*, 3 June. Available at: https://www.tagesspiegel.de/kultur/die-virologen-frei-nach-duerrenmatt-am-ende-muessen-alle-experten-in-die-irrenanstalt-bis-auf-einen/25880738.html.

Roberts, C. (2020). 'Making GDP the focus of a post-coronavirus economy would be a mistake', *The Guardian*, 3 June. Available at: https://www.theguardian.com/commentisfree/2020/jun/03/post-coronavirus-economy-gdp-growth-green-economy-million-jobs.

Roberts, M. (2020). 'Coronavirus: Europe experiencing 'pandemic fatigue'', BBC, 6 October. Available at: https://www.bbc.com/news/health-54417547.

Rohwer-Kahlmann, M. (2020). 'Will the coronavirus change the way we work from home?', *Deutsche Welle*, 20 March. Available at: https://www.dw.com/en/will-the-coronavirus-change-the-way-we-work-from-home/a-52853147.

Roose, K. (2019). 'Trump Rolls Out the Red Carpet for Right-Wing Social Media Trolls', *The New York Times*, 10 July. Available at: https://www.nytimes.com/2019/07/10/business/trump-social-media-summit.html?auth=login-facebook.

Roser M., Ritchie, H., Ortiz-Ospina, E., Beltekian, D., Mathieu, E., Hasell, J., Macdonald, B., Giattino, C. (2020). 'Coronavirus Pandemic (Covid-19)', *OurWorldInData.org*. Available at: https://ourworldindata.org/coronavirus.

Roser, M., Ortiz-Ospina, E. (2016), 'Global Education', *OurWorldInData.org*. Available at: https://ourworldindata.org/global-education.

Rotschild, M. (2020). 'Who is QAnon, the internet's most mysterious poster?', *Daily Dot*, 23 June. Available at: https://www.dailydot.com/debug/who-is-q-anon/.

Rowlatt, J. (2020). 'How coronavirus is driving a revolution in travel', *BBC*, 16 May. Available at: https://www.bbc.com/news/science-environment-52689372.

Rozsa, M. (2019). 'QAnon is the conspiracy theory that won't die: Here's what they believe, and why they're wrong', *Salon*, 18 August. Available at: https://www.salon .com/2019/08/18/qanon-is-the-conspiracy-theory-that-wont-die-heres-what-they -believe-and-why-theyre-wrong/.

RP Online (2020). 'Weltweit 292.000 Fälle binnen 24 Stunden: WHO meldet wieder Rekord bei Corona-Neuinfektionen' [Worldwide 292,000 cases within 24 hours: WHO reports record number of new corona infections], *RP Online*, 31 July. Available at: https://rp-online.de/panorama/coronavirus/who-rekord-bei-neuinfe ktionen-weltweit-292000-faelle-binnen-24-stunden_aid-52532873.

Röpcke, J. (2020a). 'Dresdner JazzFestival-Chef Behauptet: Kultur stärkt „Immunabwehr gegen Corona"' [Dresden jazz festival boss Claims: culture strengthens "immune defence against Corona"], *Bild*, 27 October. Available at: https://www.bild.de/poli tik/inland/politik-inland/dresdener-jazzfestival-chef-behauptet-kultur-staerkt -immunabwehr-gegen-corona-73614944.bild.html.

Röpcke, J. (2020b). 'Kritik an Jazzfestival in Dresden „Völlig unethischer Menschenversuch"' [Criticism of Jazz festival in Dresden "completely unethical human experiment"], *Bild*, 26 October. Available at: https://www.bild.de/politik/ inland/politik-inland/corona-hammer-freiwillige-infektionsgruppen-bei-jazz-festi val-73600166.bild.html.

SadAndUseless (2020). 'Just In Time For Coronavirus: Doorknob Licking Trend In Japan', *SadAndUseless.com*, March. Available at: https://www.sadanduseless.com/ tasty-doorknobs/.

Saunders-Hastings P.R., Krewski D. (2016). 'Reviewing the history of pandemic influenza: understanding patterns of emergence and transmission', *Pathogens*, 5(4, December), P. 66. DOI: 10.3390/pathogens5040066 .

Savage, M. (2020). 'Did Sweden's coronavirus strategy succeed or fail?', *BBC*, 23 July. Available at: https://www.bbc.com/news/world-europe-53498133.

Savulescu, J., Bostrom, N. (2009). *Human Enhancement*. Oxford: Oxford University Press.

Schäfer, J.W. (2020). 'Experte Rechnet vor: Corona-Lockdown kostet uns 3,8 Mio. Lebensjahre' [Expert calculates: Corona Lockdown costs US 3.8 million years of life], Bild, 23 October. Available at: https://www.bild.de/ bild-plus/politik/inland/politik -inland/experte-rechnet-vor-corona-lockdown-kostet-uns-3-7-mio-lebensjahre -73565552,view=conversionToLogin.bild.html.

Schäpke, N., Singer-Brodowski, M., Stelzer, F., Bergmann, M., Lang D.J. (2015). Creating Space for Change: Real-world Laboratories for Sustainability Transformations. The Case of Baden-Württemberg, *GAIA* 24 (4), pp. 281–283.

Scharmer, C.O. (1995). *Reflexive Modernisierung des Kapitalismus als Revolution von innen: auf der Suche nach Infrastrukturen für eine lernende Gesellschaft; dialogische*

BIBLIOGRAPHIC REFERENCES

Neugründung von Wissenschaft, Wirtschaft und Politik [Reflexive modernisation of capitalism as a revolution from within: in search of infrastructures for a learning society; dialogue-based refoundation of science, business and politics]. Stuttgart: M & P Verlag für Wissenschaft und Forschung.

Scharmer, C.O., Käufer, K. (2008). 'Führung vor der leeren Leinwand. Presencing als soziale Technik' [Guided tour in front of the blank canvas. Presencing as a social technique], *Zeitschrift Organisations Entwicklung*, 2, pp. 4–11. Düsseldorf: Handelsblatt Fachmedien, ISSN 0724-6110, ZDB-ID 625692-2.

Scharmer, C.O. (2009). *Theory U: Leading from the Future as It Emerges*. Oakland: Berrett-Koehler Publishers.

Scheidel, W. (2020). 'Past pandemics redistributed income between the rich and poor, according to Stanford historian'. Interviewed by Melissa de Witte for *Stanford News*, 30 April. Available at: https://news.stanford.edu/2020/04/30/pandemics-catalyze -social-economic-change/.

Schelling, T. (1978). *Micromotives and Macrobehavior*. New York: Norton.

Schneewind, J.B. (2020). 'Kantian Unsocial Sociability: Good Out of Evil' in Schneewind, J.B. *Essays on the History of Moral Philosophy*. Oxford: Oxford University Press/ Oxford Scholarship Online. DOI:10.1093/acprof:oso/9780199563012.003.0017.

Schneidewind, U. (2011). 'Auf dem Weg in die resiliente Gesellschaft' [On the way to a resilient society], *Berliner Republik*, May. http://www.b-republik.de/aktuelle-ausg abe/auf-dem-weg-in-die-resiliente-gesellschaft.

Schneidewind, U. (2014). 'Urbane Reallabore – ein Blick in die aktuelle Forschungswerkstatt' [Urban real laboratories – a look at the current research workshop], *pnd-online*, January. Available at: https://d-nb.info/1064498248/34.

Schneidewind, U., Singer-Brodowski, M. (2013). *Transformative Wissenschaft – Klimawandel im deutschen Wissenschafts- und Hochschulsystem* [Transformative Science – Climate Change in the German Science and University System]. Marburg: Metropolis Verlag.

Schnur, O. (2013). 'Resiliente Quartiersentwicklung? Eine Annäherung über das Panarchie-Modell adaptiver Zyklen' [Resilient district development? An approximation using the panarchy model of adaptive cycles], *Informationen zur Raumentwicklung*, 4 (January), pp. 337 – 350.

Schoichet, C.E., Jones, A. (2020). 'Coronavirus is making some people rethink where they want to live', *CNN*, 2 May. Available at: https://edition.cnn.com/2020/05/02/us/ cities-population-coronavirus/index.html.

Schröder, H. (2020a). 'Die Macht der Diskurse und der Kultur: Ein Interview mit Hartmut Schröder' [The power of discourse and culture: An interview with Hartmut Schröder]. Interviewed by Walder M., Isetti, G. for *Eurac Research Blog: Covid-19 And Beyond*, 30 July. Available at: https://blogs.eurac.edu/covid-19/die-macht-der-disku rse-interview-hartmut-schroeder/.

Schröder, H. (2020b). 'One health. Die Corona-Krise als ökologisches Problem?' [One health. The corona crisis as an ecological problem?], *Senate – Magazin für Politik, Gesellschaft und Ökosoziale Marktwirtschaft* [Senate – magazine for politics, society and eco-social market economy], 1 (August). Berlin: Senats der Wirtschaft Berlin, p. 38–43. Also available at: http://www.senat-magazin.de/SENATE_20-1/mobile/index.html#p=1.

Schröder, M., Schröder, H. (2020). *Heilung: Was wir verlieren, was wir gewinnen. Ein Essay* [Healing: What we lose, what we gain. An Essay]. Schriftenreihe: Die Pandemie, Band 1, Geisenheim: Remedium Verlag. Also available at: https://www.remedium-verlag.de/buecher/die-pandemie-heilung/.

Schultz, S. (2014). 'Ethik der Share Economy – Anleitung für den Uber-Menschen' [Ethics of the Share Economy – Guide for the Uber Man], *Der Spiegel*, 2 September. Available at: https://www.spiegel.de/wirtschaft/soziales/uber-und-airbnb-ethik-der-share-economy-a-988612.html.

Schultz, S. (2016). 'Milliardenverlust bei Uber – Das Übel des Knopfdruck-Kapitalismus' [Billions lost at Uber – the evil of push-button capitalism], *Der Spiegel*, 26 August. Available at: https://www.spiegel.de/wirtschaft/unternehmen/uber-deshalb-verbrennt-das-unternehmen-milliarden-a-1109596.html.

Schultz, S. (2020). 'Die neue digitale Elite' [The new digital elite], *Der Spiegel*, 11 April. Available at: https://www.spiegel.de/netzwelt/web/corona-krise-und-ihre-folgen-die-neue-digitale-elite-a-f704f9cb-b32a-48db-99ee-32c7d9b69827.

Schumpeter, J. (2006). *Theorie der wirtschaftlichen Entwicklung* [Economic development theory]. Reprint of the 1st edition from 1912. Edited by Röpke J., Stiller, O. Berlin: Duncker & Humblot.

Scuttari, A., Corradini, P. (2018). 'Multidisciplinary approaches to resilience in tourism destination studies' in Innherhofer, E., Fontanari, M., Pechlaner, H. (eds.) *Destination Resilience -Challenges and Opportunities for Destination Management and Governance*. London: Routledge. DOI:https://doi.org/10.4324/9780203701904.

Senge, P. (1990). *The Fifth Discipline: The art and practice of the learning organization.* New York: Doubleday.

Senzel, H. (2020). 'Was Singapur im Corona-Kampf anders macht' [What Singapore is doing differently in the Corona fight], *Tagesschau*, 16 March. Available at: https://www.tagesschau.de/ausland/singapur-coronakrise-101.html?utm_source=pocket-newtab.

Shallhorn, K. (2020). 'What is QAnon, the conspiracy theory group showing up to Trump rallies?', *Fox News*, 17 February. Available at: https://www.foxnews.com/politics/what-is-qanon-the-conspiracy-theory-group-showing-up-to-trump-rallies.

Shapiro, J. (2020). 'The corona election: How Trump might use the pandemic to win', *European Council on Foreign Relations*, 27 April. Available at: https://www.ecfr.eu/article/commentary_the_corona_election_how_trump_might_use_the_pandemic_to_win.

BIBLIOGRAPHIC REFERENCES

Sheahen, A. (2012). *Basic Income Guarantee: Your Right to Economic Security.* New York: Palgrave Macmillan.

Shell (2017). *World Energy Model – A View to 2100.* Shell International BV. Available at: https://www.shell.com/energy-and-innovation/the-energy-future/scenarios/shell-scenarios-energy-models/world-energy-model.html.

Shulz, B. (2020). 'Völlig unvorbereitet in die Epidemie' [Completely unprepared for the epidemic], *Zeit Online*, 28 March. Available at: https://www.zeit.de/politik/ausl and/2020-03/grossbritannien-coronavirus-boris-johnson-prince-charles-gesund heitssystem-beatmungsgeraete?utm_source=pocket-newtab.

Sibeon, R. (2004). *Rethinking Social Theory.* London: Sage Publications.

Stieb, M. (2020). 'Texas Lt. Gov. Dan Patrick: 'Lots of Grandparents' Willing to Die to Save Economy for Grandchildren', *Intelligencer*, 23 March. Available at: https://nymag.com/intelligencer/2020/03/dan-patrick-seniors-are-willing-to-die-to-save-economy.html.

Silva, C. (2020). 'China, South Korea, Taiwan sending masks and medical staff to other countries in need', *NBC NEWS*, 21 March. Available at: https://www.nbcnews.com/news/asian-america/china-south-korea-taiwan-sending-masks-medical-staff-other-countries-n1163766.

Simpol (n.d.). *Solve Global Problems.* Available at: https://simpol.org/what-we-do/solve-global-problems.

Singer, N. (2020). 'Employers Rush to Adopt Virus Screening. The Tools May Not Help Much. Symptom-checking apps and fever-screening cameras promise to keep sick workers at home and hinder the virus. But experts warn they can be inaccurate and violate privacy'. *The New York Times*, 11 May. Available at: https://www.nytimes.com/2020/05/11/technology/coronavirus-worker-testing-privacy.html?action=click&module=Top%20Stories&pgtype=Homepage.

Smith, D. (2020). 'Covid White House hot spot, vaccine progress, flu season fears: Coronavirus pandemic update', *CNET*, 5 October. Available at: https://www.cnet.com/how-to/covid-white-house-hot-spot-vaccine-progress-flu-season-fears-coronavirus-pandemic-update/.

Smith, P. (1994). *Explaining* Chaos. Cambridge: Cambridge University Press.

Snowden, D. (2000). 'Cynefin: a sense of time and space, the social ecology of knowledge management' in Despres, C., Chauvel, D. (eds.) *Knowledge Horizons: The Present and the Promise of Knowledge Management.* Oxford: Butterworth-Heinemann.

Snowden, D., Boone, M. (2007). 'A Leader's Framework for Decision Making', *Harvard Business Review*, 85 (11, November), pp. 69–76.

Sönnichsen, A. (2020). 'Covid-19: Wo ist die Evidenz?' [Covid-19: Where is the evidence?], *Deutsches Netzwerk Evidenzbasierte Medizin e.V.*, 8 September. Available at: https://www.ebm-netzwerk.de/de/veroeffentlichungen/covid-19.

Sorgner, S.L. (2018). *Schöner neuer Mensch* [Brave New Man]. Berlin: Nicolai Publishing & Intelligence.

Soros, G. (2020). 'The crisis of a lifetime' interviewed by Gregor Peter for *European Council on Foreign Affairs*, 12 May. Available at: https://www.ecfr.eu/article/commentary_the_crisis_of_a_lifetime.

South Tyrol (n.d.). *Homepage* [website] Available at: http://www.provinz.bz.it/this-is-south-tyrol/#accept-cookies.

Spacey, J. (2020). '10 Examples of Tacit Knowledge', *Simplicable*, 13 February. Available at: https://management.simplicable.com/management/new/10-examples-of-tacit-knowledge.

Spiral Dynamics Integral (n.d.). *Startseite* [home]. Available at: http://spiraldynamics-integral.de/.

Spurk, J. (2020). 'The World Before and After the Corona Crisis', *Global-e Series: Re-globalization*, 13 (36, June). Available at: https://www.21global.ucsb.edu/global-e/june-2020/world-and-after-corona-crisis.

Sritzel, B., Piatov, F., Ropcke, J. (2020). 'Coronoa-Versagen! Krisen-Saustall WHO' [Corona failure! Crisis pigsty WHO], *Bild*, 9 April. Available at: https://www.bild.de/politik/ausland/politik-ausland/corona-versagen-krisen-saustall-who-69940790.bild.html.

Stasavage, D. (2020). 'Covid-19 has exposed the weakness of America's federal government', *CNN*, 1 July. Available at: https://edition.cnn.com/2020/07/01/opinions/covid-19-america-federal-government-stasavage/index.html.

Statt, N. (2020). 'Amazon is expanding its cashierless Go model into a full-blown grocery store', *The Verge*, 25 February. Available at: https://www.theverge.com/2020/2/25/21151021/amazon-go-grocery-store-expansion-open-seattle-cashier-less.

Stauder, J. (2020). 'Covid-19 zeigt: An Grundlagenforschung zu sparen, können wir uns nicht leisten' [Covid-19 shows: We cannot afford to save on basic research], *Eurac Research Blog: Covid-19 and Beyond*, 23 April. Available at: https://blogs.eurac.edu/covid-19/grundlagenforschung/.

Steiermark.ORF.at (2020). 'CoV: Maturazeugnisse vom Roboter' [CoV: Matura certificates from the robot], *steirmark.ORF.at*, 26 June. Available at: https://steiermark.orf.at/stories/3054956/.

Steininger, K.W., Bednar-Friedl, B., Knittel, N., Kirchengast G., Nabernegg, S., Williges, K., Mestel, R., Hutter, H.-P., Kenner, L. (2020). *Klimapolitik in Österreich: Innovationschance Coronakrise und die Kosten des Nicht-Handelns* [Climate policy in Austria: Corona crisis as an innovation opportunity and the costs of inaction], Wegener Center Research Briefs, 1 (June). Graz: Wegener Center Verlag, Universität Graz.

Steinschaden, J. (2020). '14 Tech-Trends, die das Post-Corona-Zeitalter prägen werden' [14 tech trends that will shape the post-corona era], *Trending Topics*, 24 April. Available at: https://www.trendingtopics.at/digital-trends-post-corona-2020/.

BIBLIOGRAPHIC REFERENCES

Stieb, M. (2020). 'Texas Lt. Gov. Dan Patrick: "Lots of Grandparents" Willing to Die to Save Economy for Grandchildren', *Intelligencer*, 23 March. Available at: https://nymag.com/intelligencer/2020/03/dan-patrick-seniors-are-willing-to-die-to-save-economy.html.

Stiglitz, J.E., Shiller, R.J., Gopinath, G., Reinhart, C.M., Posen, A., Prasad, E., Tooze, A., D'Andrea Tyson, L., Mahbubani, K. (2020). 'How the Economy Will Look After the Coronavirus Pandemic', *Foreign Policy*, 15 April. Available at: https://foreignpolicy.com/2020/04/15/how-the-economy-will-look-after-the-coronavirus-pandemic/.

Strachan, G. (2009). 'Systems Thinking: the ability to recognize and analyse the interconnections within and between systems', in Stibben, A. (Ed.) *The Handbook of Sustainability Literacy*. Foxhole: Green Book ldt. Also available at: http://arts.brighton.ac.uk/stibbe-handbook-of-sustainability/chapters/systems-thinking.

Streeck, H. (2020). 'Hendrik Streeck 'Virologe spricht von Corona-„Dauerwelle"' [Hendrik Streeck, Virologist speaks of Corona 'perm']. Interview for *Bild*, 28 June. Available at: https://www.bild.de/politik/inland/politik-inland/hendrik-streeck-top-virologe-spricht-von-corona-dauerwelle-71553384.bild.html.

Stuenkel, O. (2015). 'China and the Rise of Competing Modernities'. Review of *When China Rules the World. The Rise of the Middle Kingdom and the End of the Western World*, by Martin Jacques (2012). London: Penguin. *Oliver Stuenkel*, 29 March. Available at: https://www.postwesternworld.com/2015/03/29/china-competing-modernities/.

Subran, L. (2020). 'Ökonom: Corona-Krise schafft den starken Staat – und er wird seinen Einfluss nutzen' [Economist: Corona crisis creates a strong state – and it will use its influence], *Online Focus*, 10 April. Available at: https://www.focus.de/finanzen/boerse/experten/gastbeitrag-von-allianz-chefvolkswirt-subran-die-welt-nach-corona-schwacher-starker-staat-oder-starker-schwacher-staat_id_11867142.html.

Südtirol News (2020a). 'Bürgerprotest gegen Migrantenankünfte auf Lampedusa' [Citizens' protest against migrant arrivals on Lampedusa], *Südtirol News*, 27 July. Available at: https://www.suedtirolnews.it/italien/buergerprotest-gegen-migrantenankuenfte-auf-lampedusa.

Südtirol News (2020b). 'Hollywoodstar Sharon Stone lobt Männer in Corona-Krise' [Hollywood star Sharon Stone praises men in the Corona crisis], *Südtirol News*, 13 May. Available at: https://www.suedtirolnews.it/unterhaltung/leute/hollywoodstar-sharon-stone-lobt-maenner-in-corona-krise.

Südtirol News (2020c). 'Immer weniger Obduktionen in Österreich – Gerichtsmediziner warnt: Morde bleiben oft unentdeck' [Fewer and fewer autopsies in Austria – coroner warns: murders often go undetected], *Südtirol News*, 10 May. Available at: https://www.suedtirolnews.it/chronik/gerichtsmediziner-warnt-morde-bleiben-oft-unentdeckt.

Südtirol News (2020d). 'Italien testet 150.000 auf Antikörper' [Italy tests 150,000 for antibodies], *Südtirol News*, 25 May. Available at: https://www.suedtirolnews.it/ital ien/italien-startet-corona-antikoerper-tests-bei-150-000-personen.

Südtirol News (2020e). 'Starke Einschränkungen für Party-Touristen auf Mallorca' [Strong restrictions for party tourists on Mallorca], *Südtirol News*, June 04. Available at: https://www.suedtirolnews.it/wirtschaft/starke-einschraenkungen-fuer-party-touristen-auf-mallorca.

Südtirol Online (2020). 'G20-Staaten erwägen Verlängerung des Schuldenmoratoriums wegen Corona' [G20 countries are considering extending the debt moratorium due to Corona], *Südtirol Online*, 19 July. Available at: https://www.stol.it/artikel/wirtsch aft/g20-staaten-erwaegen-verlaengerung-des-schuldenmoratoriums-wegen-corona.

Sudworth, J. (2020). 'Wuhan: City of silence. Looking for answers in the place where coronavirus started', *BBC*, July. Available at: https://www.bbc.co.uk/news/extra/ews u2giezk/city-of-silence-china-wuhan.

Surowiecki, J. (2004). *The wisdom of crowds. Why the many are smarter than the few and how collective wisdom shapes business, economies, societies and nations*. New York: Doubleday.

SWR (2020). 'Entwicklungsminister Müller fordert Abkehr vom Turbo-Kapitalismus' [Development Minister Müller calls for turning away from turbo-capitalism], *SWR*, 3 May. Available at: https://www.swr.de/swraktuell/mueller-kapitalismus-100.html.

Taleb, N. (2008). *The Black Swan: The Impact of the Highly Improbable*. London: Penguin.

Tambur, S. (2020). 'Addressing the coronavirus crisis like the Estonian startup community', *Estonian World*, 19 March. Available at: https://estonianworld.com/technol ogy/addressing-the-coronavirus-crisis-like-the-estonian-startup-community/.

Tan, Y. (2020). 'Covid-19 Singapore: A 'pandemic of inequality' exposed', *BBC News*, 18 September. Available at: https://www.bbc.com/news/world-asia-54082861.

Tappe, A. (2020). '30 million Americans have filed initial unemployment claims since mid-March', *CNN*, 30 April. Available at: https://edition.cnn.com/2020/04/30/ economy/unemployment-benefits-coronavirus/index.html?bt_ee= DK0bKzrj7G25ijHzvGdycuoZ28WE%2BdVVGF4%2FpSYvwKUkpgMiwuKmerqd W9EEhA %2FE&bt_ts=1588678973130.

Telebasel Schweiz & Welt (2020). 'Neue Steuern für Corona-Wiederaufbau? Plan der EU-Kommission erwartet' [New taxes for corona reconstruction? EU Commission plan expected], *Telebasel Schweiz & Welt*, 26 May. Available at: https://telebasel .ch/2020/05/26/neue-steuern-fuer-corona-wiederaufbau-plan-der-eu-kommiss ion-erwartet/?channel=105105.

Tensley, B. (2020). 'Coronavirus, face masks and America's new fault line', *CNN*, 5 May. Available at: https://edition.cnn.com/2020/05/04/politics/coronavirus-face-masks -new-fault-line-trnd/index.html.

BIBLIOGRAPHIC REFERENCES

Terra News (2020). 'Kazakhstan uses drones to patrol capital city during Covid-19 lockdown', *Terra Drone*, 9 April. Available at: https://www.terra-drone.net/global/2020/04/09/kazakhstan-drones-patrol-coronavirus-covid-19-lockdown/.

The City of Stillwater Oklahoma (2020). 'Emergency proclamation amended', *Stillwater News*, 1 May. Available at: http://stillwater.org/news/view/id/567.

The Economic Times (2020). 'Estimates suggest much deeper global downturn due to coronavirus pandemic than Great Recession: World Bank', *The Economic Times*, 17 April. Available at: https://economictimes.indiatimes.com/news/international/business/estimates-suggest-much-deeper-global-downturn-due-to-coronavirus-pandemic-than-great-recession-world-bank/articleshow/75208233.cms?from=mdr.

The Economist Intelligence Unit (EIU) (2020). 'Quality of OECD countries' response to the pandemic', *The Economist*, 17 July. Available at: https://www.eiu.com/n/quality-of-oecd-countries-response-to-the-pandemic/.

The Guardian (2020). 'Coronavirus: anger in Germany at report Trump seeking exclusive vaccine deal', *The Guardian*, 16 March. Available at: https://www.theguardian.com/world/2020/mar/16/not-for-sale-anger-in-germany-at-report-trump-seeking-exclusive-coronavirus-vaccine-deal.

The Japan Times (2020). 'Wuhan lab had three live bat coronaviruses, but none matched Covid-19', *The Japan Times*, 24 May. Available at: https://www.japantimes.co.jp/ news/2020/05/24/asia-pacific/science-health-asia-pacific/wuhan-lab-three-bat-coronaviruses-china/#.Xu-HNfLgo_U.

The Millennium Project (1996). *15 Global Challenges*. Available at: http://www.millennium-project.org/projects/challenges/.

The New York Times (2020). 'New Coronavirus cases in U.S. soar past 68,000, shattering record', *The New York Times*, 10 July. Available at: https://www.nytimes.com/2020/07/10/world/coronavirus-updates.html.

The Sofia Globe (2014). 'Valedictory speech by outgoing European Commission President Barroso', *The Sofia Globe*, 21 October. Available at: https://sofiaglobe.com/2014/10/21/valedictory-speech-by-outgoing-european-commission-president-barroso/.

The Times of India (2020). 'Coronavirus Challenge on TikTok: Video maker infected after licking public toilet seat', *The Times of India*, 28 March. Available at: https://timesofindia.indiatimes.com/gadgets-news/coronavirus-challenge-on-tiktok-video-maker-infected-after-licking-public-toilet-seat/articleshow/74839613.cms.

The Washington Post (2020). 'Why 'choosing' between the elderly and the economy is a phony, barbaric choice', *The Washington Post*, 27 March. https://www.washingtonpost.com/opinions/risking-millions-of-lives-to-save-the-economy-is-a-terrible-idea/2020/03/27/f4726236-6fa4-11ea-aa80-c2470c6b2034_story.html.

Tidey, A. (2020). 'Coronavirus in Europe: Tourism sector 'hardest hit' by Covid-19', *Euronews*, 16 April. Available at: https://www.euronews.com/2020/04/16/coronavirus-in-europe-tourism-sector-hardest-hit-by-covid-19.

Tondo, L. (2020). 'Mafia distributes food to Italy's struggling residents', *The Guardian*, 10 April. Available at: https://www.theguardian.com/world/2020/apr/10/mafia-distributes-food-to-italys-struggling-residents.

Torben M.A, Holmström, B., Honkapohja, S., Korkman, S., Söderström H.T., Vartiainen, J. (2007). *The Nordic Model. Embracing globalization and sharing risks*, The Research Institute of the Finnish Economy (ETLA), 232, (December). Helsinki: Taloustieto Oy.

t-online dpa (2021). 'Warum diese Nationen als Corona-Musterländer gelten' [Why these nations are considered Corona model countries], *t-online*. 05 August. Available at: https://www.t-online.de/nachrichten/panorama/id_90571514/schweiz-und-norwegen-warum-diese-nationen-als-corona-musterlaender-gelten-.html.

TPT Bureau Agencies (2020). 'Artificial Intelligence: Why Journalism Needs to be Human- Centric?', *The Policy Times*, 3 June. Available at: https://thepolicytimes.com/artificial-intelligence-why-journalism-needs-to-be-human-centric/.

Traegardh, L. (2007). *State And Civil Society in Northern Europe: The Swedish Model Reconsidered*. New York: Berghahn Books.

Transition Network (n.d.). *Homepage*. Available at: http://www.transitionnetwork.org/initiatives.

Transparency International (2019). *Corruption Perception Index*. Available at: http://cpi.transparency.org/cpi2011/results/.

Treehugger (n.d.). *Economics*. Available at: https://www.treehugger.com/economics-4846045.

Trend Watching (2020). WHERE NEXT? 10 CROSS-INDUSTRY TRENDS THAT ARE ACCELERATING BY THE Covid-CRISIS, *Trend Watching*. Available at: https://info.trendwatching.com/10-trends-for-a-post-coronavirus-world.

Tshidimba, D., Lateur, F., Sneyers, N. (2015). *Frugal Products*. Brussels: Roland Berger Strategy Consultants. Available at: https://www.rolandberger.com/en/Publications/Frugal-Products.html.

Tufekci, Z., Howard, J. & Greenhalgh, T. (2020). 'The Real Reason to Wear a Mask', *The Atlantic*, 22 April. Available at: https://www.theatlantic.com/health/archive/2020/04/dont-wear-mask-yourself/610336/.

Tusaie, K. & Dyer, J. (2004). Resilience: A historical review of the construct, *Holistic Nursing Practice*, 18 (1), January, pp 3–10. DOI: 10.1097/00004650-200401000-00002.

U.S. Department of Defense (2002). *DoD News Briefing – Secretary Rumsfeld and Gen. Myers. Presenter: Secretary of Defense Donald H. Rumsfeld*, 12 February. Available at: http://archive.defense.gov/Transcripts/Transcript.aspx?TranscriptID=2636.

U.S. House Committee On The Judiciary (2020). 'July 27th: Hearing on "Online Platforms and Market Power, Part 6: Examining the Dominance of Amazon, Facebook, Google

BIBLIOGRAPHIC REFERENCES

and Apple"' [Press Release]. 6 July. Available at: https://judiciary.house.gov/news/documentsingle.aspx?DocumentID=3114.

UN DESA (2020). 'The long-term impact of Covid-19 on poverty', *UN/DESA Policy Brief #86*, 15 October 2020. Available at: https://www.un.org/development/desa/dpad/publication/un-desa-policy-brief-86-the-long-term-impact-of-covid-19-on-poverty/.

UN News (2020). 'Global partners require $31 billion to speed up Covid-19 medicines for all', *United Nations*, 26 June. Available at: https://news.un.org/en/story/2020/06/1067282.

UN Secretary-General / UN Sustainable Development Group (2020). *Policy brief: the impact of Covid-19 on children.* Available at: https://reliefweb.int/report/world/policy-brief-impact-covid-19-children.

UNESCO (2019). *Global Futures Literacy Design Forum.* Available at: https://en.unesco.org/events/global-futures-literacy-design-forum.

UNESCO (2020). *Global Education Coalition #LearningNeverStops.* Available at: https://en.unesco.org/covid19/educationresponse/globalcoalition.

United Nations (2020). 'A New Era of Conflict and Violence', *United Nations.* Available at: https://www.un.org/en/un75/new-era-conflict-and-violence.

University Hospital Halle (Saale) & Medical Faculty of Martin Luther University Halle-Wittenberg (2020). *Was ist RESTART-19?* [What is RESTART-19?]. Available at: https://restart19.de/das-projekt/.

University of Aberdeen, Centre for Citizenship. Civil Society & Rule of Law (CISRUL) (2020). *Workshop: Beyond the Populist Hype. January 14–15, 2021.* Available at: https://cisrul.blog/seminarsandevents/beyond-the-populist-hype/.

University of Trento (2019). *First International Symposium of UNESCO Chairs in Anticipatory Systems, Futures Studies and Futures Literacy.* Available at: https://webmagazine.unitn.it/en/evento/sociologia/58253/first-international-symposium-of-unesco-chairs-in-anticipatory-systems.

Universität Passau (n.d.). *Multi-Resilience.* Available at:https://www.uni-passau.de/forschung/forschungsprojekte/multi-resilience/.

Uscinski, J.E., Enders, A.M., Klofstad, C.A., Seelig, M.I., Funchion, J.R., Everett, C., Wuchty, S., Premaratne, K., Murthi, M.N. (2020). 'Why do people believe Covid-19 conspiracy theories?', *The Harvard Kennedy School (HKS) Misinformation Review*, 28 April. Available at: https://doi.org/10.37016/mr-2020-015.

Uwiringiyimana, C. (2020). 'Rwanda uses drones to help catch lockdown transgressors', *Reuters*, 17 April. Available at: https://www.reuters.com/article/us-health-coronavirus-rwanda-drones/rwanda-uses-drones-to-help-catch-lockdown-transgressors-idUSKBN21Z217.

Van Til, F. (2020). 'Three scenarios for globalisation in a post-covid-19 world', *Clingendael Spectator*, 1 April. Available at: https://spectator.clingendael.org/nl/publicatie/three-scenarios-globalisation-post-covid-19-world.

Vanderklippe, N. (2020). "Stay away from here': In China, foreigners have become a target for coronavirus discrimination', *The Globe and Mail*, 9 April. Available at: https://www.theglobeandmail.com/world/article-stay-away-from-here-in-china-foreigners-have-become-a-target-for/.

Vargas Llosa, M. (2020). 'Nobelpreisträger Mario Vargas Llosa: «Freiheit ist eine Kraftquelle für den Kampf gegen das Virus»' [Nobel Prize winner Mario Vargas Llosa: "Freedom is a source of strength for the fight against the Virus"], interviewed by René Scheu for *Neue Zürcher Zeitungi*, 2 November. Available at: https://www.nzz.ch/feuilleton/mario-vargas-llosa-ueber-corona-lockdown-und-die-freiheit-ld.1584005?reduced=true.

Vendettuoli, G. (2020). 'Il coronavirus è l'Apocalisse per alberghi e ristoranti' [Coronavirus is the apocalypse for hotels and restaurants], *AGI – Agenzia Italiana*, 4 April. Available at: https://www.agi.it/economia/news/2020-04-04/coronavirus-crollo-ristoranti-alberghi-8179853/.

Volksgruppen.orf.at (2020). 'Coronakrise beeinträchtigt Kinderrechte' [Corona crisis affects children's rights], *volksgruppen.orf.at*, 26 May. Available at: https://volksgruppen.orf.at/diversitaet/stories/3050475/.

Von Schönburg, A. (2020). 'Warum weite Teile der Elite Hardliner lieben: Wir leiden am Stockholm-Syndrom!' [Why large sections of the elite love hardliners: We suffer from Stockholm syndrome!], *Bild*, 4 May. Available at: https://www.bild.de/ politik/inland/politik-inland/corona-krise-warum-weite-teile-der-elite-hardliner-gegen-oeffnungen-bleiben-70426322.bild.html.

Von Stefenelli, A. (2020). 'Ein Blick in die Zukunft nach der Corona-Krise' [A look into the future after the corona crisis], *Zett – Die Sonntagszeitung*, 21 June 21, pp. 8–9. https://www.suedtirolnews.it/chronik/nach-corona-ein-blick-in-die-zukunft.

Von Westphalen, A. (2020). 'Fehler im System' [Error in System], *Telepolis*, 10 June. Available at: https://www.heise.de/tp/features/Fehler-im-System-4779301.html.

Voros, J. (2003). 'A generic foresight process framework', *Foresight*, 5 (3), pp. 10–21. DOI:10.1108/14636680310698379.

Voros, J. (2017). 'Big History and anticipation: Using Big History as a framework for global foresight', in Poli, R.(ed.) *Handbook of anticipation: Theoretical and applied aspects of the use of future in decision making*. Cham: Springer International. DOI:10.1007/978-3-319-31737-3_95-1.

Wagner, M., Hammond, E. & Hayes, M. (2020). 'Coronavirus Pandemic in the US', *CNN*, 30 April. Available at: https://edition.cnn.com/us/live-news/us-coronavirus-update-04-30-20/h_e90047bd263620ce7d71d643abao2edo.

Wakabayashi, D., Alba, D. & Tracey, M. (2020). 'Bill Gates, at Odds With Trump on Virus, Becomes a Right-Wing Target', *The New York Times*, 17 April. Available at: https://www.nytimes.com/2020/04/17/technology/bill-gates-virus-conspiracy-theories.html.

BIBLIOGRAPHIC REFERENCES

Wakefield, J. (2020). 'Coronavirus: AI steps up in battle against Covid-19', *BBC News*, 17 April. Available at: https://www.bbc.com/news/technology-52120747.

Wallas, F. (2020). 'Doing Business After Corona: How the Business World Will Change After Coronavirus', *Payments Journal*, 28 April. Available at: https://www.payments journal.com/doing-business-after-corona-how-the-business-world-will-change -after-coronavirus/.

Wallerstein, I.M. (2004). The Uncertainties of Knowledge. Philadelphia: Temple University Press.

Watts, J. (2020a). 'Clean air in Europe during lockdown 'leads to 11,000 fewer deaths'', *The Guardian*, 30 April. Available at: https://www.theguardian.com/environment/ 2020/apr/30/clean-air-in-europe-during-lockdown-leads-to-11000-fewer-deaths.

Watts, J. (2020b). 'Is the Covid-19 crisis the catalyst for greening the world's airlines?', *The Guardian*, 17 May. Available at: https://www.theguardian.com/world/2020/ may/17/is-covid-19-crisis-the-catalyst-for-the-greening-of-worlds-airlines?CMP= Share_iOSApp_Other.

Weick, K.E., Sutcliffe, K.M. (2001). *Managing the unexpected: assuring high performance in an age of complexity*. San Francisco: Jossey-Bass.

Weisbrod, L. (2020). David Graeber: "Werden wir danach so tun, als sei alles nur ein Traum gewesen?" [Afterwards, will we pretend it was all just a dream?], *Zeit Online*, 31 March. Available at: https://www.zeit.de/arbeit/2020-03/david-graebner-coro navirus-kapitalismus-bullshitjobs.

Welt (2020). 'Die Maßstäbe setzen jetzt die Popstars der Pandemie' [The standards are now set by pop stars of the pandemic], *Welt*, 4 April. Available at: https://www .welt.de/politik/ausland/plus207003303/Corona-Virologen-sind-die-neuen-Popst ars.html.

Widmann, V. (2019). 'Was will eigentlich der Transhumanismus?' [What does transhumanism actually want?], *The European*, 3 May. Available at: https://www.theeurop ean.de/valentin-widmann/15745-nietzsche-ein-transhumanist.

Widmann, V. (2020a). 'Coronaphobie – Die Macht der Angst und ihre Folgen' [Coronaphobia – The power of fear and its consequences.], *Telepolis*, 16 March. Available at: https://www.heise.de/tp/features/Coronaphobie-Die-Macht-der -Angst-und-ihre-Folgen-4683052.html.

Widmann, V. (2020b). 'Die Kontroverse in der Krise – Die Sache mit der Menschenwürde und dem Wert des Lebens' [The controversy in the crisis – The matter of human dignity and the value of life], *Salto*, 12 May. Available at: https://www.salto.bz/de/arti cle/12052020/warum-dieser-dissens.

Widmann, V. (2020c). 'Letter to Roland Benedikter', 14 May. Archive of Roland Benedikter.

Widmann, V. (2020d). 'Über den Tod sprechen' [Talking about death], *Telepolis*, 10 May. Available at: https://www.heise.de/tp/features/Ueber-den-Tod-sprechen-4717 624.html.

Wiegrefe, K. (2020). 'Als die Grippe in Nachkriegsdeutschland wütete' [When the flu raged in post-war Germany], *Der Spiegel*, 20 April. Available at: https://www.spie gel.de/geschichte/pandemien-als-die-grippe-im-nachkriegsdeutschland-wuetete-a-00000000-0002-0001-0000-000170518603.

Wiener Zeitung (2020). 'Klaus Bachler sieht neue Opernzeiten'[Klaus Bachler sees new opera times]. *Wiener Zeitung,*11 June. Available at: https://www.wienerzeitung.at/ nachrichten/kultur/buehne/2063902-Klaus-Bachler-sieht-neue-Opernzeiten.html.

Wike, R., Fetterolf, J. (2018). 'Liberal Democracy's Crisis of Confidence', Journal of Democracy, 29 (4, October), pp. 136–150. DOI: 10.1353/jod.2018.0069.

Wilkinson, R.G., Pickett, K. (2009). *The Spirit Level: Why More Equal Societies Almost Always Do Better*. London: Allen Lane.

Williams, S. (2020). 'I can recover at home': Cosmetic surgeons see rise in patients amid pandemic, *BBC*, 10 July. Available at: https://www.bbc.com/news/world-53341771.

Wilson, J., Swyngedouw, E. (2014). *The Post-Political and Its Discontents*. Edinburgh: Edinburgh University Press. Available at: https://www.euppublishing.com/ userimages/ContentEditor/1416314452198/Wilson%20%26%20Swyngedouw%20 -%20The%20Post-Political%20and%20its%20Discontents%20-%20Introduction .pdf.

Wimer, C., Collyer, S., Jaravel, X., (2019). The Costs of Being Poor: Inflation Inequality Leads to Three Million More People in Poverty. The Groundwork Collaborative, Center on Poverty & Social Policy at Columbia University. Available at: https://grou ndworkcollaborative.org/wp-content/uploads/2019/11/The-Costs-of-Being-Poor -Groundwork-Collaborative.pdf.

Wischer, G. (2020). 'China's Covid-19 Propaganda Playbook – Part 1', *International Policy Digest*, 17 April. Available at: https://intpolicydigest.org/2020/04/17/china-s -covid-19-propaganda-playbook-part-1/.

Wissenschaftlicher Beirat der Bundesregierung Globale Umweltveränderungen [German Advisory Council on Global Change] (2011). *World in Transition – A Social Contract for Sustainability*. Berlin: WBGU. Available at: https://www.wbgu.de/fileadmin/user_upl oad/wbgu/publikationen/hauptgutachten/hg2011/pdf/wbgu_jg2011_en.pdf.

Wolfram, M., Ravetz, J, Scholl, C. (2020). 'Beyond Urban Living Labs: The making of transformative urban innovation systems', *BioMed Central Ltd*, 31 August. Available at: https://www.biomedcentral.com/collections/urbanll.

Wood, A.W. (1991). 'Unsociable Sociability: The Anthropological Basis of Kantian Ethics', *Philosophical Topics*, 19 (1), 325–351. Available at: http://www.jstor.org/sta ble/43154098.

Woodward, A. (2020). 'Both the new coronavirus and SARS outbreaks likely started in Chinese 'wet markets'. Historic photos show what the markets looked like', *Business Insider*, 26 February. Available at: https://www.businessinsider.com/wuhan-coro navirus-chinese-wet-market-photos-2020-1?IR=T.

BIBLIOGRAPHIC REFERENCES

Woolley, A.W., Chabris, C.F., Pentland, A., Hashmi, N., Malone, T.W. (2010). 'Evidence for a Collective Intelligence Factor in the Performance of Human Groups', *Science*, 330 (6004, 29 October), Pp. 686–688. DOI: 10.1126/science.1193147.

World Economic Forum (2020). *The Global Risk Report 2020*. Geneva: World Economic Forum. Available at: https://reports.weforum.org/global-risks-report-2020/.

World Health Organization (2017). *PANDEMIC INFLUENZA SEVERITY ASSESSMENT (PISA)*. Geneva: WHO. Available at: https://apps.who.int/iris/bitstream/handle/10665/259392/WHO-WHE-IHM-GIP-2017.2-eng.pdf?sequence=1.

World Health Organization (2020a). 'As more go hungry and malnutrition persists, achieving Zero Hunger by 2030 in doubt, UN report warns. Securing healthy diets for the billions who cannot afford them would save trillions in costs', *UN*, 13 July. Available at: https://www.who.int/news-room/detail/13-07-2020-as-more-go-hungry-and-malnutrition-persists-achieving-zero-hunger-by-2030-in-doubt-un-report-warns.

World Health Organization (2020b). Coronavirus disease (Covid-19) pandemic [Press Conference]. https://www.who.int/emergencies/diseases/novel-coronavirus-2019?gclid=EAIaIQobChMIgLeVi4Xf6QIVxaQYCh1_DQEeEAAYASAAEgLyd_D_BwE.

World Health Organization (2020c). 'Inoculating against the 'infodemic' in Africa', *UN*, 5 March. Available at: https://www.afro.who.int/news/inoculating-against-infodemic-africa. .

World Health Organization (2020d). Timeline of WHO's response to Covid-19, *WHO*, 29 June. Available at: https://www.who.int/news-room/detail/29-06-2020-covidtimeline.

World Health Organization (2020e). 'WHO Director-General's opening remarks at the media briefing on Covid-19 – 30 July 2020', 30 July. Available at: https://www.who.int/dg/speeches/detail/who-director-general-s-opening-remarks-at-the-media-briefing-on-covid-19---30-july-2020.

World Health Organization (2020f). 'WHO Director-General's opening remarks at the media briefing on Covid-19 – 3 August 2020' [announcement], 3 August. Available at: https://www.who.int/dg/speeches/detail/who-director-general-s-opening-remarks-at-the-media-briefing-on-covid-19---3-august-2020.

World Health Organization (n.d.). *Tool for Influenza Pandemic Risk Assessment* (TIPRA). Available at: https://www.who.int/influenza/areas_of_work/human_animal_interface/tipra/en/.

Worldometer (2021). *Age, Sex, Existing Conditions of Covid-19 Cases and Deaths*, Last updated: September 27, 2021. Available at: https://www.worldometers.info/coronavirus/coronavirus-age-sex-demographics/.

Worldometer (2020a). *Age, Sex, Existing Conditions of Covid-19 Cases and Deaths*, Last updated: May 13, 2020. Available at: https://www.worldometers.info/coronavirus/coronavirus-age-sex-demographics/.

Worldometer (2020b). *Coronavirus: Cuba*. Available at: https://www.worldometers .info/coronavirus/country/cuba/.

Worldometer (2020d). *Coronavirus: Germany*. Available at: https://www.worldomet ers.info/coronavirus/country/germany/.

Worldometer (2020d). *Current World Population*. Available at: https://www.worldomet ers.info/world-population/.

Worldometer (2020e). *Info Coronavirus*. Available at: https://www.worldometers.info/ coronavirus/.

Worldometer (2020f). *United States Coronavirus Cases*. Available at: https://www .worldometers.info/coronavirus/country/us/.

Xiao, Y., Fan, Z. (2020). '10 technology trends to watch in the Covid-19 pandemic', *World Economic Forum*, 27 April. Available at: https://www.weforum.org/agenda/2020/04/ 10-technology-trends-coronavirus-covid19-pandemic-robotics-telehealth/.

Yang, J., Wang, W., Hu, P., Han, L., Wang, D., Yang, Z., Yu, C., Li, Y., Ma, A. (2020). *Examining China's Response to the Covid-19 Outbreak (September 2019-January 2020): The Catastrophe That Could Have Been Avoided*. Translated by Matthew Trueman. USA: Citizen Press.

Yang, W. (2020). 'Taiwans erfolgreicher Kampf gegen Corona' [Taiwan's successful fight against corona], *Deutsche Welle*, 16 March. Available at: https://www.dw.com/de/ taiwans-erfolgreicher-kampf-gegen-corona/a-52737708.

Yokomatsu, M., Hochrainer-Stigler, S. (2020). *Disaster Risk Reduction and Resilience*. Singapore: Springer Singapore. DOI: 10.1007/978-981-15-4320-3.

Yong, E. (2020). 'Why the Coronavirus Is So Confusing', *The Atlantic*, 29 April. Available at: https://www.theatlantic.com/ health/archive/2020/04/pandemic-confusing-uncertainty/610819/?utm_source=Nature+Briefing&utm_campaign=743f0c9604-briefing-dy-20200430&utm_medium=email&utm_term=0_c9dfd39373-743f0c9604-43812713.

Yonhap News (2020). 'Korea's mass virus testing capability contributes to better quarantine', *Yonhap News*, 5 March. Available at: https://m-en.yna.co.kr/view/AEN20 200305002900320?section=science/medicine.

Yuk Wah, C., Haines, D. (2020). 'Diseasescape: Coping with Coronavirus, Mobility, and Politics', *Global-e series: Pandemic – Border Crossing Caveats*, 13 (33, May). Available at: https://www.21global.ucsb.edu/global-e/may-2020/diseasescape-coping-coro navirus-mobility-and-politics.

Yunus, M. (2020). 'Post-Corona Recovery Programme: No Going Back', *la Repubblica*, 19 April. Available at: https://www.repubblica.it/esteri/2020/04/19/news/post -corona_recovery_programme_no_going_back-254431614/.

Zarocostas, J. (2020). 'How to fight an infodemic', *World Report*, 395 (10225, February), p.676. DOI:https://doi.org/10.1016/S0140-6736(20)30461-X.

BIBLIOGRAPHIC REFERENCES

ZDF Heute (2020). 'Wegen Corona-Maßnahmen: Zeitweise 17 Prozent weniger CO2-Emissionen' [Because of corona measures: At times 17 percent less CO2 emissions], *ZDF Heute*, 19 May. Available at:. https://www.zdf.de/nachrichten/panorama/coronavirus-weniger-co2-emissionen-100.html.

Zenker, H. (2020). 'Gezielt Risikogruppen isolieren – Ausgangssperren für über 70-Jährige?' [Targeted isolation of risk groups – curfews for people over 70?], *Mob*, 27 March. Available at: https://www.moz.de/ nachrichten/politik/corona-massnahmen-gezielt-risikogruppen-isolieren-ausgangssperren-fuer-ueber-70-jaehrige_-49382596.html.

Žižek, S. (2020). *Pandemic! Covid-19 Shakes the World*. Cambridge: Polity Press.

Zolli, A (2012). 'Learning to Bounce Back', *The New York Times*, 2 November. Available at: https://www.nytimes.com/2012/11/03/opinion/forget-sustainability-its-about-resilience.html.

Zolli, A., Healy, A.M. (2013). *Resilience. Why Things Bounce Back*. London: Headline Publishing Group.

Zovatto, D. (2020) 'The rapidly deteriorating quality of democracy in Latin America', *Brookings*, 28 February. Available at: https://www.brookings.edu/blog/order-from-chaos/2020/02/28/the-rapidly-deteriorating-quality-of-democracy-in-latin-america/.

Zur, O. (n.d.). 'TeleMental Health Services Across State Lines', *Zur Institute*. Available at: https://www.zurinstitute.com/telehealth-across-state-lines/.

Index

Action-learning 171, 276, 338
Africa 6, 9, 15, 21, 35, 48–50, 117, 134, 286
Artificial Intelligence (AI) 34f, 50, 66f, 71,
     203, 230
     Super-intelligent AI 230, 241
Ashby's Law 146
Asia 15, 100, 135, 140, 268
Australia
     See Countries
Austria
     See Countries

Bangladesh
     See Countries
Belgium
     See Countries
Brazil
     See Countries
Britain
     See Countries
Belt and Road Initiative (BRI) 281, 283
Biological espionage 70f
Black Swan 173, 175, 332
Bostrom, Nick 229–231, 242
Bundle crisis 53, 59, 122, 151, 157
     See also Crisis bundles (both notions are
          not identical)

Cambodia
     See Countries
Canada
     See Countries
China
     See Countries
Croatia
     See Countries
Czech Republic
     See Countries
Climate
     Climate change 11, 14, 25, 59, 123–125, 145,
          211f, 214, 224, 300–303
     Climate crisis 86, 296f, 299, 302f,
          332–334
Collaborative Innovation Networks
     (CoIN)

Collective
     Collective intelligence 141, 148, 176f 180,
          219, 229–231, 239–242, 246, 251–254,
          277, 329, 336, 340
     Collective wisdom 231, 239–243, 246, 251,
          253f, 329, 336, 339f
     Collective immunity 134, 139, 197
          See also herd immunity
Complexify 153, 159, 169, 245, 254
Complexity
     Complexity management 26, 147, 254, 277
     Complexity worker 277–279
Conflict
     Conflict line 103, 157, 179, 205, 208, 213,
          237, 278
Conspiration
     Conspiration belief 208
     Conspiration theory 53
Contagion 46f, 56, 264
Countries
     Arab Emirates 19
     Australia 6, 108, 198, 201, 214, 217, 319f
     Austria 10, 19, 25, 26–28, 34, 99, 117f, 151,
          171, 181, 217, 328
     Bangladesh
     Belgium 181, 328
     Brazil 40, 45f, 104, 150, 198, 324, 329
     Britain
          See United Kingdom (UK)
     Cambodia 314
     Canada 72, 320, 329
     China 5, 36–42, 61f, 71f, 88f, 100, 103–105,
          135f, 171, 184f, 189–191, 319f, 353
     Croatia 181
     Czech Republic 181
     Denmark 4, 181
     Finland 181, 276
     France 5, 40, 104, 125, 134, 139, 151, 171, 181,
          194, 210, 217
     Germany 8, 21, 31f, 74f, 93f, 104, 135f, 139f,
          151, 168, 177–179, 194f, 307, 328f
     Greece 276
     Hungary 181, 314, 329
     India 20, 40, 44f, 48, 58, 77, 198, 207, 229,
          276, 280, 311f, 324

INDEX

Iran 83, 104, 106, 111, 209, 320
Israel 7, 106, 206, 320
Italy 5f, 19, 21, 28–30, 40, 64f, 98, 103f, 109, 123, 130f, 135f, 139, 166, 171, 181, 214, 262, 276, 301, 325f
Japan 108, 134, 328, 338
Kazakhstan 64
Latvia 181
Luxemburg 181
Libya 106
Malaysia 276
Netherlands 181, 268, 276, 301
New Zealand 151, 182, 210f, 217, 235, 320, 328, 342
Nigeria 40, 50, 106
North Korea 320
Norway 151
Russia 72, 104, 135, 157, 171, 320, 324
Rwanda 64
Saudi Arabia 324
Singapore 19f, 33, 135, 182, 209, 251, 269
Slovenia 181
South Africa 22, 50, 324
South Korea 40, 58, 75, 80, 104, 108, 110, 135, 235, 328, 342
Spain 6, 40, 98, 103, 136, 181, 216, 325
Switzerland 130, 151, 171
Sweden 19, 75, 137f, 181, 234
Syria 106
Taiwan 40, 58, 75, 104f, 135, 190, 235, 353
Thailand 182, 338
Tunisia 51, 63, 276
United Kingdom (UK) 64, 85f, 134, 201, 250, 276, 299f, 313, 320, 328
United States of America (USA) 36, 83, 104f, 151, 185, 209f, 217f, 237, 242, 250, 328
Uruguay 276
Vietnam 135, 182, 198
Yemen 106
Covid Resilience Ranking 151f
Crisis
　Crisis bundles xxiv, 56, 59, 124, 145
Cross
　Cross-national 186, 281, 335f
　Cross-sectoral 142, 147, 176–178, 251, 253, 277, 335, 339
Curfew
　See Lockdown

Cyber-attack 70, 89, 247, 280, 320
Cyber-espionage 329
Cybernetics 159, 163, 177
Cynefin 173–175

Deaths xviii, 5–7, 13, 25, 41, 46, 48, 80, 99, 104, 111, 116, 130, 134, 137, 151, 170, 197f, 263, 298f, 328
Democracy 180, 223, 236, 299, 305, 312–315, 340, 353
　Liquid democracy 250
　e-democracy 250
Democrat 43, 83, 76
Democratisation 40, 237
Denmark
　See Countries
　Degrowth
　See Post-Growth
Development paradox 228, 233
Digital education 201
Diseasescape 189–192
Doughnut Economy 219–221
　See also Post-growth

Ebola xiii, 125
Europe 5f, 8, 28, 34, 40, 44, 60f, 74f, 77, 100f, 120, 124, 132, 178, 181, 184, 189, 198, 217, 247f, 301, 309–311, 316, 329, 348–351
European Union (EU) 227, 284, 294, 297, 300, 309, 316–318, 325, 330, 350f
Existential risk
　See Risk

Fatalities
　See deaths
Finland
　See Countries
Flu
　Asian Flu 116, 196
　Hong Kong Flu 116
　Spanish Flu 196
France
　See Countries
Frugal 222, 280f
Futures
　Futures Cone 270f, 335
　Futures Diamond 270–272, 274

Futures *(cont.)*
Futures Literacy   170f, 240, 267f, 270,
   273–277, 281, 285, 288, 335, 337–341, 352

Generation Corona   34
Germany
   See Countries
Globalism   58, 90, 192, 205, 207
Globalisation
   Hyper-Globalisation   xvii
   Re-Globalisation   185, 349, 356
   Globalisation 2.0   335
Global Governance   189, 256, 282f, 308, 336
Governance panarchy   250
Greece
   See Countries
Grey goo-scenario   230

Hackathon   177
Herd immunity   4, 46, 138, 197, 305
Humanism
Hungary
   See Countries
Hyper-globalisation
   See Globalisation

India
   See Countries
Infections   4, 6–8, 41f, 46, 54, 69, 76, 98, 104,
   111f, 129f, 136, 140, 198, 307, 342
Infectious upper limits   140
Infektions-Obergrenzen
   See Infectious upper limits
Infodemic   xiii, 53, 116, 237
Interdisciplinary   xxiv, 150, 152, 231, 242,
   252, 254–256, 261, 276, 279, 282,
   285, 343
Iran
   See Countries
Israel
   See Countries
Italy
   See Countries

Jagannath wagon   229
Japan
   See Countries
Jinping, Xi   39, 103f, 301

Kazakhstan
   See Countries
Krastev, Ivan   58, 101, 194f, 205, 207

Latvia
   See Countries
Learning organisation   169
Leverage point   244, 246, 249, 267,
   281, 321
Libya
   See Countries
Lockdown   7f, 10f, 16f, 20f, 24f, 27–32,
   35f, 45–51, 64–66, 75–80, 94, 103,
   106–110, 136–138, 197–199, 261f,
   302f, 325
Luxemburg
   See Countries

Malaysia
   See Countries
Merkel, Angela   xv, 109, 140
MERS   xiii
Miller, Riel   273f, 285, 288, 338
Mode 3 (science)   252
Multi-level governance   xxiii, 166, 279
Multi-resilience   156, 163, 169, 184, 228, 243,
   253, 266, 279, 328, 335
Multi-Stakeholder-Initiative (MSI)   253f

Nationalism   19, 58f, 205–207, 325
Neoliberal   xvi, xxiii, 38, 57, 59, 62, 74, 77,
   88–90, 101, 194, 222, 229, 355
Netherlands
   See Countries
New Silk Road
   See Belt and Road Initiative (BRI)
New Zealand
   See Countries
Nigeria
   See Countries
North Korea
   See Countries
Norway
   See Countries

OECD   40, 48, 157, 286, 328
One Belt One Road (OBOR)
   See Belt and Road Initiative (BRI)

INDEX

Panarchy Model of Adaptive Cycles   159–165
Patient zero   5
Pierson trilemma   217f
Post-growth   213, 219–224, 235, 269, 281, 336
Prevention paradox   137

QAnon   120

Reflexive modernity   229, 252
Re-Globalisation
　See Globalisation
Republican   76, 84
Resilience
　Organisational resilience   176
　Psychological resilience   169
　Resilience culture   158, 180f
　Societal resilience   149, 151, 158, 176
　　See also resilient society
Resilient society
　See Society
Risk
　Existential risk   58, 229f, 241f
　Risk group   140, 234
Russia
　See Countries
Rwanda
　See Countries

SARS   xiii, 4, 89, 116, 135, 190
Saudi Arabia
　See Countries
Shutdown
　See Lockdown
Side-effects   202
Simplify   153, 159, 169, 244
Singapore
　See Countries
Slovenia
　See Countries
Social change   244, 246f, 249f, 252
Social distancing   37, 47f, 53, 76, 96, 99, 113, 135f, 138, 142, 197, 262, 264, 355
Society
　Learning society   169
　Multi-resilient society   213, 235, 247, 249
　Open society   38, 41, 57, 60, 66, 75, 77f, 83, 85, 87, 124, 126, 132f, 147f, 186, 238, 261, 314f, 318, 324, 347–349, 352

Resilient society   234f, 239, 290
Sustainable society   213, 221, 223, 233–235, 238f, 241, 244, 247, 335
South Africa
　See Countries
South Korea
　See Countries
Spain
　See Countries
Super-intelligent
　See Artificial Intelligence
Sustainability   123, 143, 213, 228, 232–239, 246, 250, 256, 278, 330, 332–336, 339, 347f
Sustainable society
　See Society
Switzerland
　See Countries
Sweden
　See Countries
Systems Thinking   156, 158f, 164, 169, 244
Syria
　See Countries

Taiwan
　See Countries
Telehealth   202
Thailand
　See Countries
Tansdisciplinary   147–150, 153, 159, 169, 177–179, 244f, 247, 251f, 268f, 285, 293, 335, 356f
Transhumanism   63, 68f, 241, 339
Transition Town   250f, 267
Tunisia
　See Countries

UNESCO   18, 201, 240, 268, 273, 276f, 281, 285, 295f
United Kingdom (UK)
　See Countries
United Nations (UN)   8, 15, 19, 32, 35, 220, 222, 284f, 295, 308
United States of America (USA)
　See Countries
Uruguay
　See Countries

INDEX

Universal Basic Income 213, 216, 218f, 224, 250, 269, 299f

Vaccine xviii, 4, 6, 39, 71–73, 138, 186, 196–198, 233, 237, 284, 287–289, 296, 319–323, 350, 353
Vaccine nationalism 320–323
Viable Systems Model (vsm) 146, 159, 163–165, 278
Vietnam
   See Countries

Wave (infection) 42, 95, 110, 137, 140, 149, 151, 168, 196, 306f, 312
World Trade Organization (wto) 88, 186, 284
Wuhan xxii, 4f, 41, 54, 353

Yemen
   See Country

Zero-growth 219–221, 336

Printed in the United States
by Baker & Taylor Publisher Services